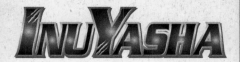

VOL. 41
Shonen Sunday Edition

Story and Art by
RUMIKO TAKAHASHI

English Adaptation by Gerard Jones

Translation/Mari Morimoto
Touch-up Art & Lettering/Bill Schuch
Cover & Interior Graphic Design/Yuki Ameda
Editor/Shaenon K. Garrity

VP, Production/Alvin Lu
VP, Publishing Licensing/Rika Inouye
VP, Sales & Product Marketing/Gonzalo Ferreyra
VP, Creative/Linda Espinosa
Publisher/Hyoe Narita

Printed in the U.S.A.

Published by VIZ Media, LLC
P.O. Box 77010
San Francisco, CA 94107

10 9 8 7 6 5 4 3 2 1
First printing, October 2009

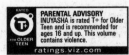

www.viz.com   WWW.SHONENSUNDAY.COM

INUYASHA

VOL. 41

Shonen Sunday Edition

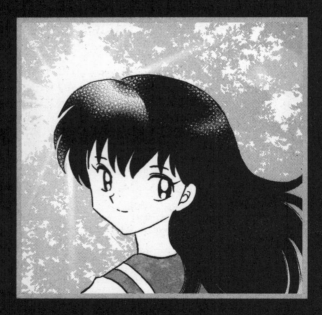

STORY AND ART BY
RUMIKO TAKAHASHI

CONTENTS

THE STORY THUS FAR

Long ago, in the "Warring States" era of Japan's Muromachi period (*Sengoku-jidai*, approximately 1467-1568 CE), a legendary dog-like half-demon called "Inuyasha" attempted to steal the Shikon Jewel—or "Jewel of Four Souls"—from a village, but was stopped by the enchanted arrow of the village priestess, Kikyo. Inuyasha fell into a deep sleep, pinned to a tree by Kikyo's arrow, while the mortally wounded Kikyo took the Shikon Jewel with her into the fires of her funeral pyre. Years passed.

Fast-forward to the present day. Kagome, a Japanese high school girl, is pulled into a well one day by a mysterious centipede monster and finds herself transported into the past—only to come face to face with the trapped Inuyasha. She frees him, and Inuyasha easily defeats the centipede monster.

The residents of the village, now 50 years older, readily accept Kagome as the reincarnation of their deceased priestess Kikyo, a claim supported by the fact that the Shikon Jewel emerges from a cut on Kagome's body. Unfortunately, the jewel's rediscovery means that the village is soon under attack by a variety of demons in search of this treasure. Then, the jewel is accidentally shattered into many shards, each of which may have the fearsome power of the entire jewel.

Although Inuyasha says he hates Kagome because of her resemblance to Kikyo, the woman who "killed" him, he is forced to team up with her when Kaede, the village leader, binds him to Kagome with a powerful spell. Now the two grudging companions must fight to reclaim and reassemble the shattered shards of the Shikon Jewel before they fall into the wrong hands...

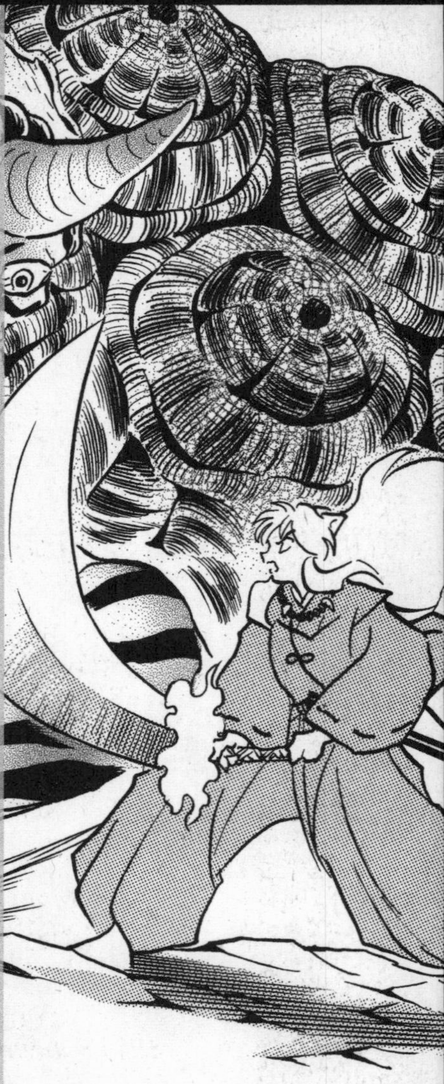

THIS VOLUME Inuyasha's sword Tetsusaiga has acquired a new power, the Dragon Scale, which draws demonic power out of opponents. But Inuyasha doesn't seem to be able to use the Dragon Scale without injuring himself. Meanwhile, Naraku has created a new incarnation, the sorcerer Byakuya, and sent him to follow Inuyasha's group for unknown reasons...

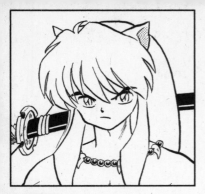

INUYASHA
Half-demon hybrid, son of a human mother and demon father. His necklace is enchanted, allowing Kagome to control him with a word.

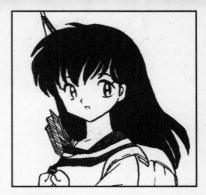

KAGOME
Modern-day Japanese schoolgirl who can travel back and forth between the past and present through an enchanted well.

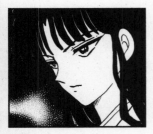

NARAKU
Enigmatic demon-mastermind behind the miseries of nearly everyone in the story.

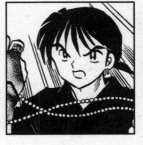

MIROKU
Lecherous Buddhist priest cursed with a mystical "hellhole" in his hand that's slowly killing him.

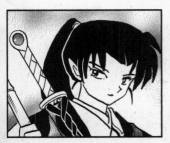

BYAKUYA
A powerful sorcerer and master of illusions created by Naraku.

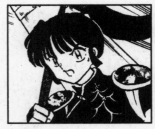

SANGO
"Demon Exterminator" or slayer from the village where the Shikon Jewel was first born.

SCROLL 1
THE INVINCIBLE BLADE

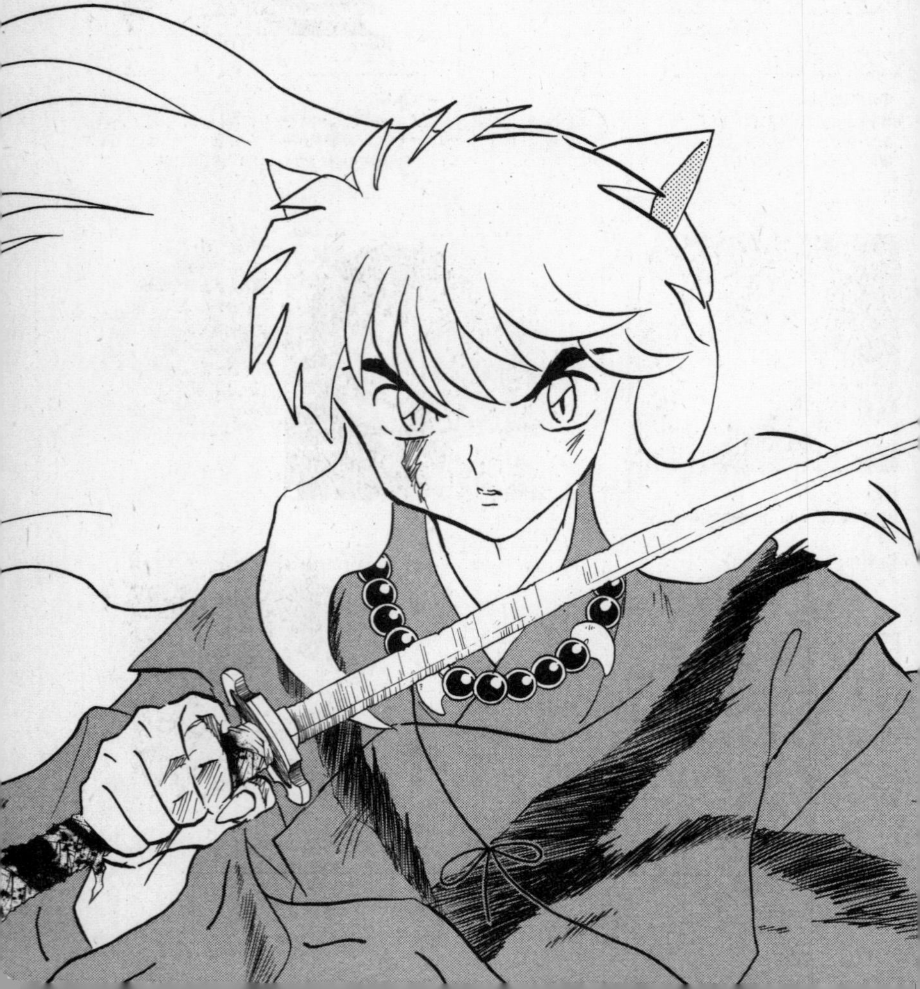

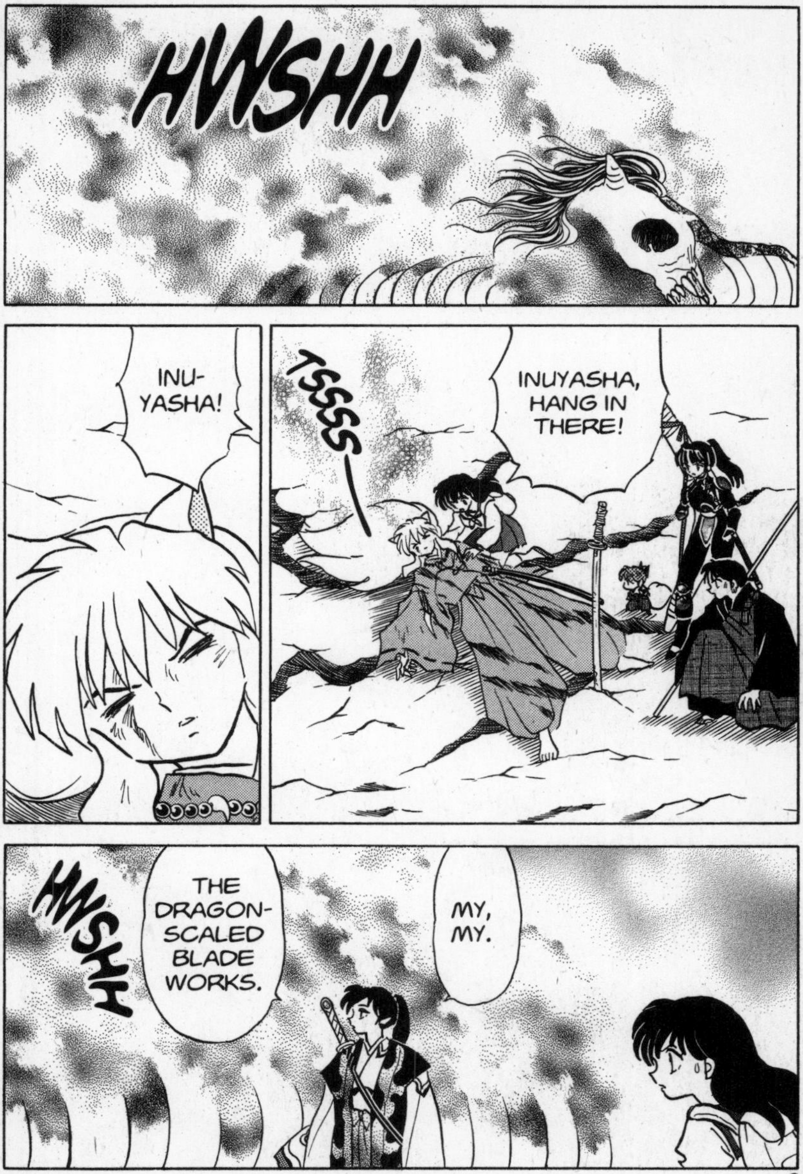
HWSHH
INUYASHA, HANG IN THERE!
TSSSS—
INU-YASHA!
MY, MY.
THE DRAGON-SCALED BLADE WORKS.
HWSHH

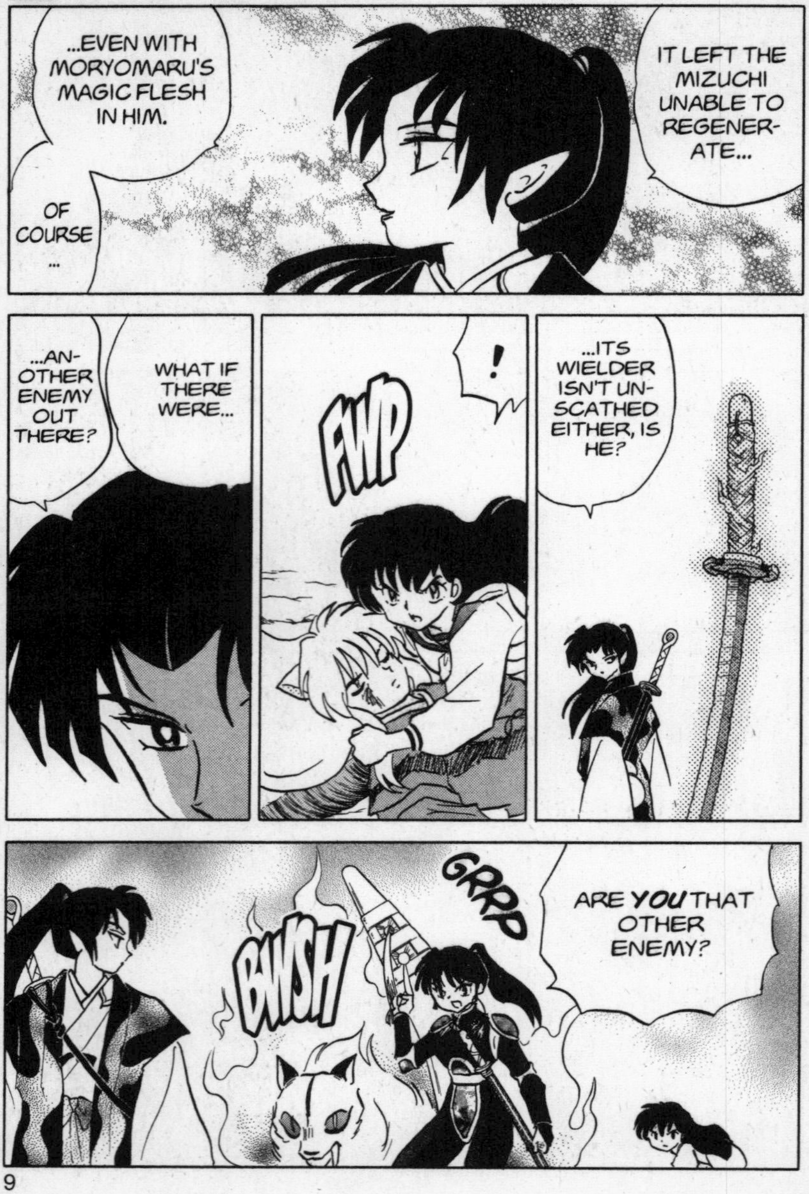
IT LEFT THE MIZUCHI UNABLE TO REGENERATE...
...EVEN WITH MORYOMARU'S MAGIC FLESH IN HIM.
OF COURSE ...
...ITS WIELDER ISN'T UNSCATHED EITHER, IS HE?
!
FWP
WHAT IF THERE WERE...
...ANOTHER ENEMY OUT THERE?
ARE **YOU** THAT OTHER ENEMY?
GRRP
BWISH

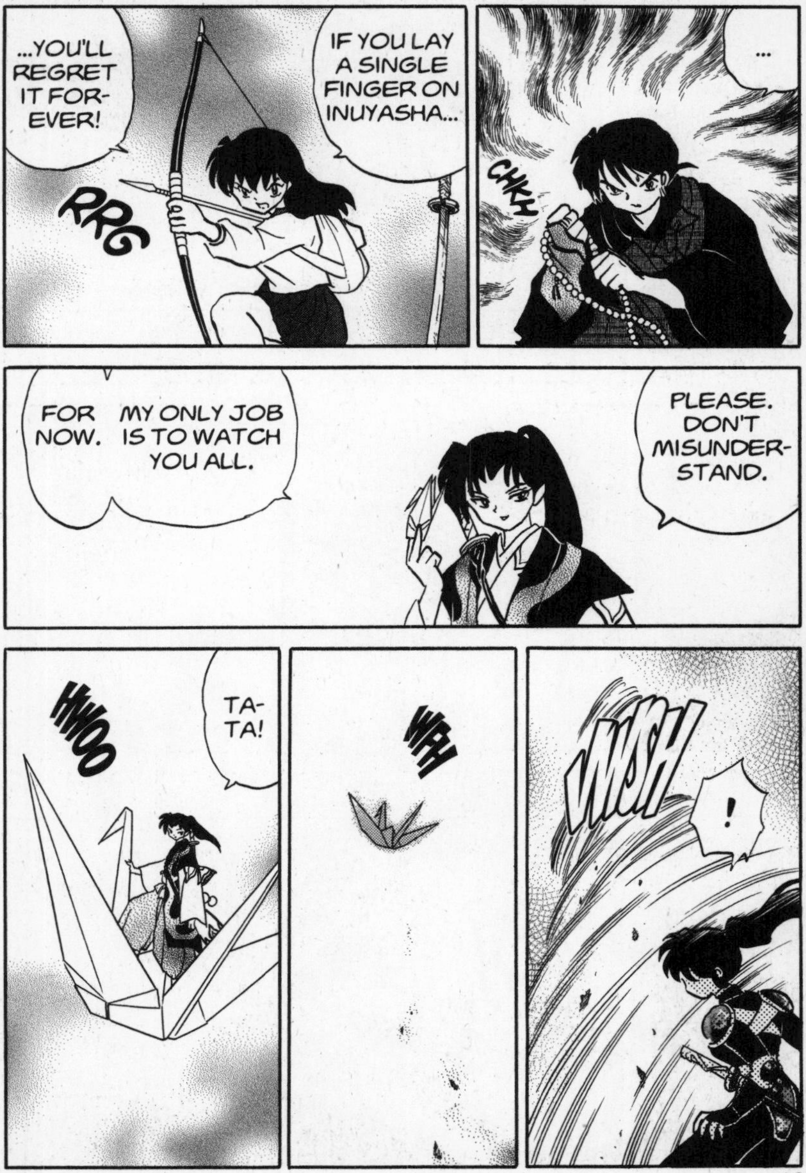
...
CHKH
IF YOU LAY A SINGLE FINGER ON INUYASHA...
...YOU'LL REGRET IT FOR-EVER!
RRG
PLEASE. DON'T MISUNDER-STAND.
MY ONLY JOB IS TO WATCH YOU ALL.
FOR NOW.
!
TA-TA!
HWOO

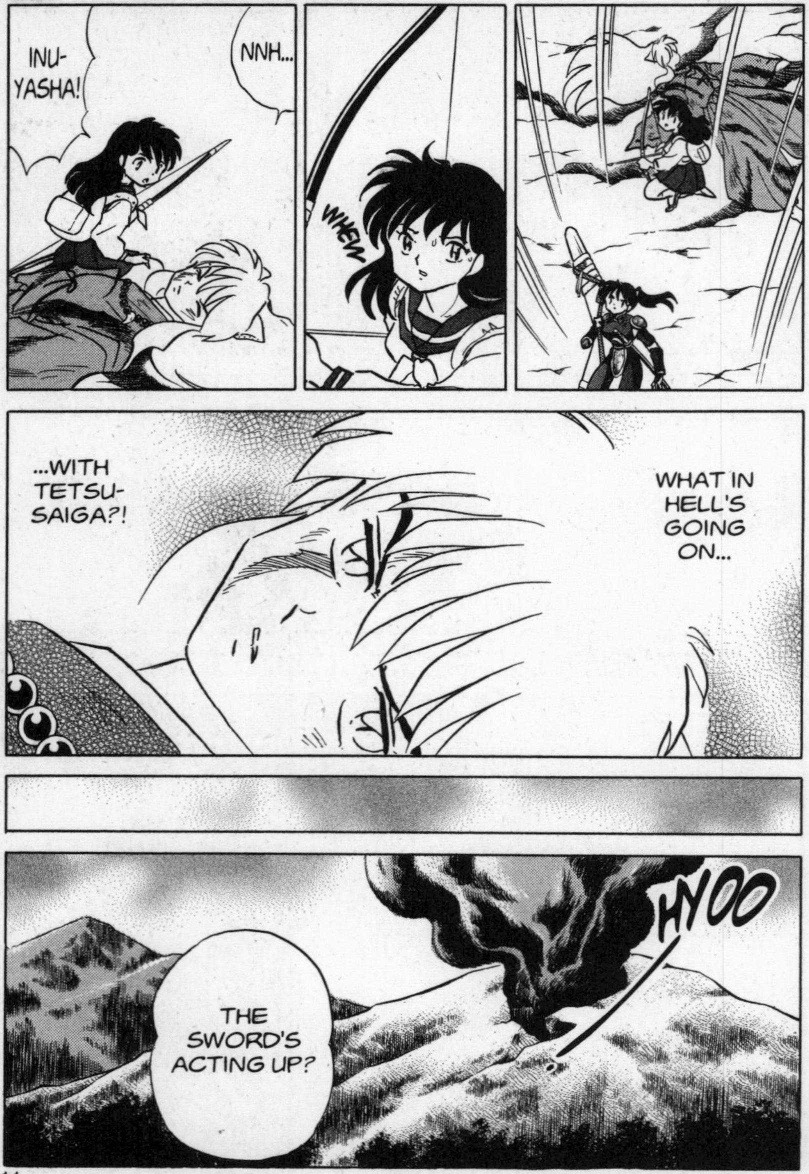
WHEW
NNH...
INU-YASHA!
WHAT IN HELL'S GOING ON...
...WITH TETSU-SAIGA?!
HYOO
THE SWORD'S ACTING UP?

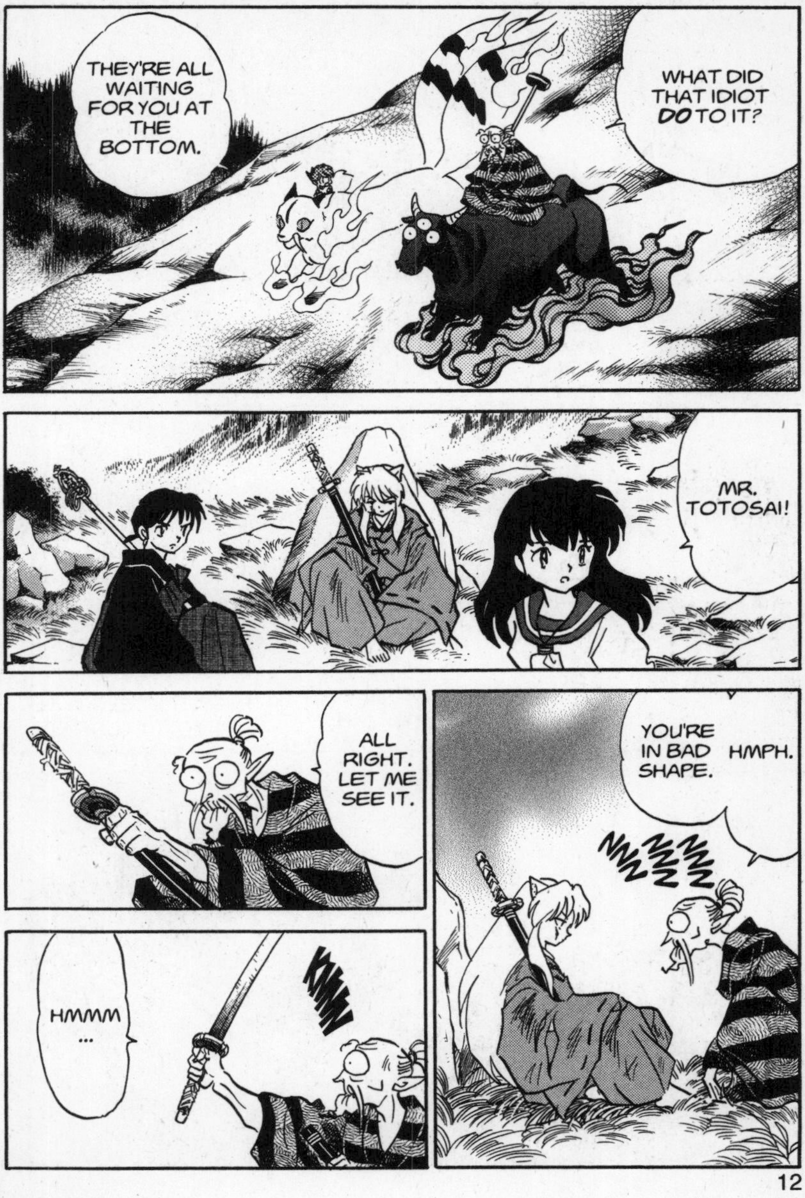
WHAT DID THAT IDIOT *DO* TO IT?
THEY'RE ALL WAITING FOR YOU AT THE BOTTOM.
MR. TOTOSAI!
YOU'RE IN BAD SHAPE.
HMPH.
ALL RIGHT. LET ME SEE IT.
HMMM ...

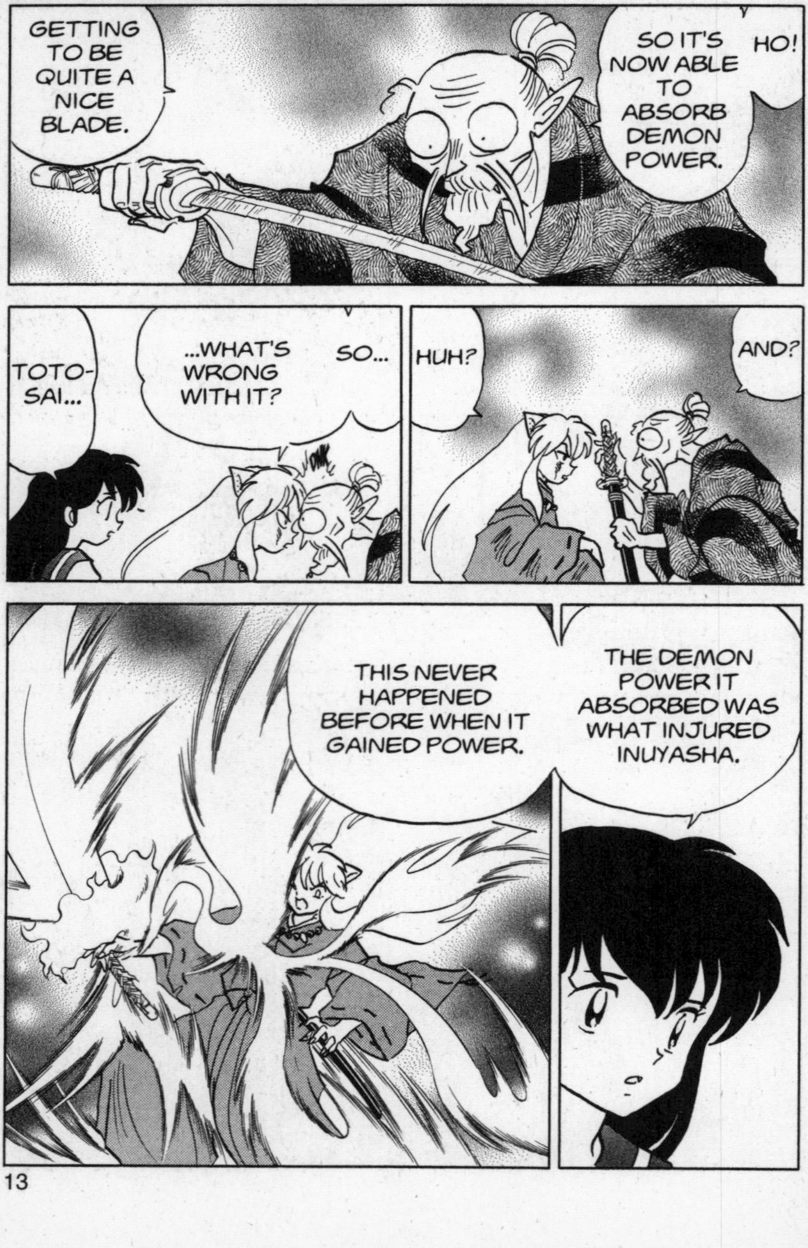
HO!
SO IT'S NOW ABLE TO ABSORB DEMON POWER.
GETTING TO BE QUITE A NICE BLADE.
AND?
HUH?
SO...
...WHAT'S WRONG WITH IT?
TOTO-SAI...
THE DEMON POWER IT ABSORBED WAS WHAT INJURED INUYASHA.
THIS NEVER HAPPENED BEFORE WHEN IT GAINED POWER.

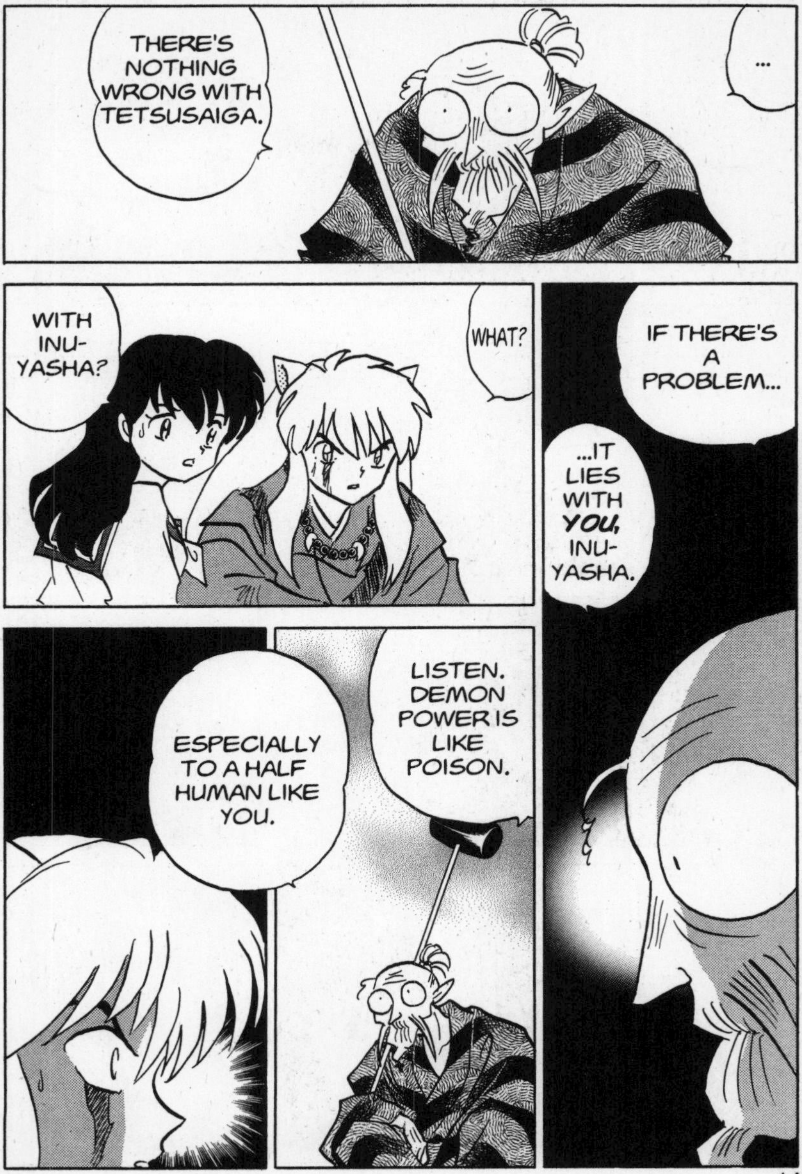
...
THERE'S NOTHING WRONG WITH TETSUSAIGA.
IF THERE'S A PROBLEM...
...IT LIES WITH *YOU,* INU-YASHA.
WHAT?
WITH INU-YASHA?
LISTEN. DEMON POWER IS LIKE POISON.
ESPECIALLY TO A HALF HUMAN LIKE YOU.

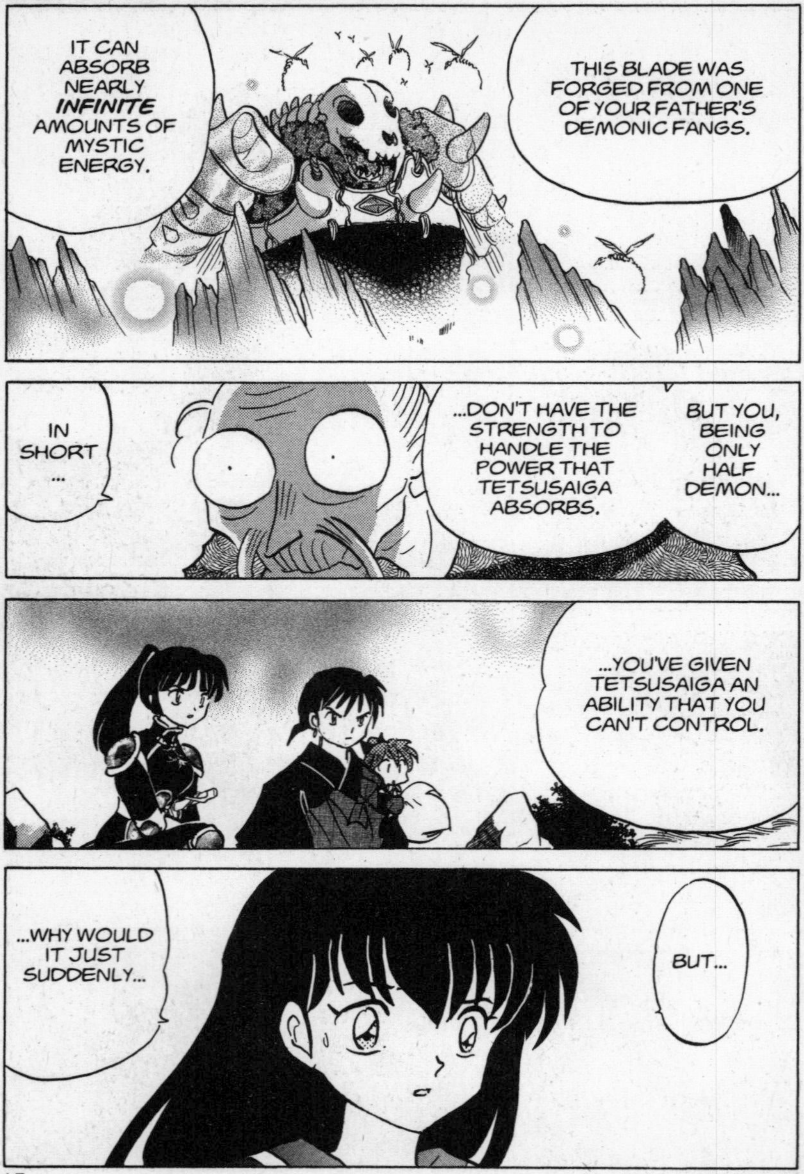
THIS BLADE WAS FORGED FROM ONE OF YOUR FATHER'S DEMONIC FANGS.
IT CAN ABSORB NEARLY *INFINITE* AMOUNTS OF MYSTIC ENERGY.
BUT YOU, BEING ONLY HALF DEMON...
...DON'T HAVE THE STRENGTH TO HANDLE THE POWER THAT TETSUSAIGA ABSORBS.
IN SHORT...
...YOU'VE GIVEN TETSUSAIGA AN ABILITY THAT YOU CAN'T CONTROL.
BUT...
...WHY WOULD IT JUST SUDDENLY...

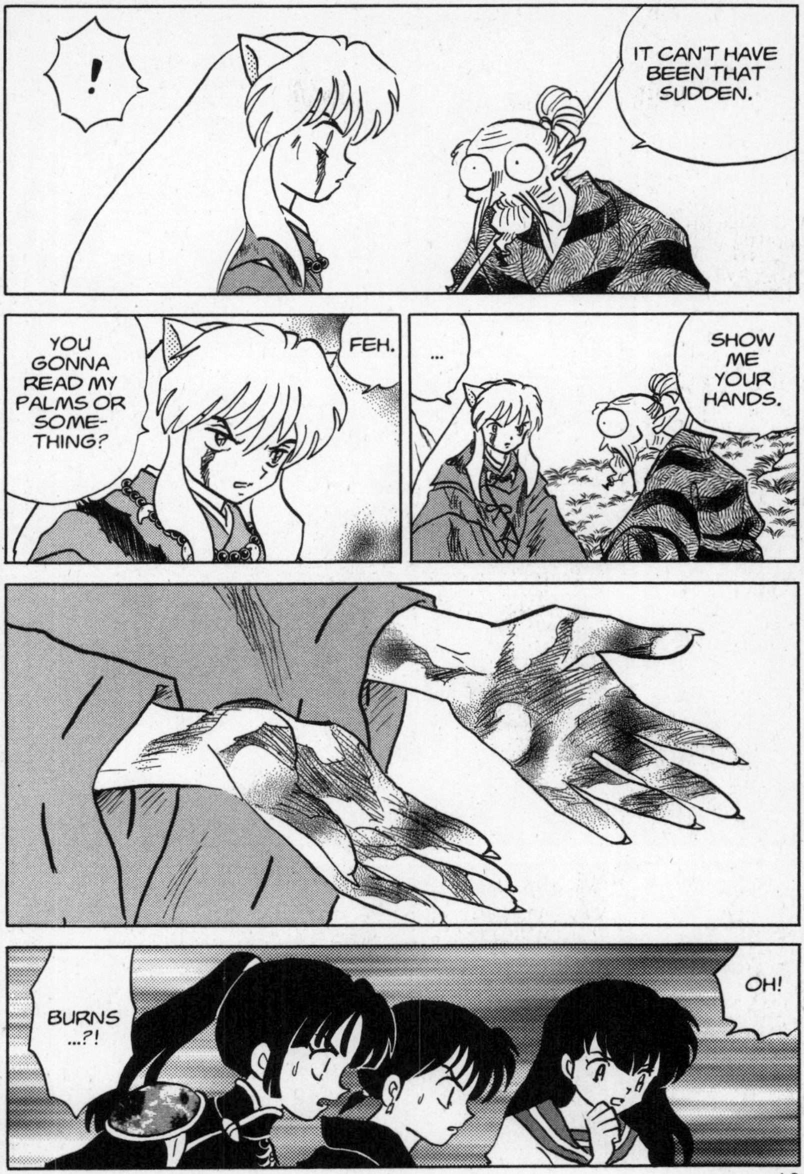
IT CAN'T HAVE BEEN THAT SUDDEN.
!
SHOW ME YOUR HANDS.
...
FEH.
YOU GONNA READ MY PALMS OR SOME-THING?
OH!
BURNS ...?!

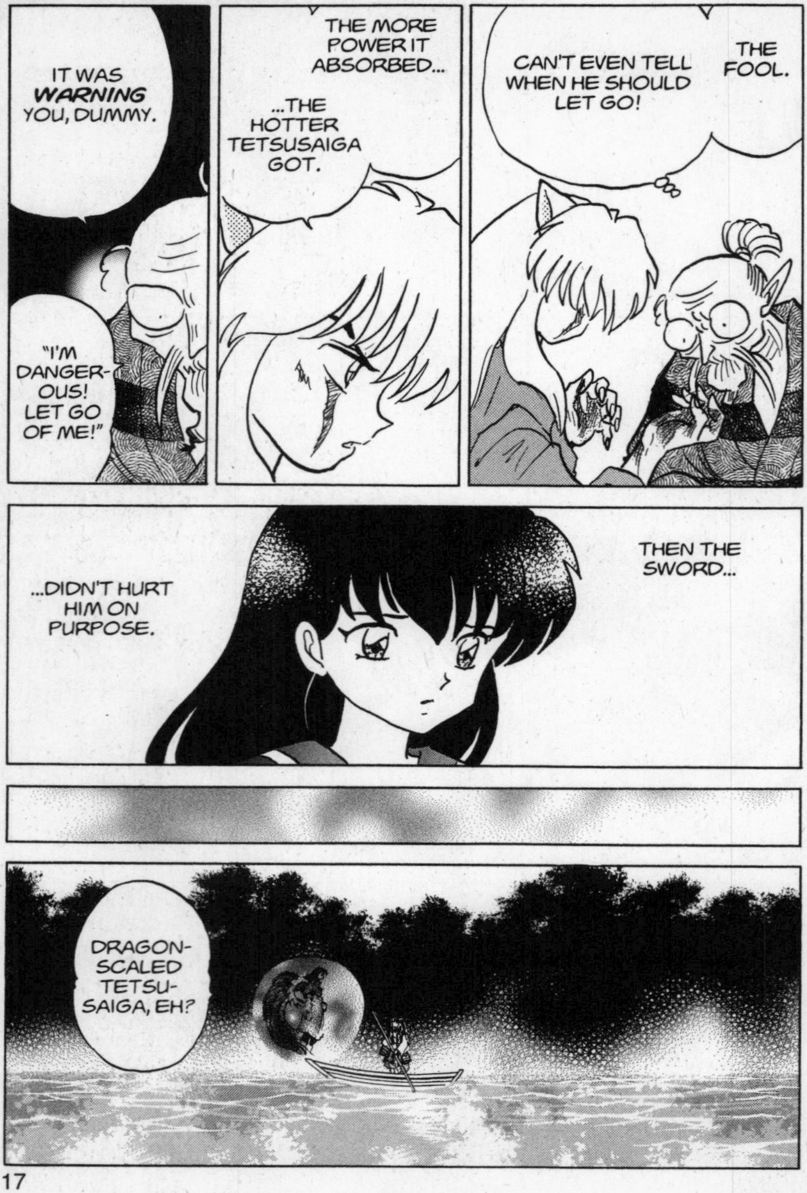
THE FOOL.
CAN'T EVEN TELL WHEN HE SHOULD LET GO!
THE MORE POWER IT ABSORBED...
...THE HOTTER TETSUSAIGA GOT.
IT WAS *WARNING* YOU, DUMMY.
"I'M DANGER-OUS! LET GO OF ME!"
THEN THE SWORD...
...DIDN'T HURT HIM ON PURPOSE.
DRAGON-SCALED TETSU-SAIGA, EH?

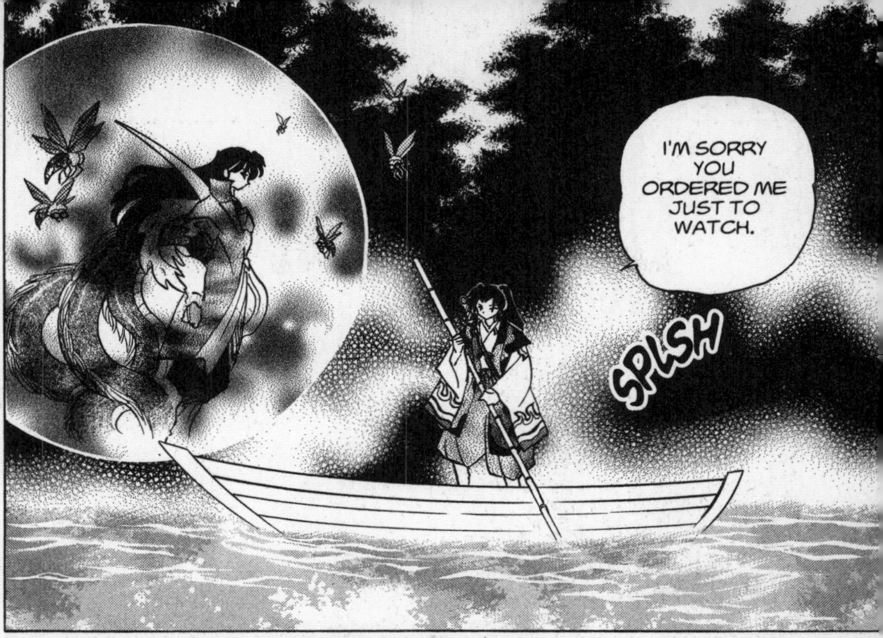
I'M SORRY YOU ORDERED ME JUST TO WATCH.
SPLSH

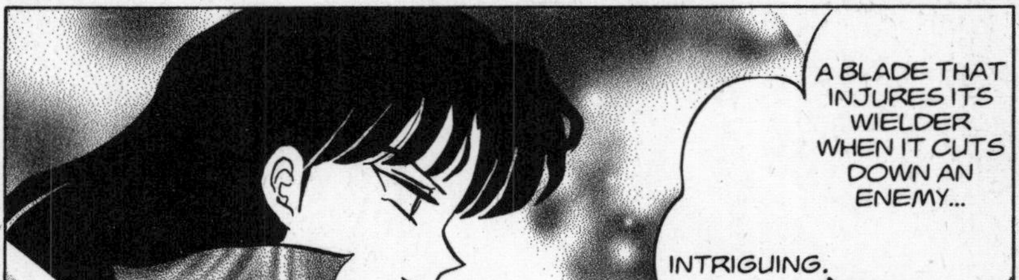
A BLADE THAT INJURES ITS WIELDER WHEN IT CUTS DOWN AN ENEMY...
INTRIGUING.

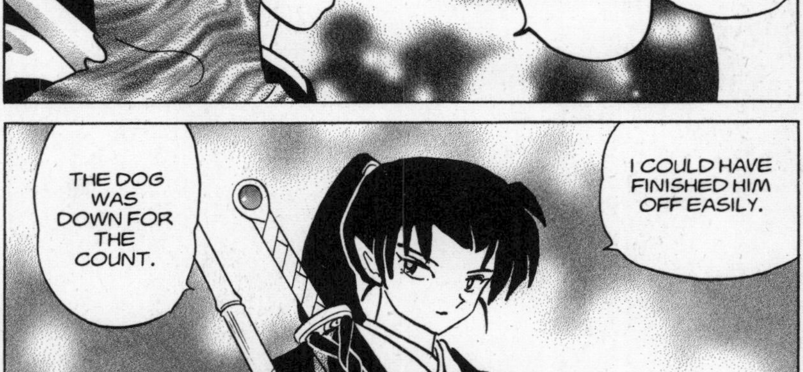
I COULD HAVE FINISHED HIM OFF EASILY.
THE DOG WAS DOWN FOR THE COUNT.

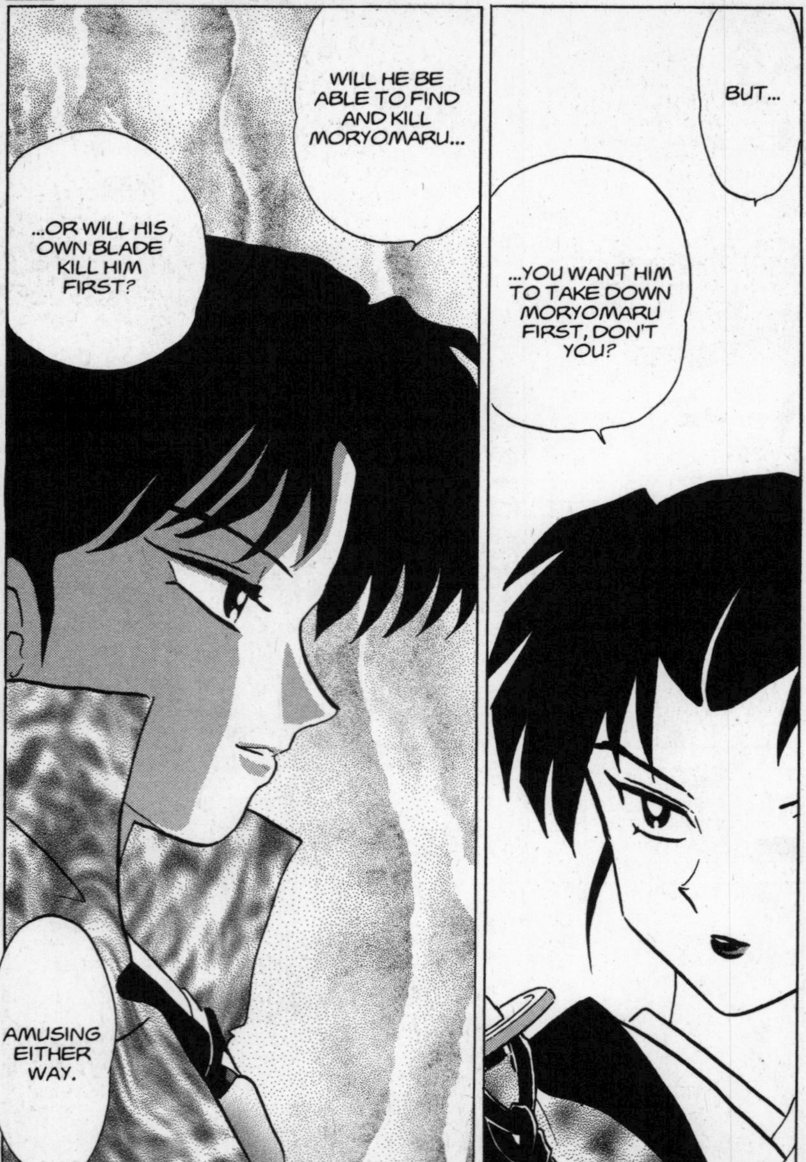
WILL HE BE ABLE TO FIND AND KILL MORYOMARU...
...OR WILL HIS OWN BLADE KILL HIM FIRST?
AMUSING EITHER WAY.
BUT...
...YOU WANT HIM TO TAKE DOWN MORYOMARU FIRST, DON'T YOU?

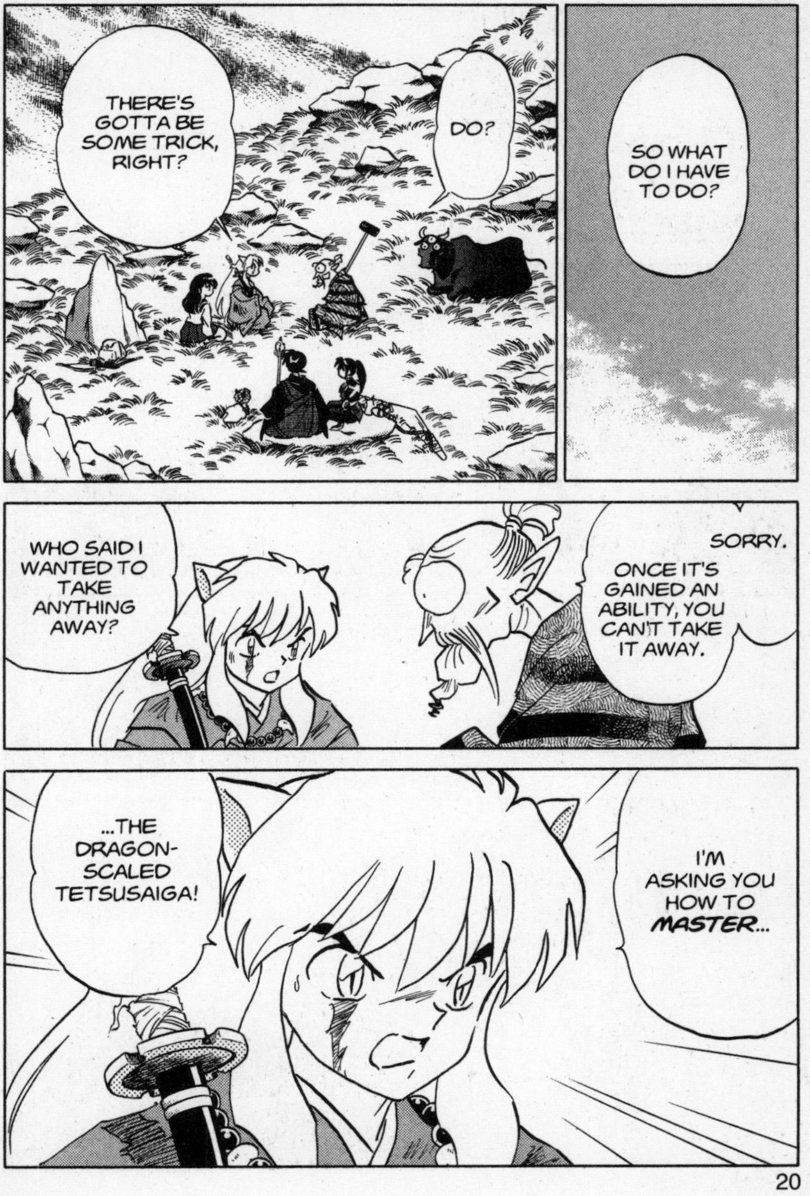
SO WHAT DO I HAVE TO DO?
DO?
THERE'S GOTTA BE SOME TRICK, RIGHT?
SORRY. ONCE IT'S GAINED AN ABILITY, YOU CAN'T TAKE IT AWAY.
WHO SAID I WANTED TO TAKE ANYTHING AWAY?
I'M ASKING YOU HOW TO MASTER...
...THE DRAGON-SCALED TETSUSAIGA!

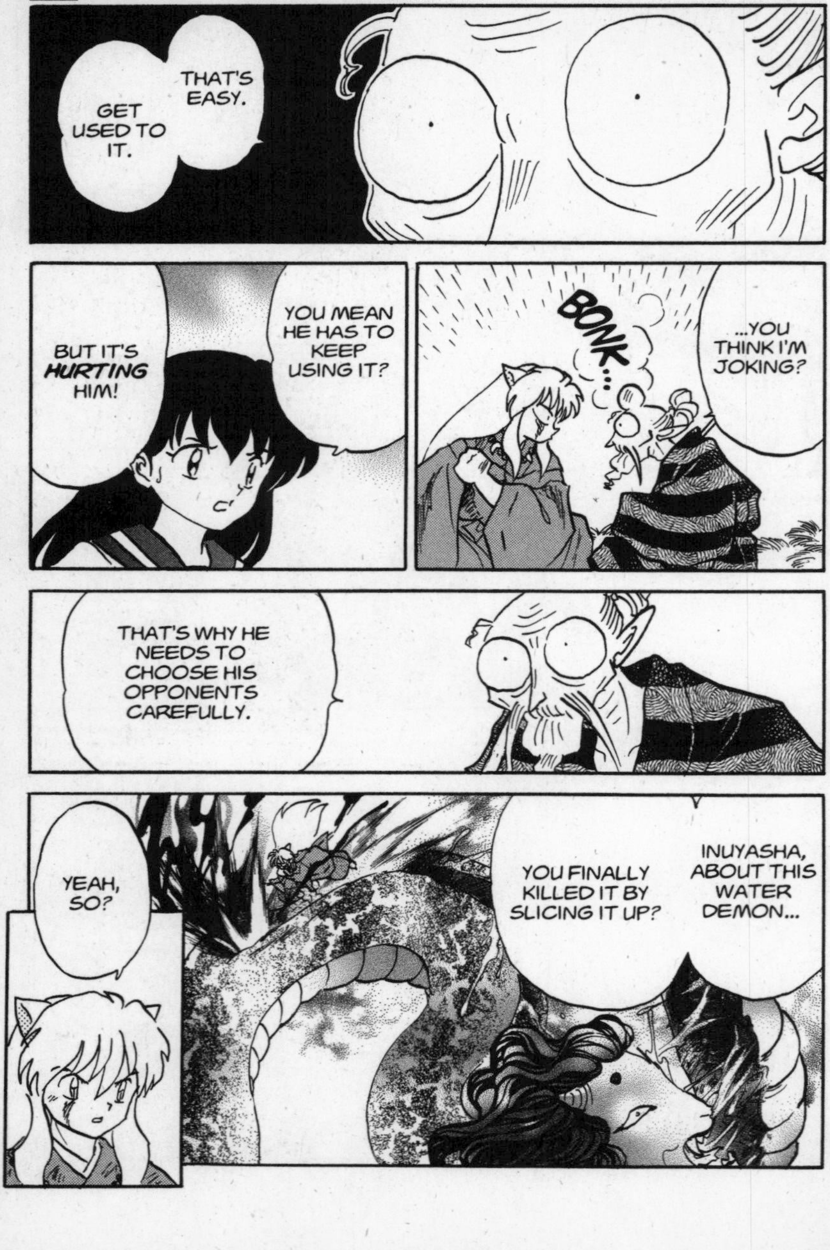
THAT'S EASY.
GET USED TO IT.
...YOU THINK I'M JOKING?
BONK...
YOU MEAN HE HAS TO KEEP USING IT?
BUT IT'S *HURTING* HIM!
THAT'S WHY HE NEEDS TO CHOOSE HIS OPPONENTS CAREFULLY.
INUYASHA, ABOUT THIS WATER DEMON...
YOU FINALLY KILLED IT BY SLICING IT UP?
YEAH, SO?

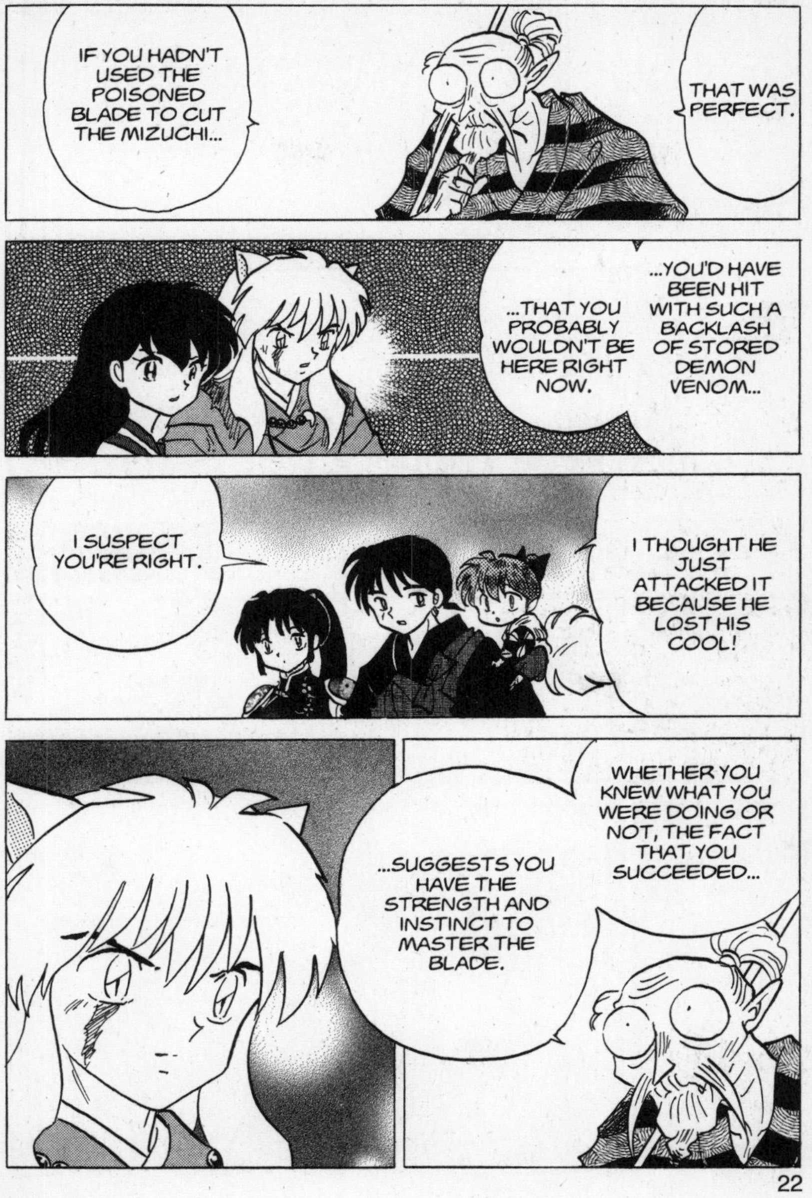
THAT WAS PERFECT.
IF YOU HADN'T USED THE POISONED BLADE TO CUT THE MIZUCHI...
...YOU'D HAVE BEEN HIT WITH SUCH A BACKLASH OF STORED DEMON VENOM...
...THAT YOU PROBABLY WOULDN'T BE HERE RIGHT NOW.
I THOUGHT HE JUST ATTACKED IT BECAUSE HE LOST HIS COOL!
I SUSPECT YOU'RE RIGHT.
WHETHER YOU KNEW WHAT YOU WERE DOING OR NOT, THE FACT THAT YOU SUCCEEDED...
...SUGGESTS YOU HAVE THE STRENGTH AND INSTINCT TO MASTER THE BLADE.

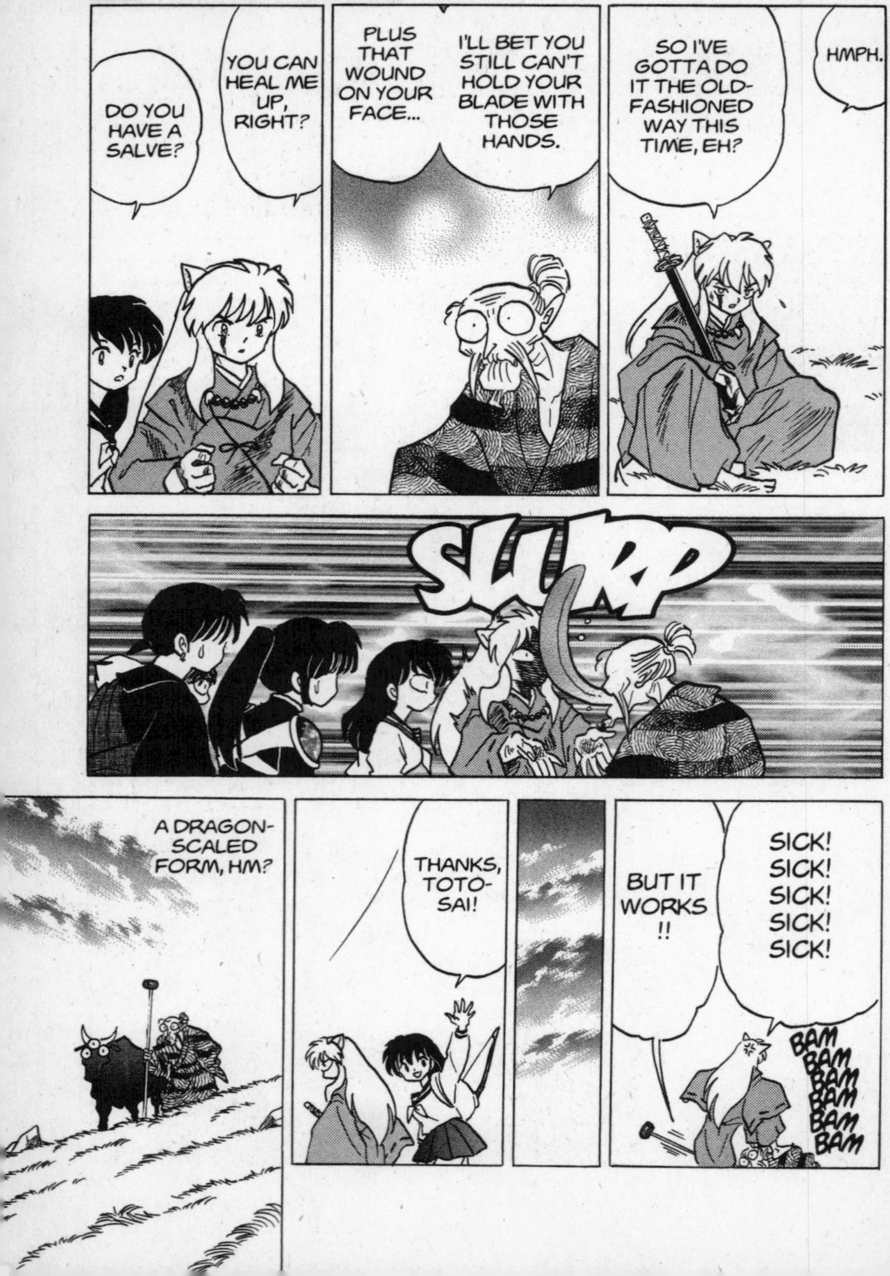
DO YOU HAVE A SALVE?
YOU CAN HEAL ME UP, RIGHT?
PLUS THAT WOUND ON YOUR FACE...
I'LL BET YOU STILL CAN'T HOLD YOUR BLADE WITH THOSE HANDS.
SO I'VE GOTTA DO IT THE OLD-FASHIONED WAY THIS TIME, EH?
HMPH.
SLURP
A DRAGON-SCALED FORM, HM?
THANKS, TOTO-SAI!
SICK! SICK! SICK! SICK! SICK!
BUT IT WORKS !!
BAM BAM BAM BAM BAM BAM

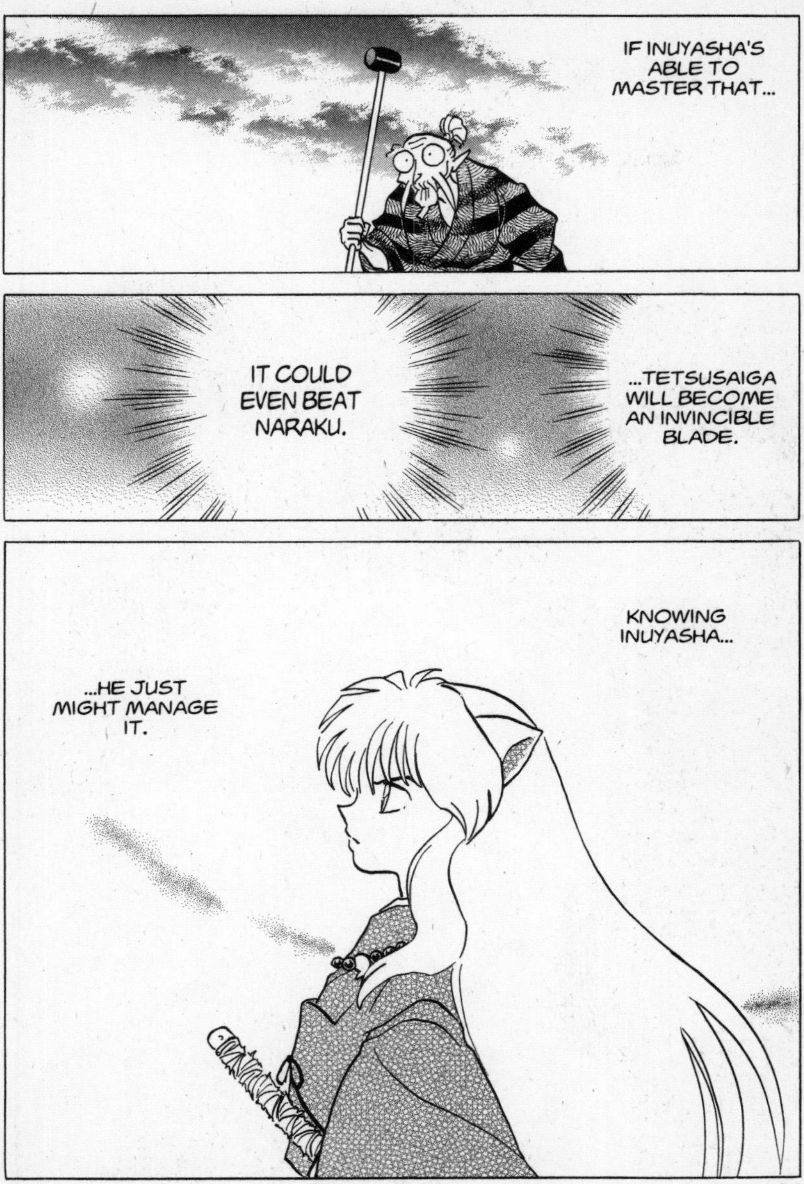
IF INUYASHA'S ABLE TO MASTER THAT...
...TETSUSAIGA WILL BECOME AN INVINCIBLE BLADE.
IT COULD EVEN BEAT NARAKU.
KNOWING INUYASHA...
...HE JUST MIGHT MANAGE IT.

SCROLL 2
MEIOJU

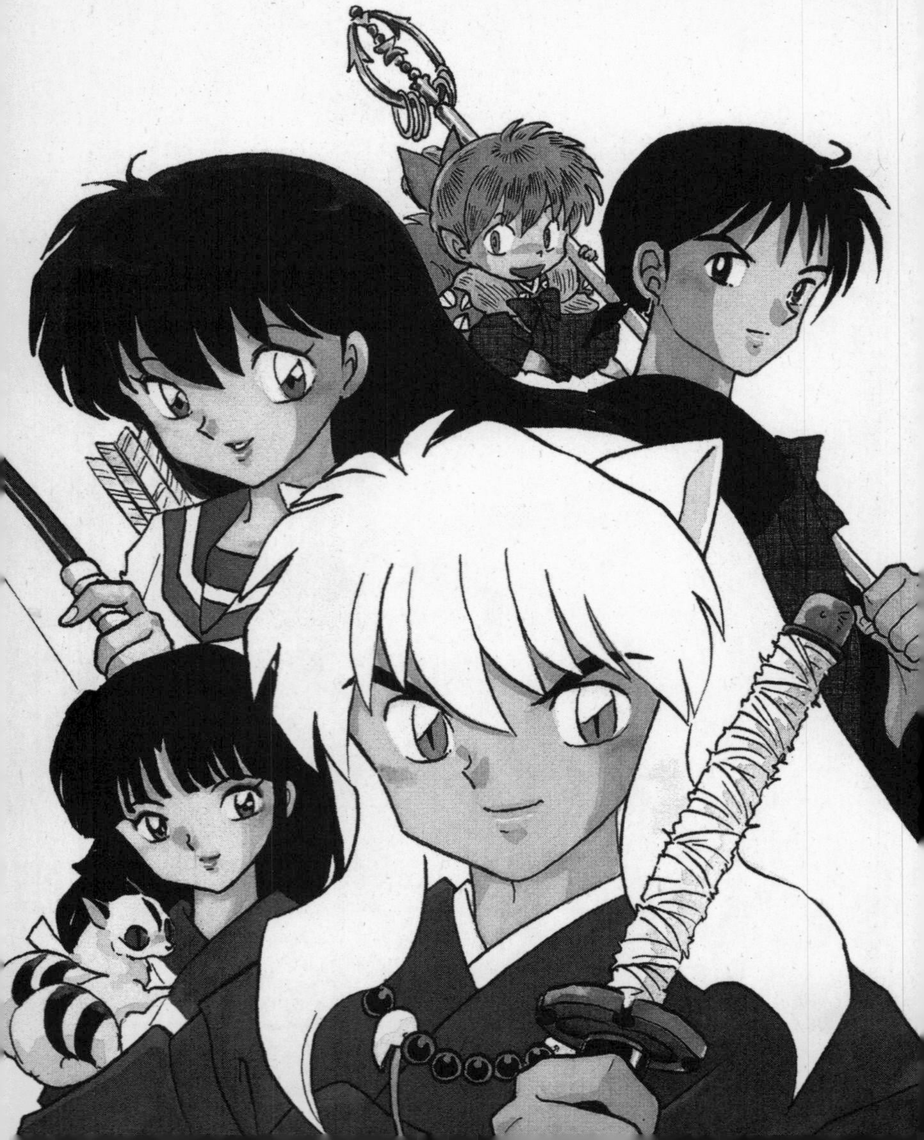

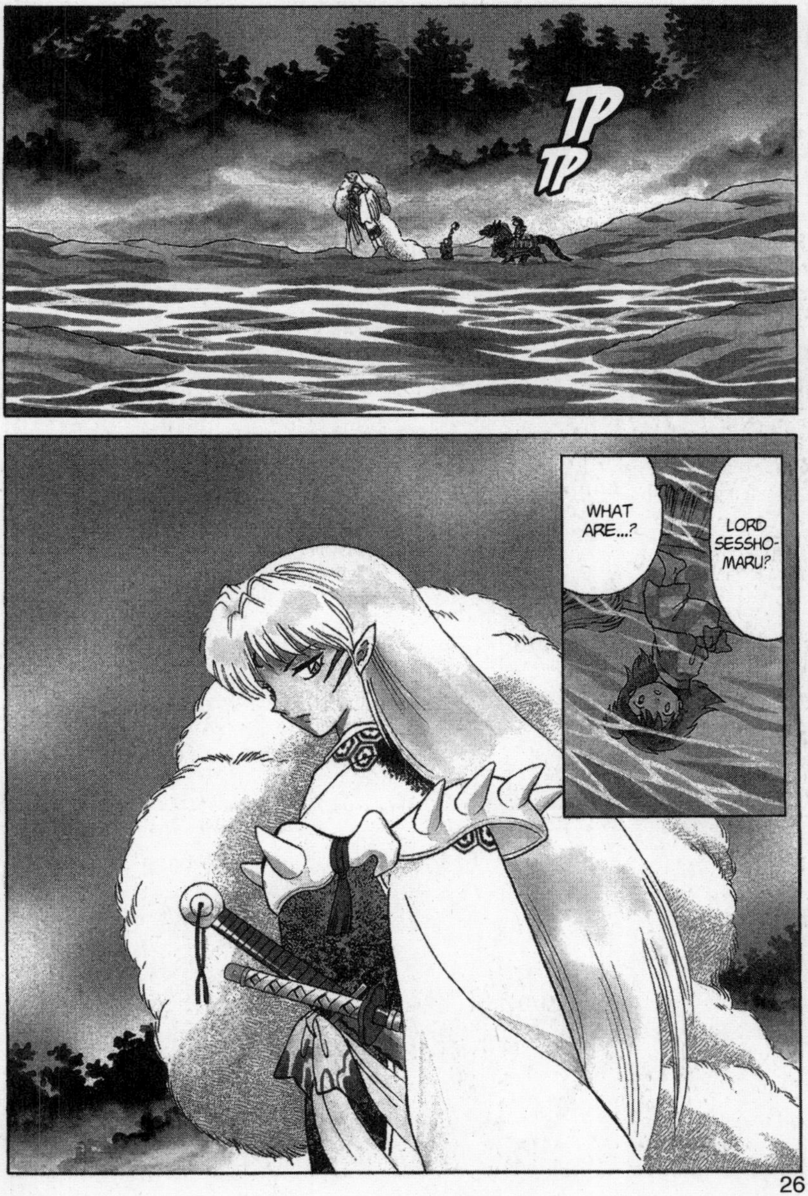
TP
TP
LORD SESSHO-MARU?
WHAT ARE...?

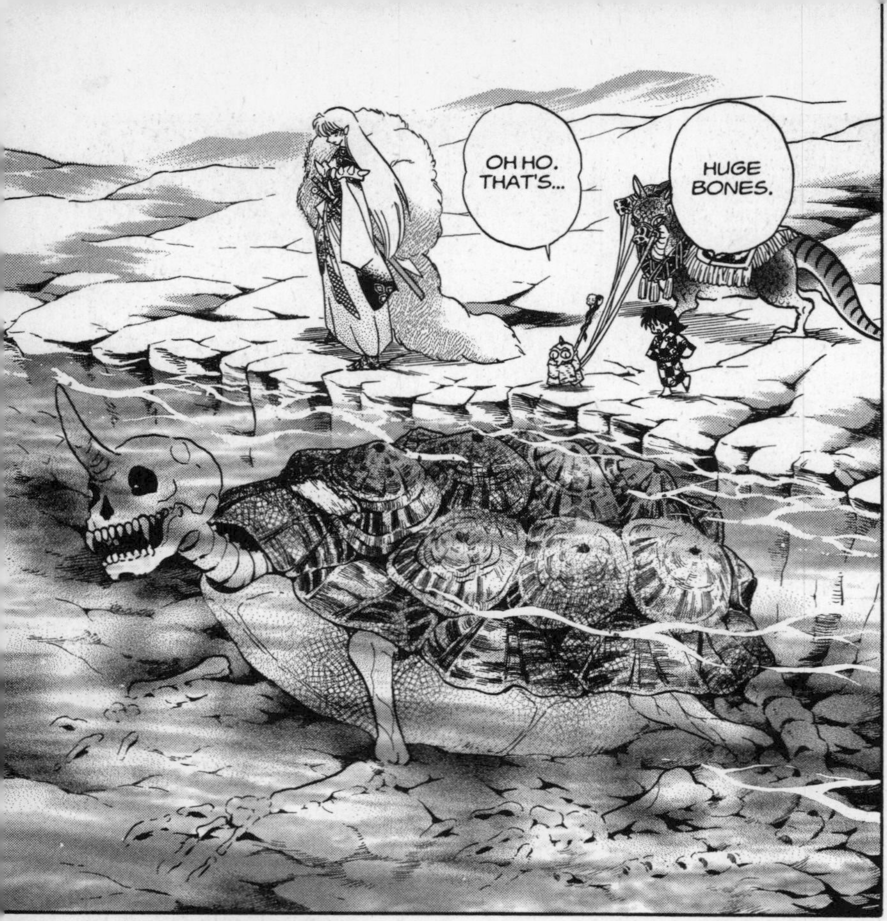
HUGE BONES.
OH HO. THAT'S...

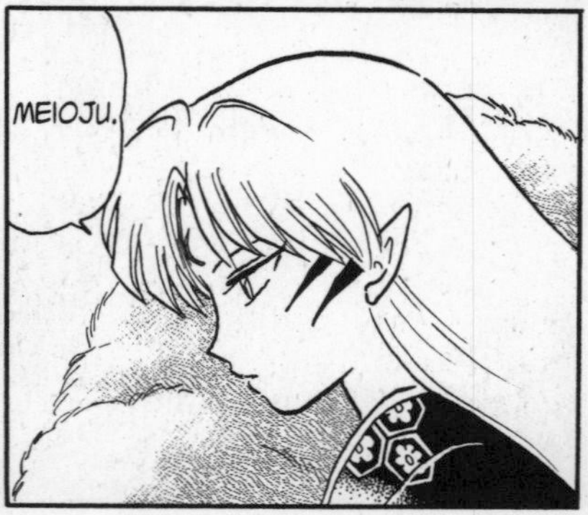
MEIOJU.

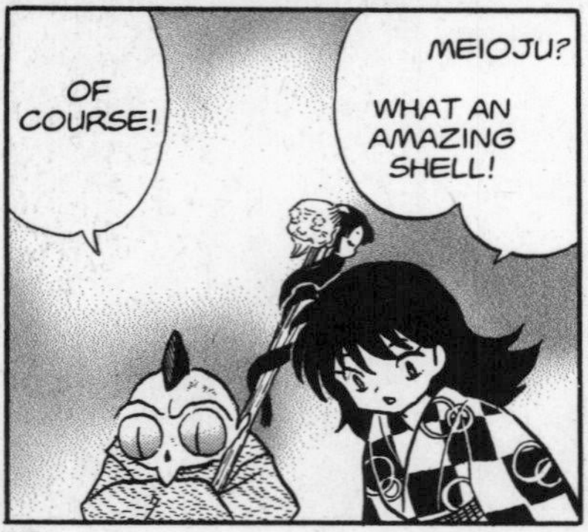
MEIOJU?
WHAT AN AMAZING SHELL!
OF COURSE!

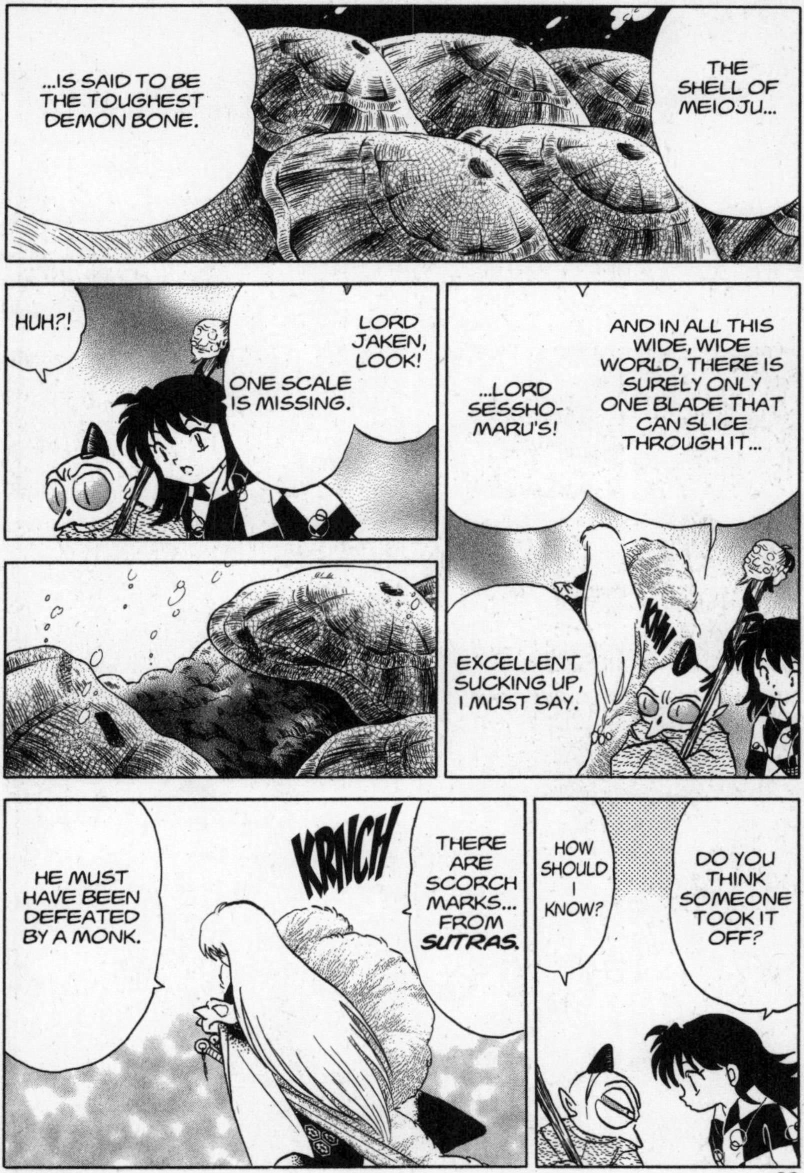
THE SHELL OF MEIOJU...
...IS SAID TO BE THE TOUGHEST DEMON BONE.
AND IN ALL THIS WIDE, WIDE WORLD, THERE IS SURELY ONLY ONE BLADE THAT CAN SLICE THROUGH IT...
...LORD SESSHO-MARU'S!
KNW
EXCELLENT SUCKING UP, I MUST SAY.
LORD JAKEN, LOOK!
ONE SCALE IS MISSING.
HUH?!
DO YOU THINK SOMEONE TOOK IT OFF?
HOW SHOULD I KNOW?
THERE ARE SCORCH MARKS... FROM *SUTRAS*.
KRNCH
HE MUST HAVE BEEN DEFEATED BY A MONK.

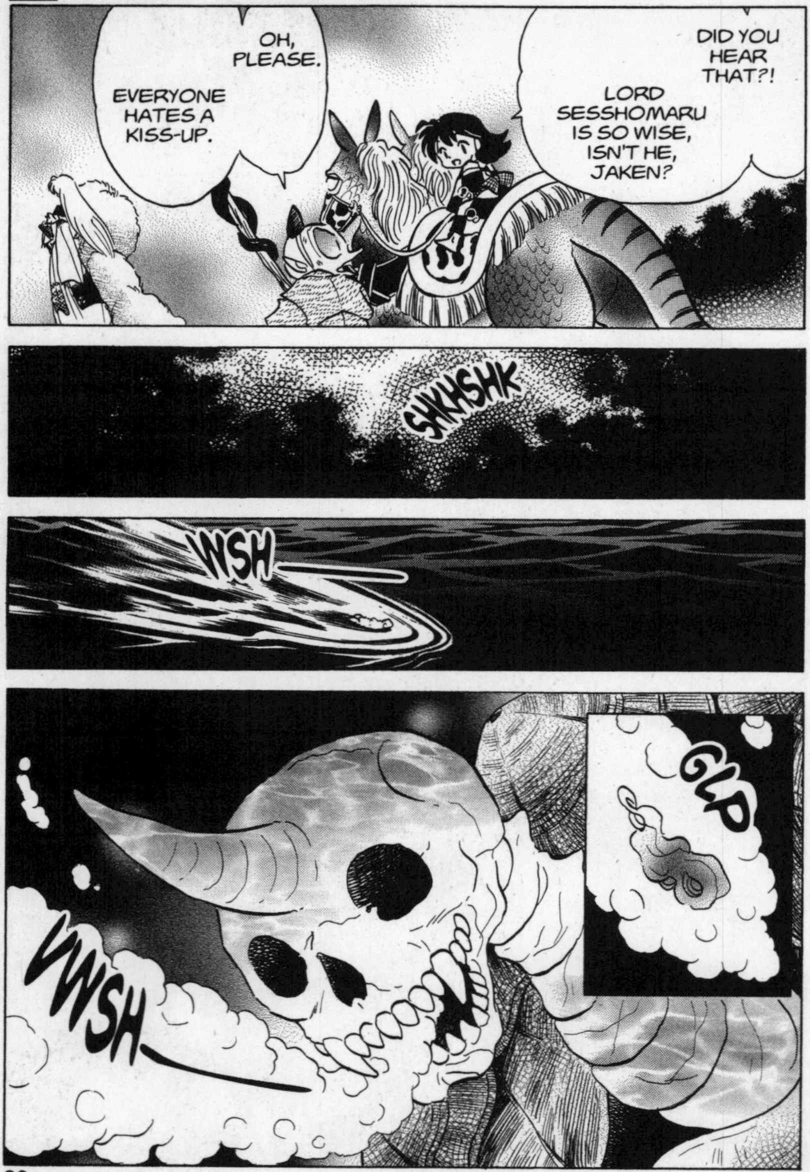
DID YOU HEAR THAT?! LORD SESSHOMARU IS SO WISE, ISN'T HE, JAKEN?
OH, PLEASE. EVERYONE HATES A KISS-UP.
SHKHSHK
WSH
GLP
VWSH

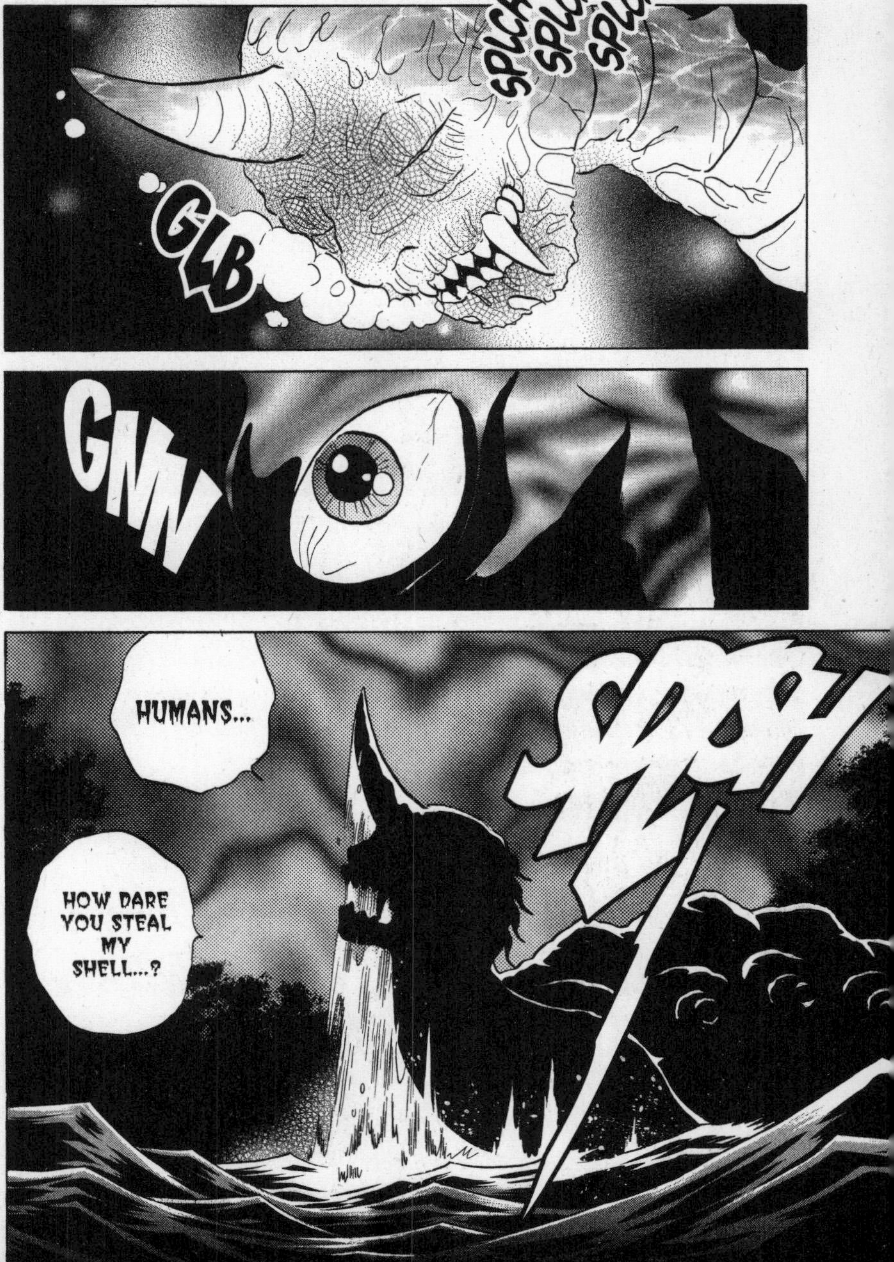
SPLCH SPLCH SPLCH
GLB
GNN
SPPH
HUMANS...
HOW DARE YOU STEAL MY SHELL...?

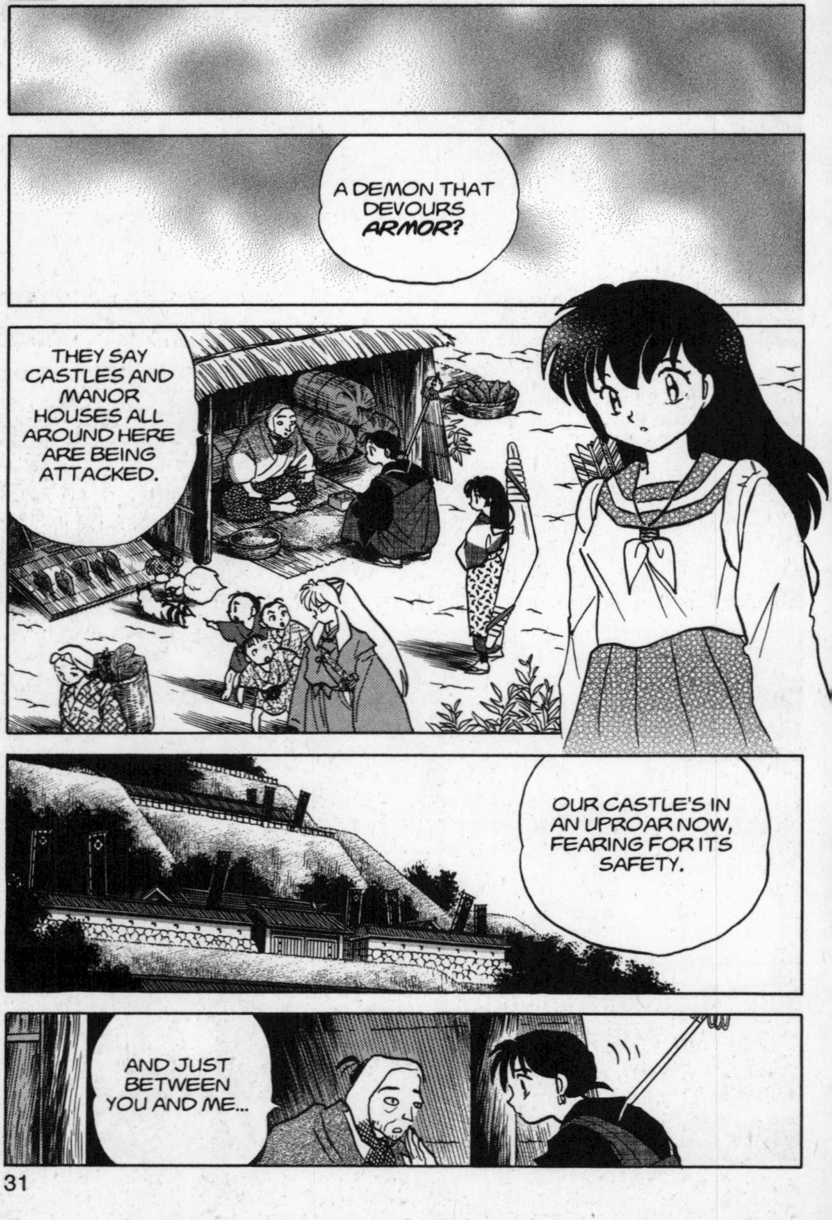
A DEMON THAT DEVOURS *ARMOR?*
THEY SAY CASTLES AND MANOR HOUSES ALL AROUND HERE ARE BEING ATTACKED.
OUR CASTLE'S IN AN UPROAR NOW, FEARING FOR ITS SAFETY.
AND JUST BETWEEN YOU AND ME...

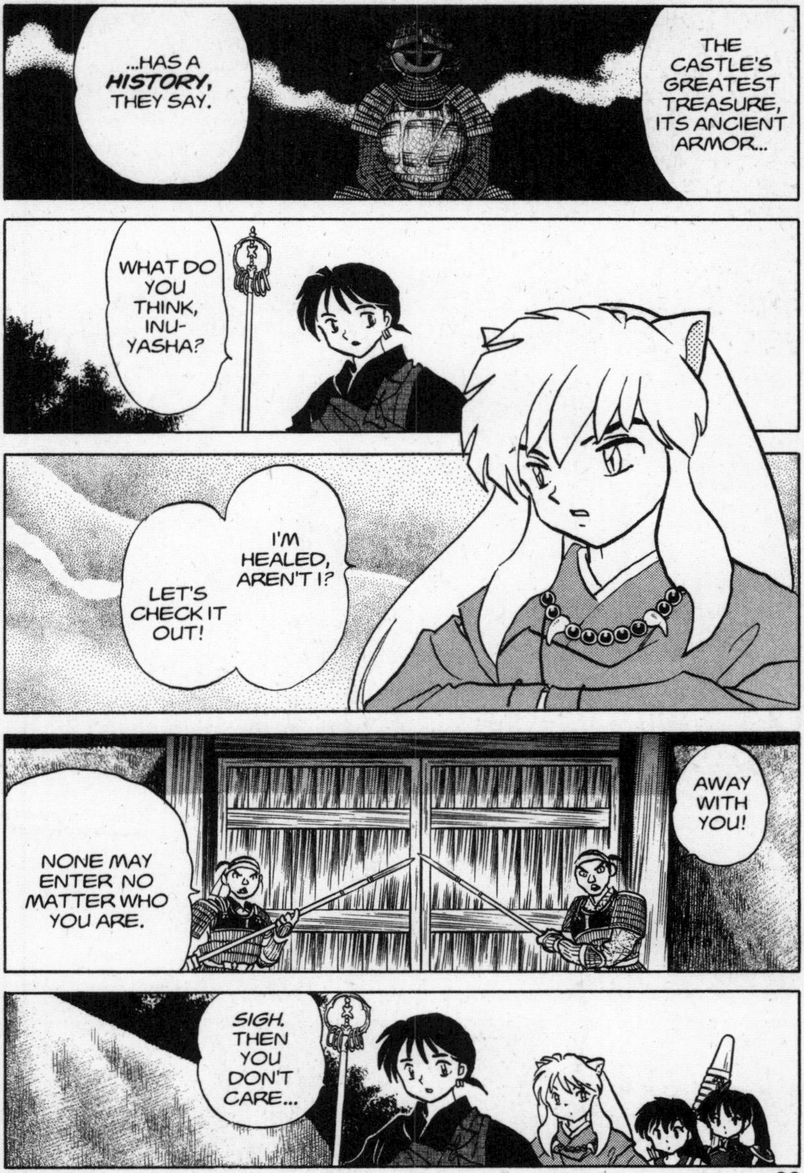
THE CASTLE'S GREATEST TREASURE, ITS ANCIENT ARMOR...
...HAS A HISTORY, THEY SAY.
WHAT DO YOU THINK, INU-YASHA?
I'M HEALED, AREN'T I?
LET'S CHECK IT OUT!
AWAY WITH YOU!
NONE MAY ENTER NO MATTER WHO YOU ARE.
SIGH. THEN YOU DON'T CARE...

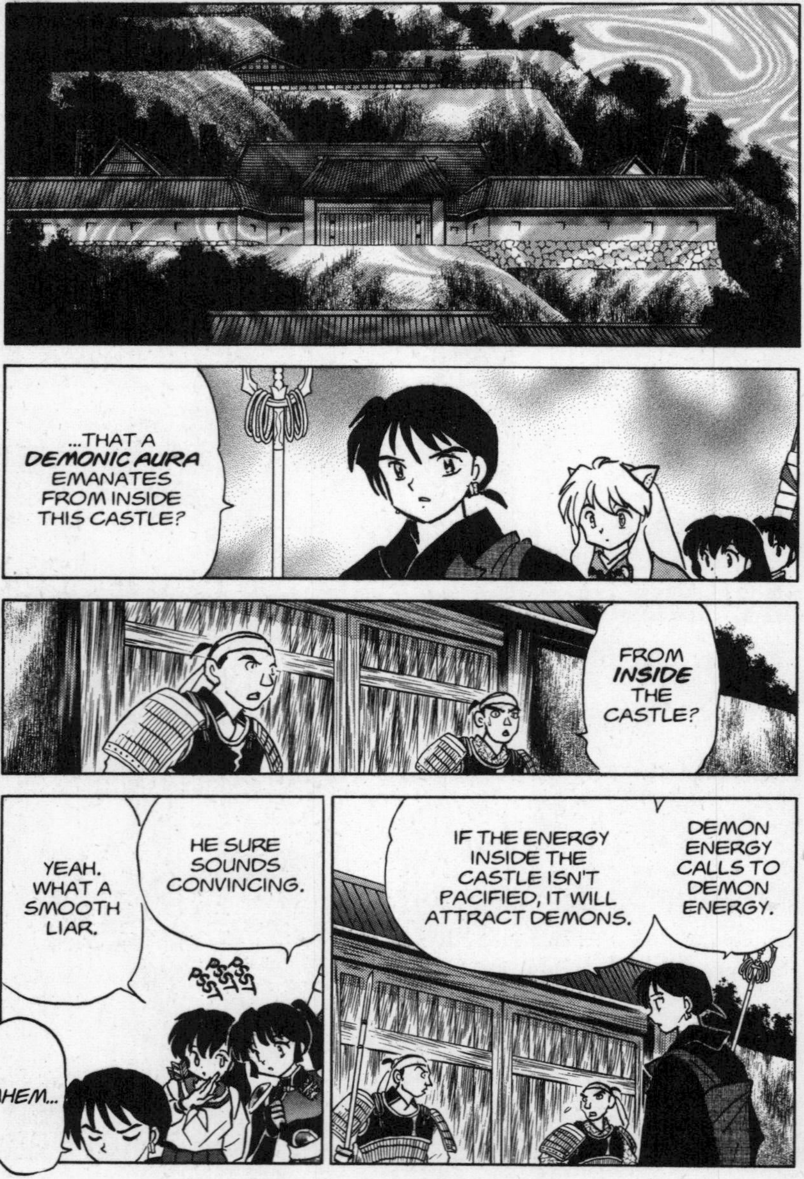
...THAT A DEMONIC AURA EMANATES FROM INSIDE THIS CASTLE?
FROM INSIDE THE CASTLE?
DEMON ENERGY CALLS TO DEMON ENERGY.
IF THE ENERGY INSIDE THE CASTLE ISN'T PACIFIED, IT WILL ATTRACT DEMONS.
HE SURE SOUNDS CONVINCING.
YEAH. WHAT A SMOOTH LIAR.
PSST PSST PSST
AHEM...

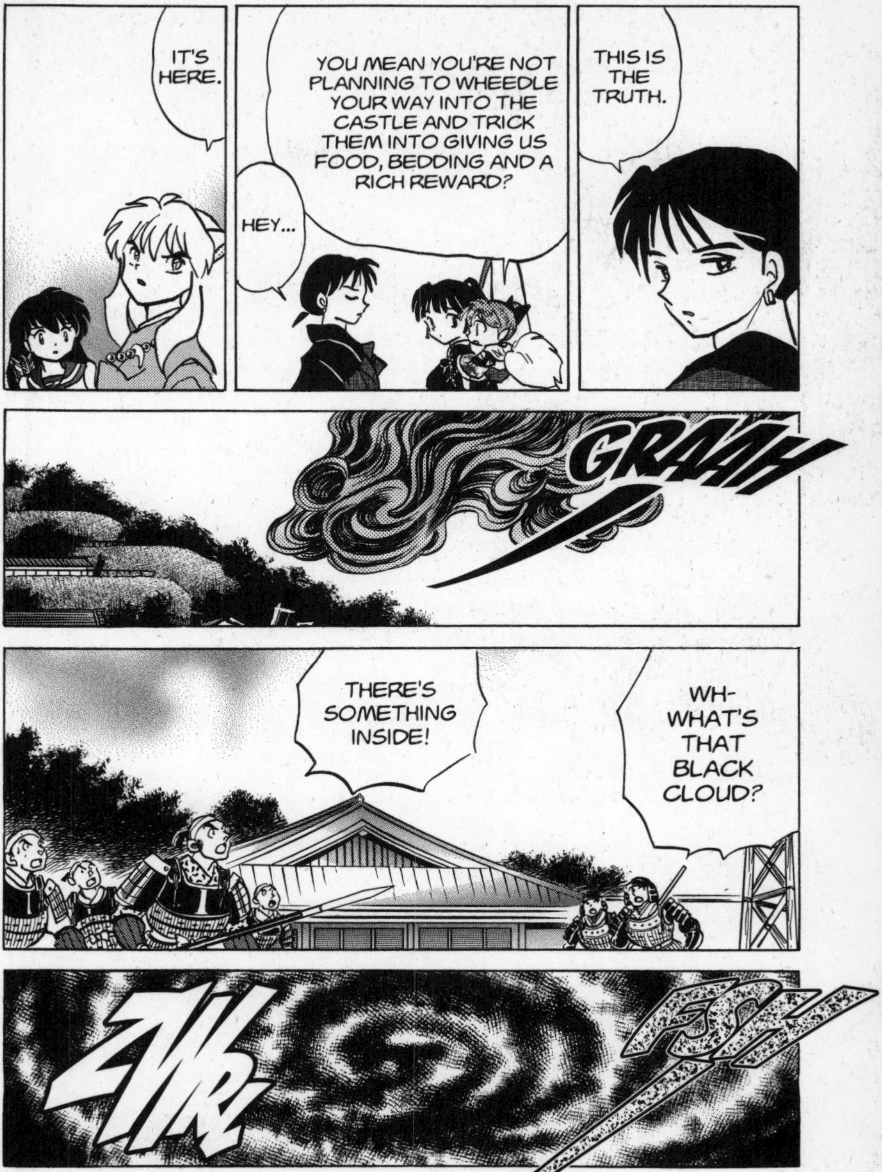
IT'S HERE.
YOU MEAN YOU'RE NOT PLANNING TO WHEEDLE YOUR WAY INTO THE CASTLE AND TRICK THEM INTO GIVING US FOOD, BEDDING AND A RICH REWARD?
HEY...
THIS IS THE TRUTH.
GRAAH
THERE'S SOMETHING INSIDE!
WH-WHAT'S THAT BLACK CLOUD?
ZWR
FSSH

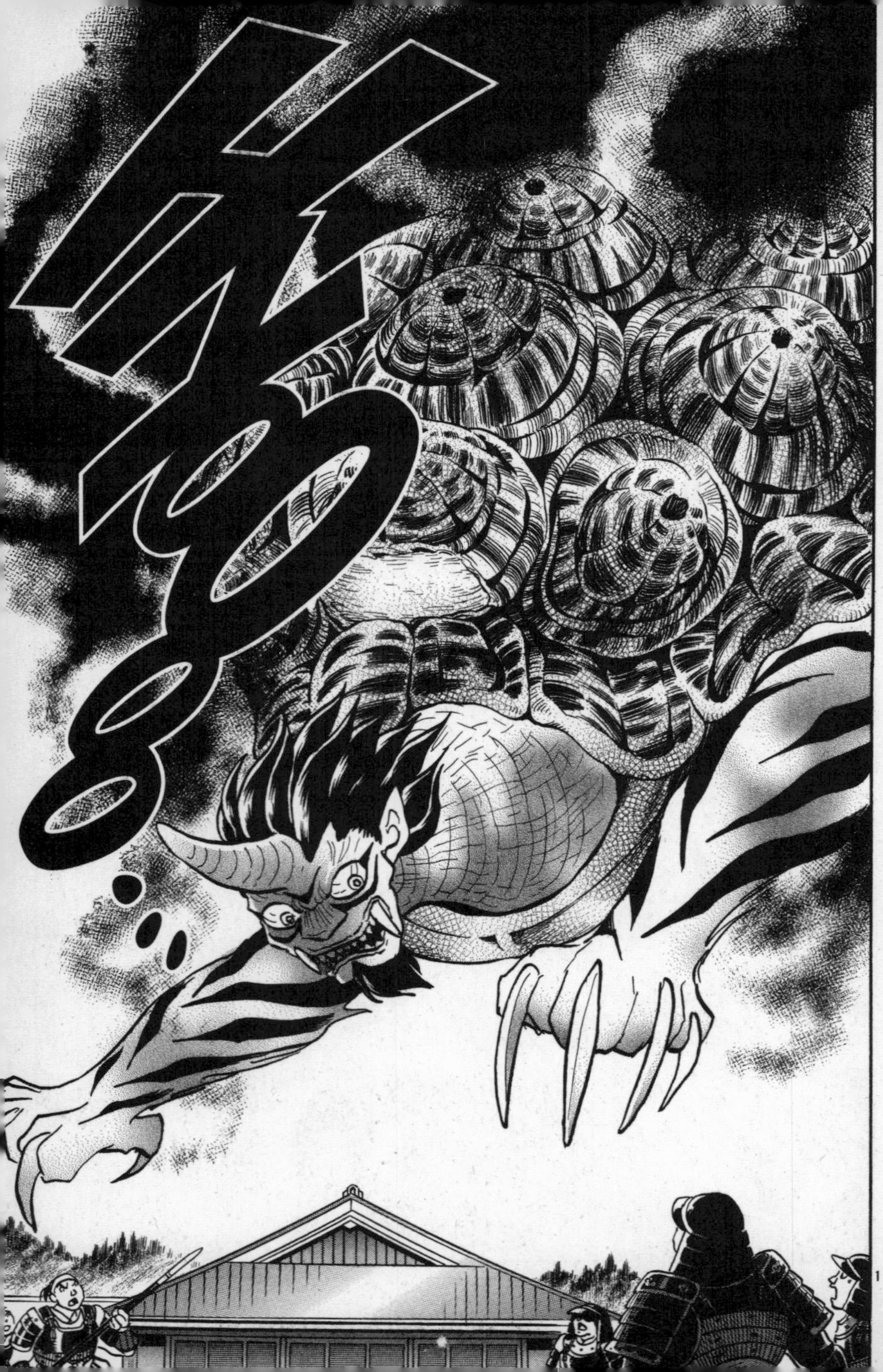

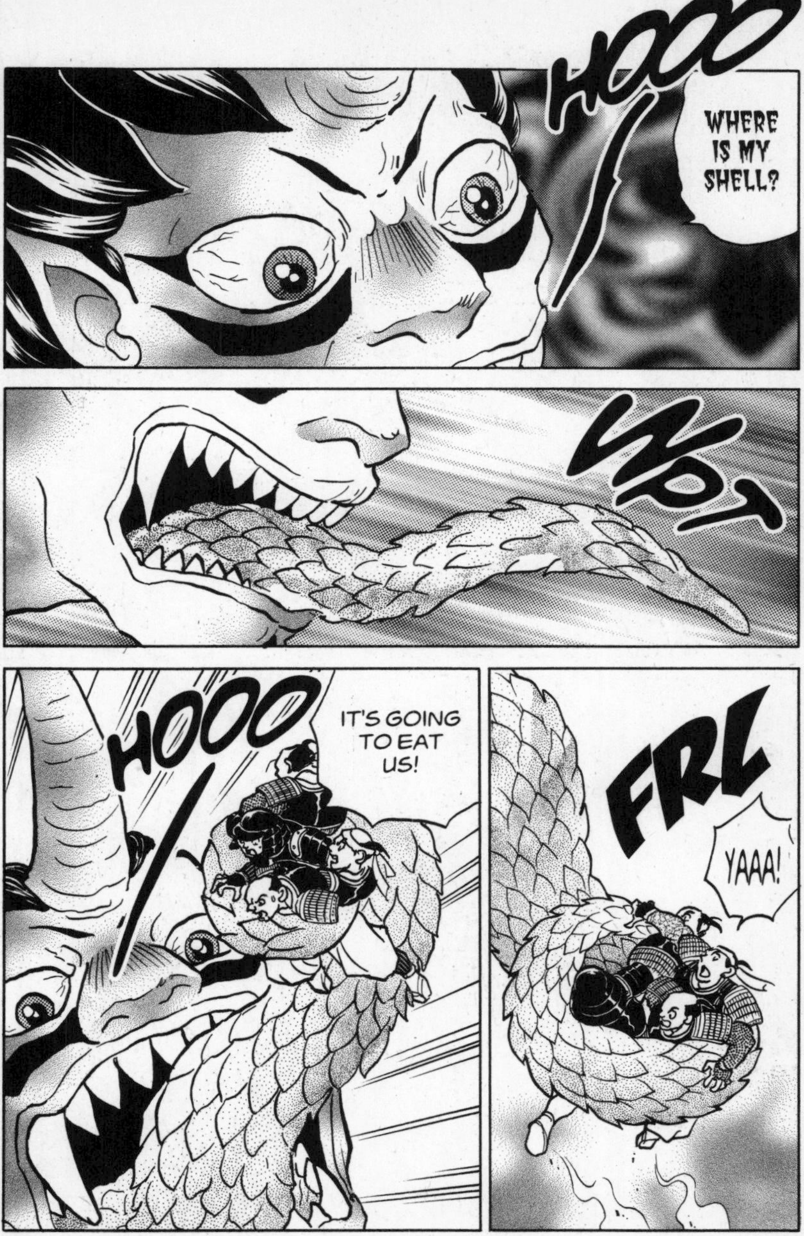
HOOO
WHERE IS MY SHELL?
WPT
FRL
YAAA!
HOOO
IT'S GOING TO EAT US!

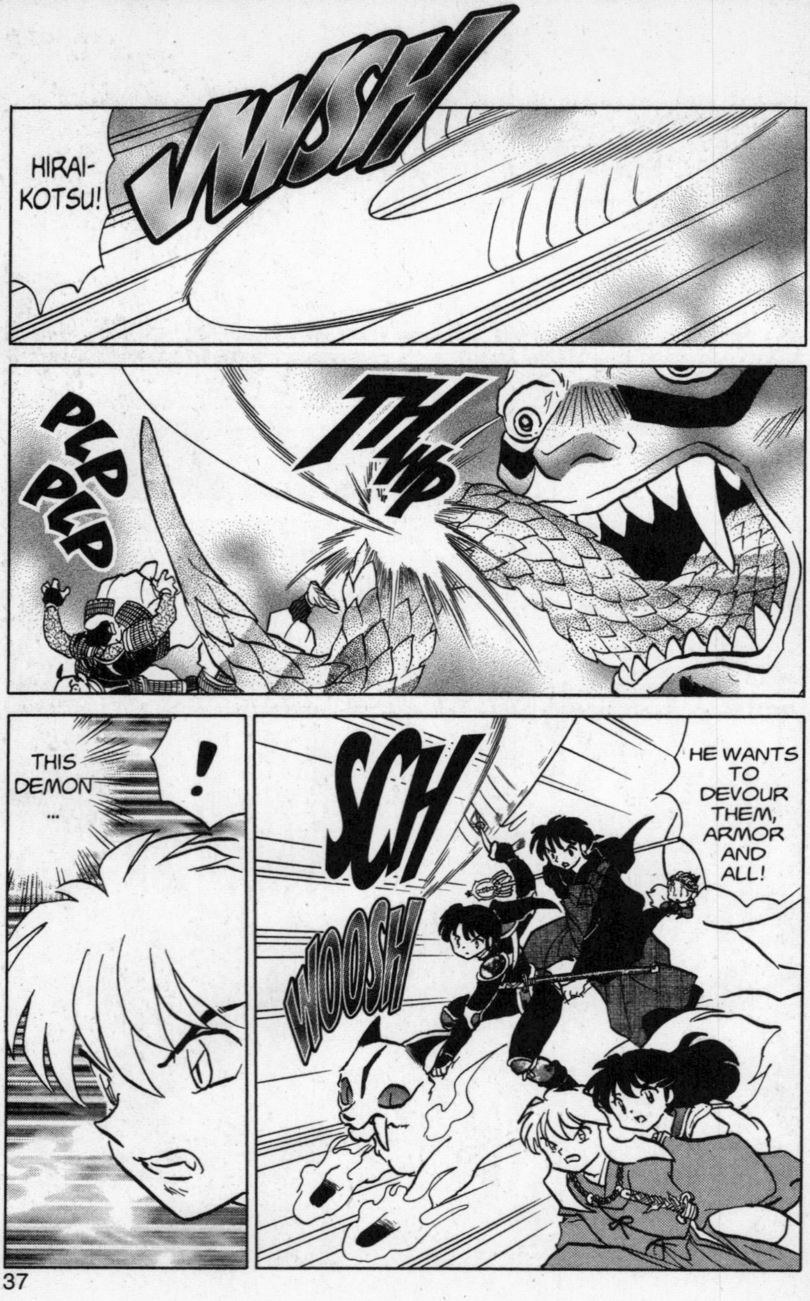
JWSH
HIRAI-KOTSU!
THWP
PLP PLP
HE WANTS TO DEVOUR THEM, ARMOR AND ALL!
SCH
WOOSH
THIS DEMON ...
!

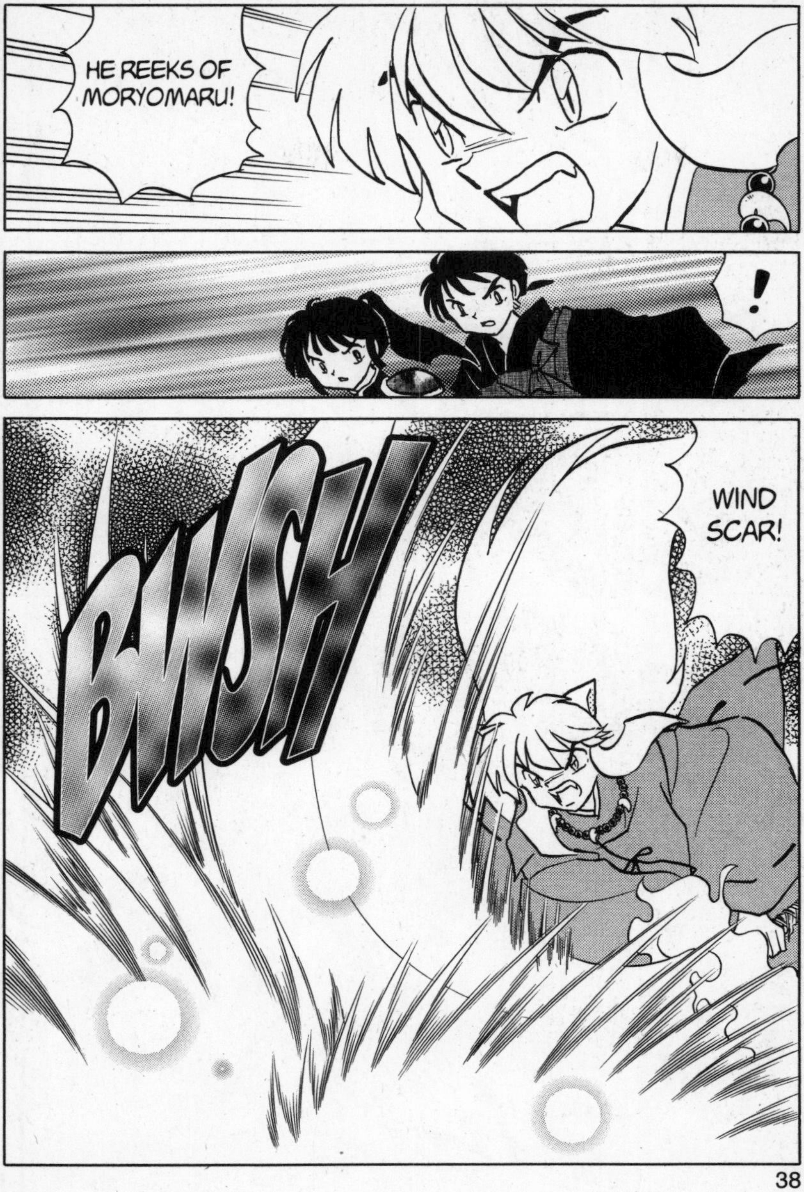
HE REEKS OF MORYOMARU!
!
WIND SCAR!
BWSH

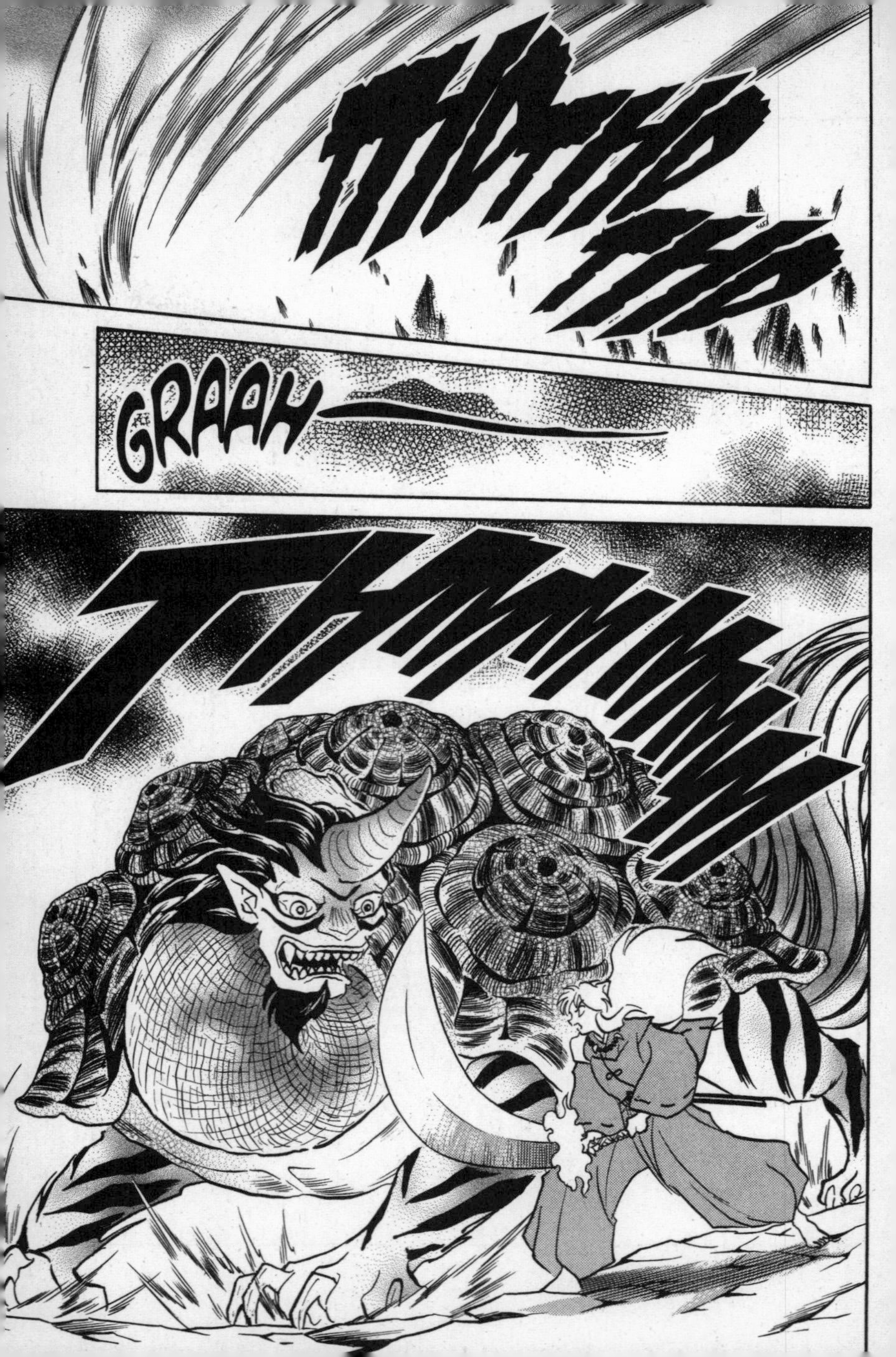
GRAAH

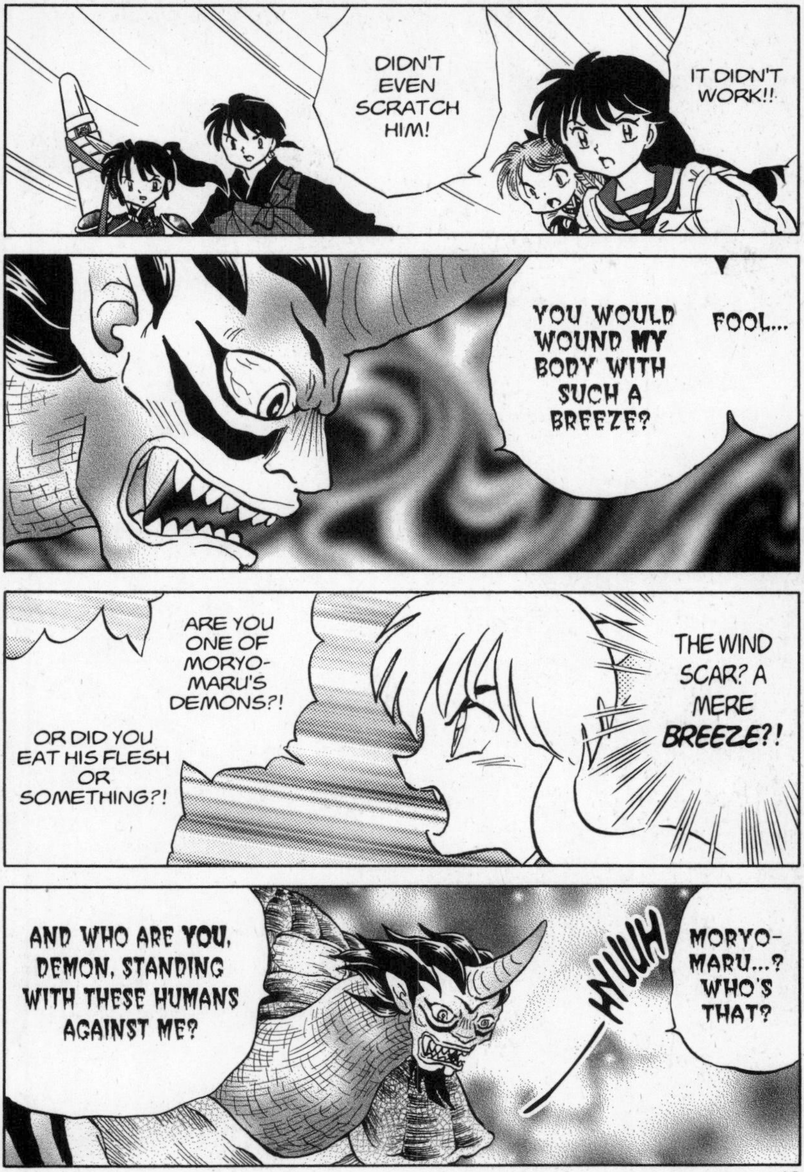
IT DIDN'T WORK!!
DIDN'T EVEN SCRATCH HIM!
FOOL...
YOU WOULD WOUND MY BODY WITH SUCH A BREEZE?
THE WIND SCAR? A MERE BREEZE?!
ARE YOU ONE OF MORYO-MARU'S DEMONS?!
OR DID YOU EAT HIS FLESH OR SOMETHING?!
MORYO-MARU...? WHO'S THAT?
HYUUH
AND WHO ARE YOU, DEMON, STANDING WITH THESE HUMANS AGAINST ME?

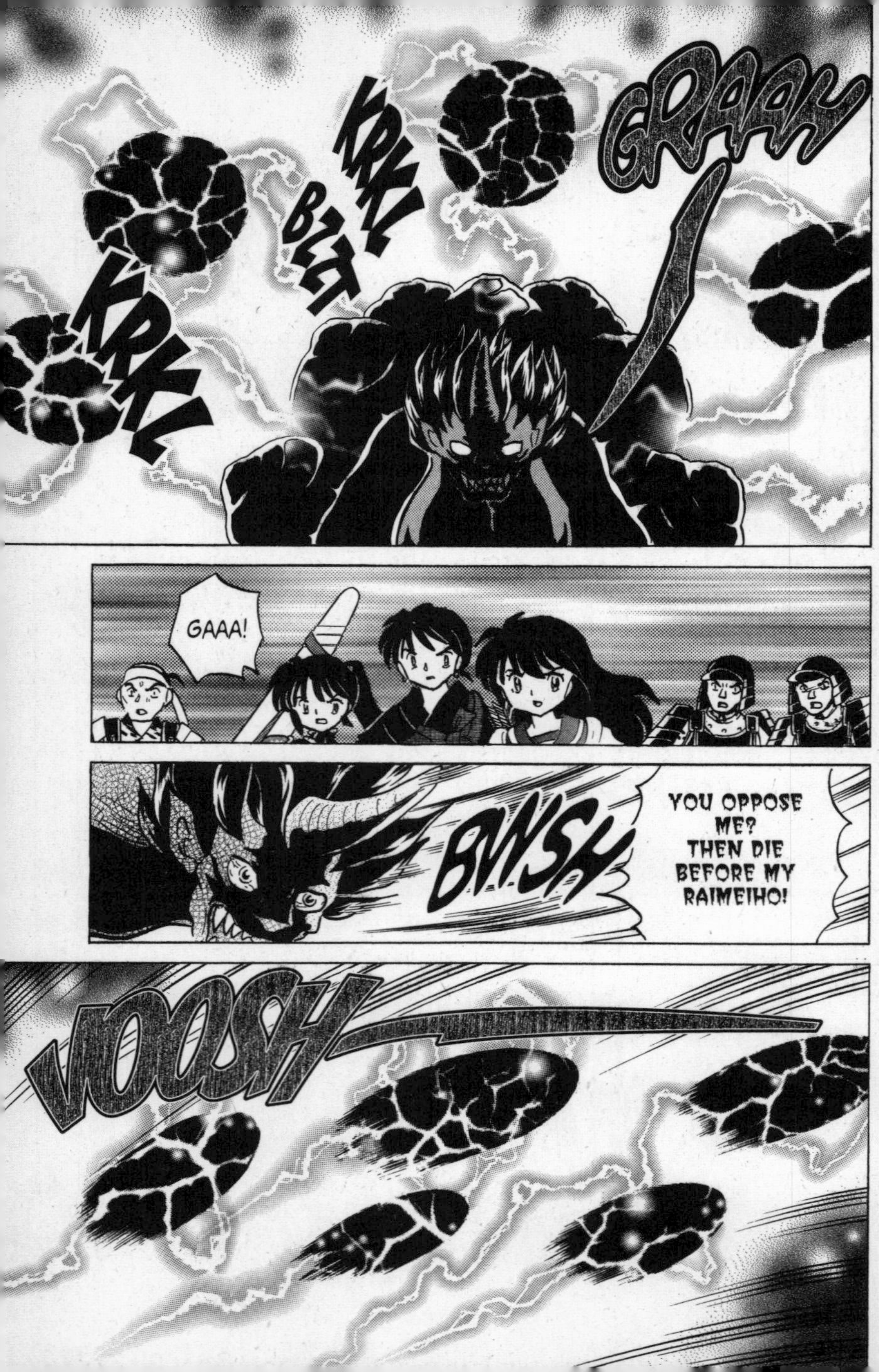
GRAAAH
KRKL!
BZZT
KRKL
GAAA!
YOU OPPOSE ME? THEN DIE BEFORE MY RAIMEIHO!
BWSH
VOOOSH

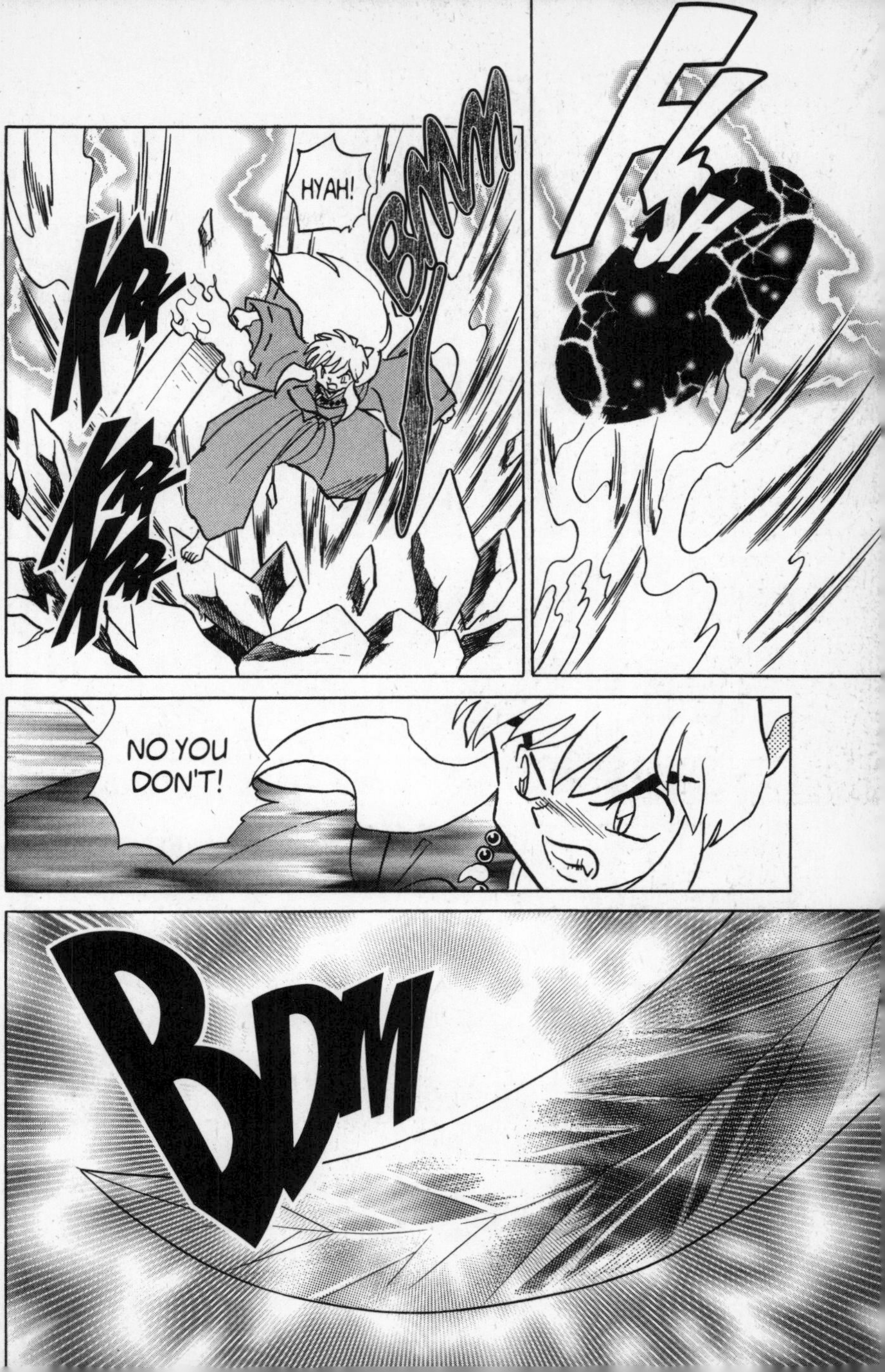
HYAH!
NO YOU DON'T!
BDM

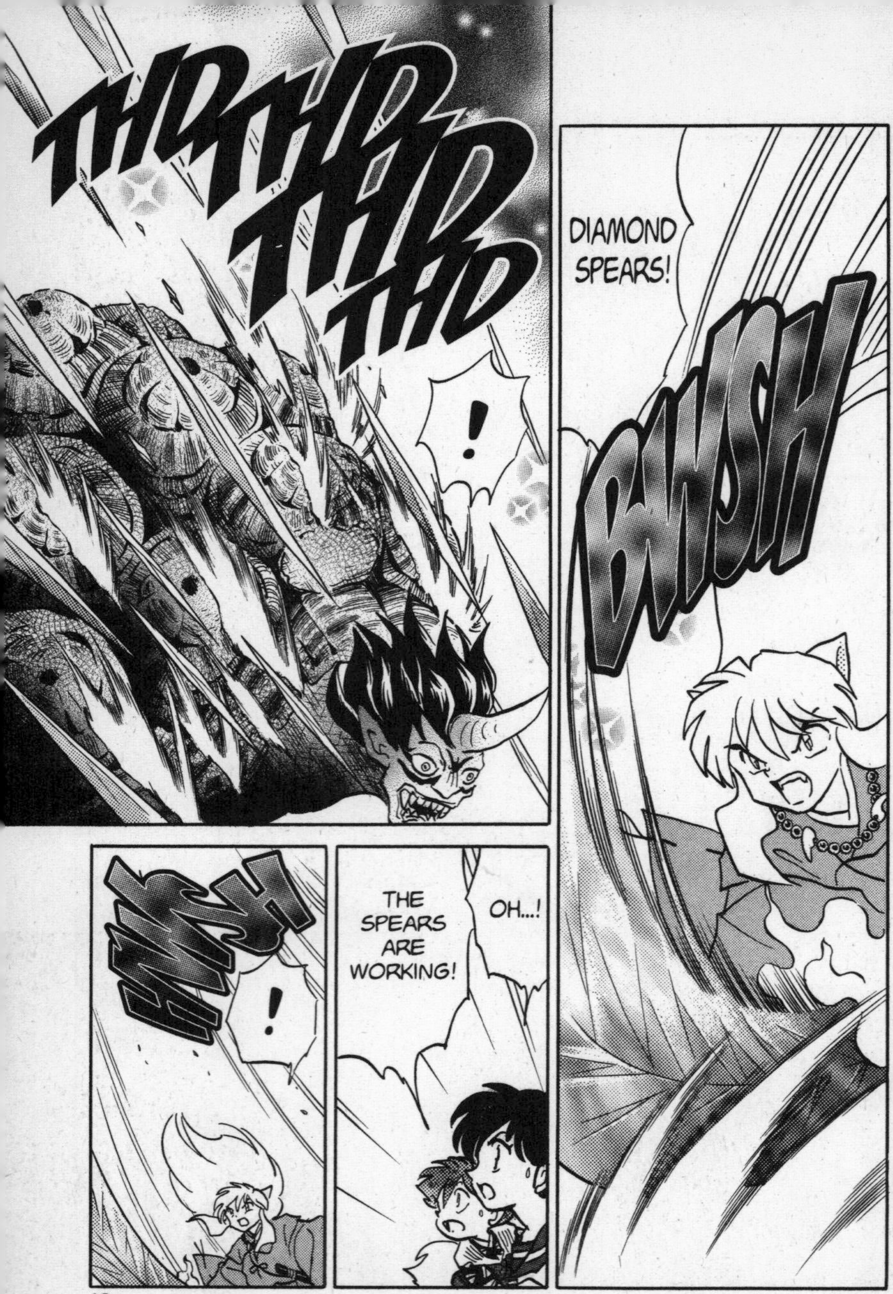
DIAMOND SPEARS!
BWSH
THD THD THD
!
OH...!
THE SPEARS ARE WORKING!
WHSH
!

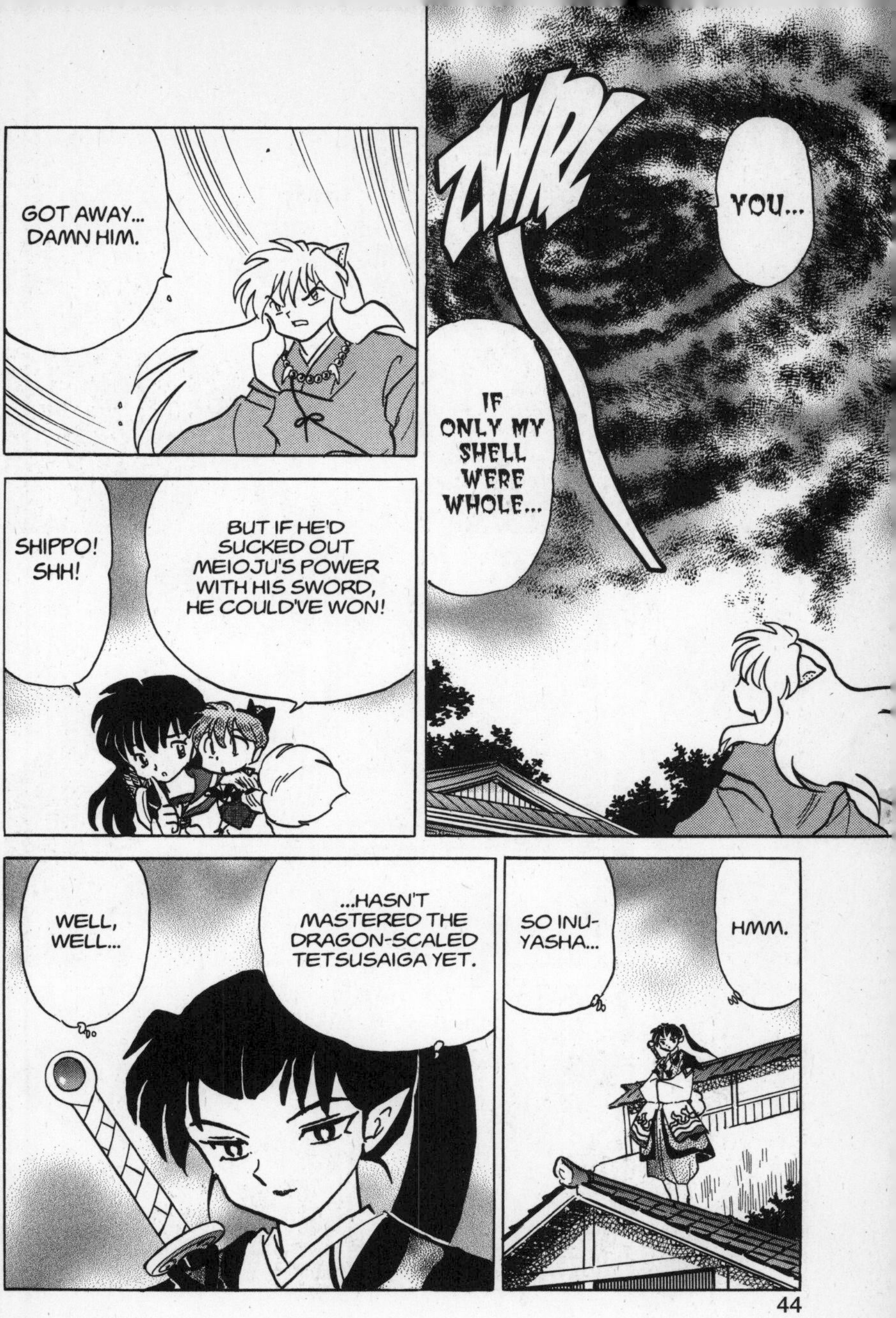
ZWR!
YOU...
IF ONLY MY SHELL WERE WHOLE...
GOT AWAY... DAMN HIM.
BUT IF HE'D SUCKED OUT MEIOJU'S POWER WITH HIS SWORD, HE COULD'VE WON!
SHIPPO! SHH!
HMM.
SO INU-YASHA...
...HASN'T MASTERED THE DRAGON-SCALED TETSUSAIGA YET.
WELL, WELL...

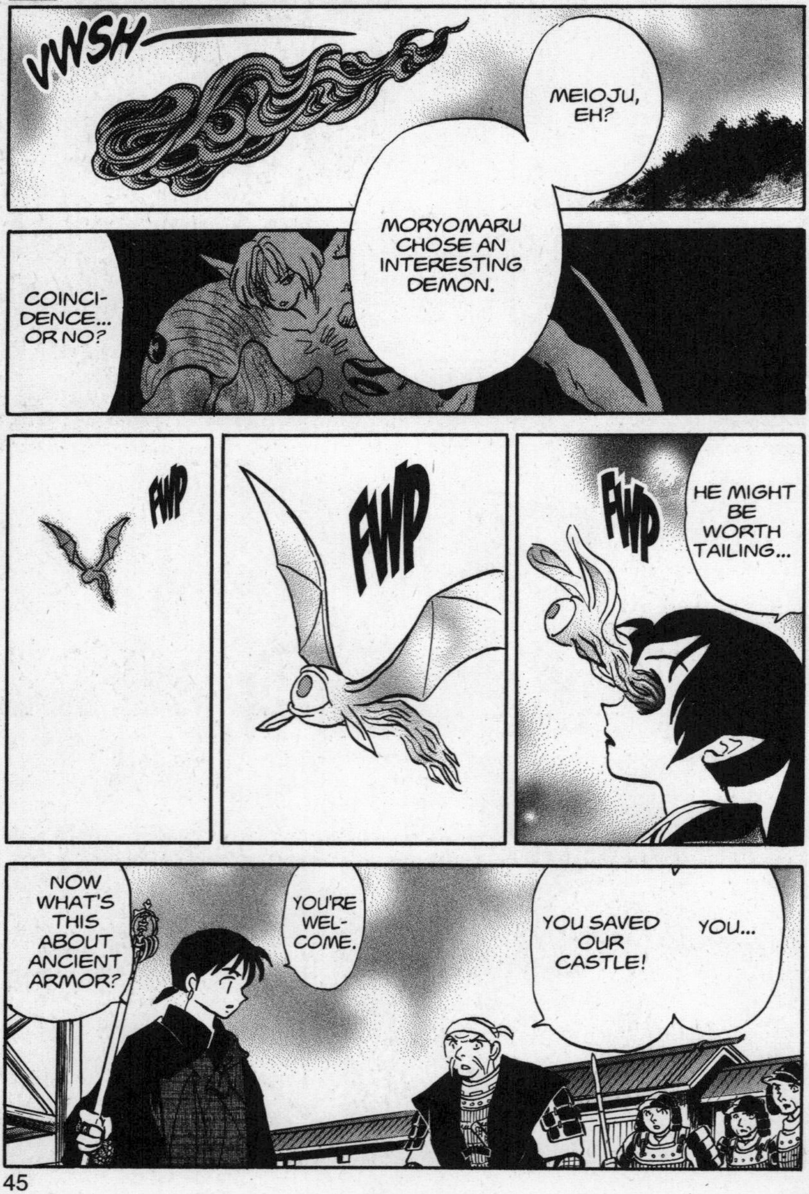
VWSH
MEIOJU, EH?
MORYOMARU CHOSE AN INTERESTING DEMON.
COINCIDENCE... OR NO?
HE MIGHT BE WORTH TAILING...
FWP
FWP
FWP
YOU...
YOU SAVED OUR CASTLE!
YOU'RE WELCOME.
NOW WHAT'S THIS ABOUT ANCIENT ARMOR?

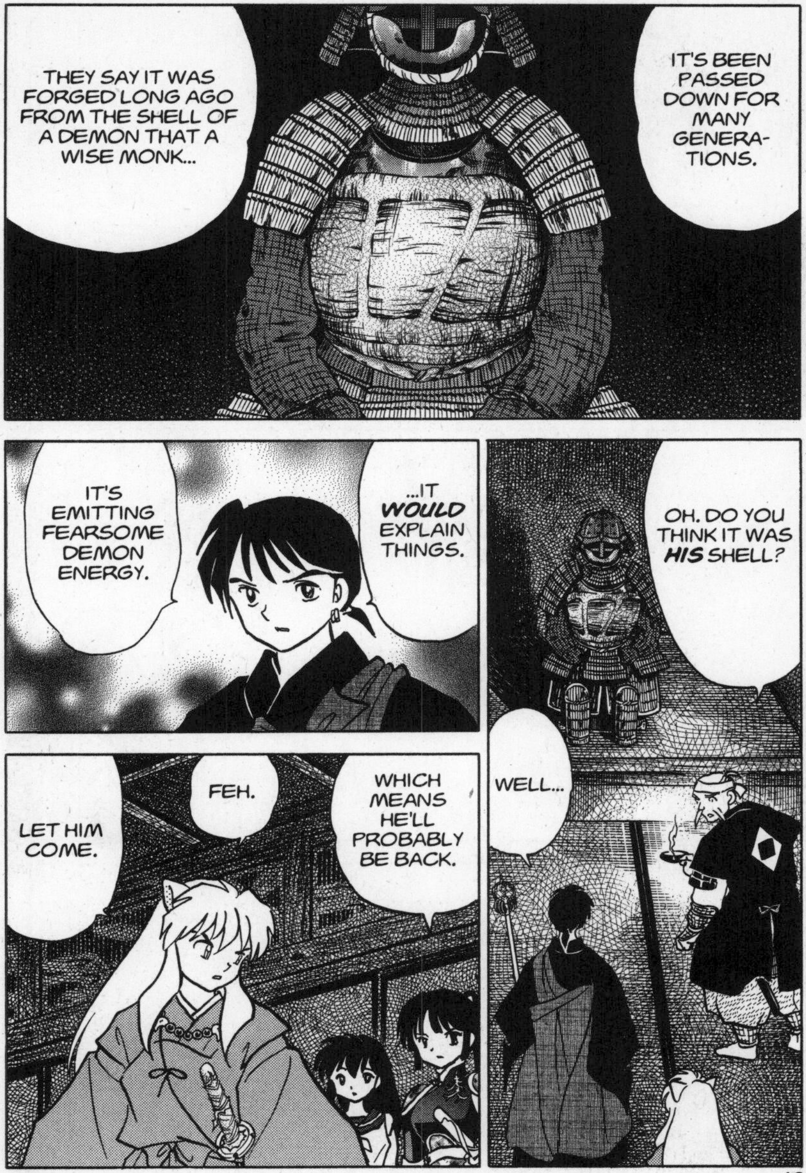
IT'S BEEN PASSED DOWN FOR MANY GENERA- TIONS.
THEY SAY IT WAS FORGED LONG AGO FROM THE SHELL OF A DEMON THAT A WISE MONK...
OH. DO YOU THINK IT WAS HIS SHELL?
WELL...
...IT WOULD EXPLAIN THINGS.
IT'S EMITTING FEARSOME DEMON ENERGY.
WHICH MEANS HE'LL PROBABLY BE BACK.
FEH.
LET HIM COME.

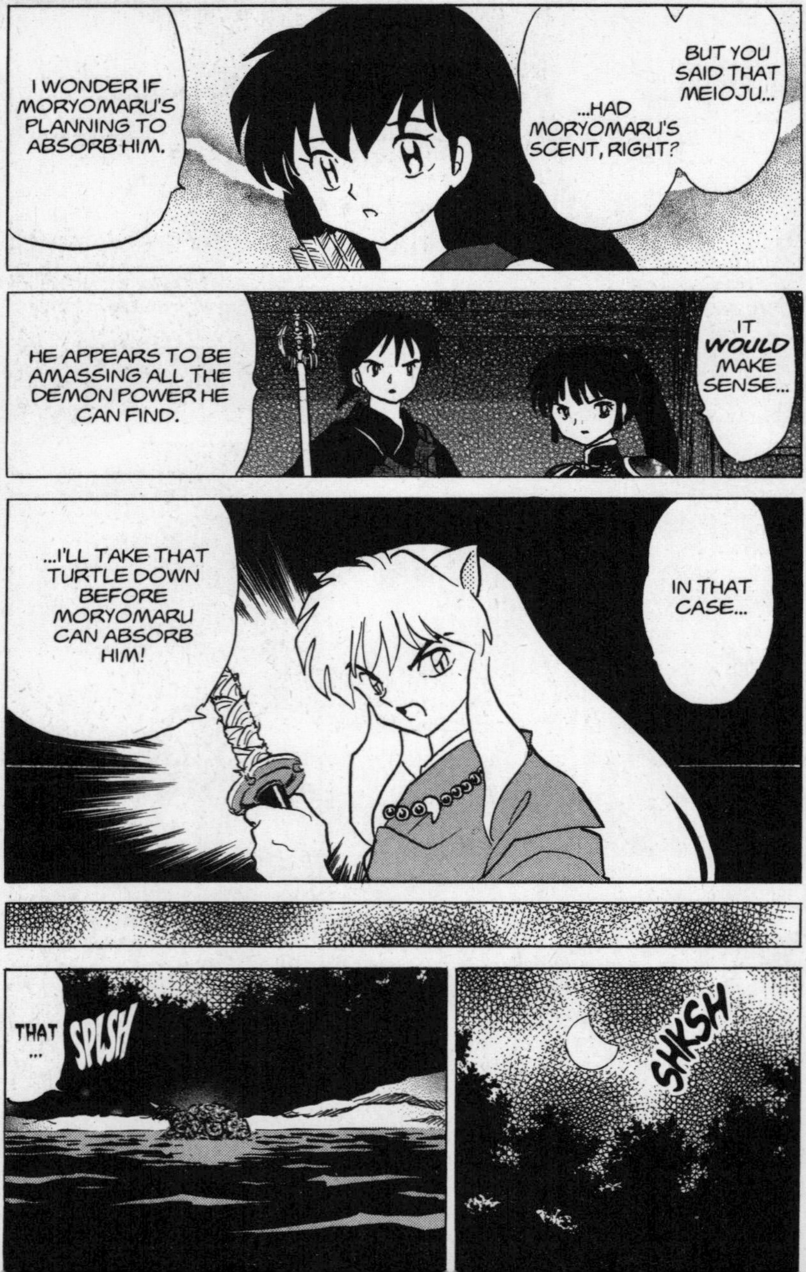
BUT YOU SAID THAT MEIOJU...
...HAD MORYOMARU'S SCENT, RIGHT?
I WONDER IF MORYOMARU'S PLANNING TO ABSORB HIM.
IT *WOULD* MAKE SENSE...
HE APPEARS TO BE AMASSING ALL THE DEMON POWER HE CAN FIND.
IN THAT CASE...
...I'LL TAKE THAT TURTLE DOWN BEFORE MORYOMARU CAN ABSORB HIM!
SHKSH
SPLSH
THAT ...

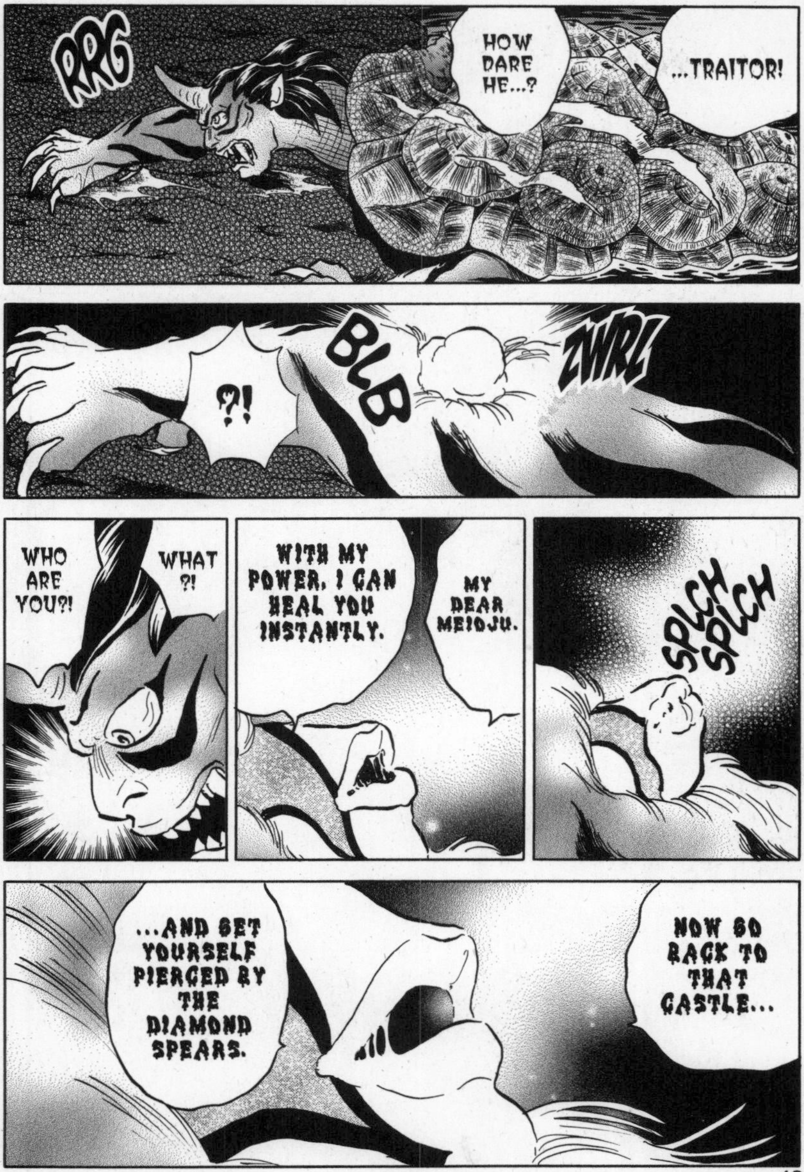
...TRAITOR!
HOW DARE HE...?
RRG
ZWRL
BLB
?!
SPLCH SPLCH
MY DEAR MEIDJU.
WITH MY POWER, I CAN HEAL YOU INSTANTLY.
WHAT ?!
WHO ARE YOU?!
NOW GO BACK TO THAT CASTLE...
...AND GET YOURSELF PIERCED BY THE DIAMOND SPEARS.

SCROLL 3
THE ARMORED SHELL

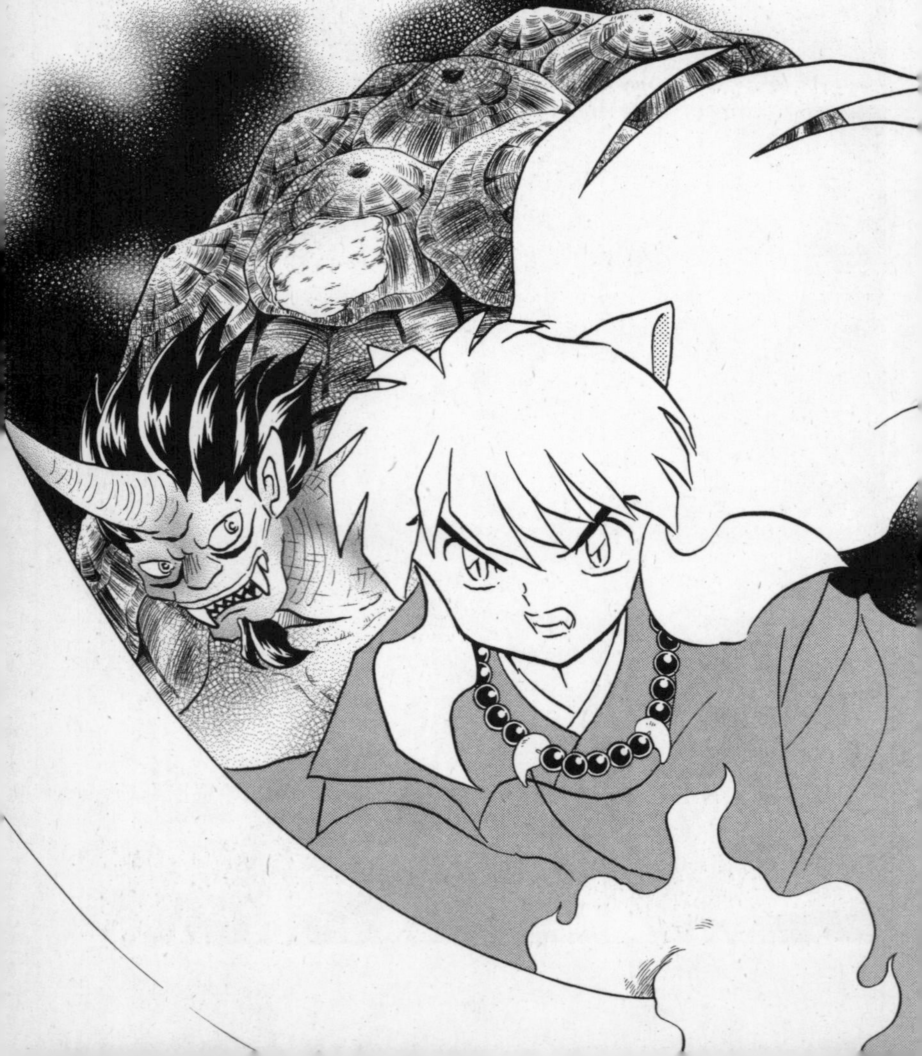

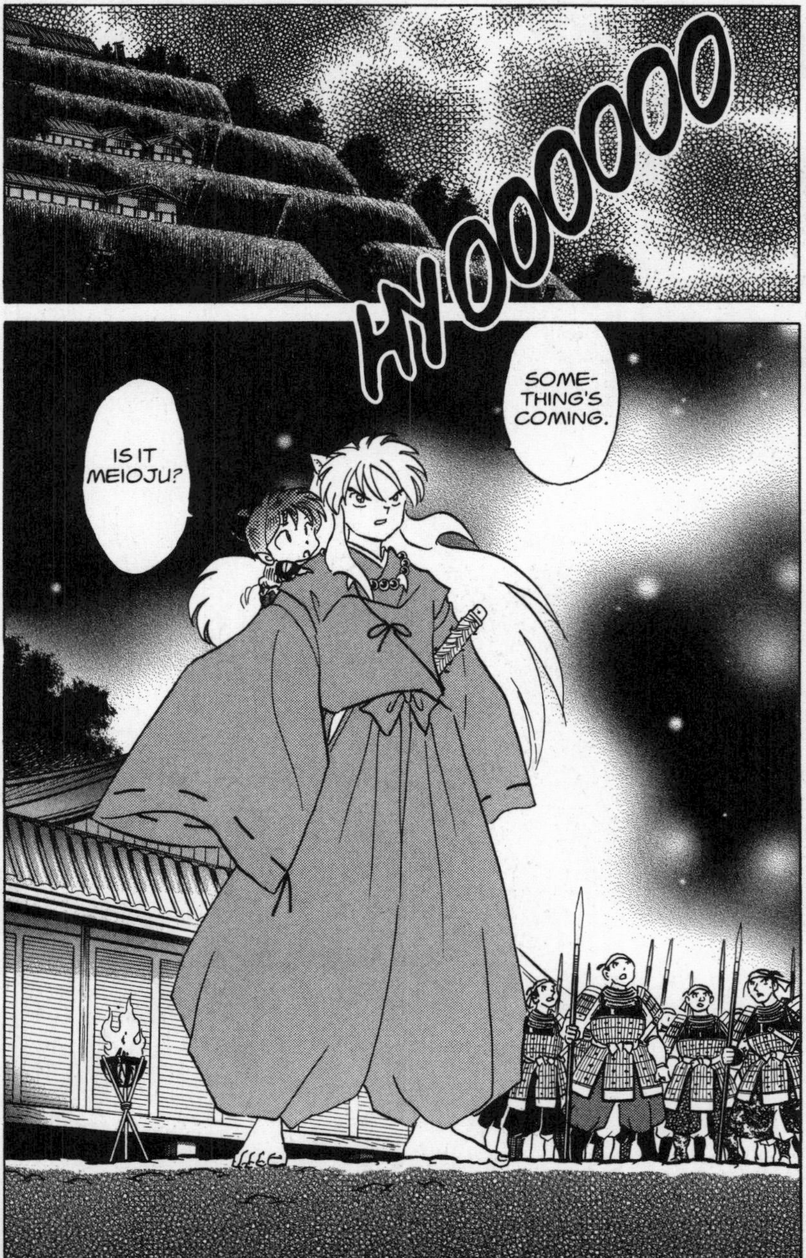
HYOOOOOO
SOME-THING'S COMING.
IS IT MEIOJU?

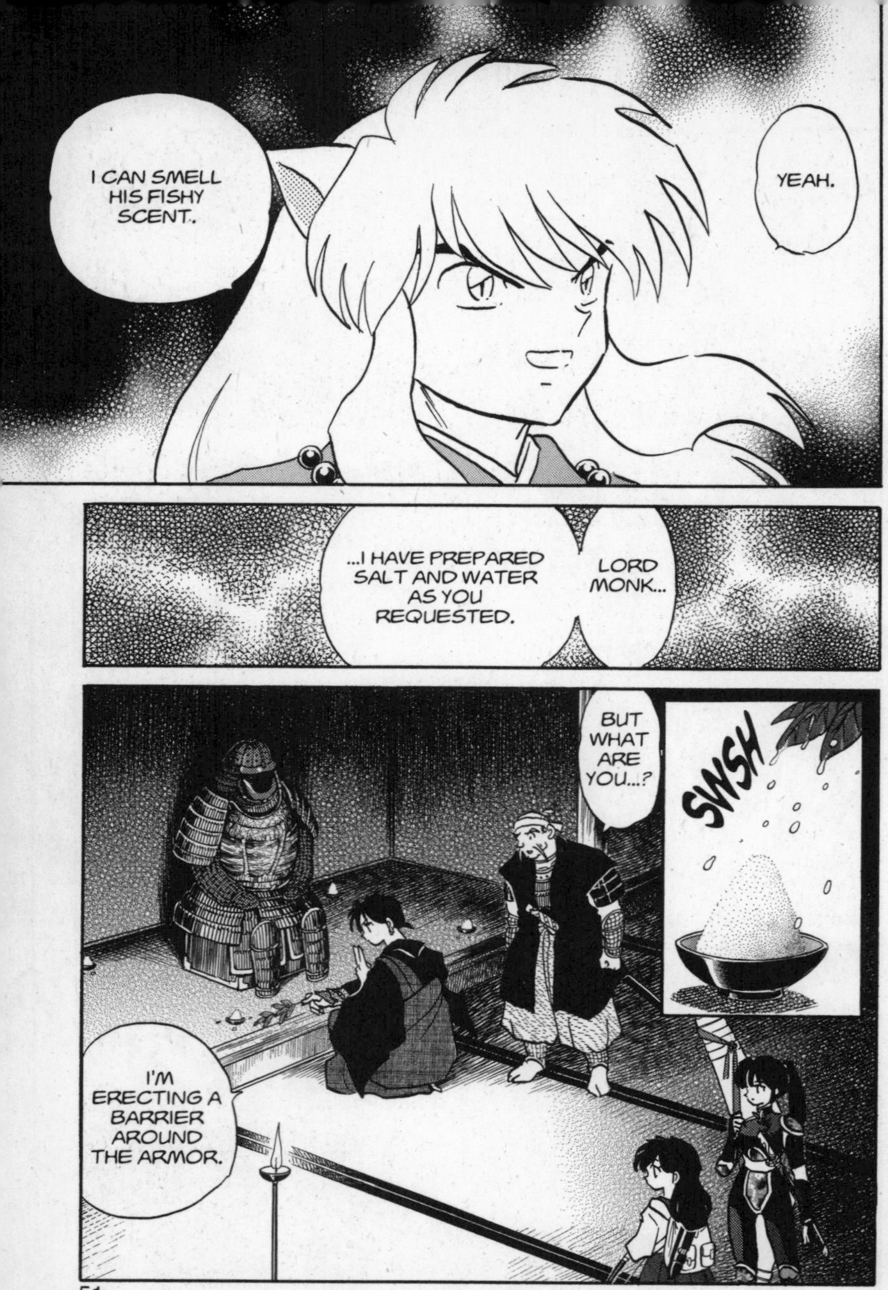
YEAH.
I CAN SMELL HIS FISHY SCENT..
LORD MONK...
...I HAVE PREPARED SALT AND WATER AS YOU REQUESTED.
SWSH
BUT WHAT ARE YOU...?
I'M ERECTING A BARRIER AROUND THE ARMOR.

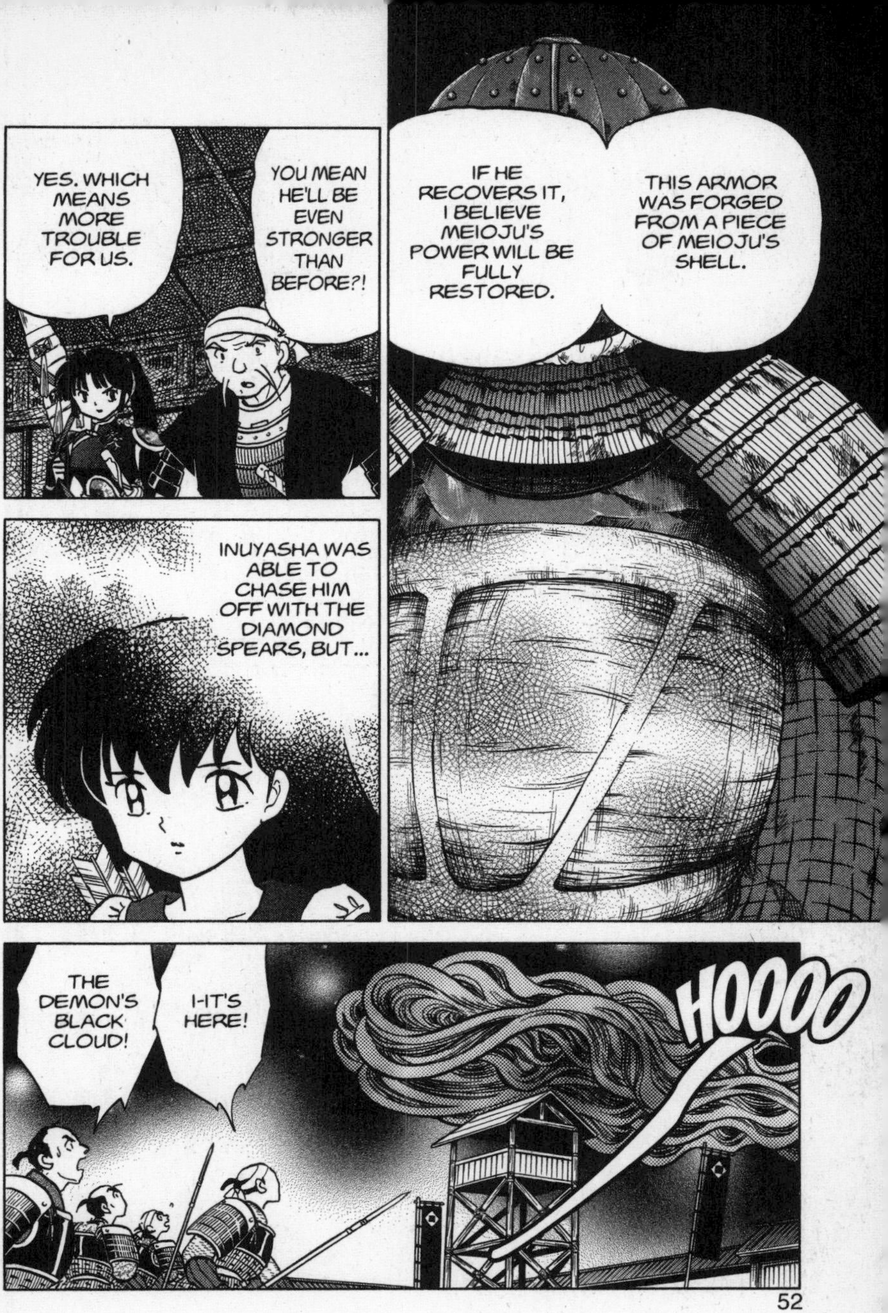
THIS ARMOR WAS FORGED FROM A PIECE OF MEIOJU'S SHELL.
IF HE RECOVERS IT, I BELIEVE MEIOJU'S POWER WILL BE FULLY RESTORED.
YOU MEAN HE'LL BE EVEN STRONGER THAN BEFORE?!
YES. WHICH MEANS MORE TROUBLE FOR US.
INUYASHA WAS ABLE TO CHASE HIM OFF WITH THE DIAMOND SPEARS, BUT...
HOOOO
I-IT'S HERE!
THE DEMON'S BLACK CLOUD!

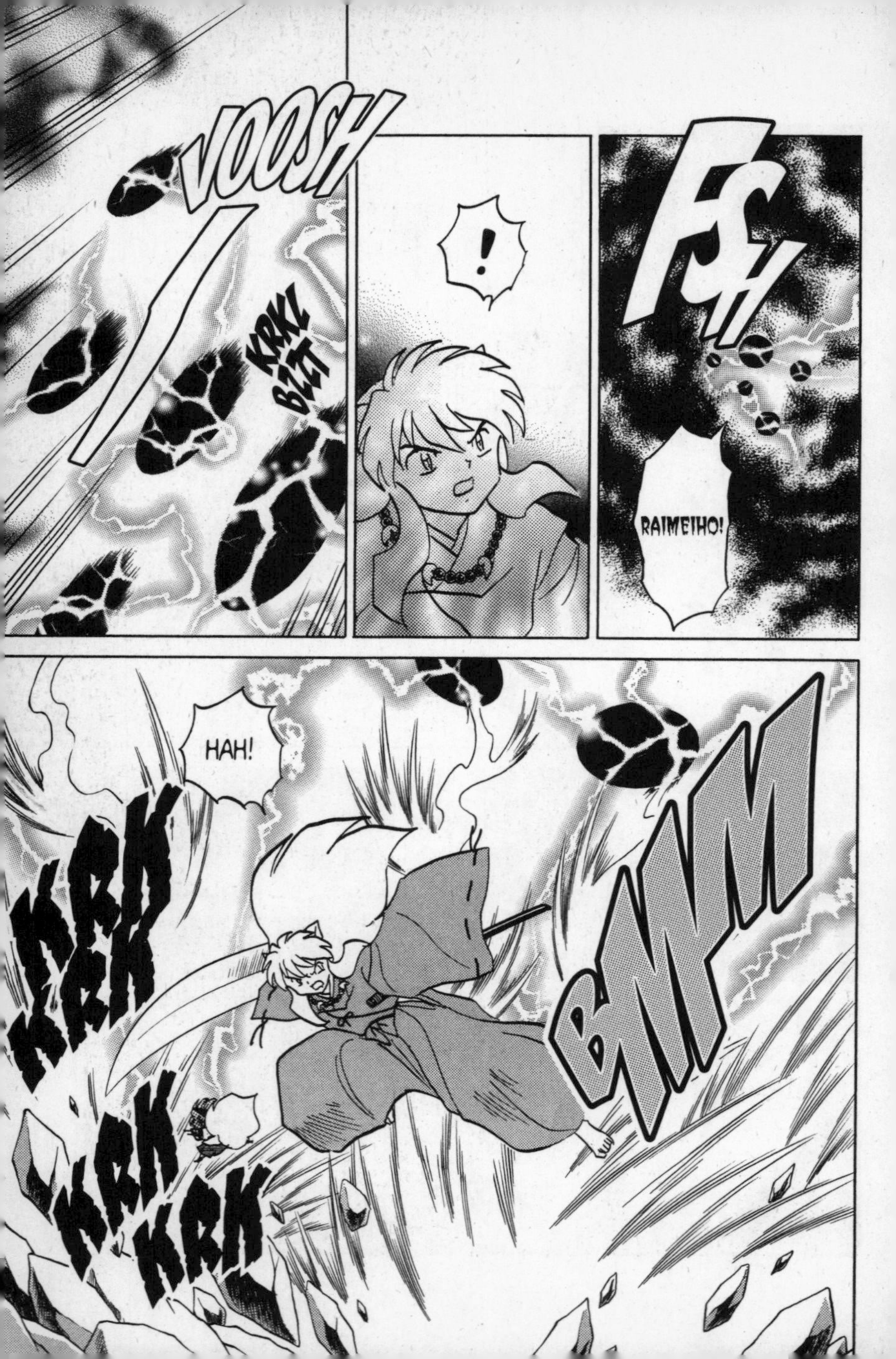
FSH
RAIMEIHO!
!
VOOSH
KRKL BZZT
HAH!
BMMM
KRK KRK
KRK KRK

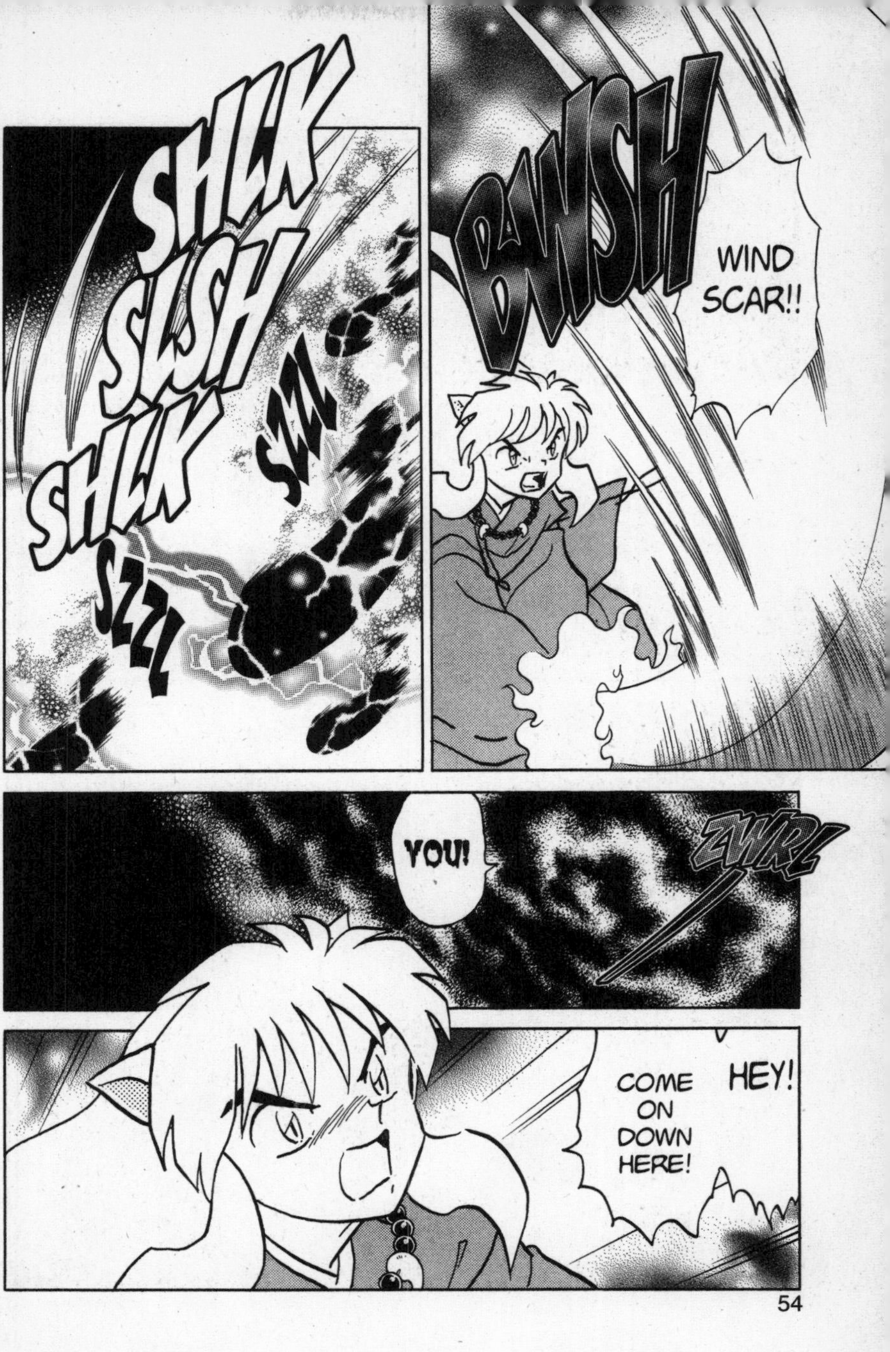
BWISH
WIND SCAR!!
SHCK
SLSH
SHCK
SZZZ
SZZZ
ZWIRL
YOU!
HEY!
COME ON DOWN HERE!

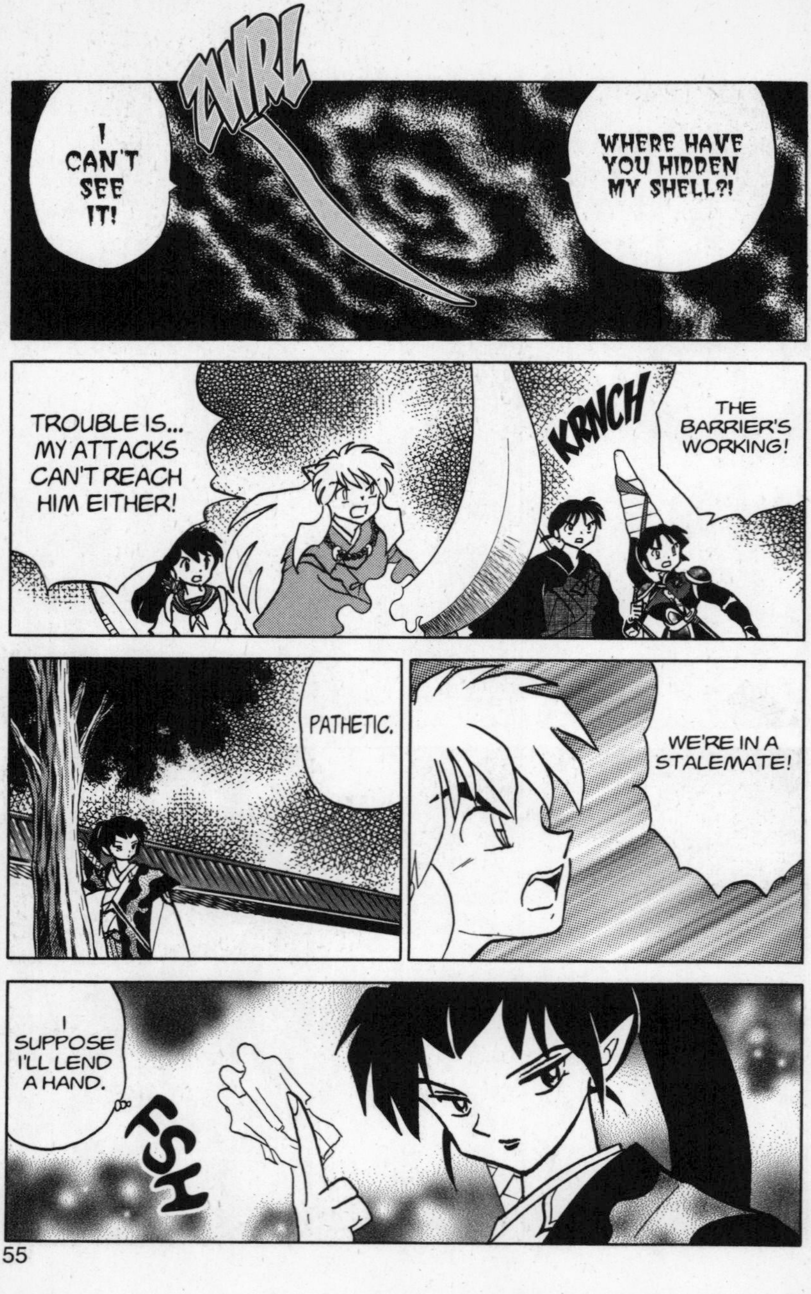
WHERE HAVE YOU HIDDEN MY SHELL?!
ZWRL
I CAN'T SEE IT!
THE BARRIER'S WORKING!
KRNCH
TROUBLE IS... MY ATTACKS CAN'T REACH HIM EITHER!
WE'RE IN A STALEMATE!
PATHETIC.
I SUPPOSE I'LL LEND A HAND.
FSH

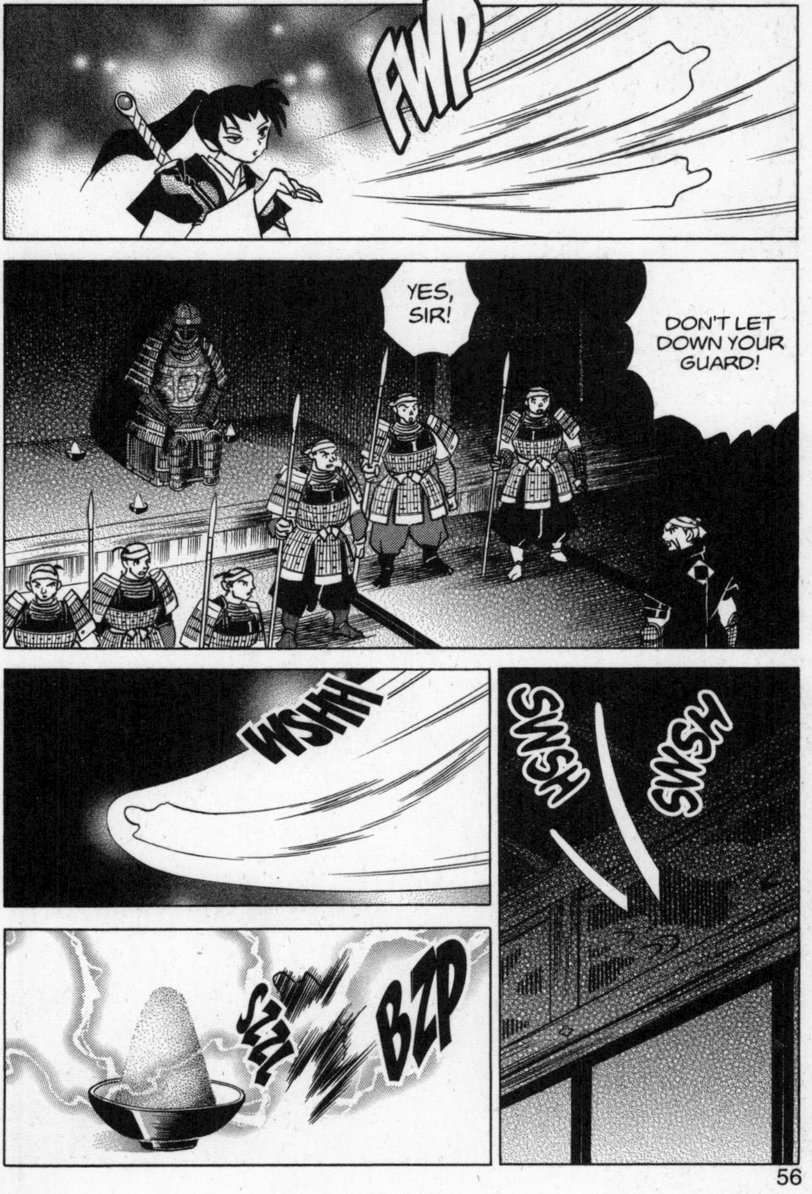
FWP
DON'T LET DOWN YOUR GUARD!
YES, SIR!
SWSH
SWSH
WSHH
SZZZ
BZP

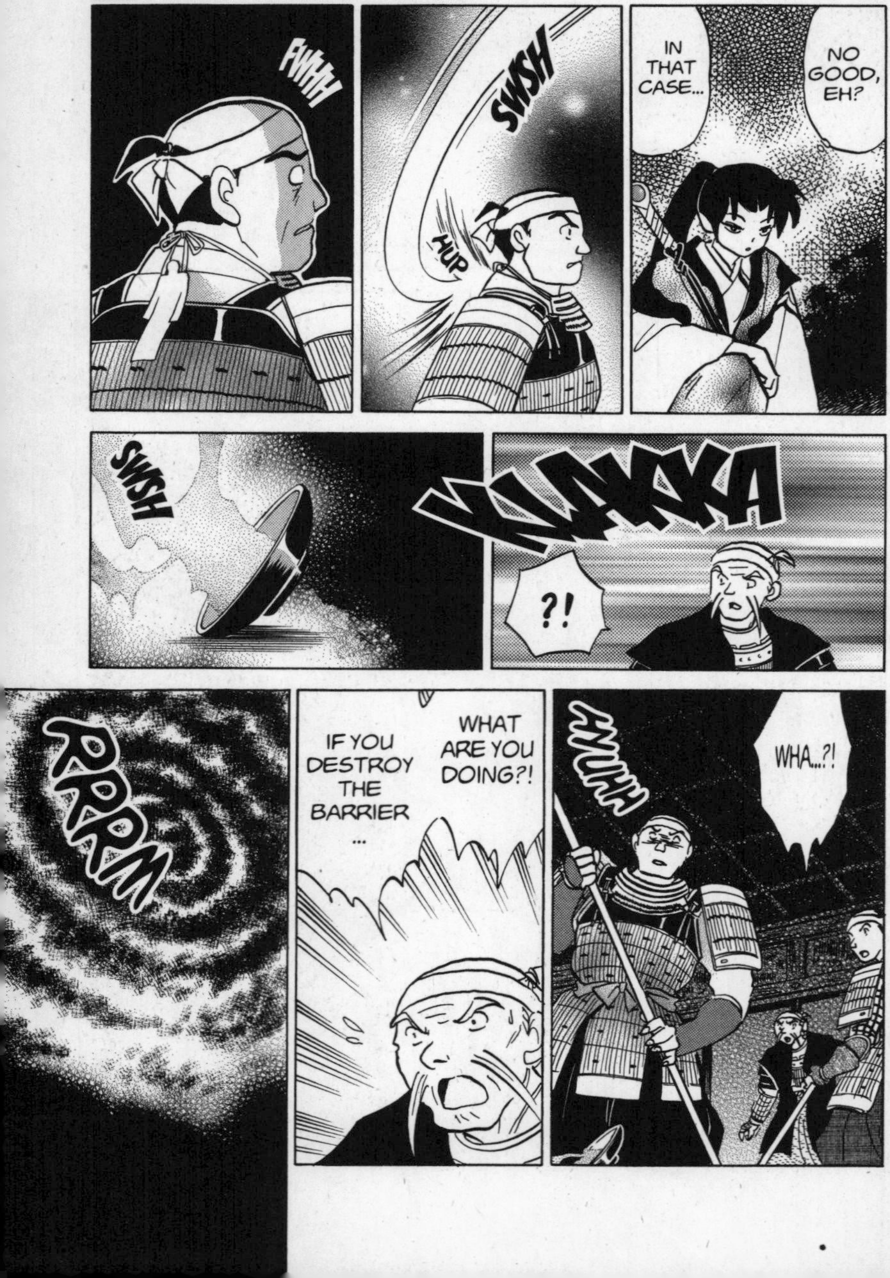
NO GOOD, EH?
IN THAT CASE...
SWSH
HUP
FWHH
?!
SWSH
WHA...?!
WHAT ARE YOU DOING?!
IF YOU DESTROY THE BARRIER ...
RRRM

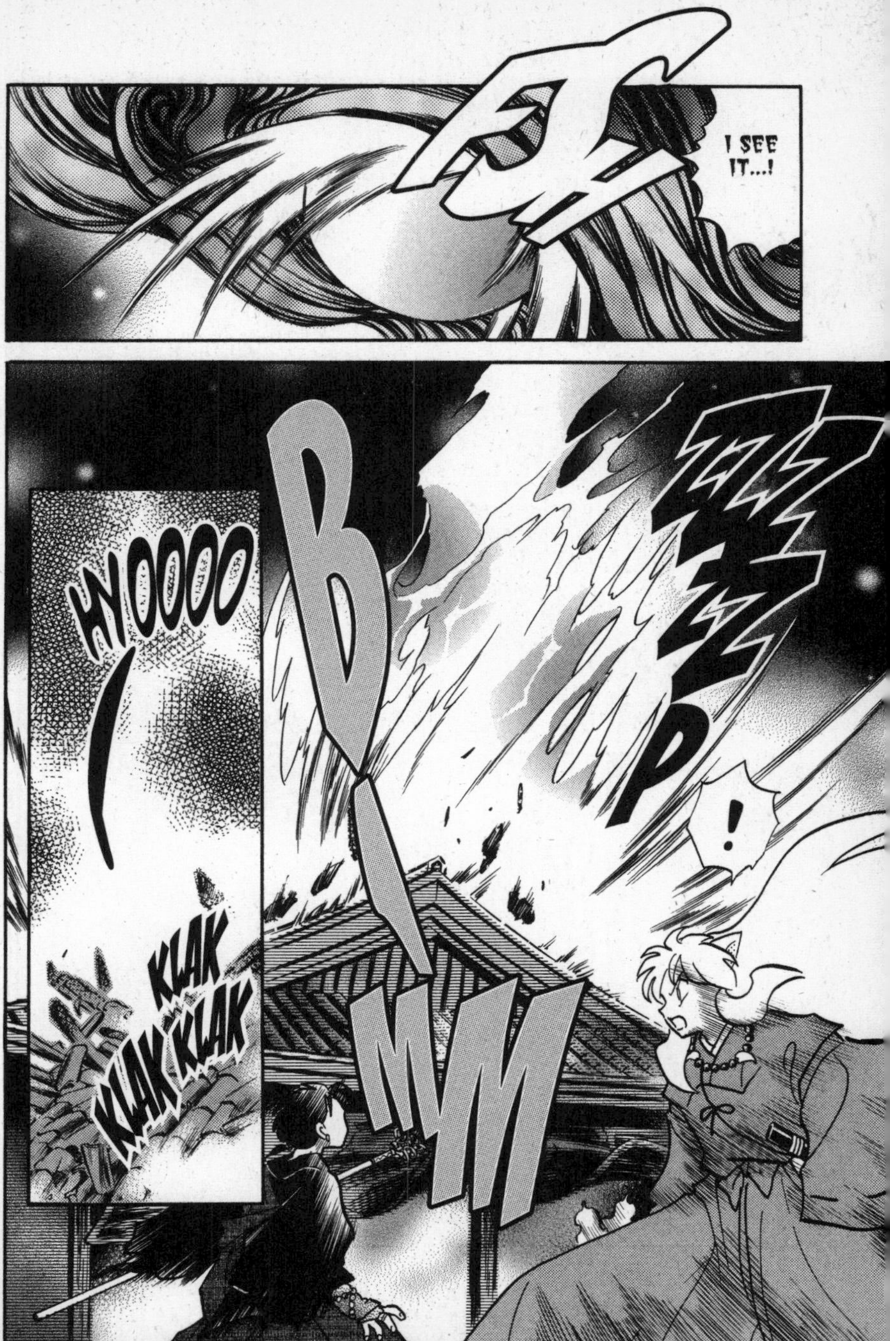
I SEE IT...!
ZZZZP
!
BMMM
HYOOOO
KLAK KLAK KLAK

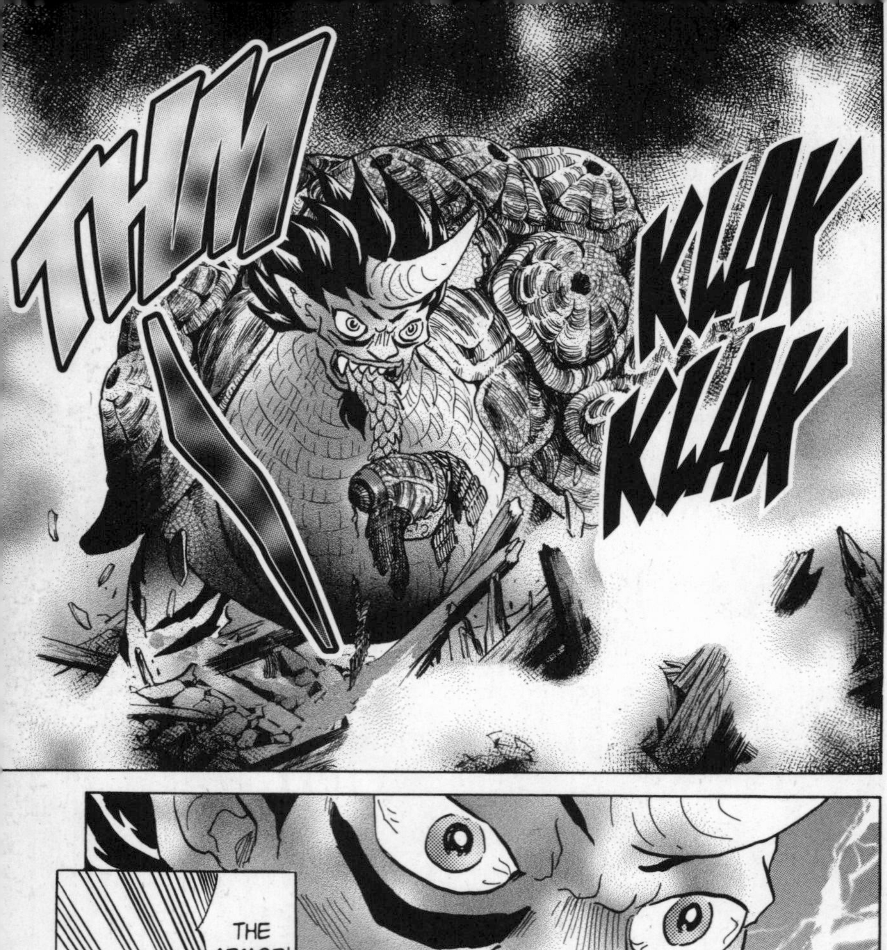
KLAK
KLAK
THM
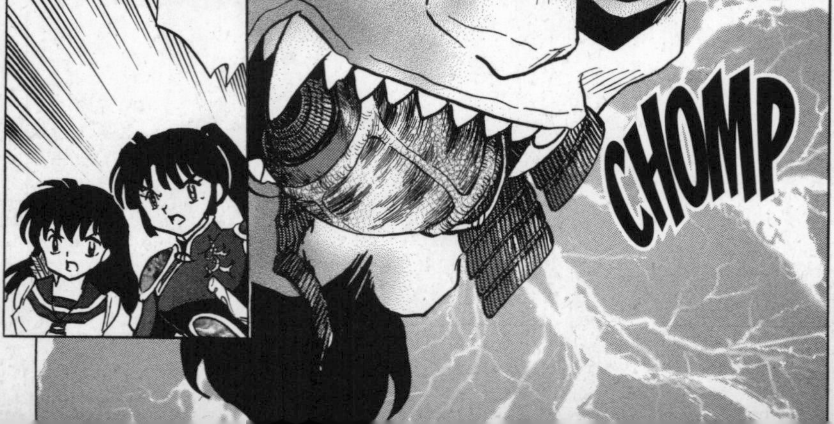
CHOMP
THE ARMOR!

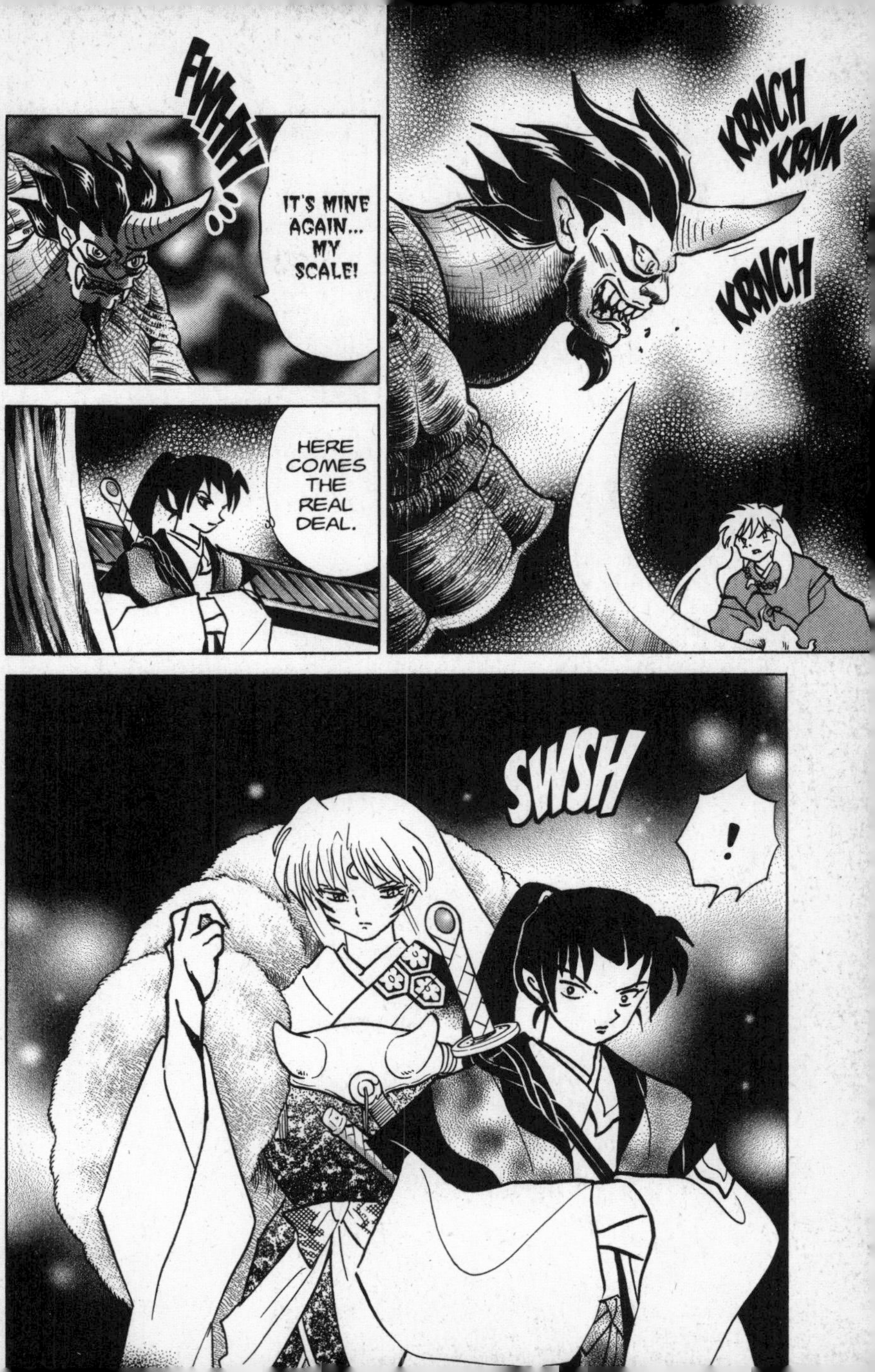
KRNCH
KRNK
KRNCH
FWHH
IT'S MINE AGAIN... MY SCALE!
HERE COMES THE REAL DEAL.
SWSH
!

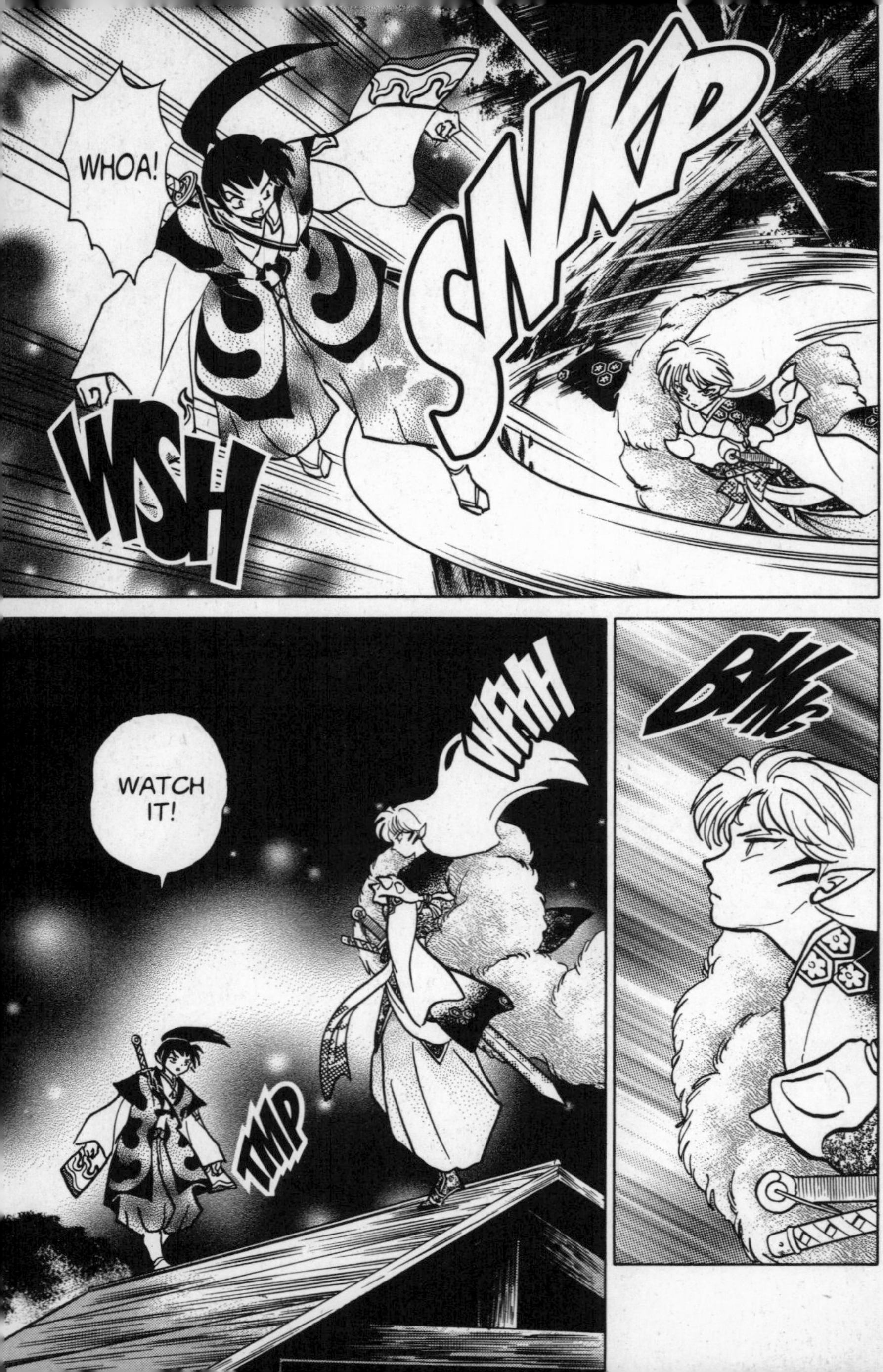
SNKP
WHOA!
WSH
BING
WFHH
WATCH IT!
TMP

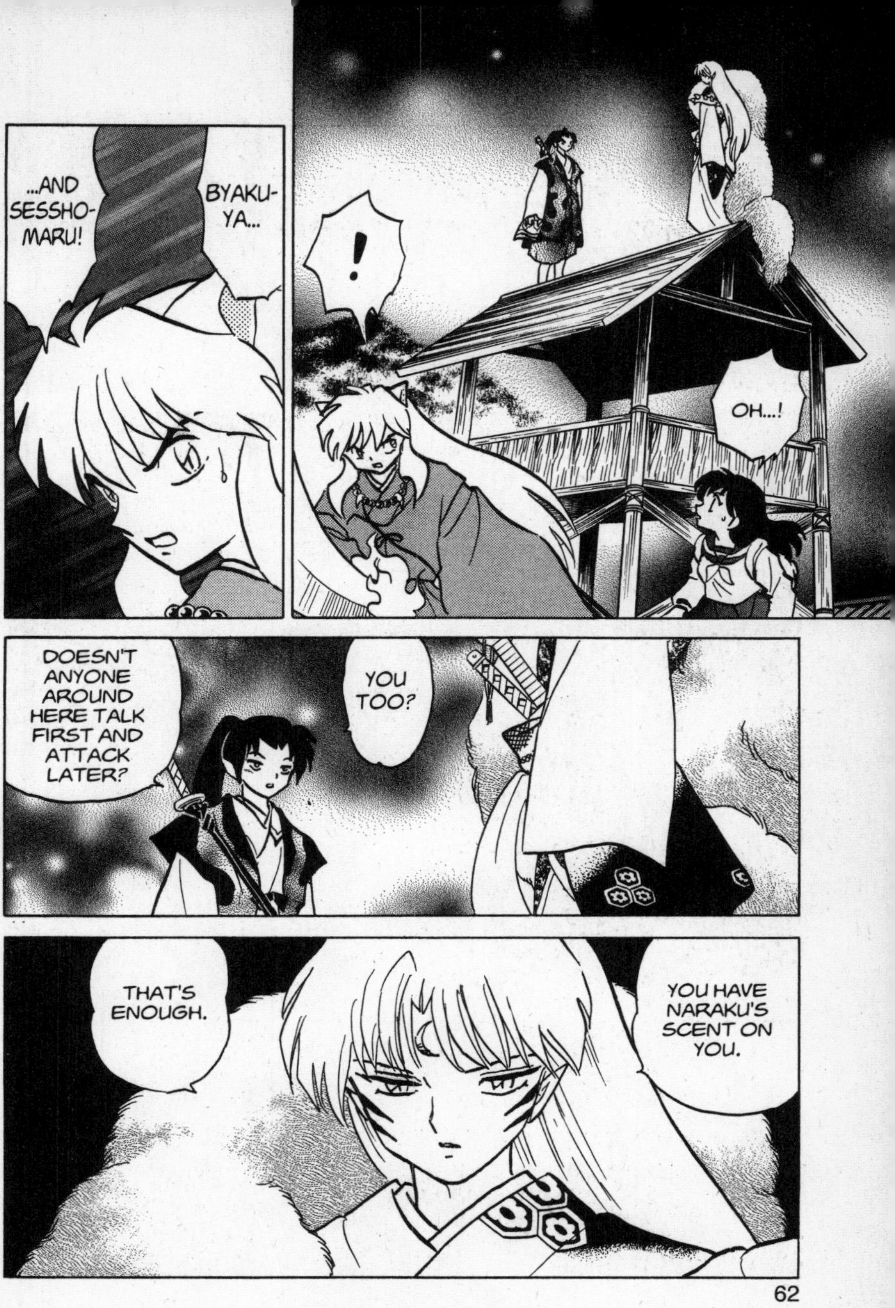
OH...!
!
BYAKU-YA...
...AND SESSHO-MARU!
YOU TOO?
DOESN'T ANYONE AROUND HERE TALK FIRST AND ATTACK LATER?
YOU HAVE NARAKU'S SCENT ON YOU.
THAT'S ENOUGH.

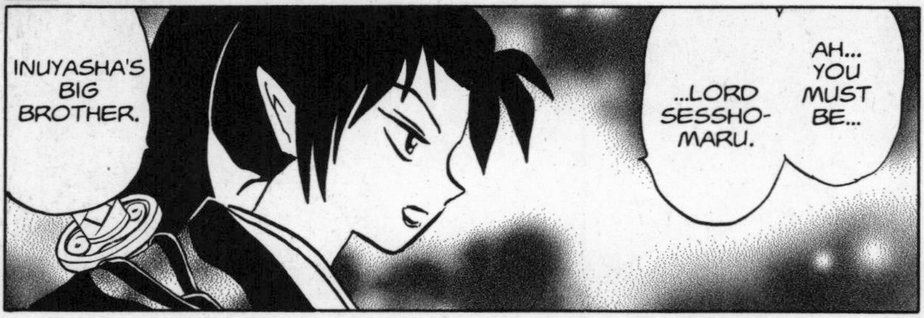
AH... YOU MUST BE...
...LORD SESSHO-MARU.
INUYASHA'S BIG BROTHER.

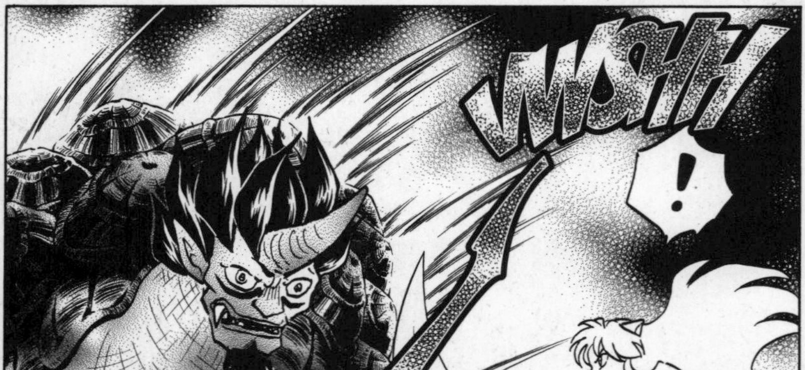
WSHH
!

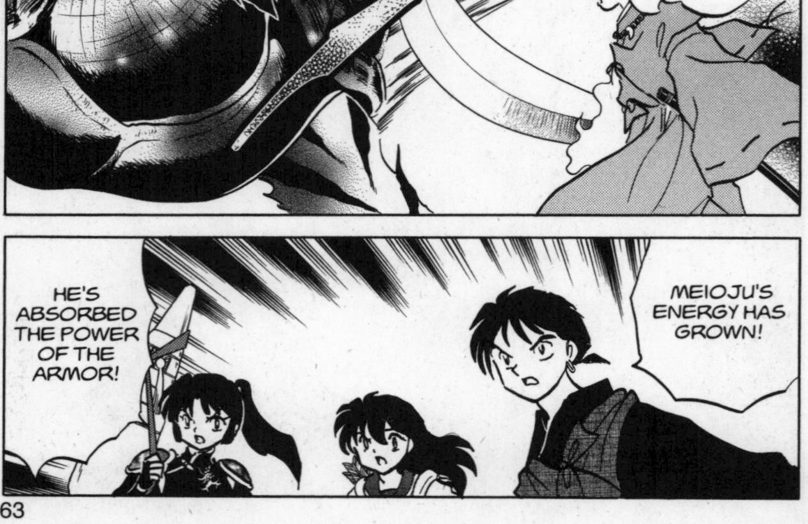
MEIOJU'S ENERGY HAS GROWN!
HE'S ABSORBED THE POWER OF THE ARMOR!

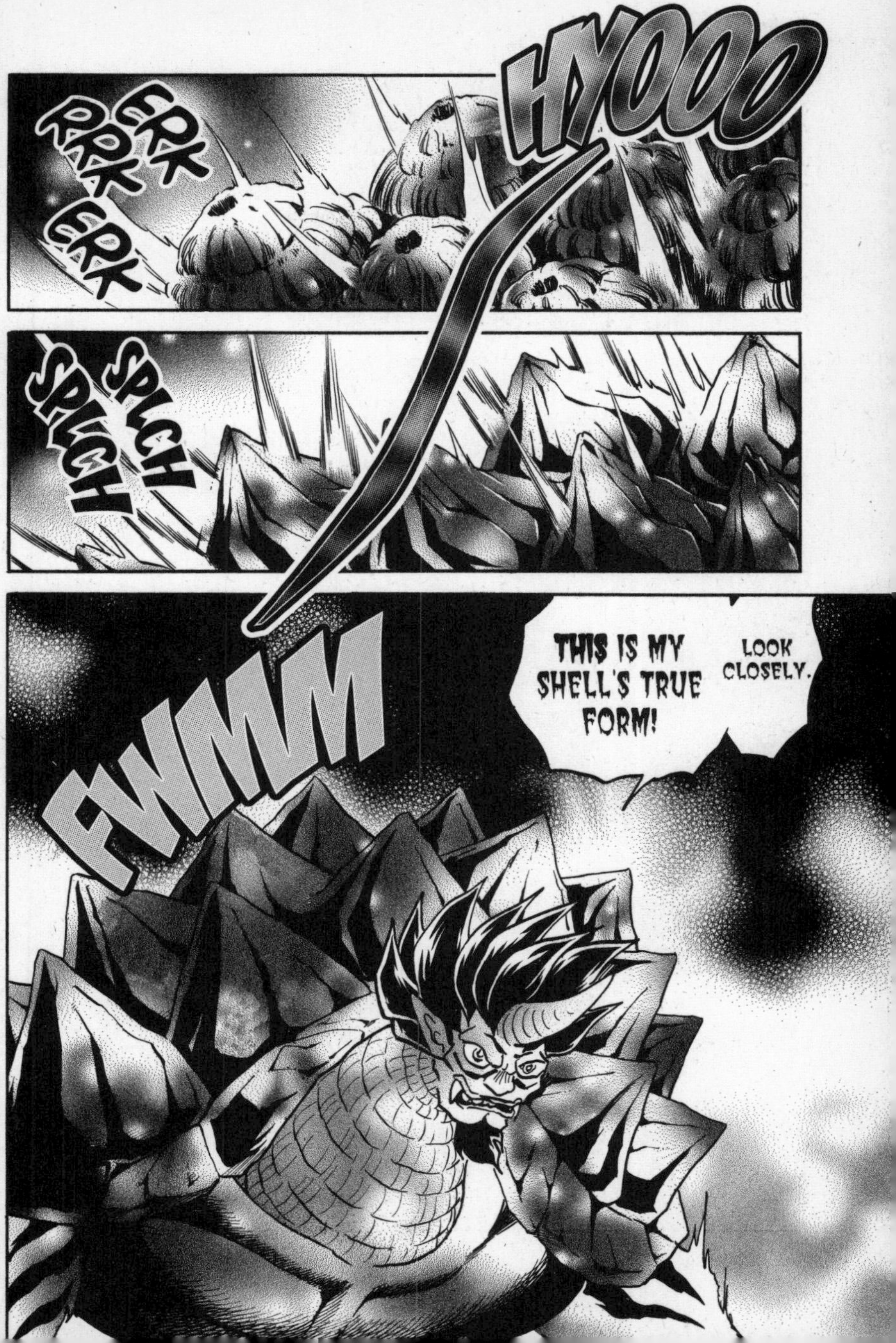
HYOOO
ERK RRK ERK ERK
SPLCH SPLCH
LOOK CLOSELY.
THIS IS MY SHELL'S TRUE FORM!
FWMMM

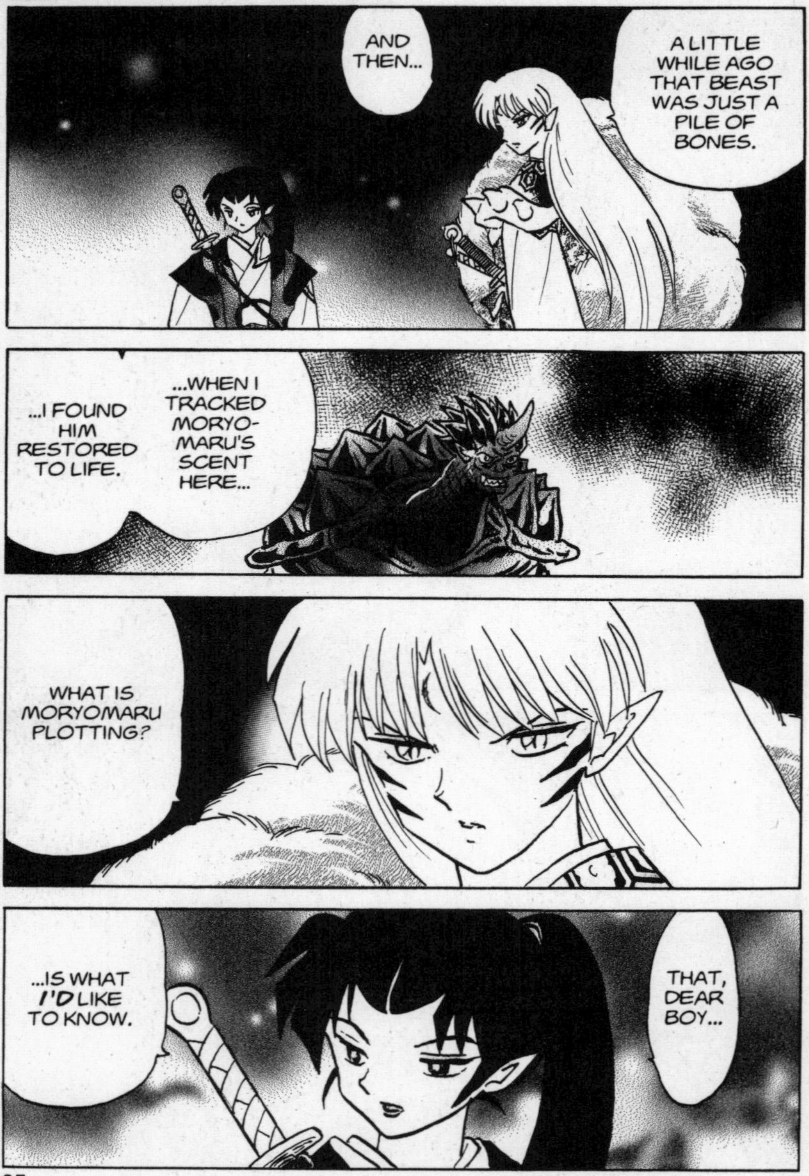
A LITTLE WHILE AGO THAT BEAST WAS JUST A PILE OF BONES.
AND THEN...
...WHEN I TRACKED MORYO-MARU'S SCENT HERE...
...I FOUND HIM RESTORED TO LIFE.
WHAT IS MORYOMARU PLOTTING?
THAT, DEAR BOY...
...IS WHAT *I'D* LIKE TO KNOW.

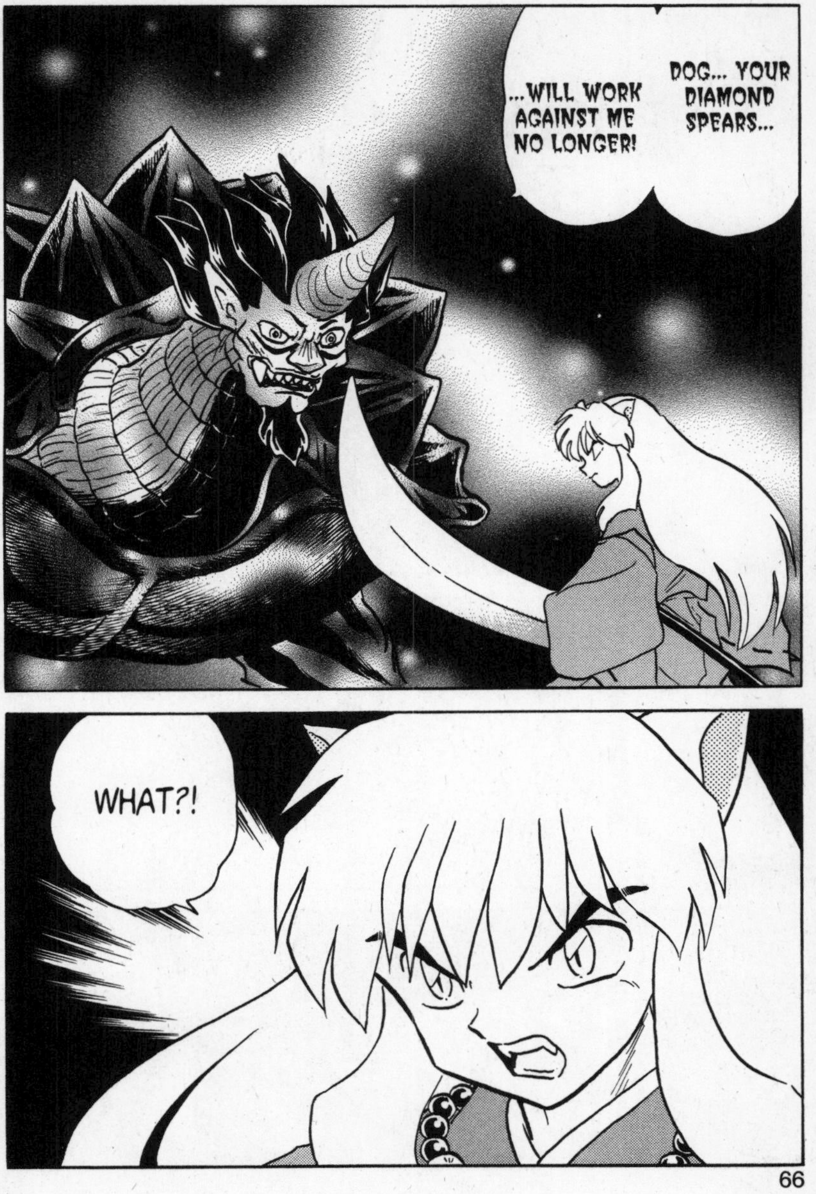
DOG... YOUR DIAMOND SPEARS...
...WILL WORK AGAINST ME NO LONGER!
WHAT?!

SCROLL 4

MORYOMARU'S TARGET

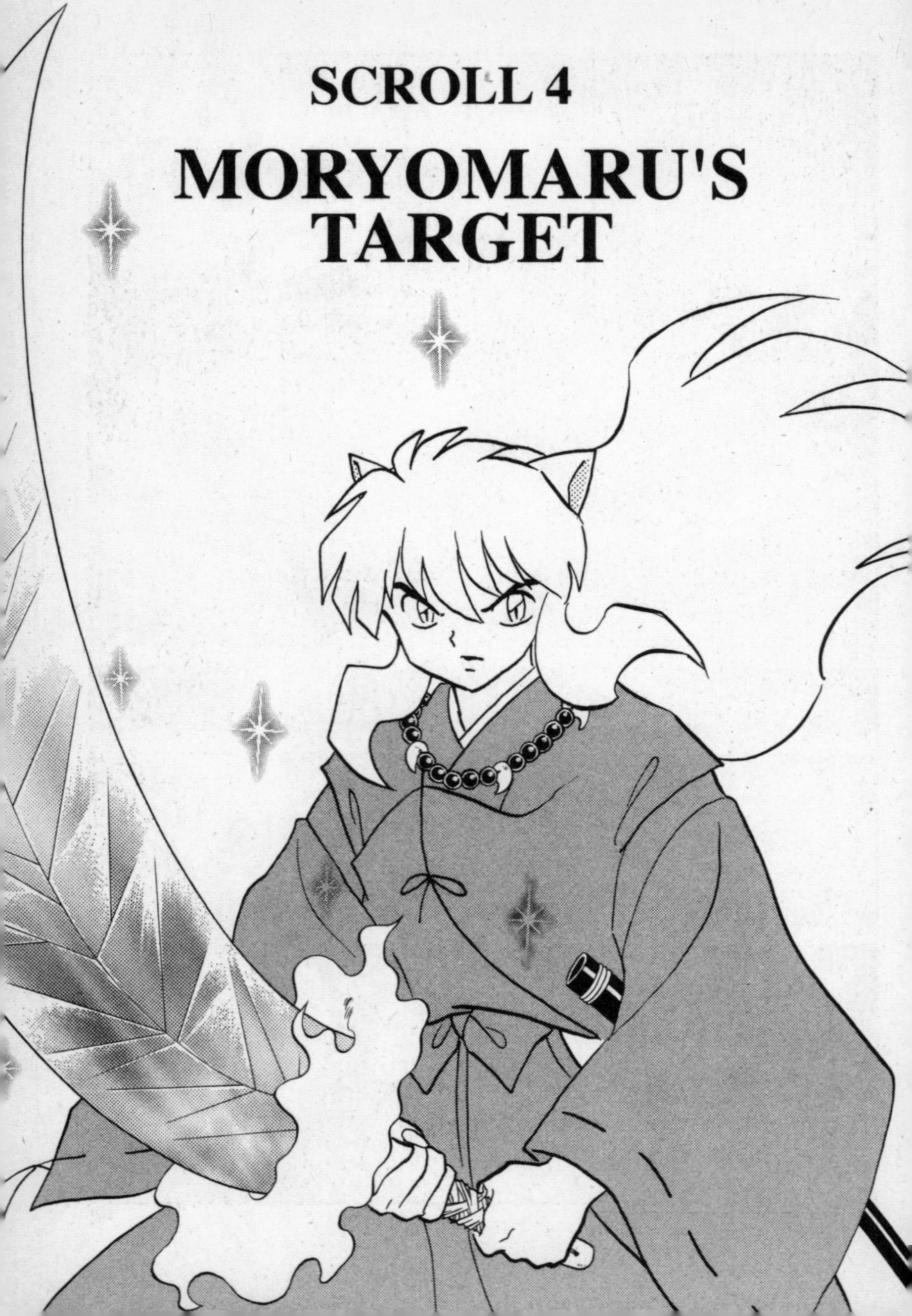

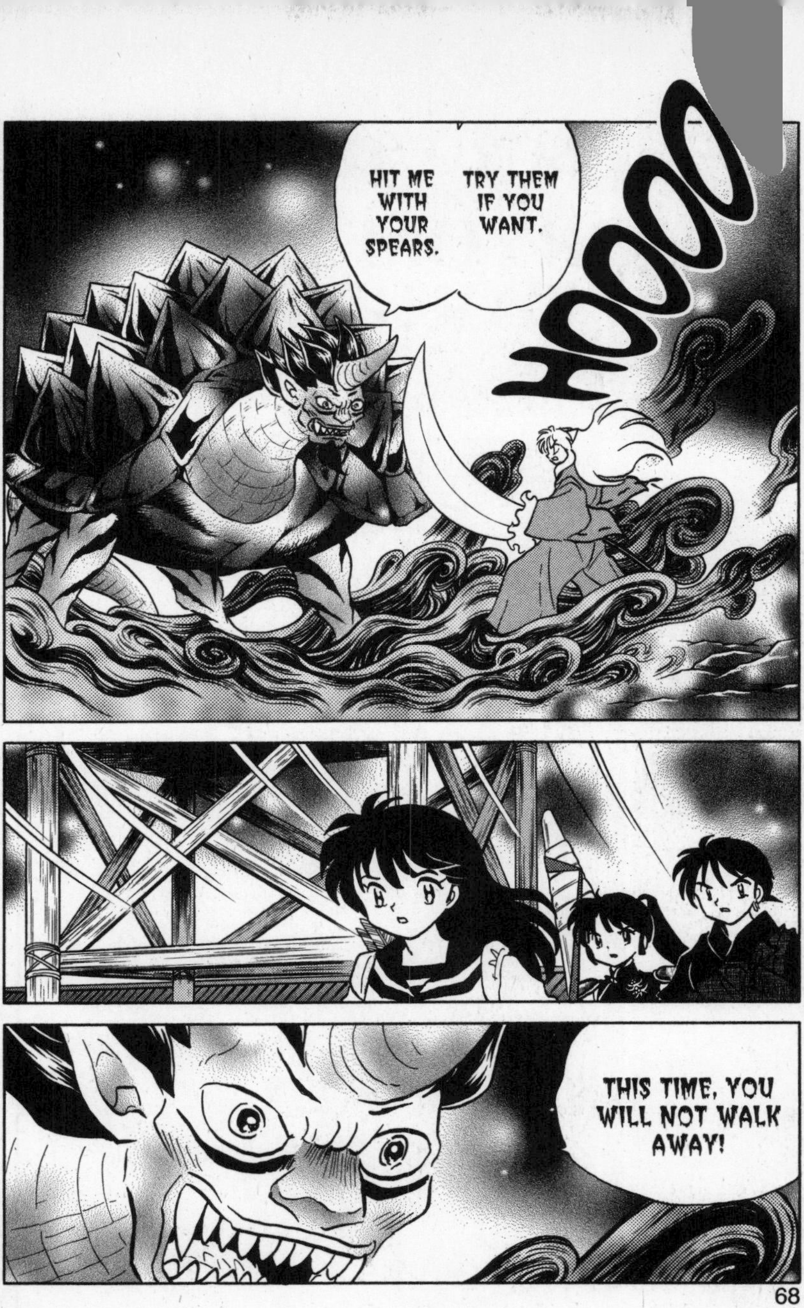
TRY THEM IF YOU WANT.
HIT ME WITH YOUR SPEARS.
HOOOO
THIS TIME, YOU WILL NOT WALK AWAY!

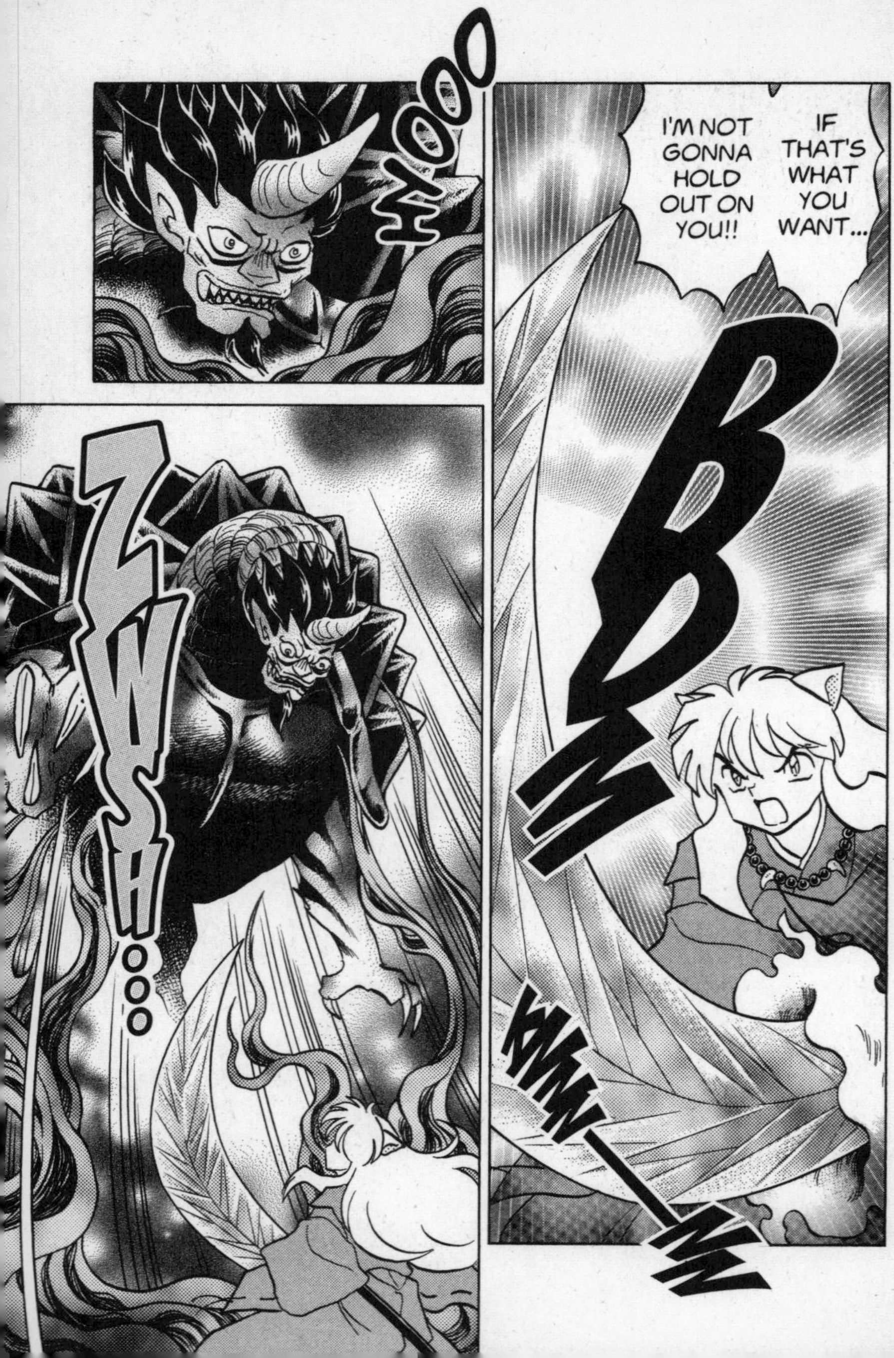
IF THAT'S WHAT YOU WANT...
I'M NOT GONNA HOLD OUT ON YOU!!
WHOOOO
ZWSH...

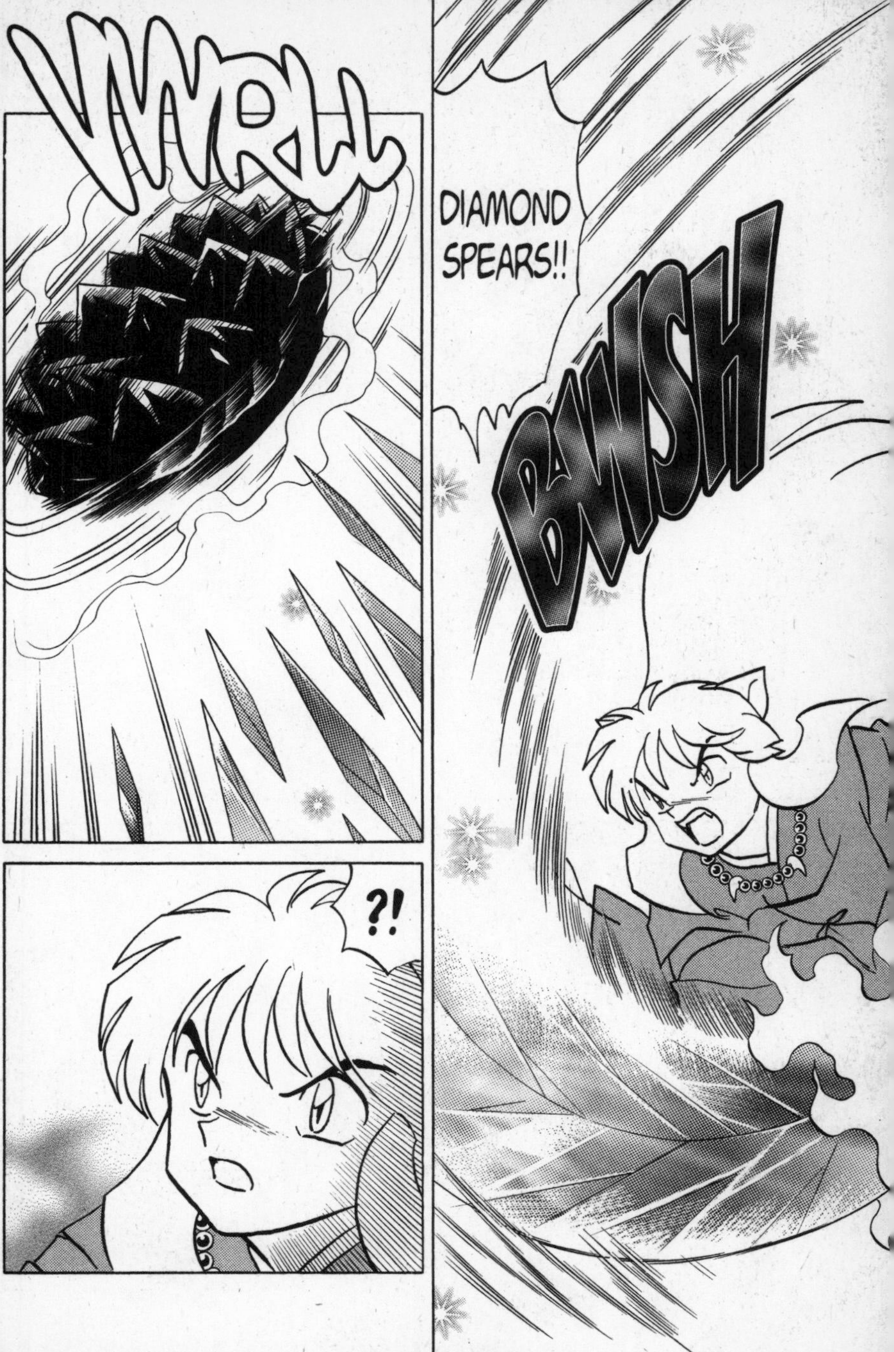
DIAMOND SPEARS!!
BWISH
?!

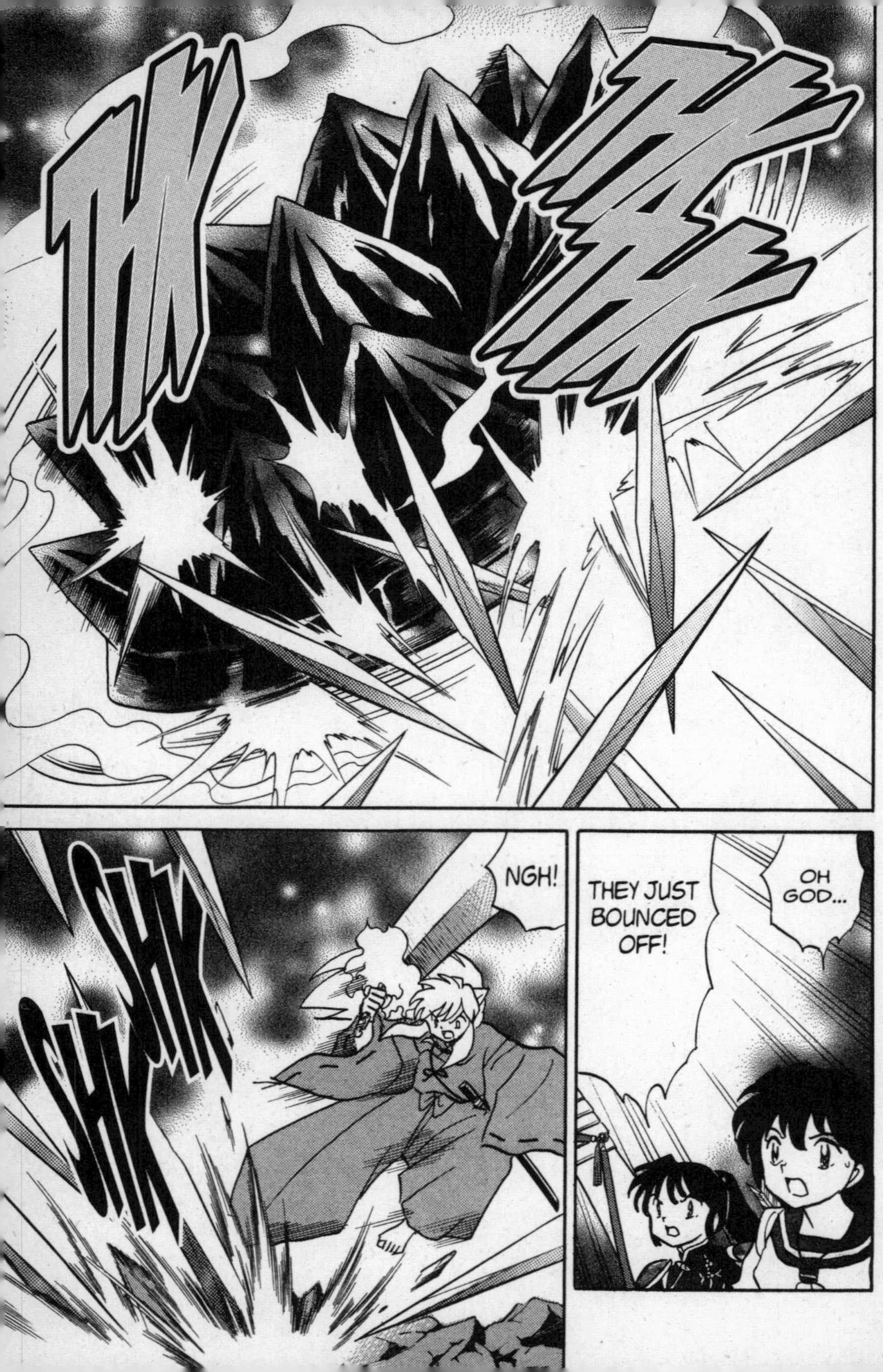
OH GOD...
THEY JUST BOUNCED OFF!
NGH!
SHK
SHK

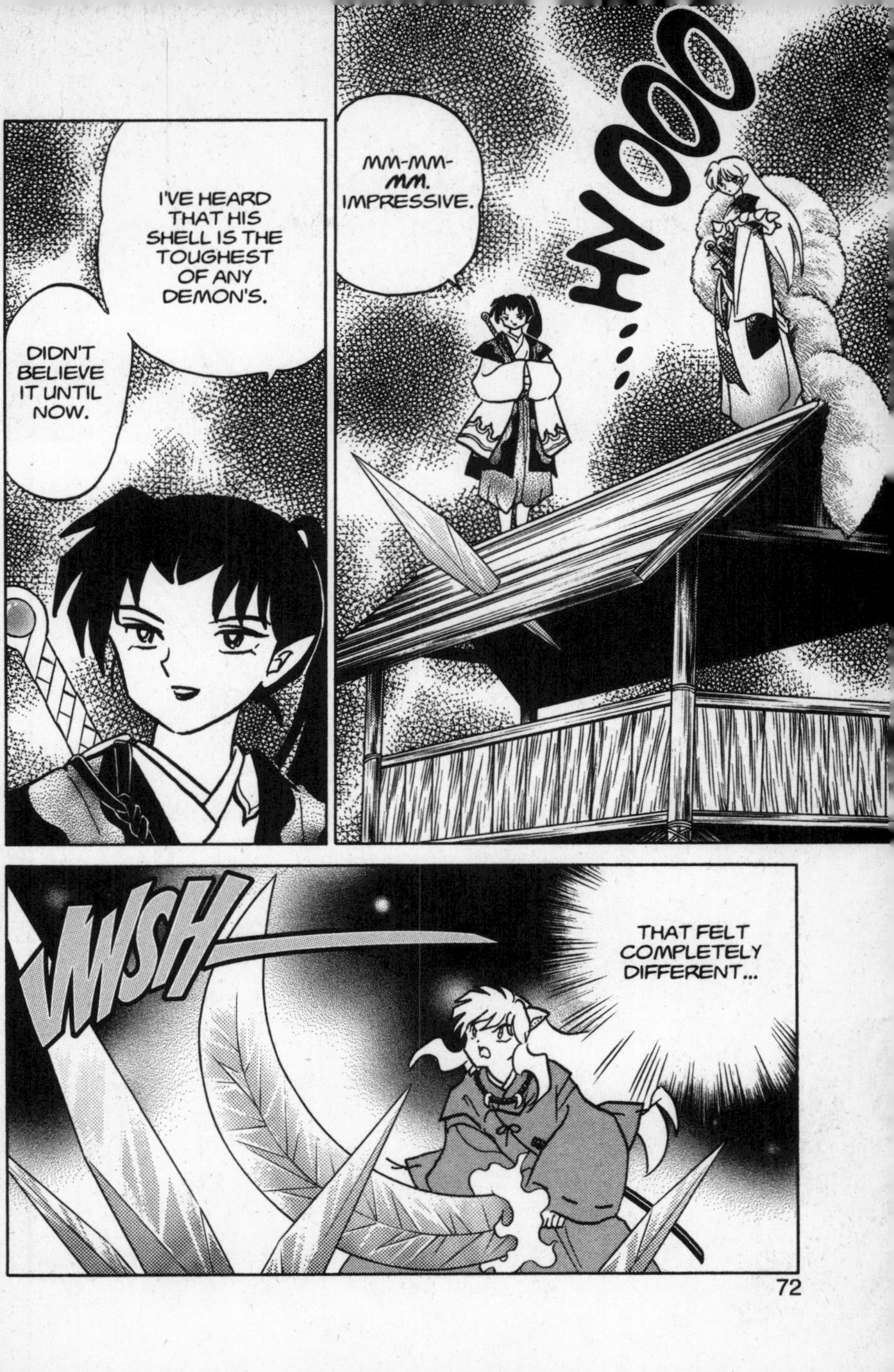
HYOOO...
MM-MM-MM. IMPRESSIVE.
I'VE HEARD THAT HIS SHELL IS THE TOUGHEST OF ANY DEMON'S.
DIDN'T BELIEVE IT UNTIL NOW.
VWSH
THAT FELT COMPLETELY DIFFERENT...

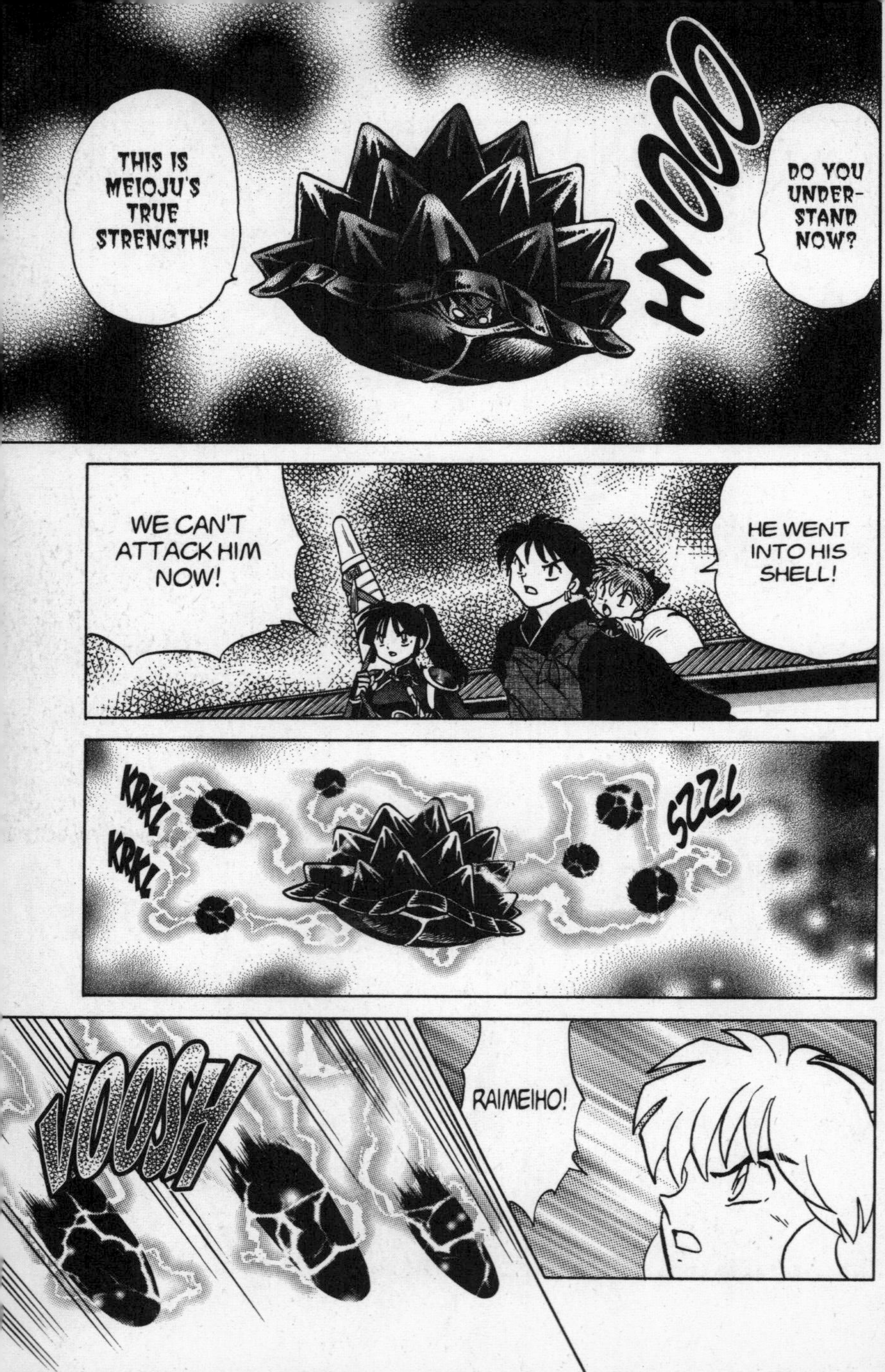
DO YOU UNDER-STAND NOW?
HYOOO
THIS IS MEIOJU'S TRUE STRENGTH!
HE WENT INTO HIS SHELL!
WE CAN'T ATTACK HIM NOW!
SZZZ
KRKL
KRKL
RAIMEIHO!
JOOSH

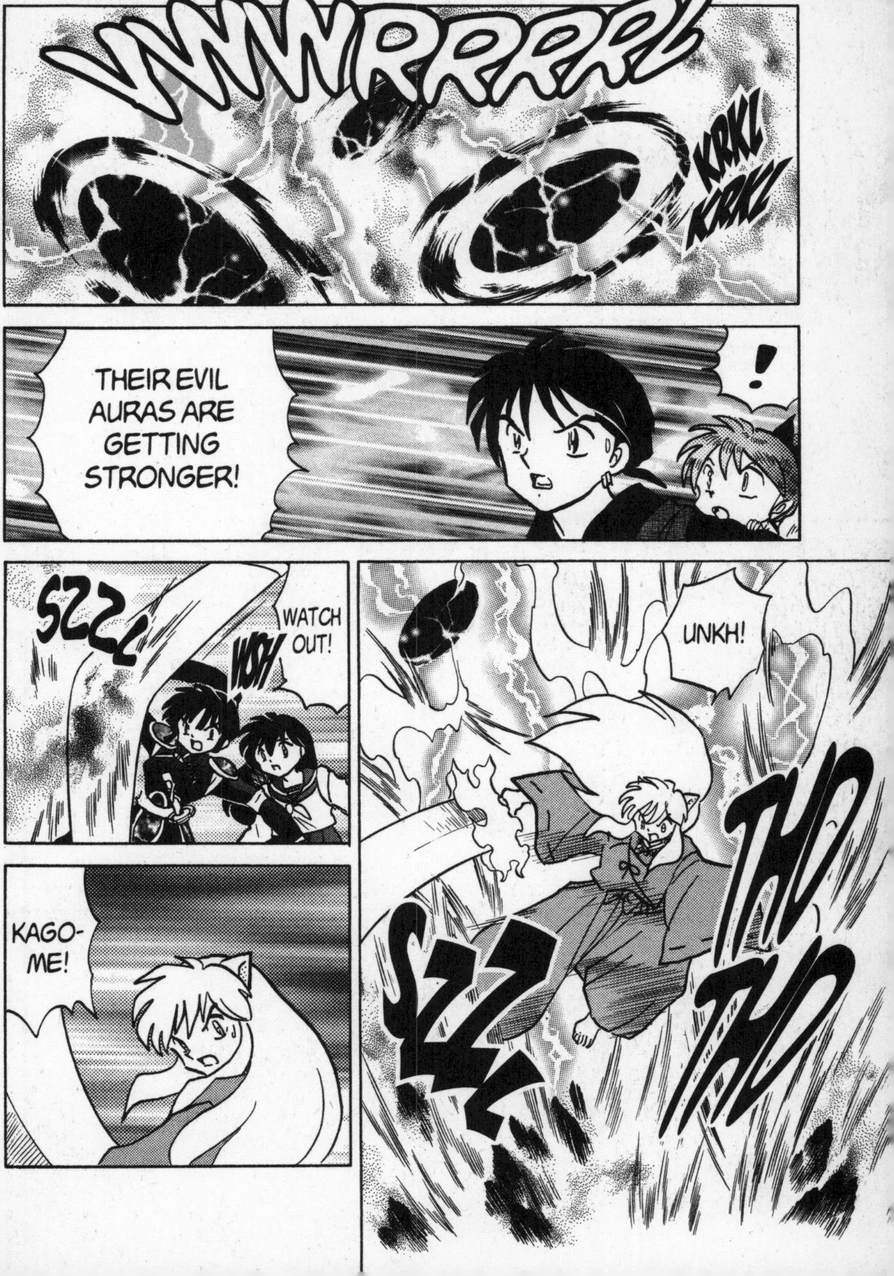
VVWWRRRR!
KRKL KRKL
!
THEIR EVIL AURAS ARE GETTING STRONGER!
UNKH!
THD THD
SZZ
SZZZ
WSH
WATCH OUT!
KAGO-ME!

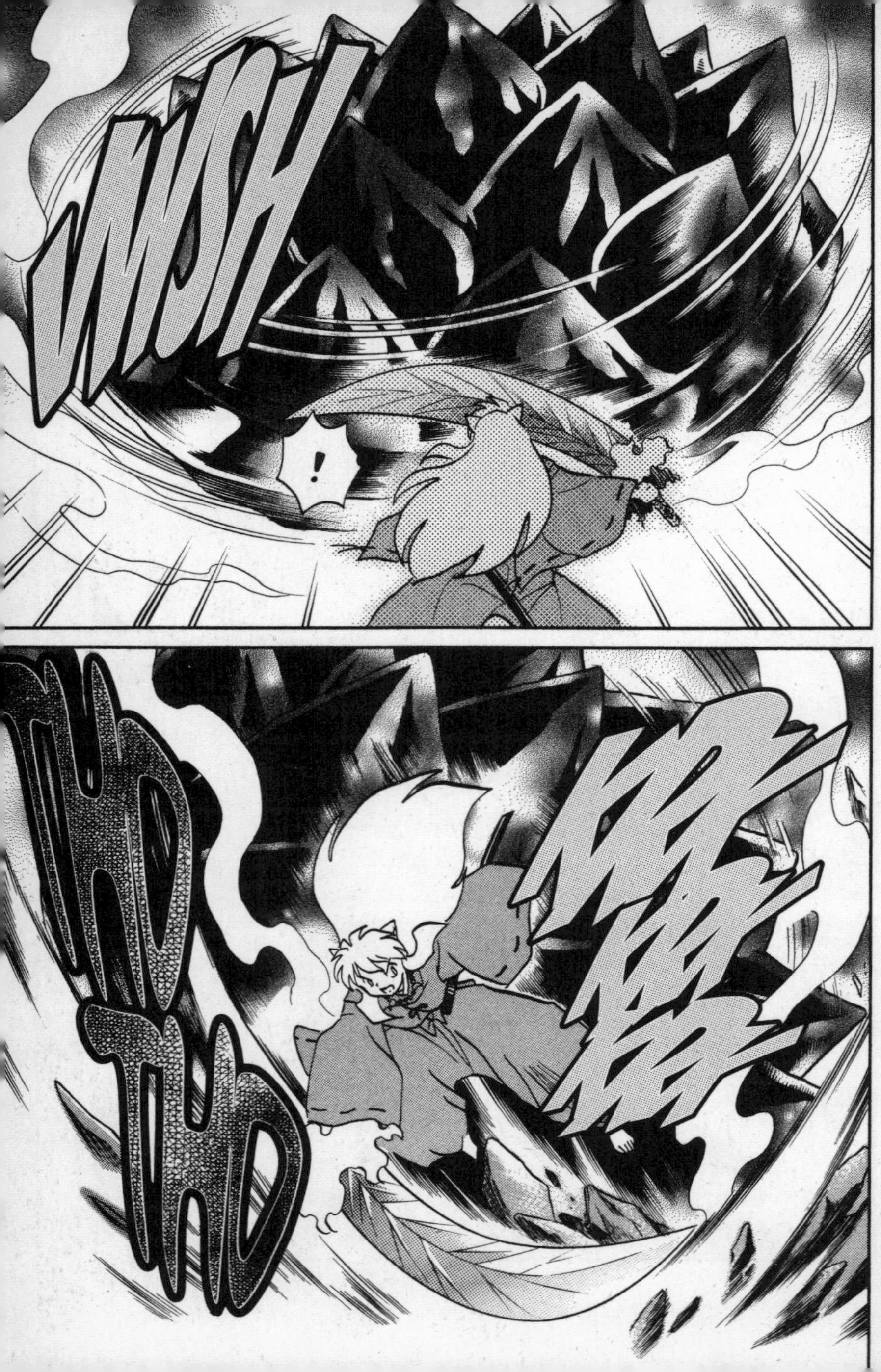
!
THD
THD

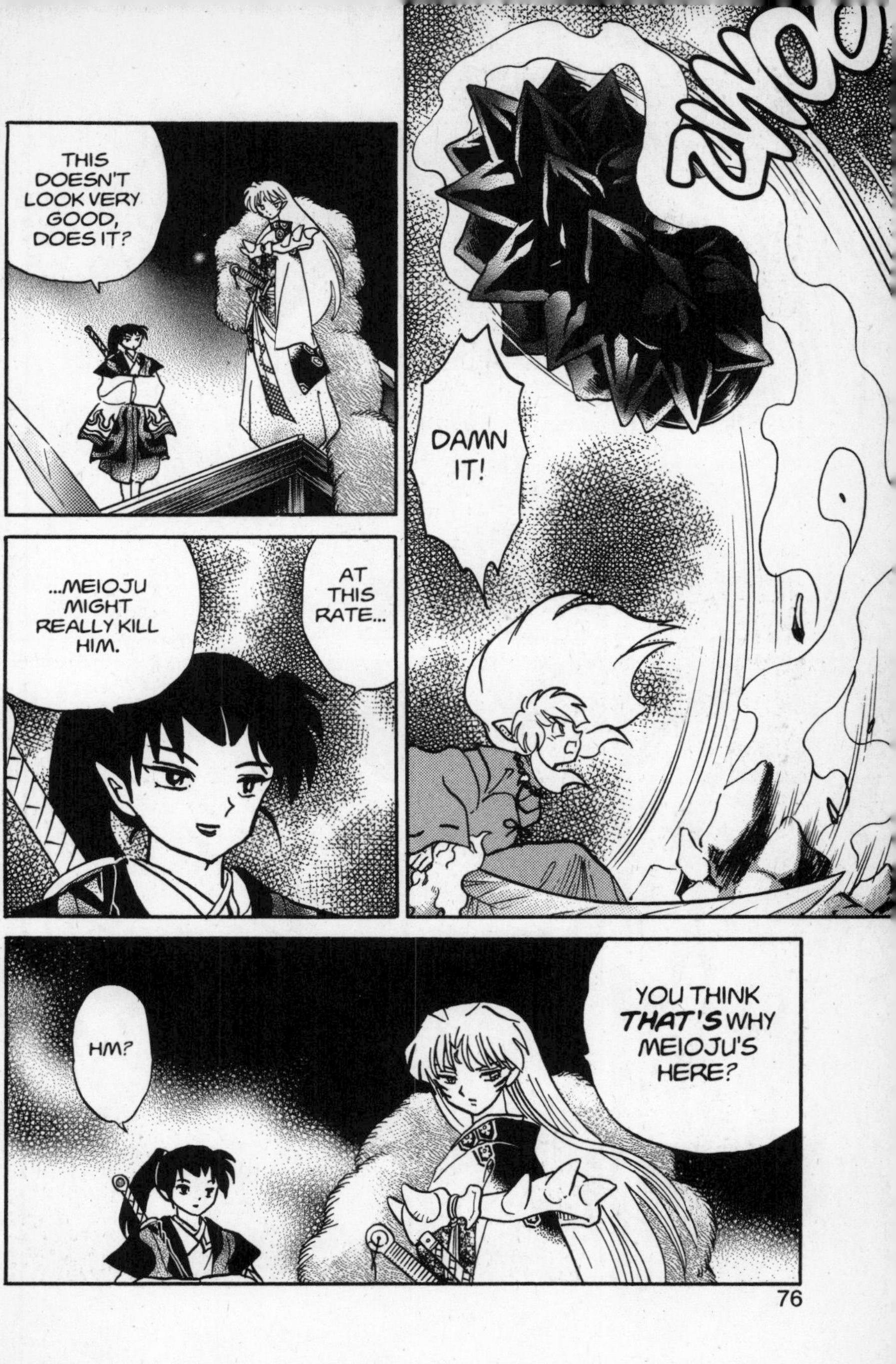
DAMN IT!
THIS DOESN'T LOOK VERY GOOD, DOES IT?
AT THIS RATE...
...MEIOJU MIGHT REALLY KILL HIM.
YOU THINK **THAT'S** WHY MEIOJU'S HERE?
HM?

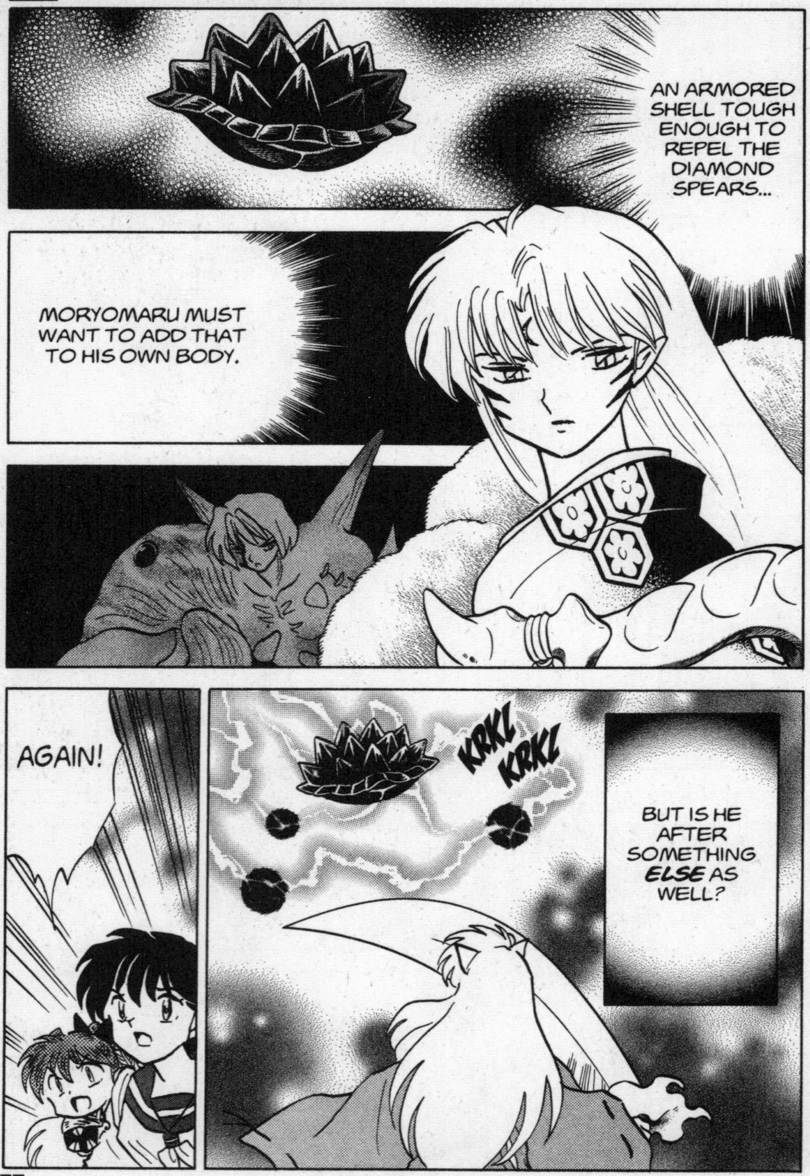
AN ARMORED SHELL TOUGH ENOUGH TO REPEL THE DIAMOND SPEARS...
MORYOMARU MUST WANT TO ADD THAT TO HIS OWN BODY.
KRKL KRKL
BUT IS HE AFTER SOMETHING *ELSE* AS WELL?
AGAIN!

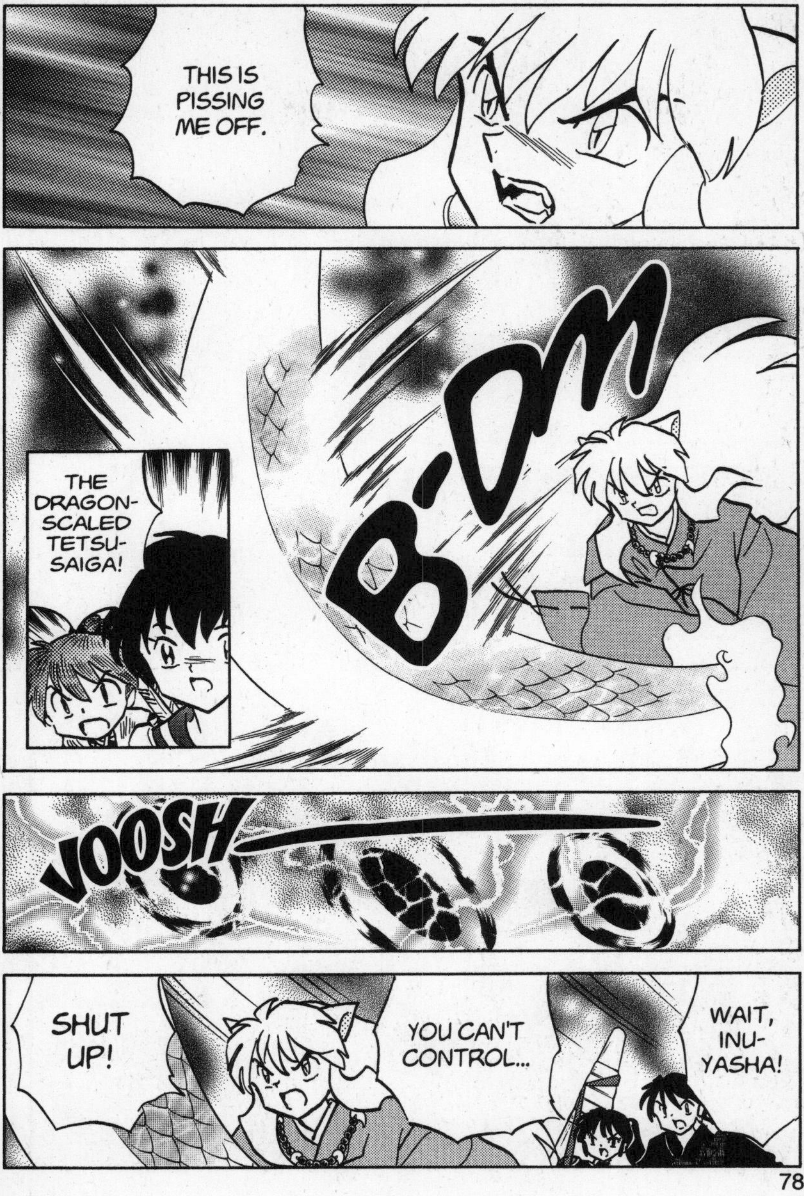
THIS IS PISSING ME OFF.
B-DM
THE DRAGON-SCALED TETSU-SAIGA!
VOOSH
WAIT, INU-YASHA!
YOU CAN'T CONTROL...
SHUT UP!

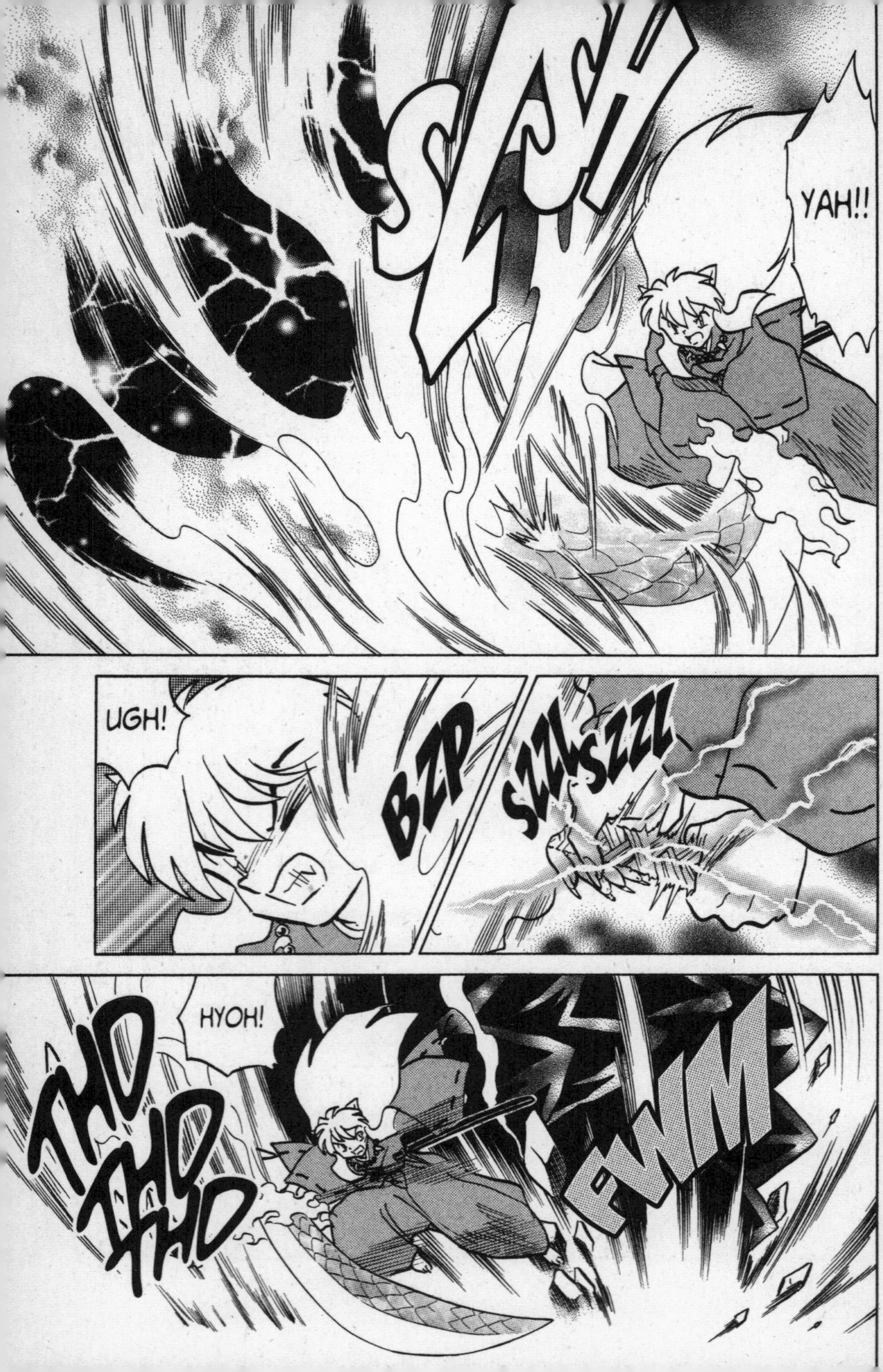
YAH!!
SLASH
SZZLSZZL
UGH!
BZP
FWM
HYOH!
THD THD THD THD

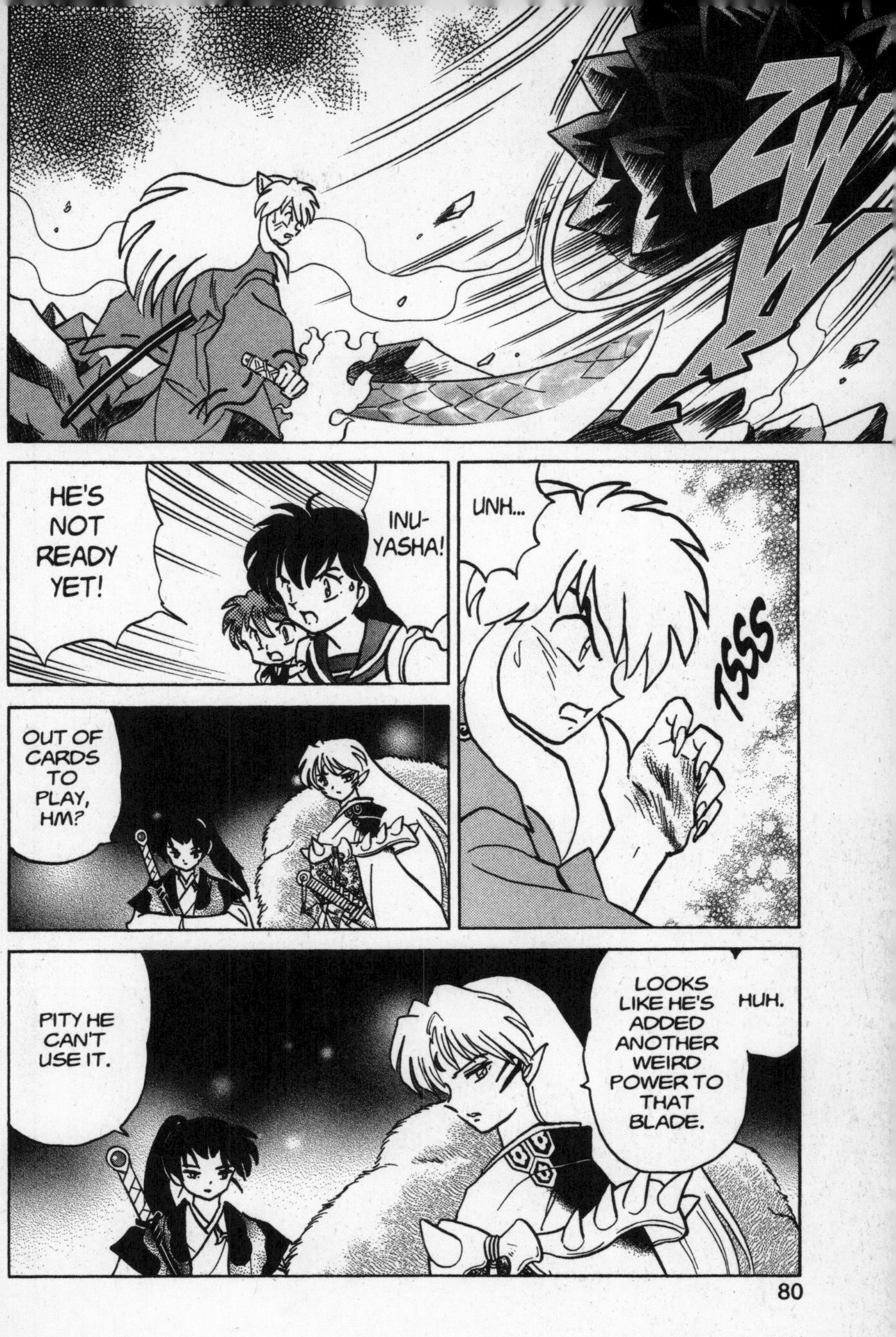
UNH...
TSSS
INU-YASHA!
HE'S NOT READY YET!
OUT OF CARDS TO PLAY, HM?
HUH.
LOOKS LIKE HE'S ADDED ANOTHER WEIRD POWER TO THAT BLADE.
PITY HE CAN'T USE IT.

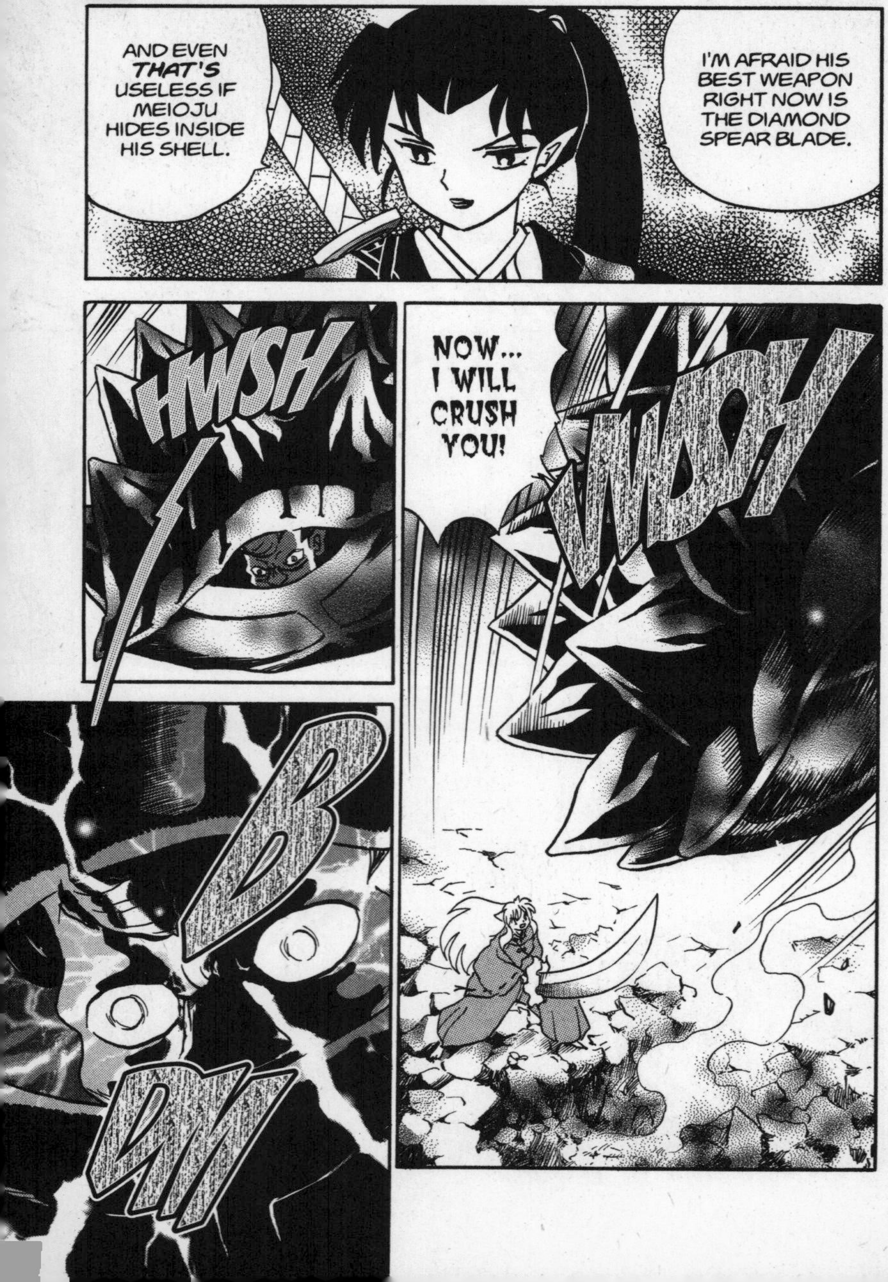
I'M AFRAID HIS BEST WEAPON RIGHT NOW IS THE DIAMOND SPEAR BLADE.
AND EVEN *THAT'S* USELESS IF MEIOJU HIDES INSIDE HIS SHELL.
NOW... I WILL CRUSH YOU!
WDOH
HWSH
B
WM

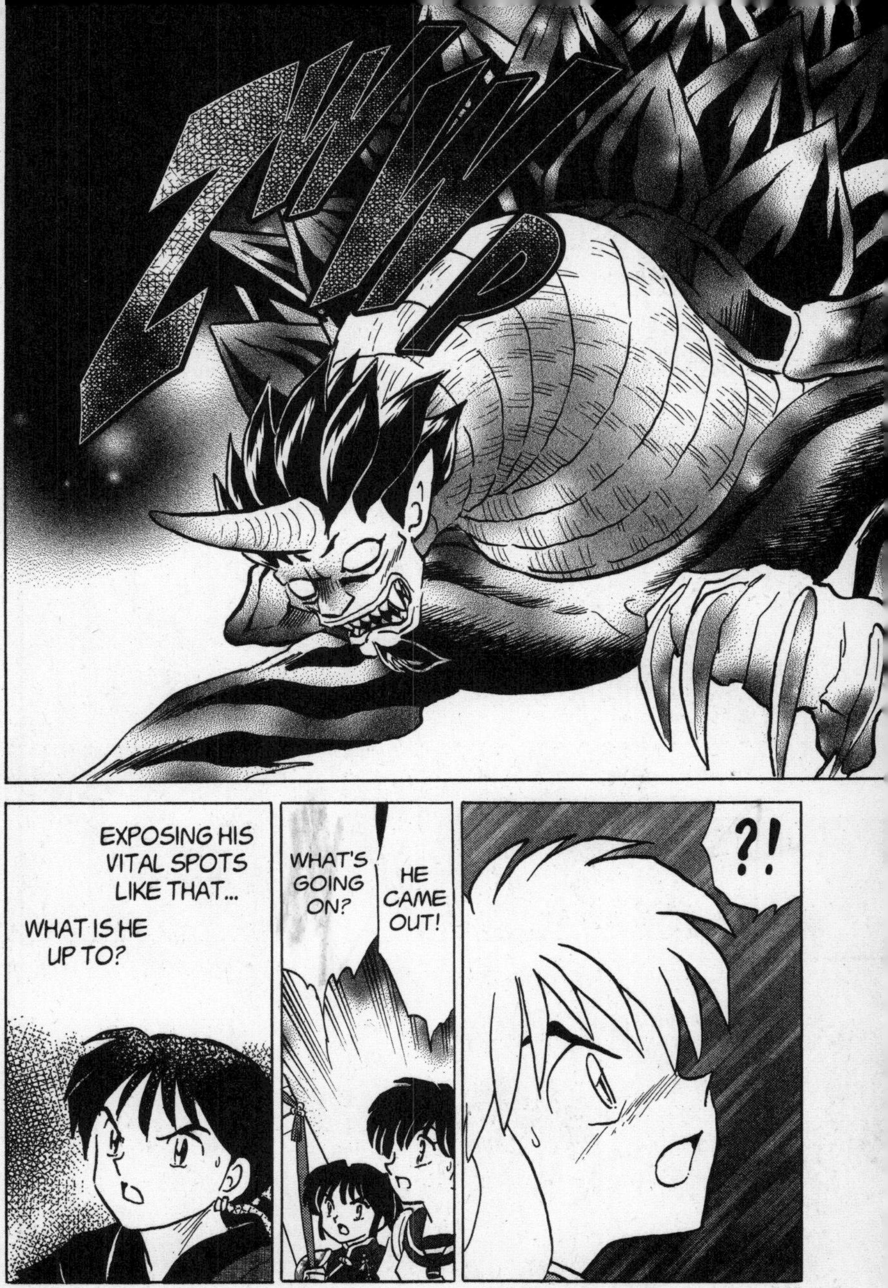
ZWHIP
?!
HE CAME OUT!
WHAT'S GOING ON?
EXPOSING HIS VITAL SPOTS LIKE THAT...
WHAT IS HE UP TO?

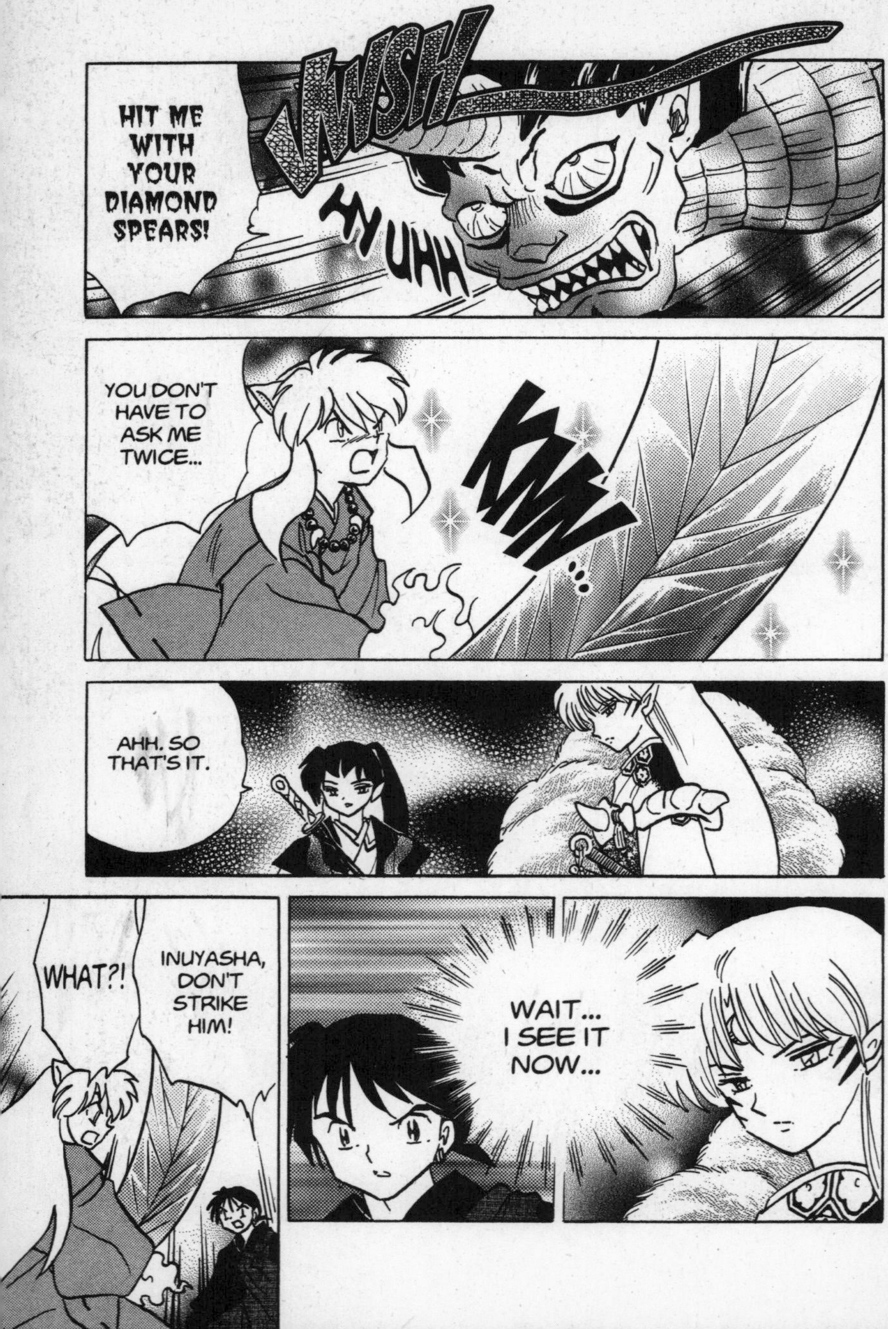
WSH
HIT ME WITH YOUR DIAMOND SPEARS!
HN UHH
YOU DON'T HAVE TO ASK ME TWICE...
KWM...
AHH. SO THAT'S IT.
WAIT... I SEE IT NOW...
INUYASHA, DON'T STRIKE HIM!
WHAT?!

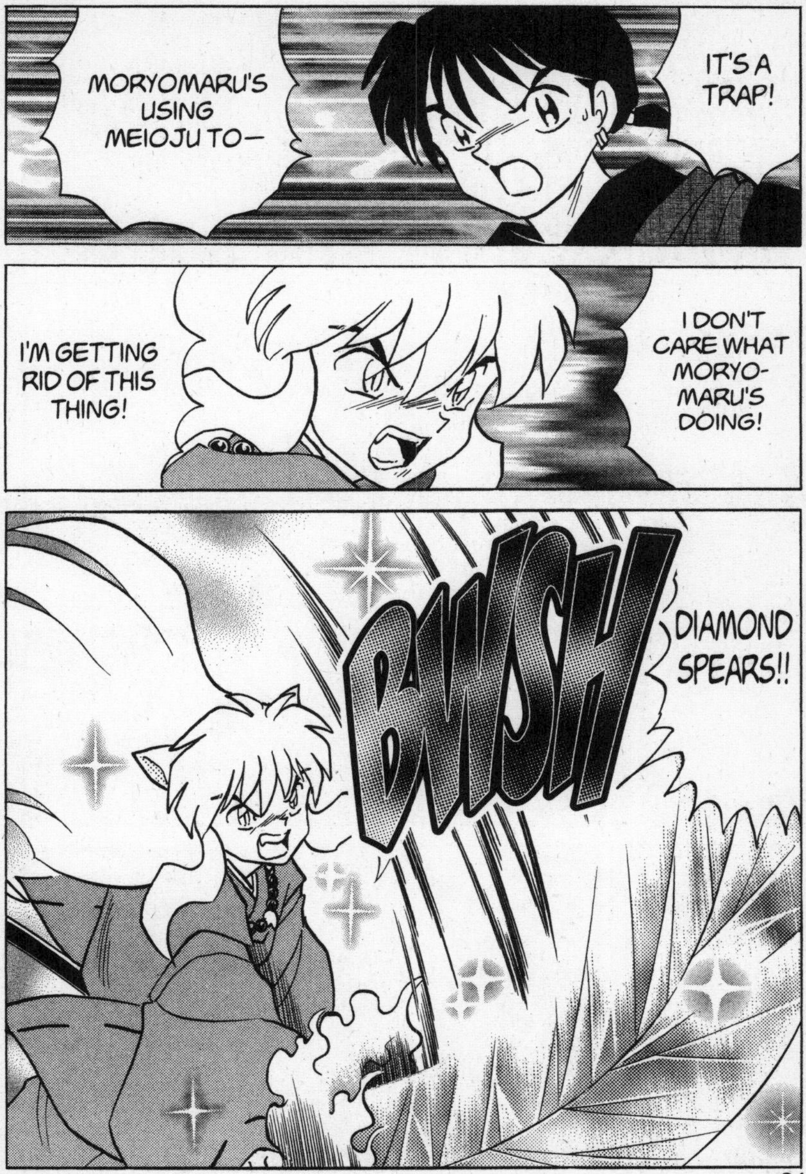
IT'S A TRAP!
MORYOMARU'S USING MEIOJU TO—
I DON'T CARE WHAT MORYO-MARU'S DOING!
I'M GETTING RID OF THIS THING!
DIAMOND SPEARS!!
BWSH

SCROLL 5

THE STOLEN DIAMOND SPEARS

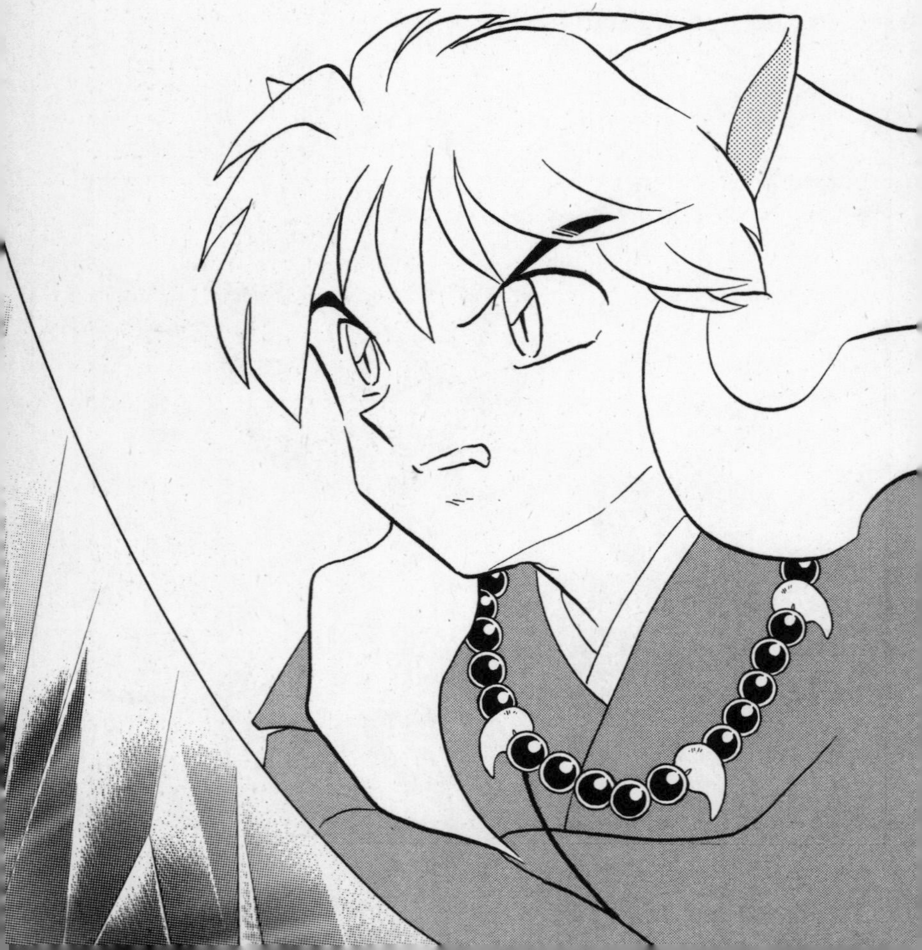

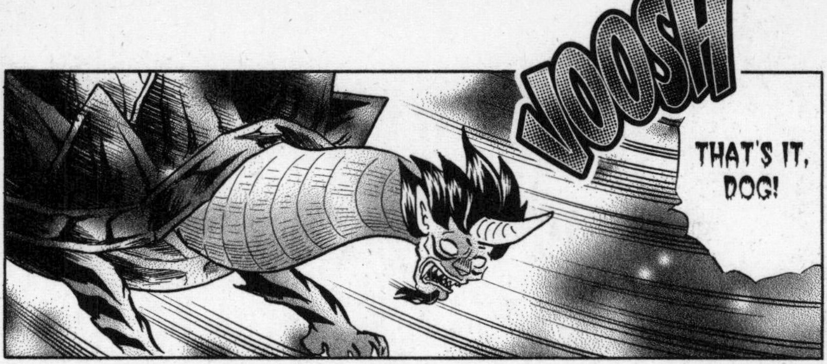
VOOSH
THAT'S IT, DOG!

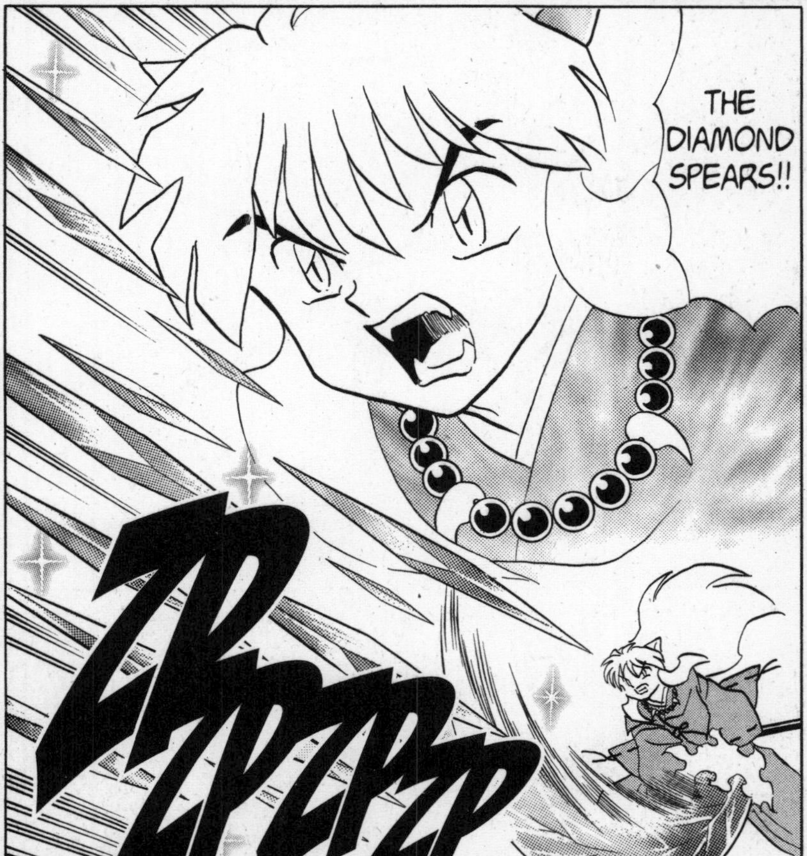
THE DIAMOND SPEARS!!
ZRRRRP

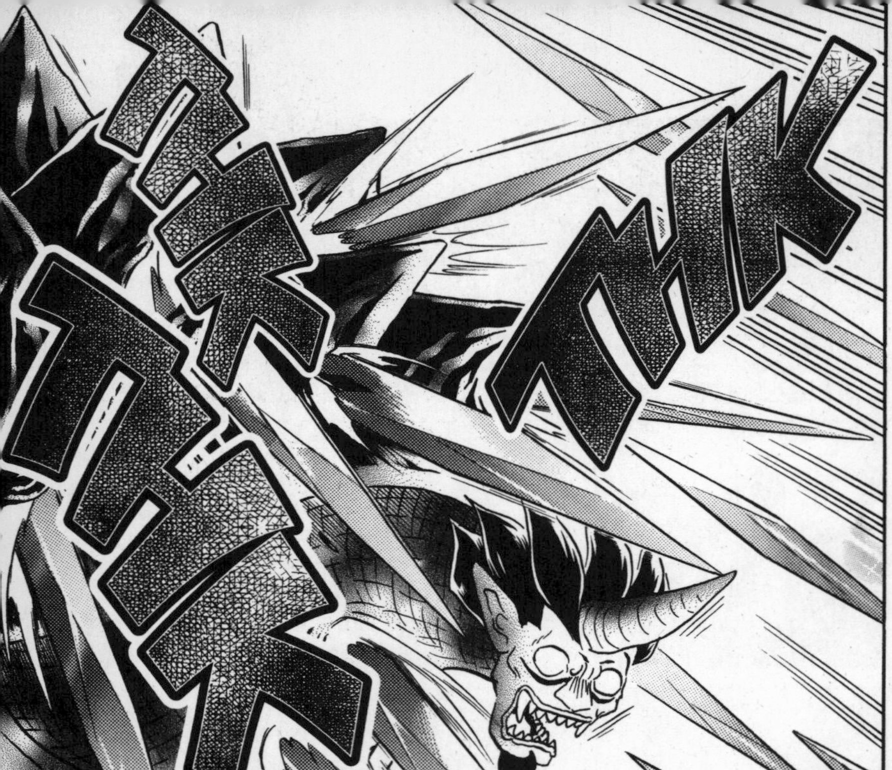
CHINK

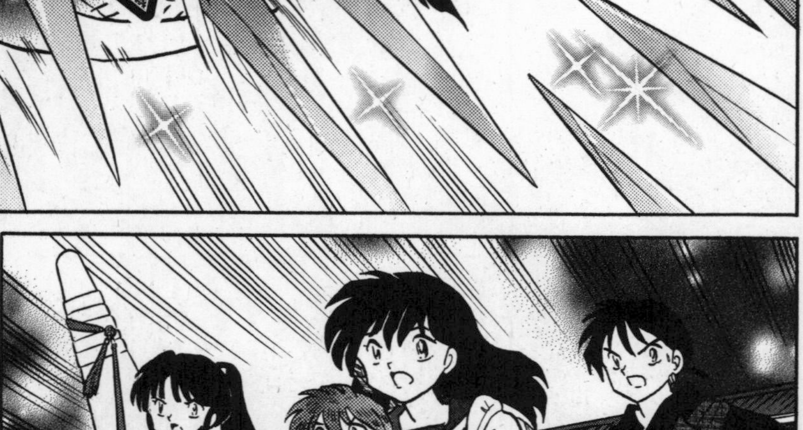

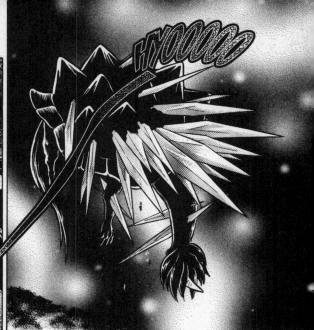

HYOOOOO

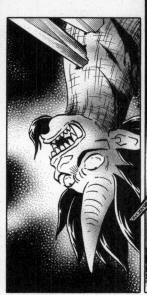

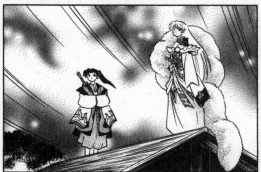

H... HE DID IT...

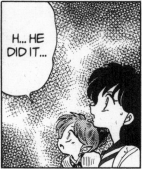

HUH?

CHAK

GET BACK, INUYASHA!

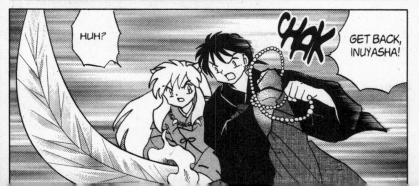

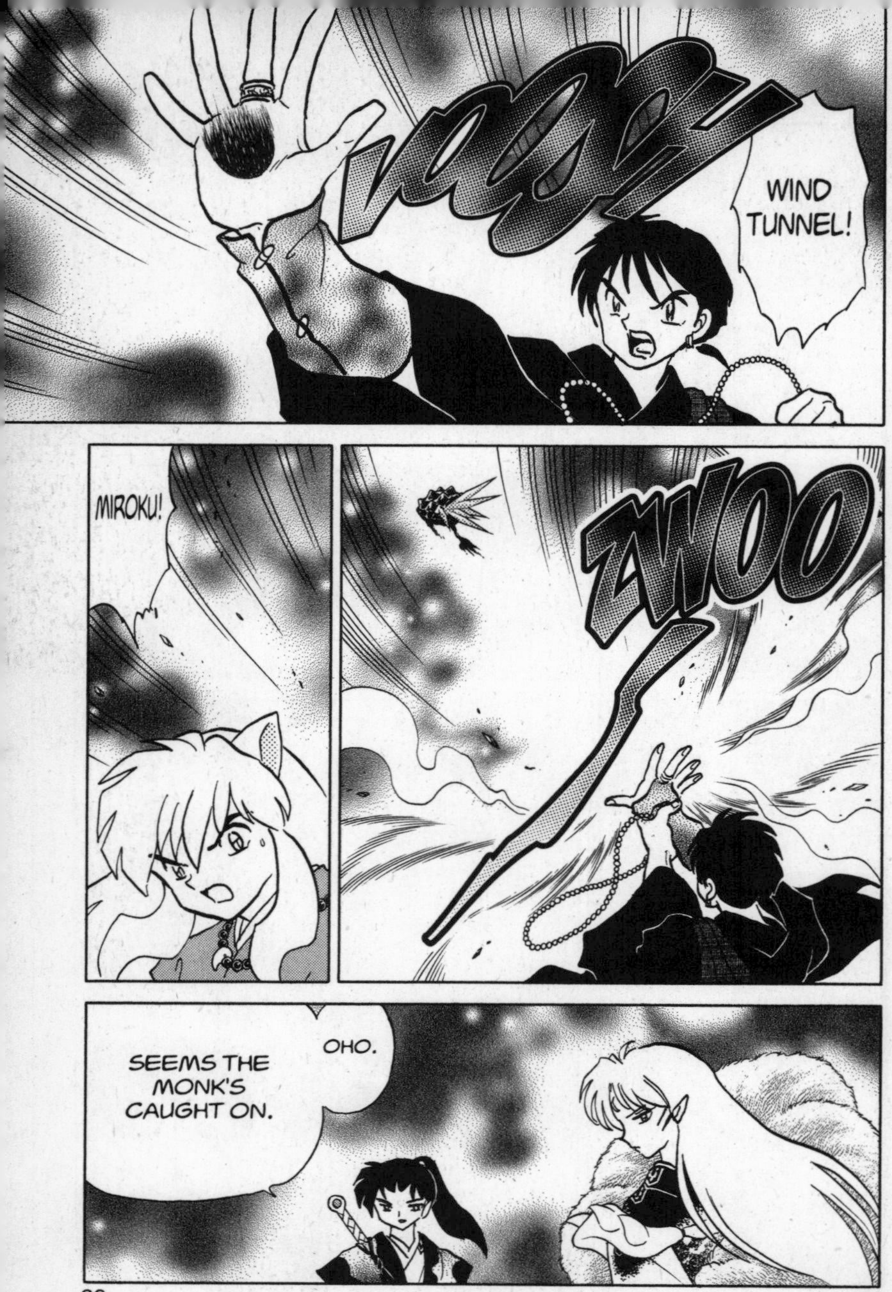
VOOSH
WIND TUNNEL!
ZWOO
MIROKU!
OHO.
SEEMS THE MONK'S CAUGHT ON.

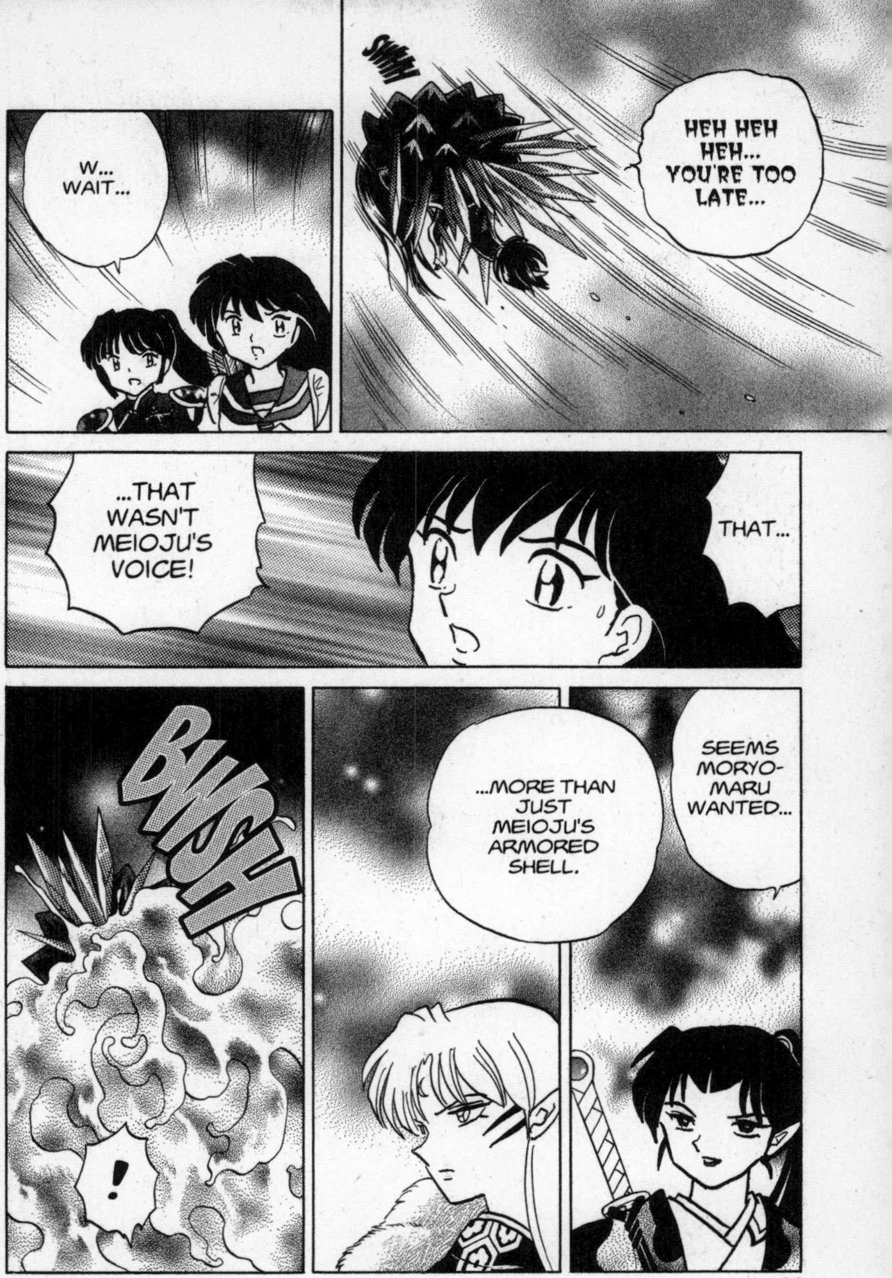
SWHH
HEH HEH HEH... YOU'RE TOO LATE...
W... WAIT...
THAT...
...THAT WASN'T MEIOJU'S VOICE!
SEEMS MORYO-MARU WANTED...
...MORE THAN JUST MEIOJU'S ARMORED SHELL.
BWSH
!

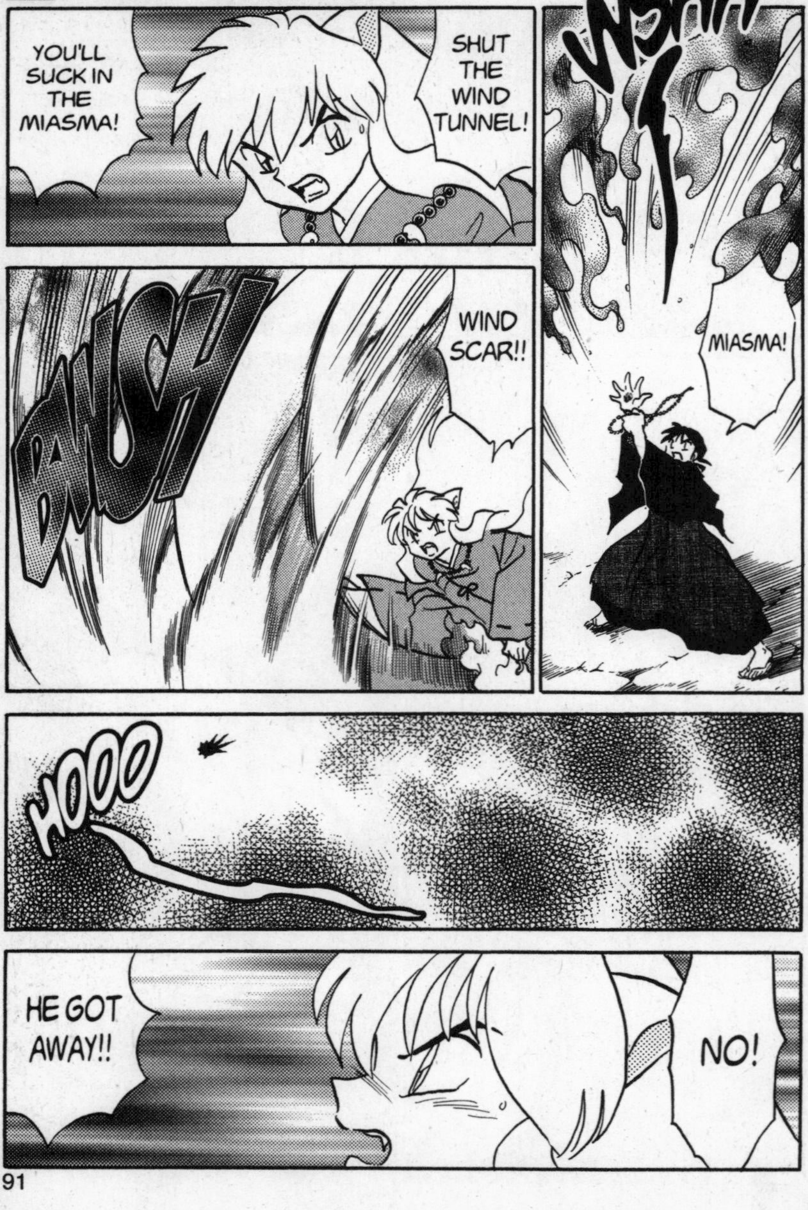
WSHH
MIASMA!
SHUT THE WIND TUNNEL!
YOU'LL SUCK IN THE MIASMA!
WIND SCAR!!
BWSH
HOOO
NO!
HE GOT AWAY!!

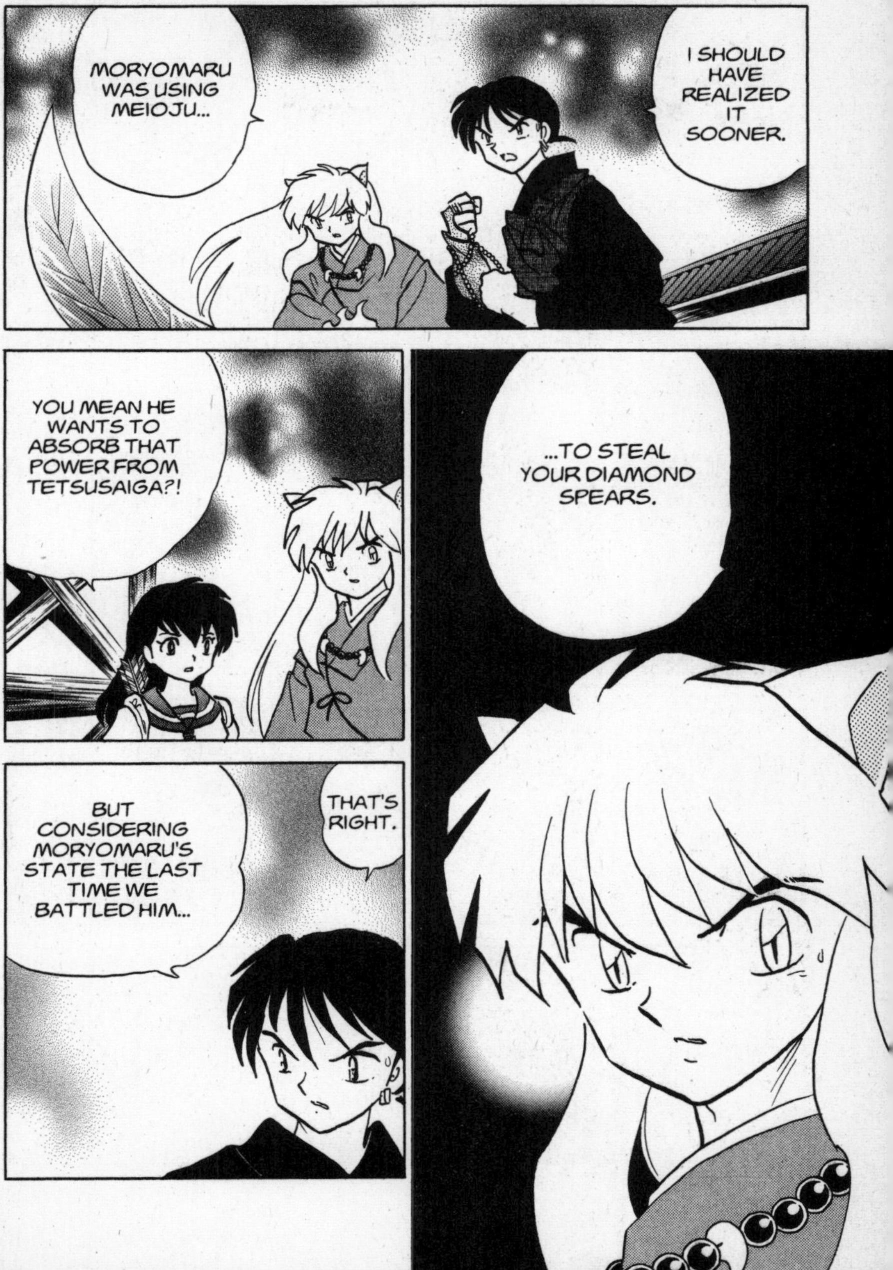
I SHOULD HAVE REALIZED IT SOONER.
MORYOMARU WAS USING MEIOJU...
...TO STEAL YOUR DIAMOND SPEARS.
YOU MEAN HE WANTS TO ABSORB THAT POWER FROM TETSUSAIGA?!
THAT'S RIGHT.
BUT CONSIDERING MORYOMARU'S STATE THE LAST TIME WE BATTLED HIM...

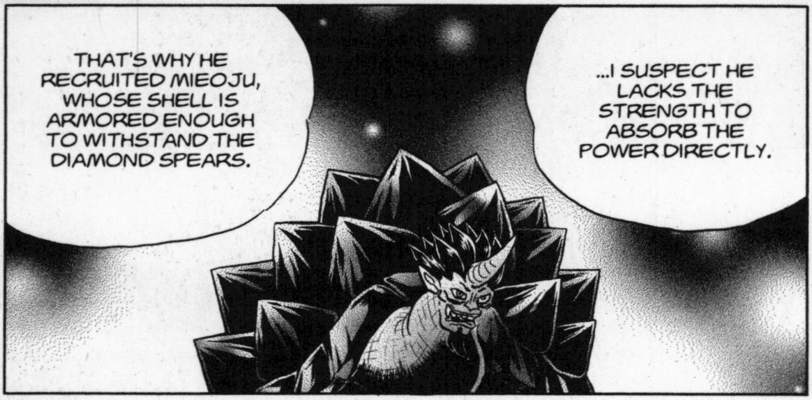
...I SUSPECT HE LACKS THE STRENGTH TO ABSORB THE POWER DIRECTLY.
THAT'S WHY HE RECRUITED MIEOJU, WHOSE SHELL IS ARMORED ENOUGH TO WITHSTAND THE DIAMOND SPEARS.

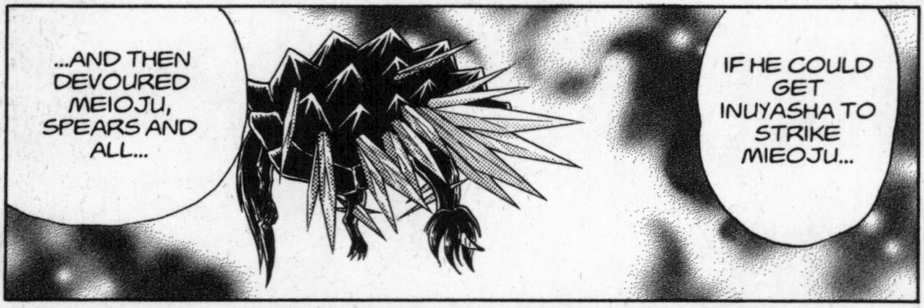
IF HE COULD GET INUYASHA TO STRIKE MIEOJU...
...AND THEN DEVOURED MEIOJU, SPEARS AND ALL...

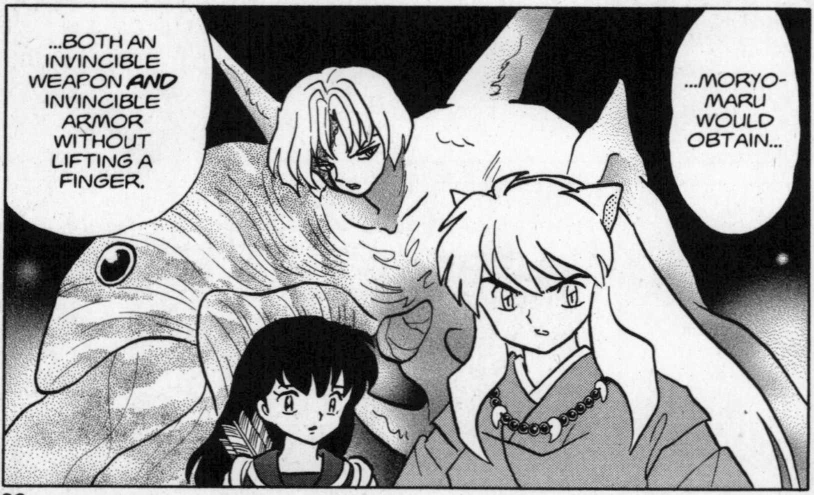
...MORYO-MARU WOULD OBTAIN...
...BOTH AN INVINCIBLE WEAPON *AND* INVINCIBLE ARMOR WITHOUT LIFTING A FINGER.

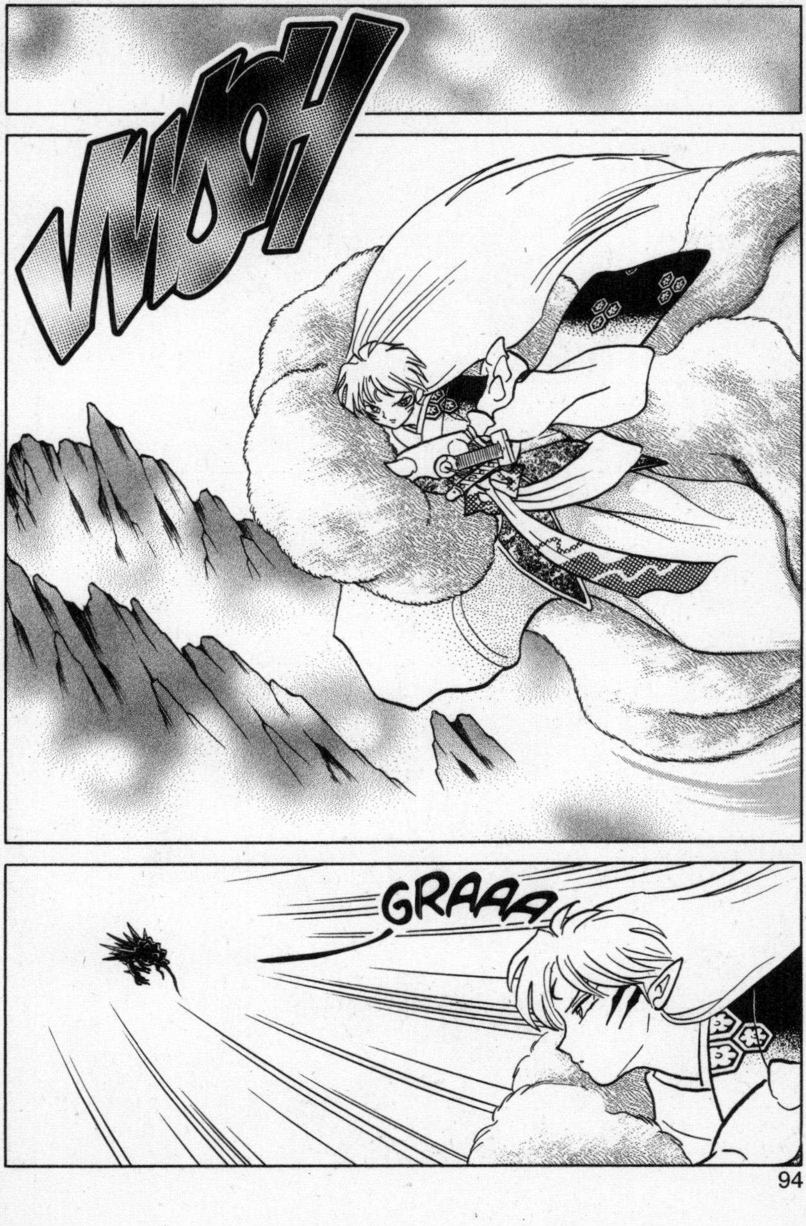
WHOOSH
GRAAA

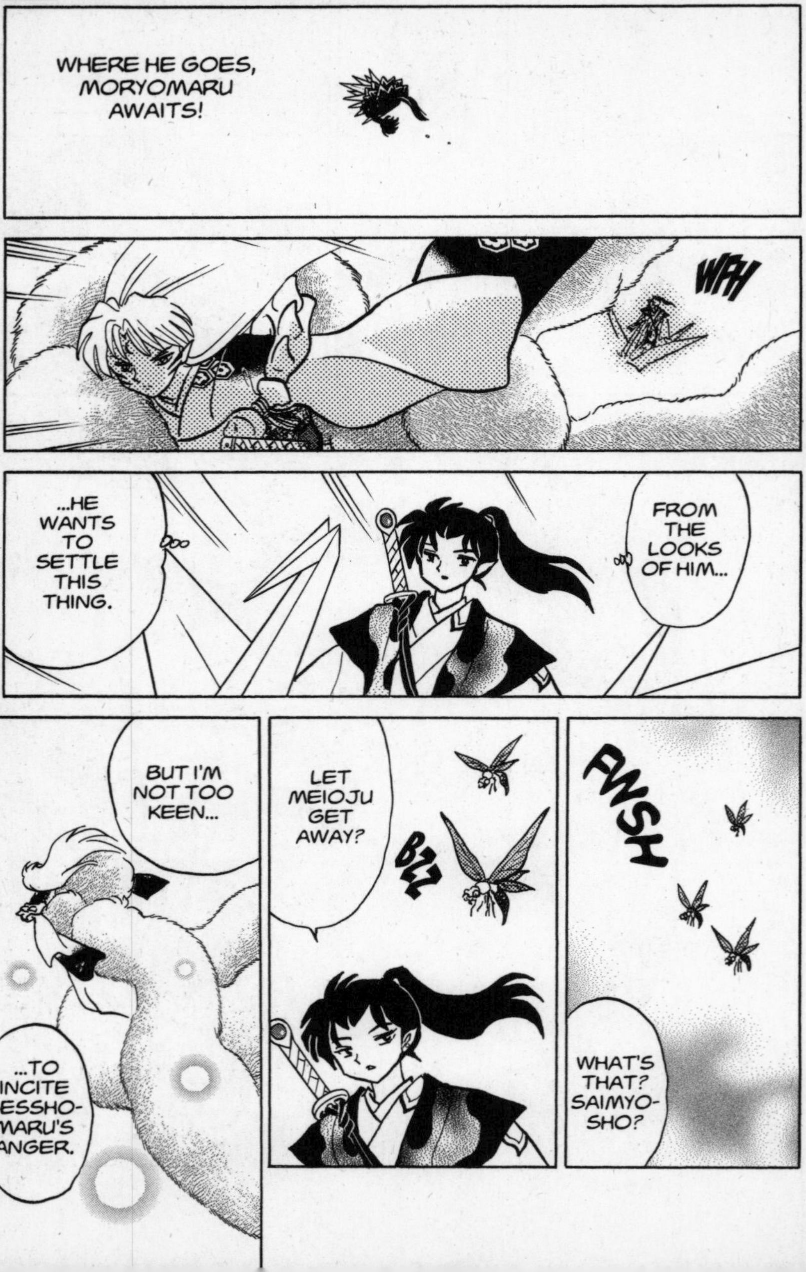
WHERE HE GOES, MORYOMARU AWAITS!
WPH
FROM THE LOOKS OF HIM...
...HE WANTS TO SETTLE THIS THING.
FWSH
WHAT'S THAT? SAIMYOSHO?
BZZ
LET MEIOJU GET AWAY?
BUT I'M NOT TOO KEEN...
...TO INCITE SESSHOMARU'S ANGER.

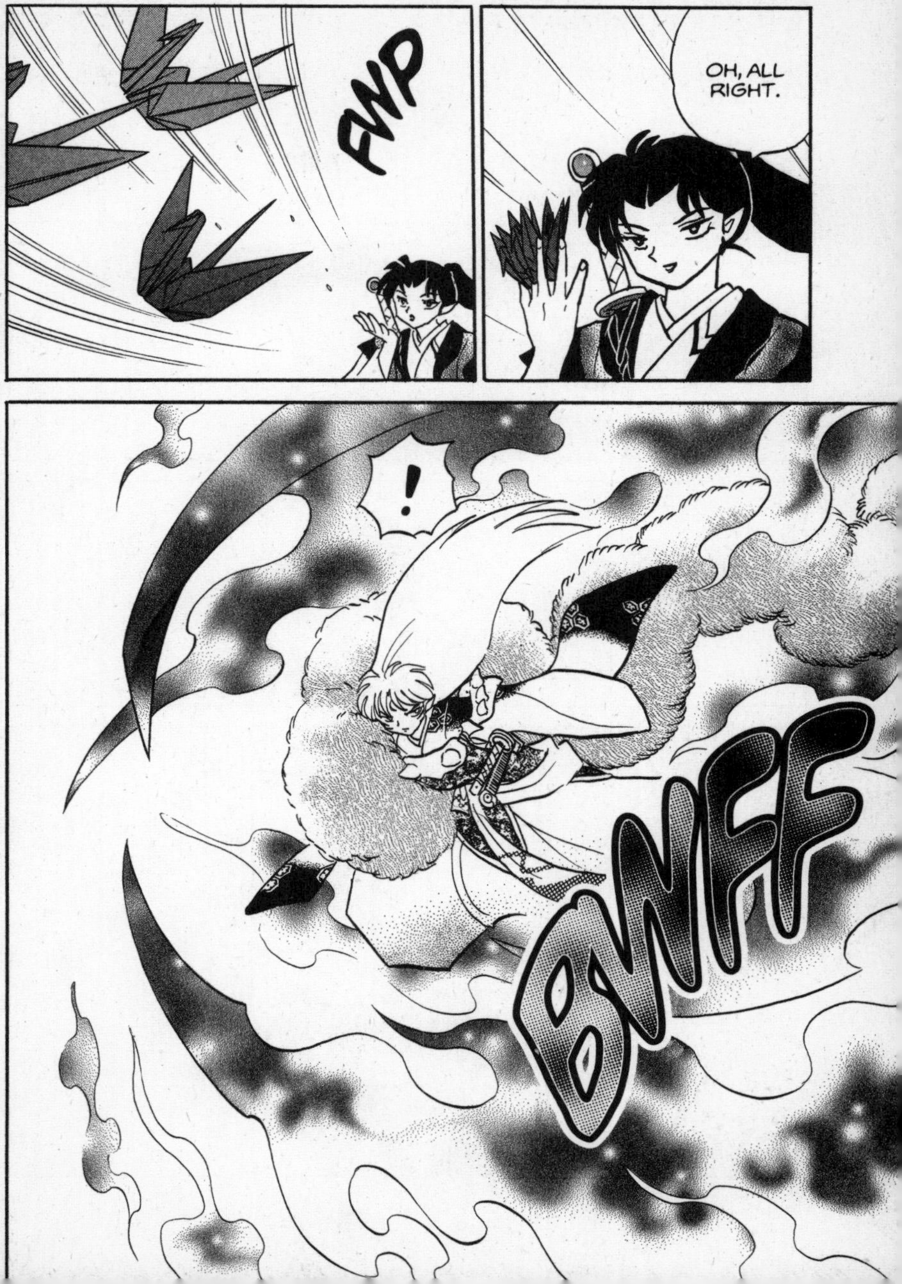
OH, ALL RIGHT.
FWP
!
BWFF

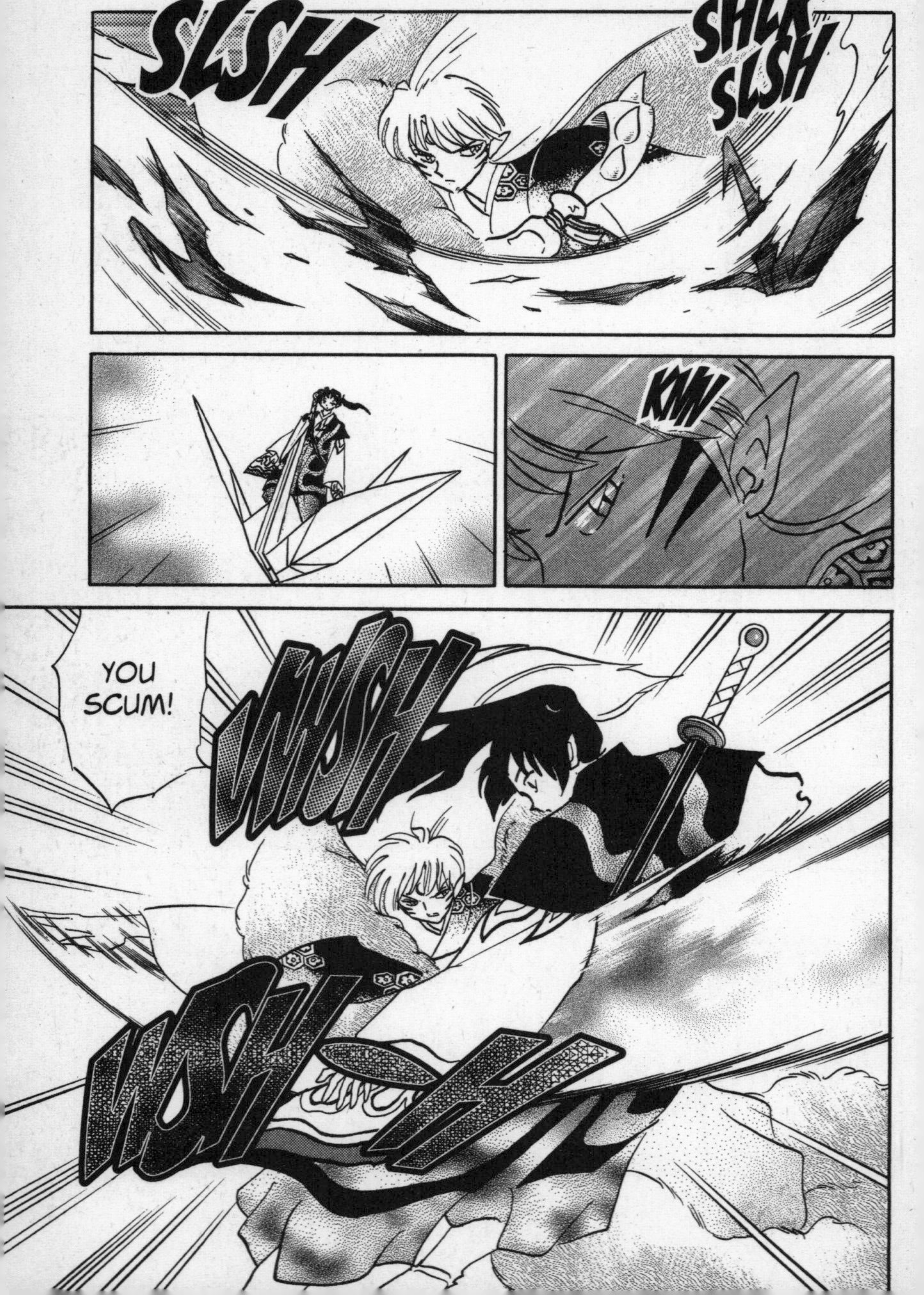
SHLK
SLSH
SLSH
KNN
YOU SCUM!
WHSH
WHSH

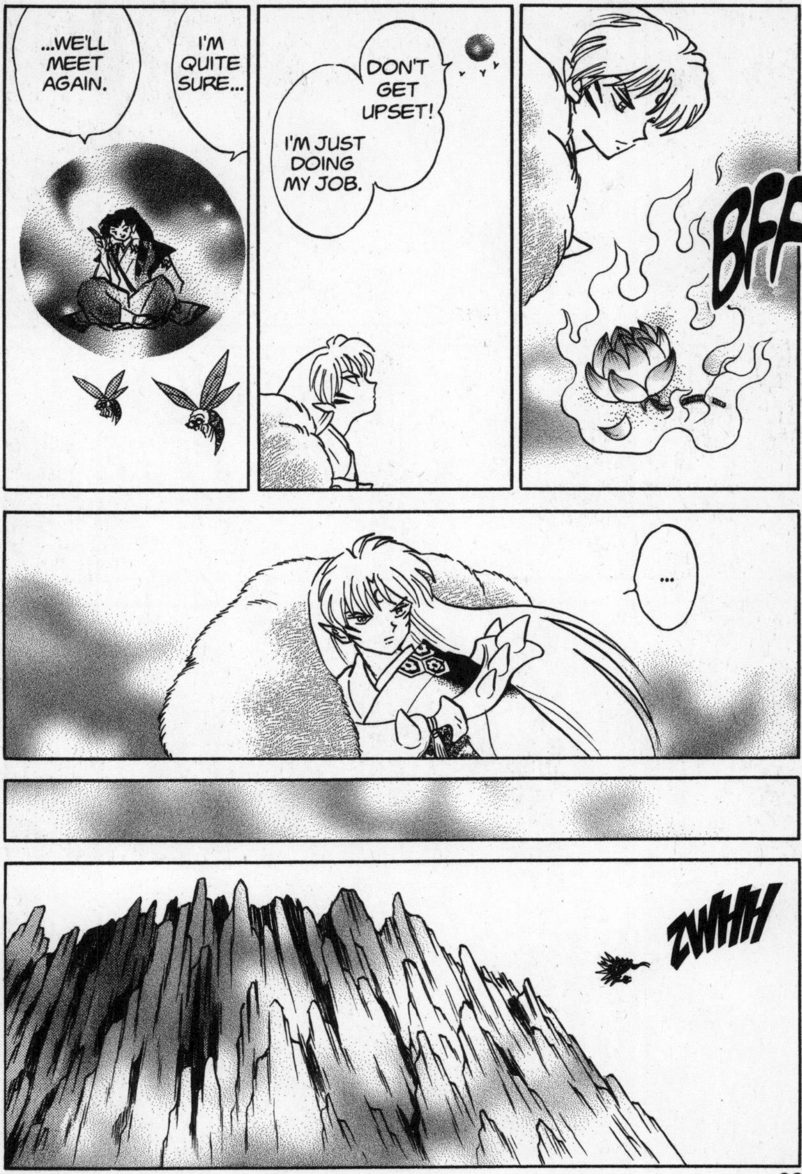
BFF
DON'T GET UPSET!
I'M JUST DOING MY JOB.
I'M QUITE SURE...
...WE'LL MEET AGAIN.
...
ZWHH

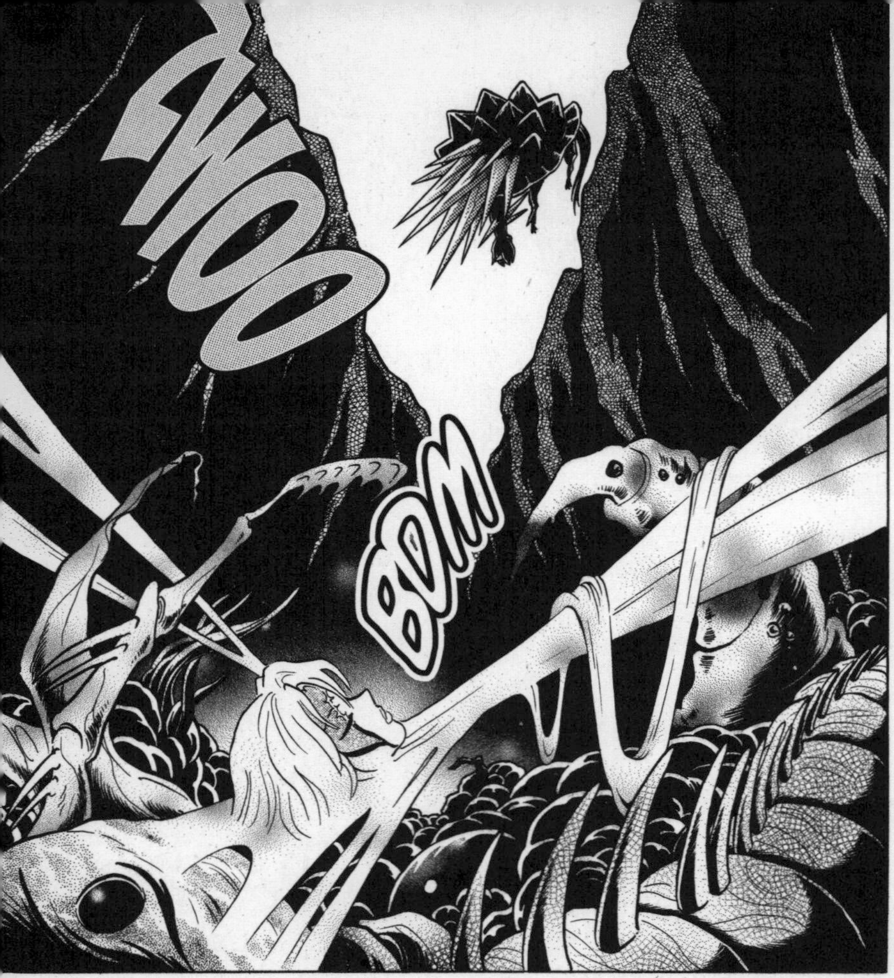

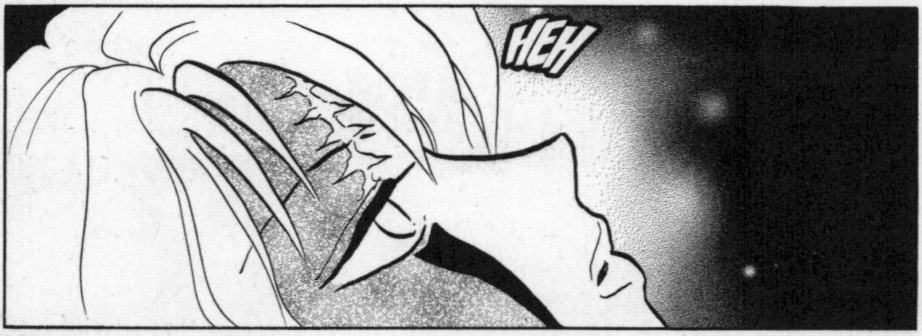
HEH

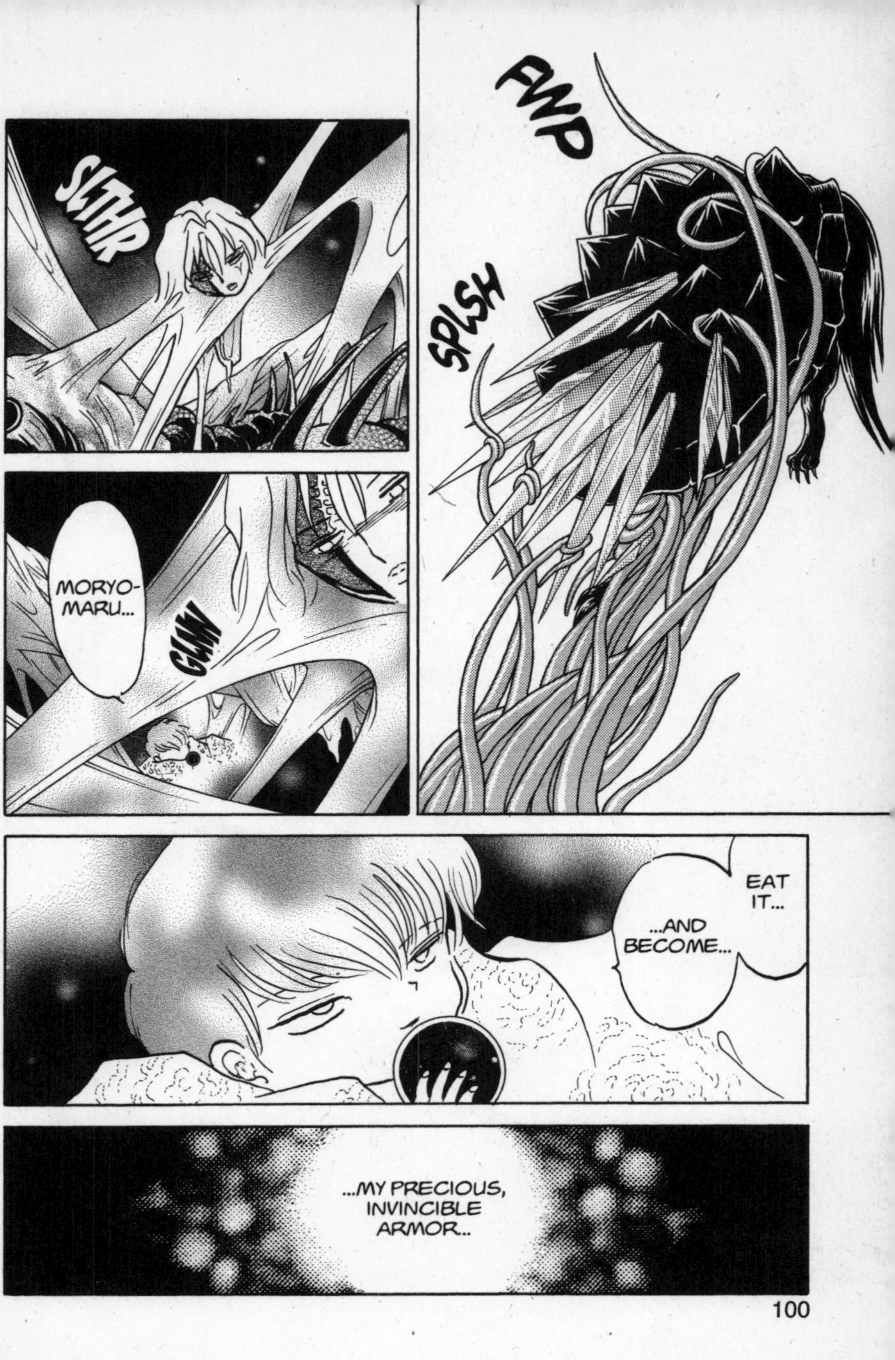
FWP
SPLSH
SLTHR
MORYO-MARU...
GLMM
EAT IT... ...AND BECOME...
...MY PRECIOUS, INVINCIBLE ARMOR...

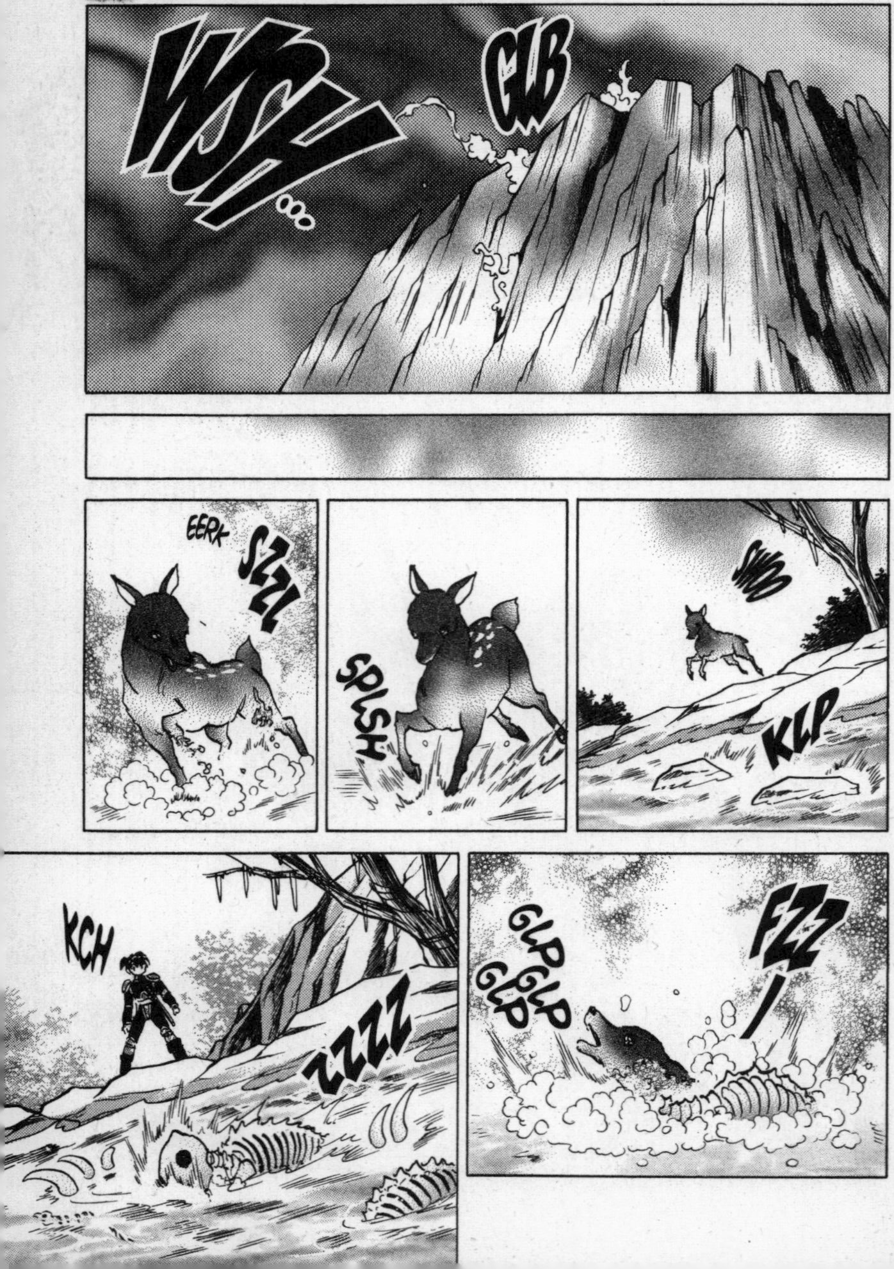
GLB
WSSH
SWOO
KLP
SPLSH
SZZZ
EERK
FZZ
GLP GLP GLP
KCH
ZZZZ

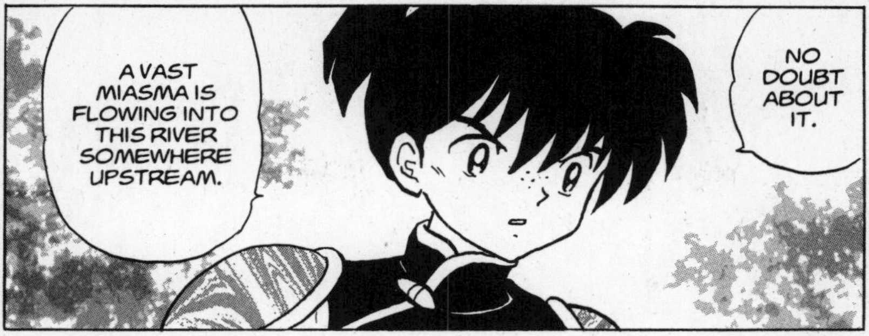
NO DOUBT ABOUT IT.
A VAST MIASMA IS FLOWING INTO THIS RIVER SOMEWHERE UPSTREAM.

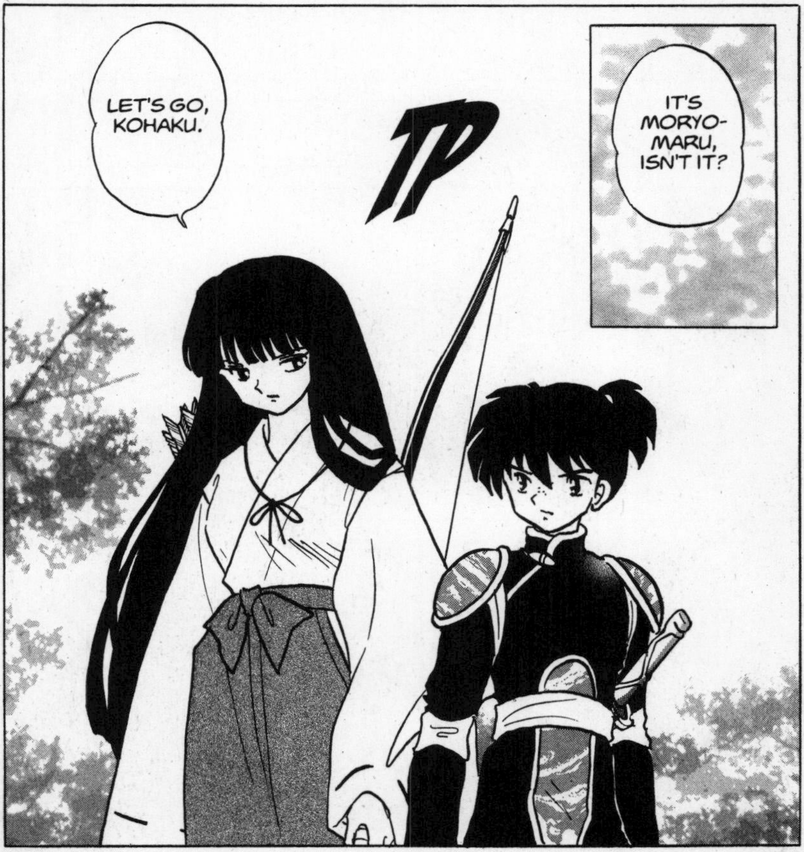
IT'S MORYO-MARU, ISN'T IT?
LET'S GO, KOHAKU.

SCROLL 6

MORYOMARU'S TRANSFORMATION

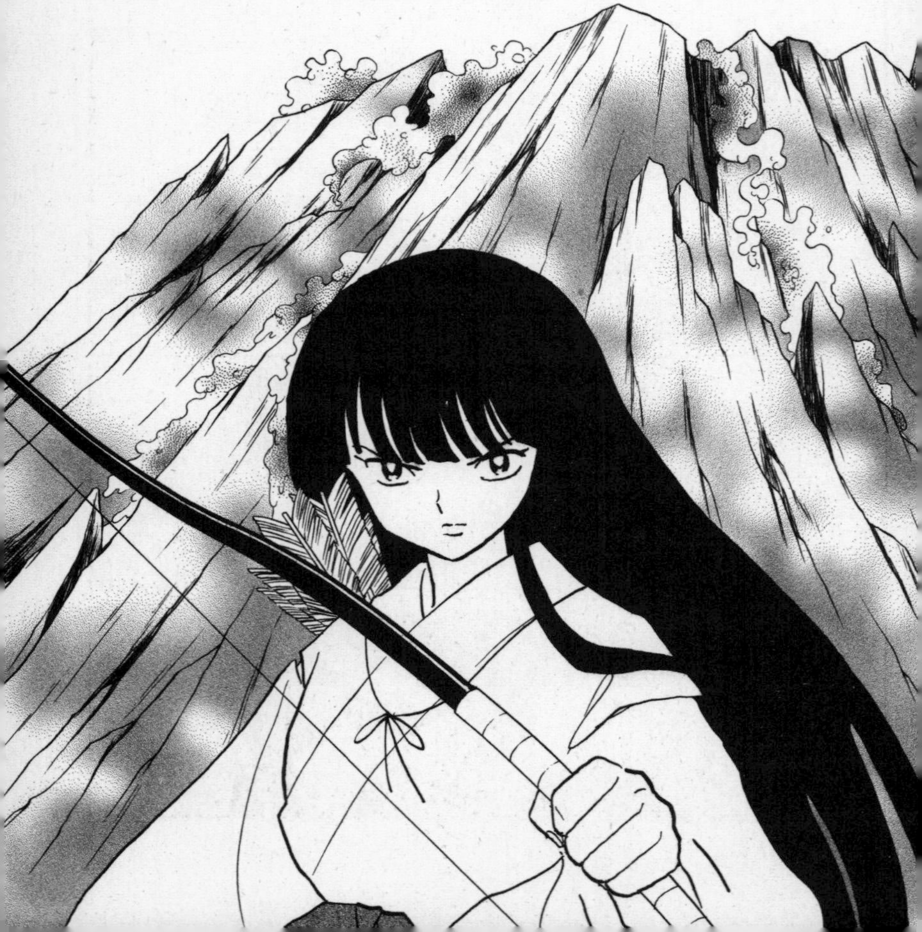

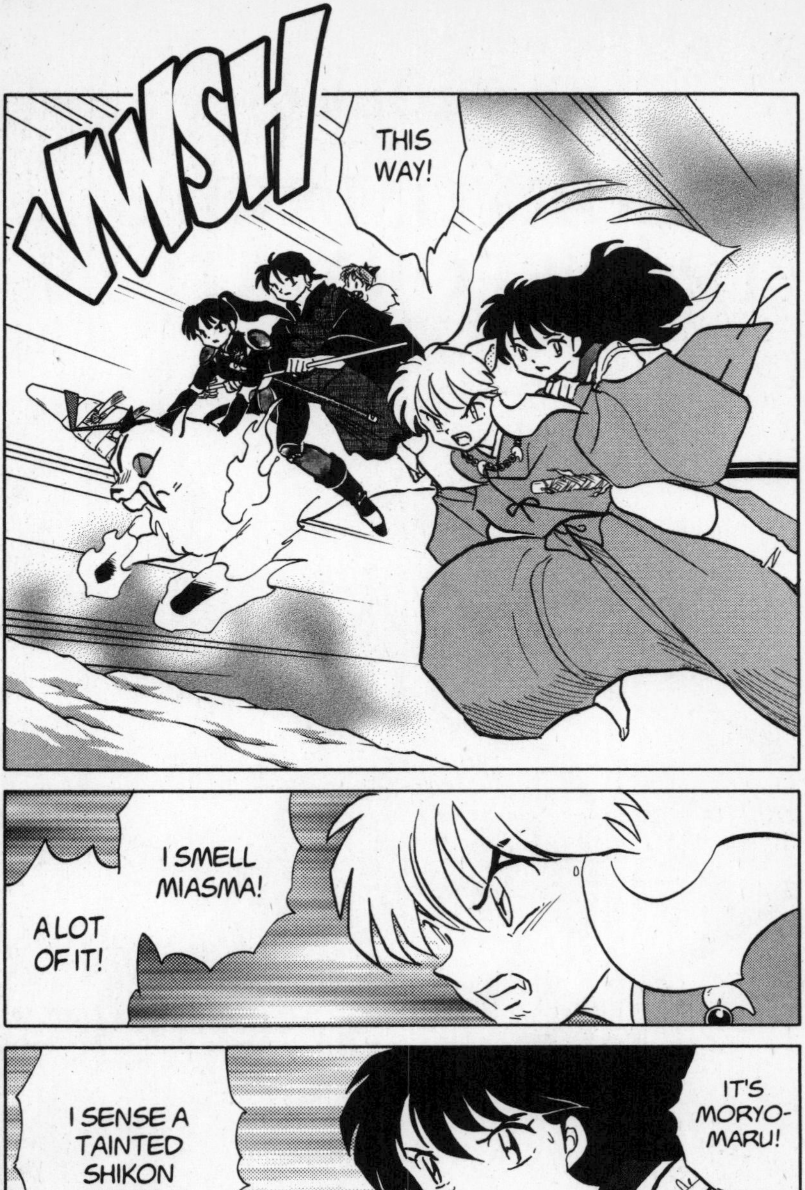
VWSH
THIS WAY!
I SMELL MIASMA!
A LOT OF IT!
I SENSE A TAINTED SHIKON SHARD!
IT'S MORYO-MARU!

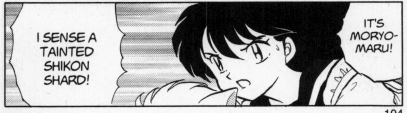

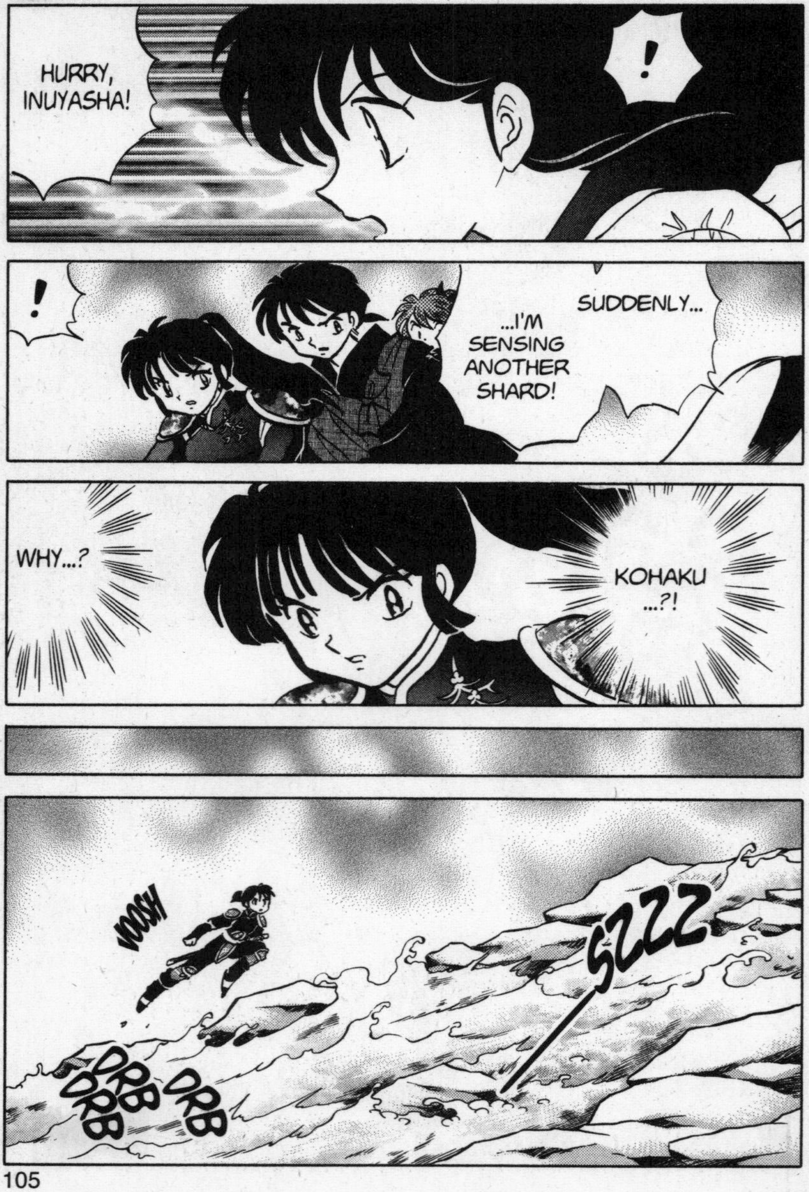
!
HURRY, INUYASHA!
SUDDENLY...
...I'M SENSING ANOTHER SHARD!
!
KOHAKU ...?!
WHY...?
SZZZ
VOOSH
DRB DRB
DRB

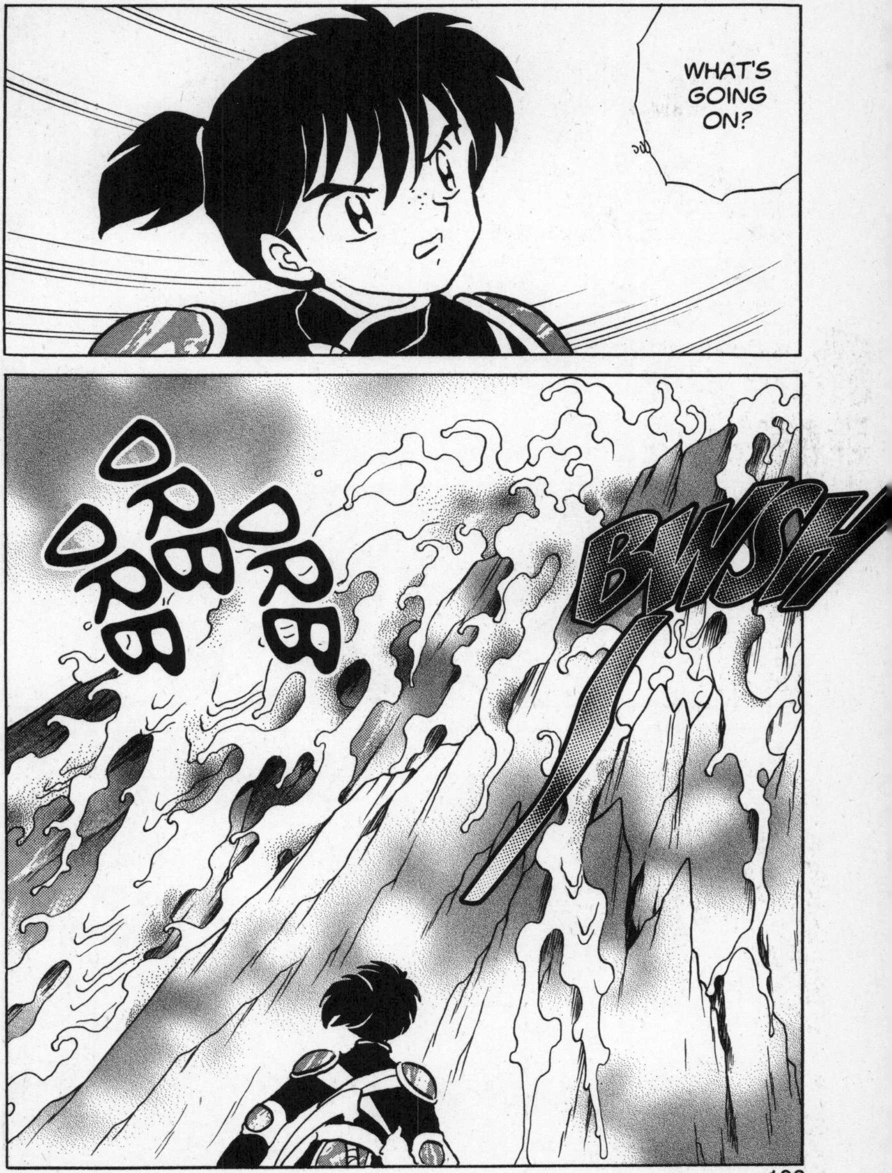
WHAT'S GOING ON?
DRB DRB
DRB DRB
BWSH

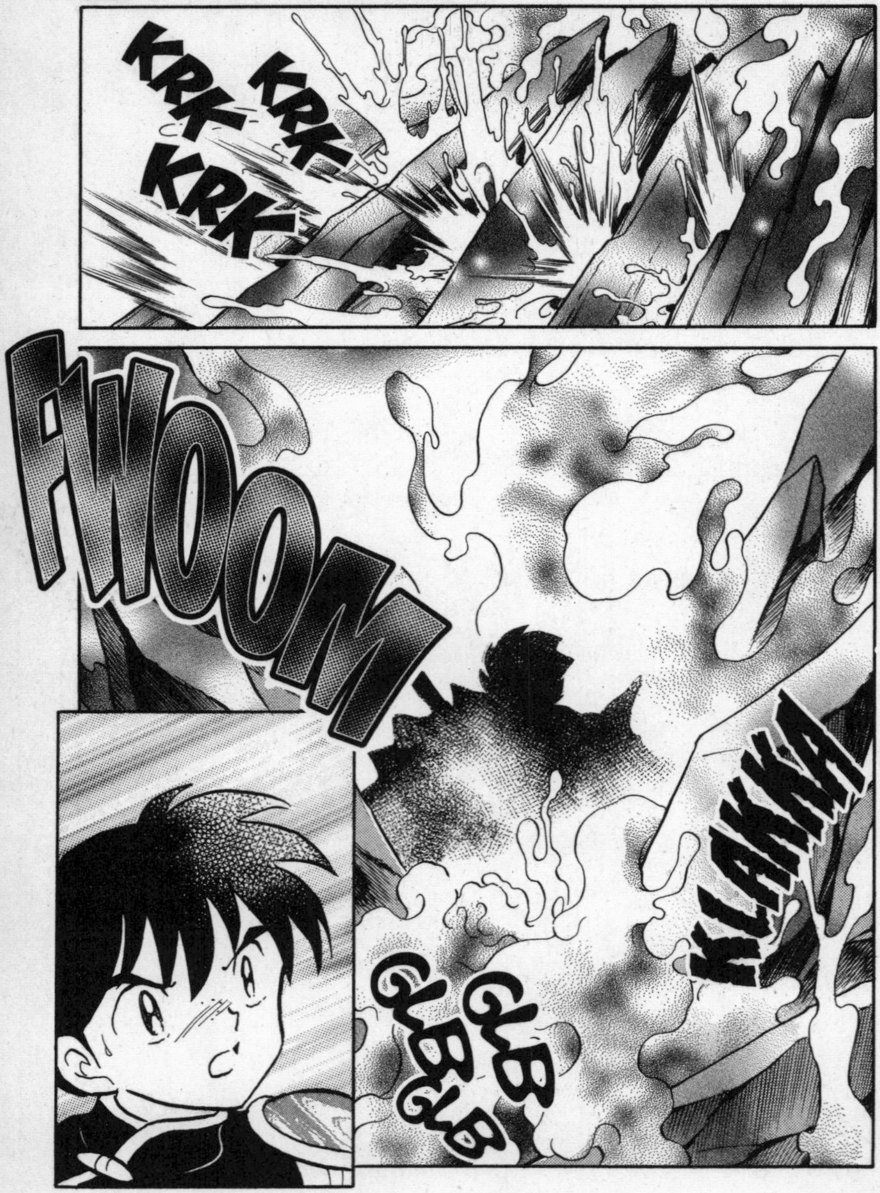
KRK KRK
KRK KRK
FWOOM
KLANKA
GLB
GLBGLB

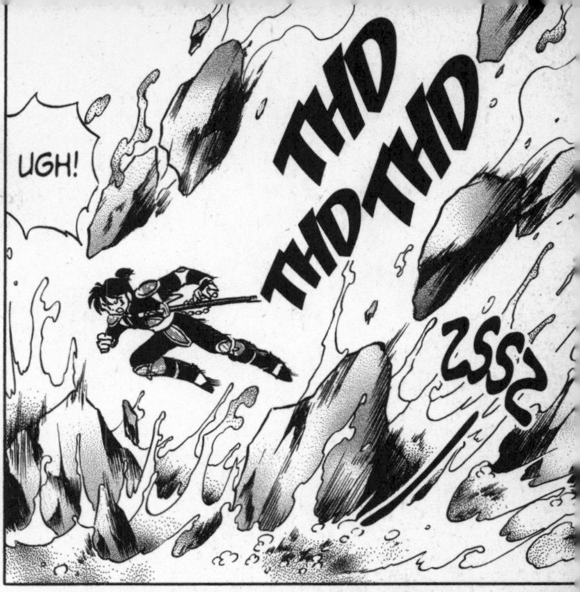
UGH!
THD THD THD
ZSSS
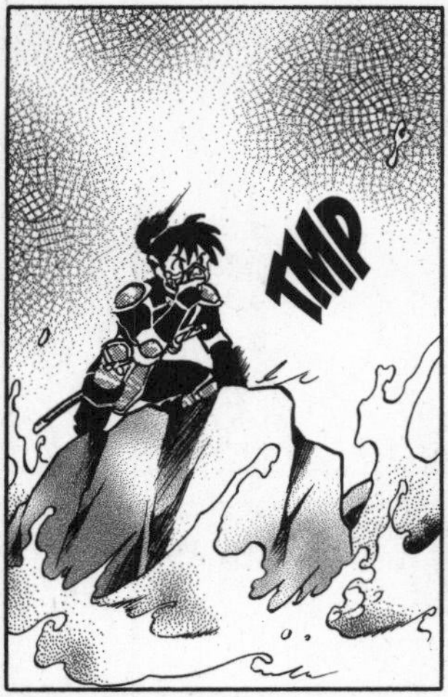
TMP
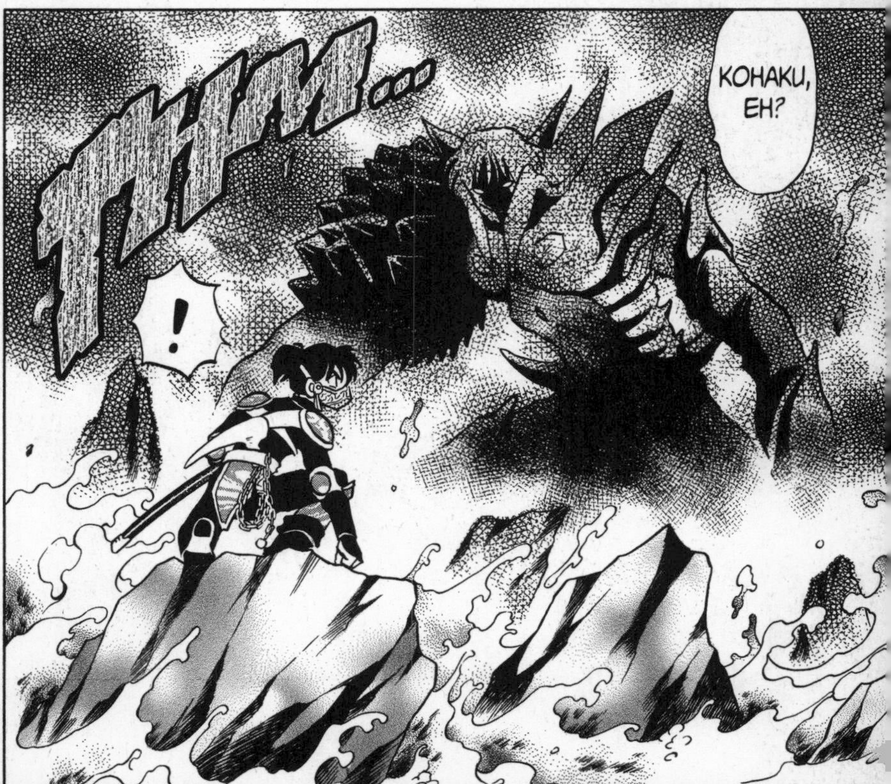
KOHAKU, EH?
THM...
!

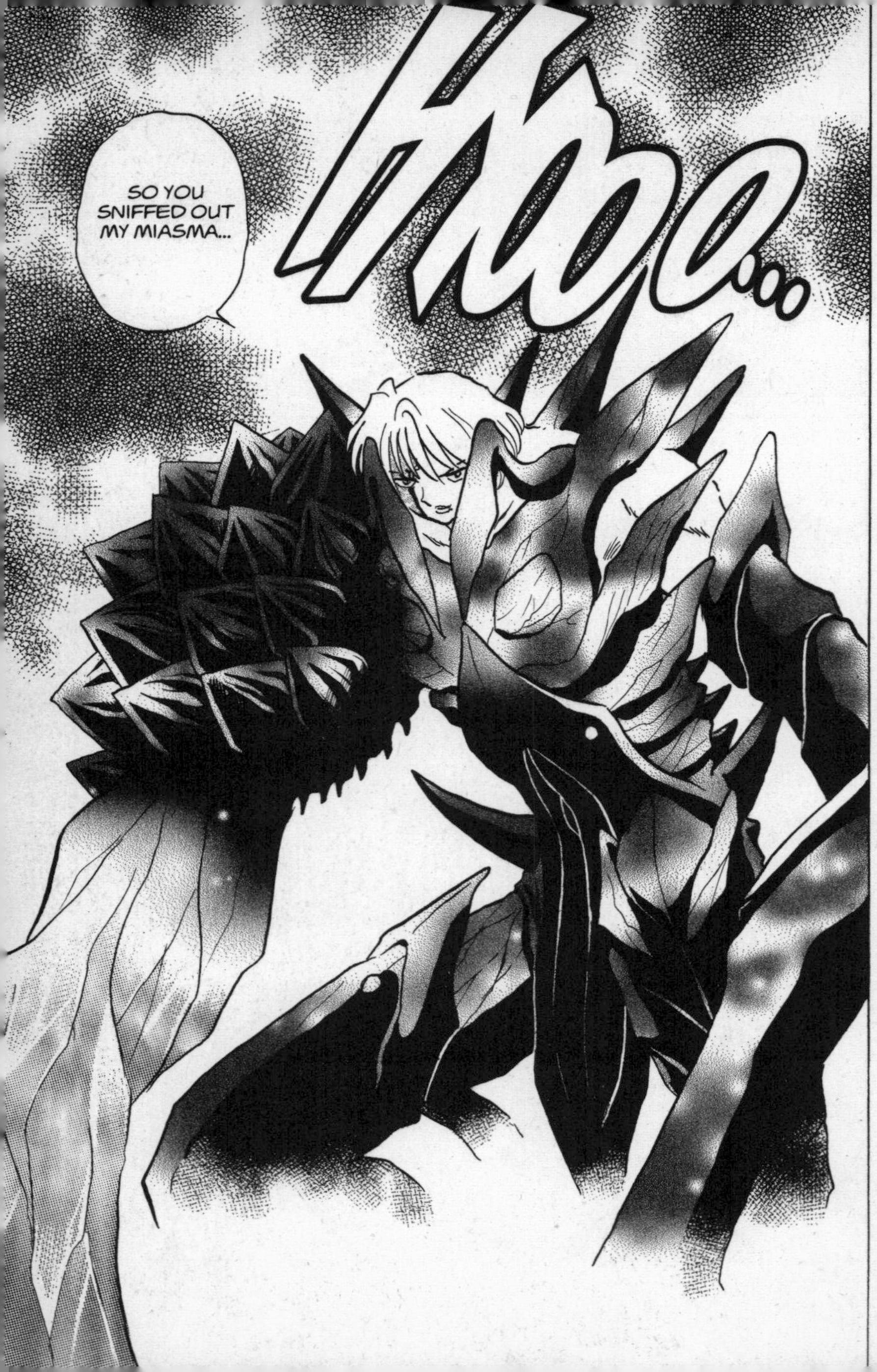
SO YOU SNIFFED OUT MY MIASMA...

MORYOMARU...
YOU TRANS-
FORMED...
HEH HEH HEH.
IF YOU CAME KNOWING I WAS HERE...
...THAT MEANS YOU WON'T MIND...
...IF I DEVOUR YOU... YES?
!

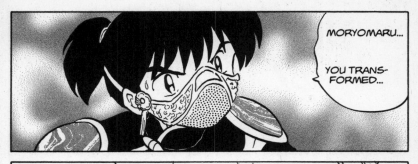

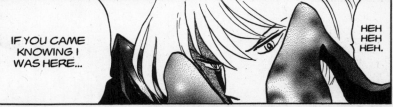

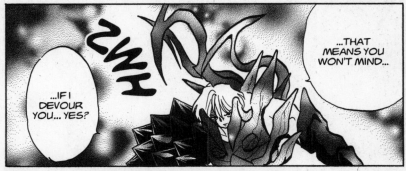

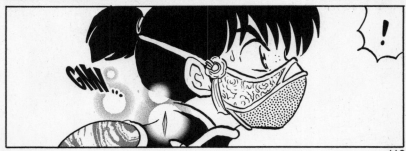

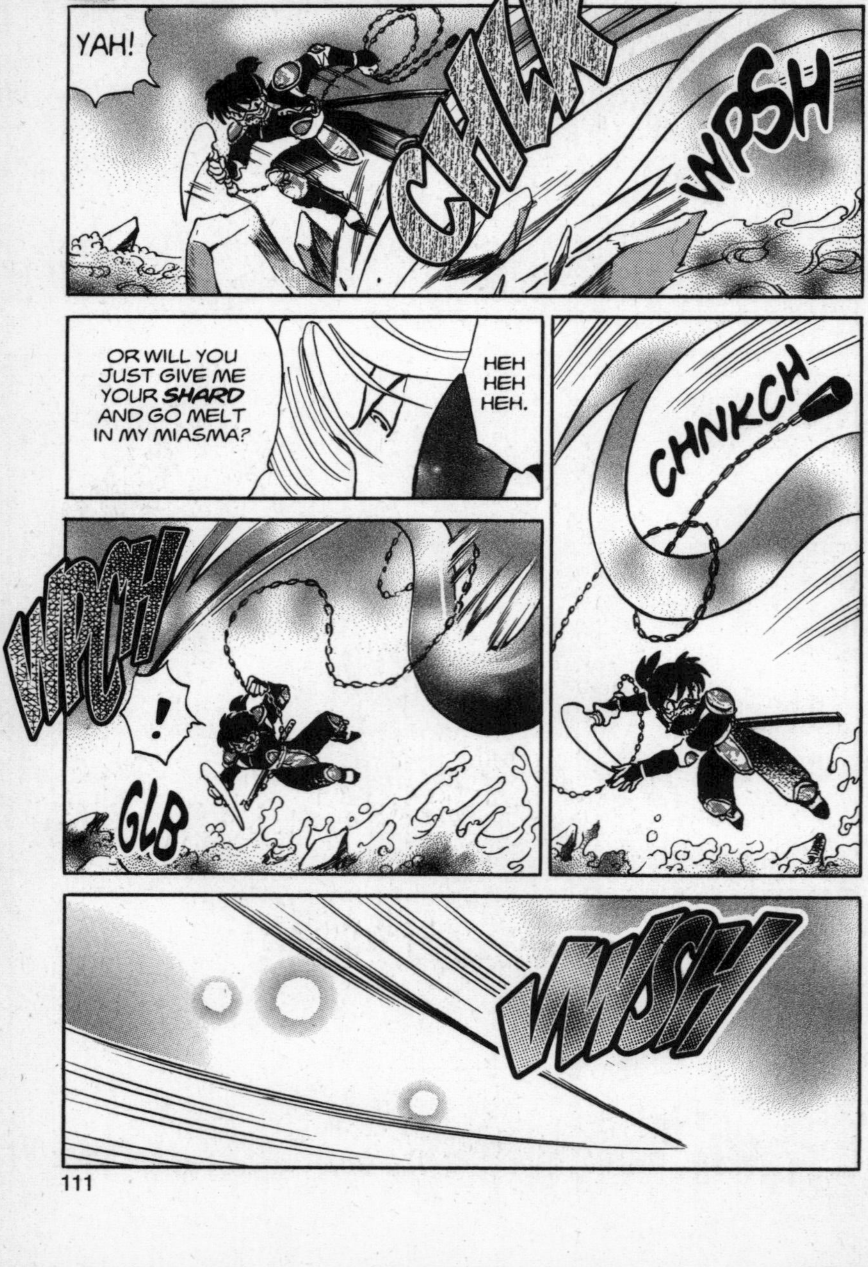
WPSH
CHNK
YAH!
CHNKCH
HEH HEH HEH.
OR WILL YOU JUST GIVE ME YOUR **SHARD** AND GO MELT IN MY MIASMA?
!
WPCH
GLB
WMSH

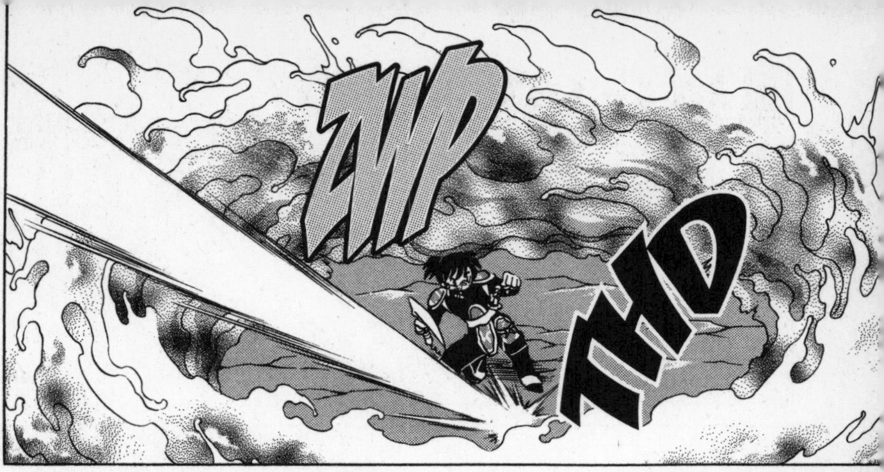
ZWIP
THD
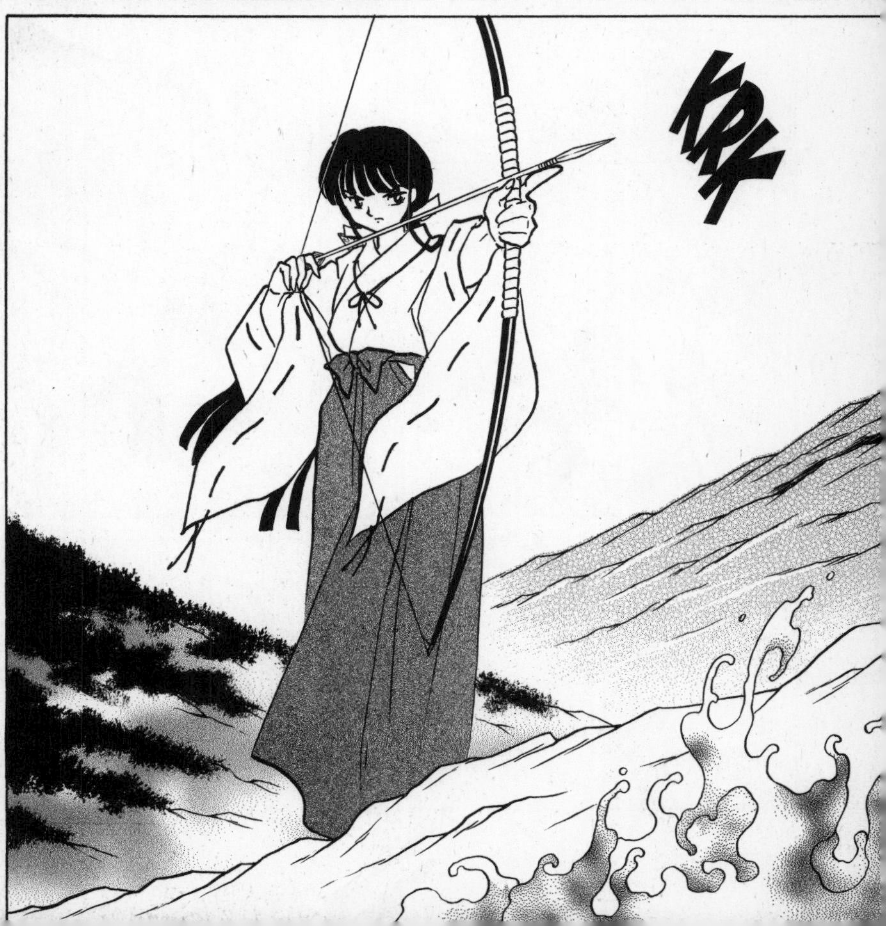
KRK

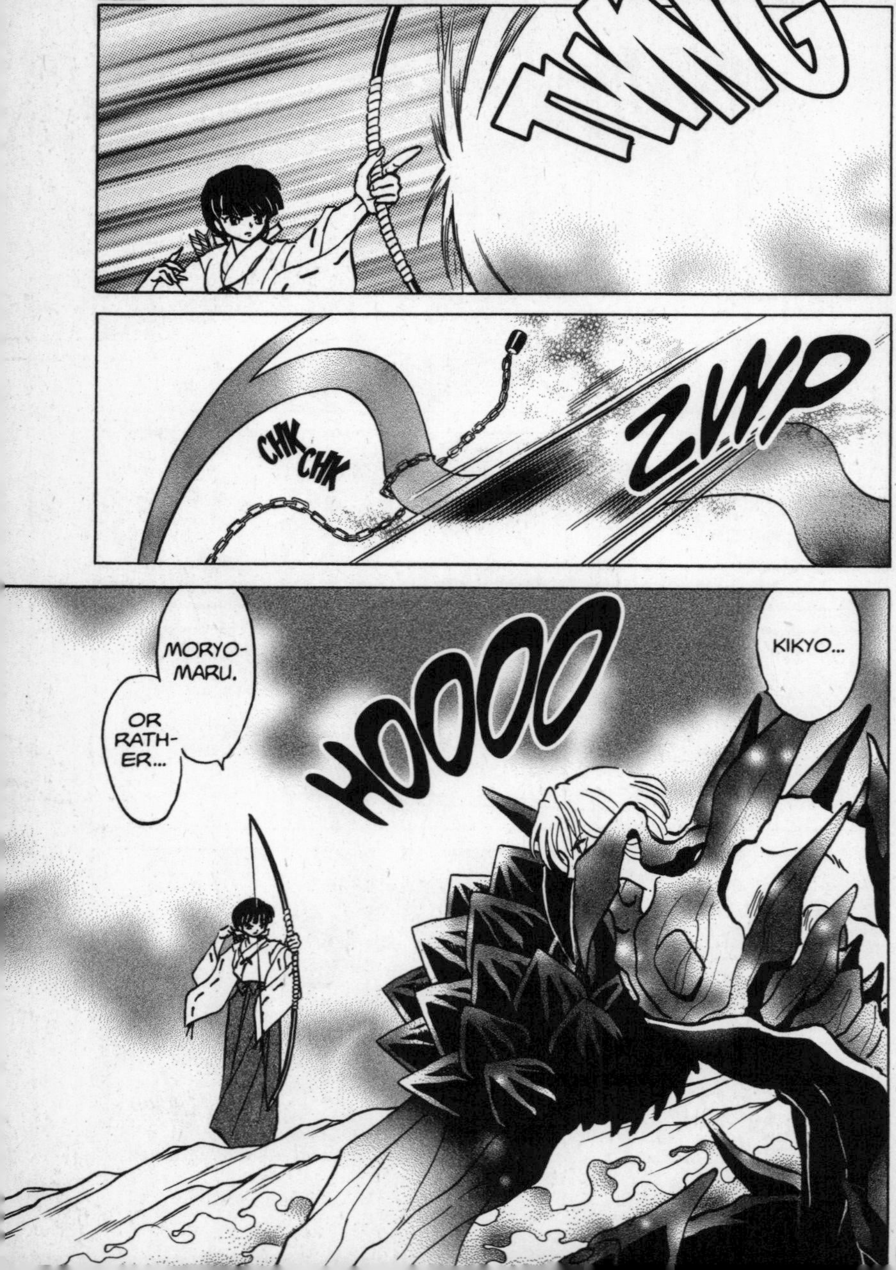
TWNG
ZWIP
CHK-CHK
KIKYO...
HOOOO
MORYO-MARU.
OR RATHER...

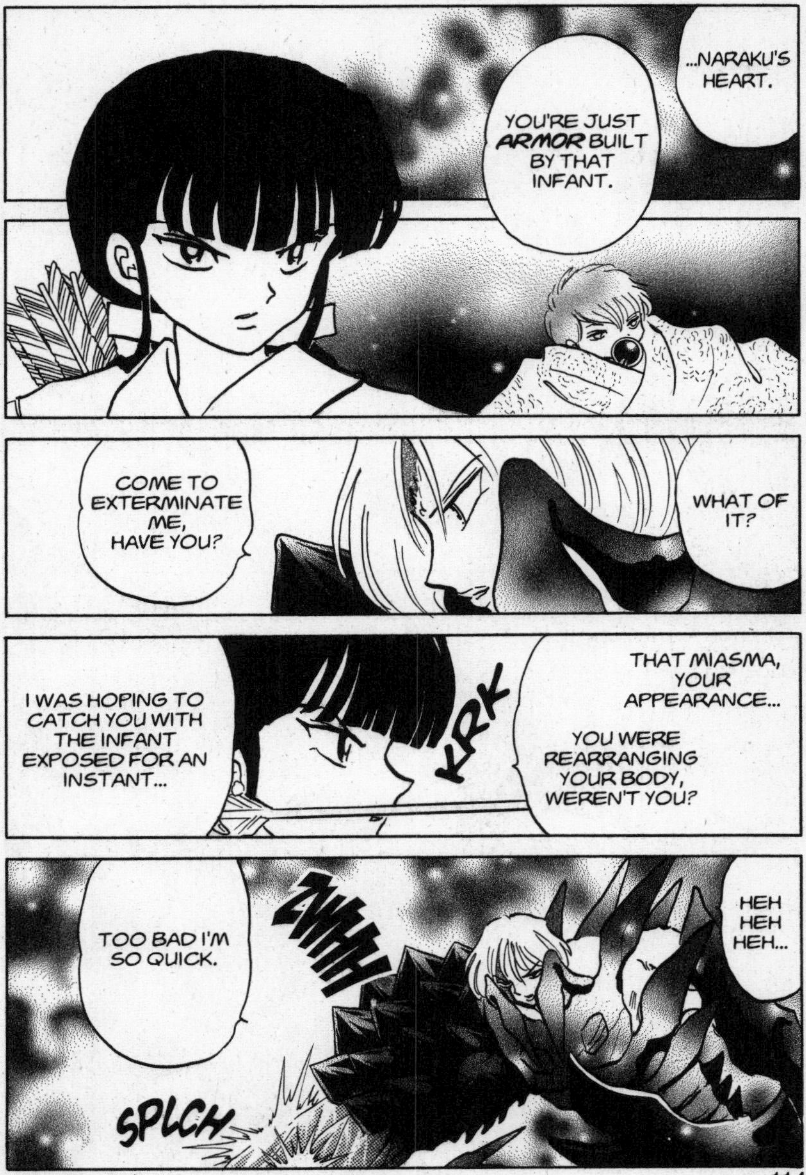
...NARAKU'S HEART.
YOU'RE JUST ARMOR BUILT BY THAT INFANT.
WHAT OF IT?
COME TO EXTERMINATE ME, HAVE YOU?
THAT MIASMA, YOUR APPEARANCE...
YOU WERE REARRANGING YOUR BODY, WEREN'T YOU?
KRK
I WAS HOPING TO CATCH YOU WITH THE INFANT EXPOSED FOR AN INSTANT...
HEH HEH HEH...
TOO BAD I'M SO QUICK.
SPLCH

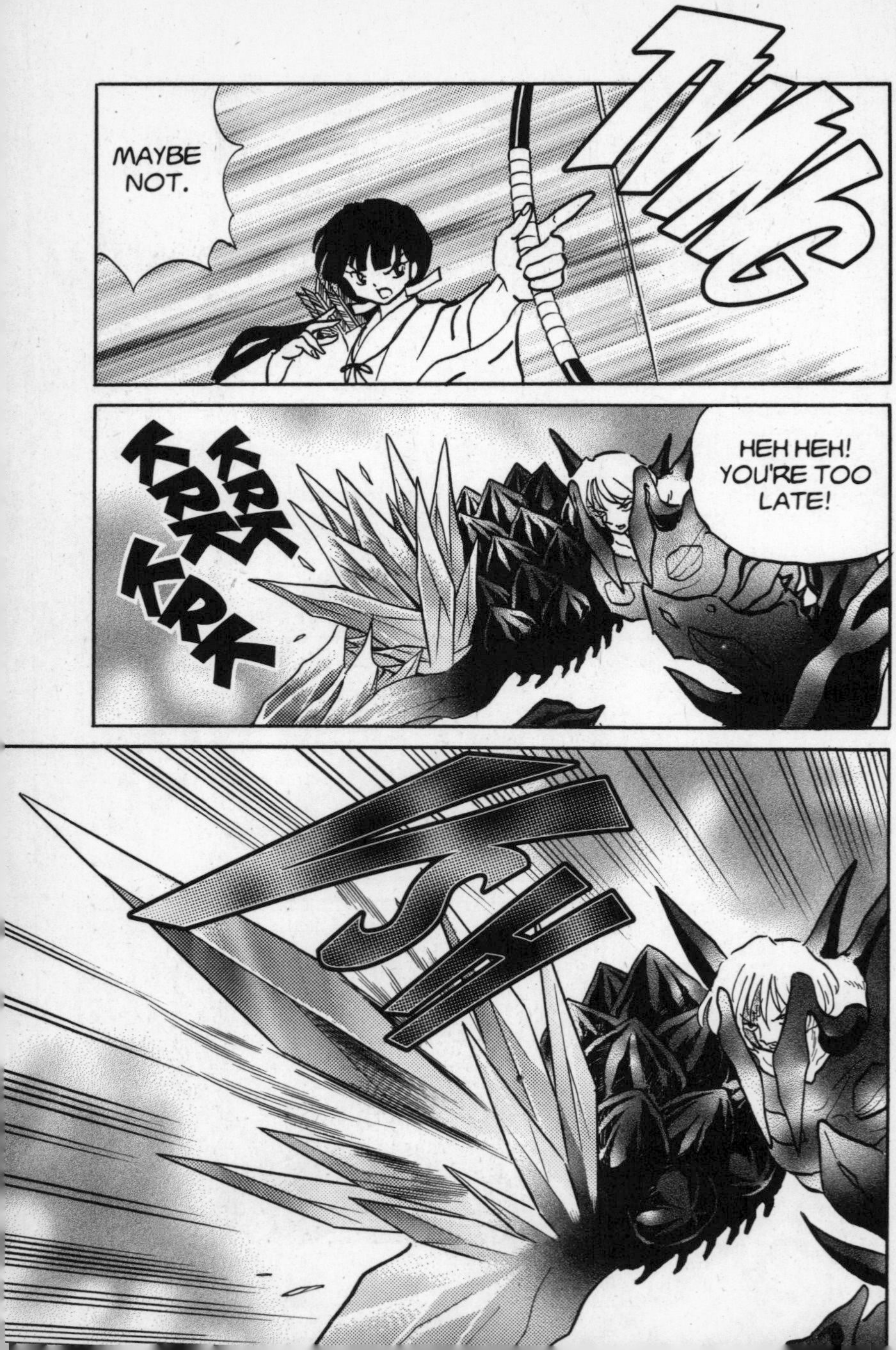
MAYBE NOT.
ZING
HEH HEH! YOU'RE TOO LATE!
KRK KRK KRK

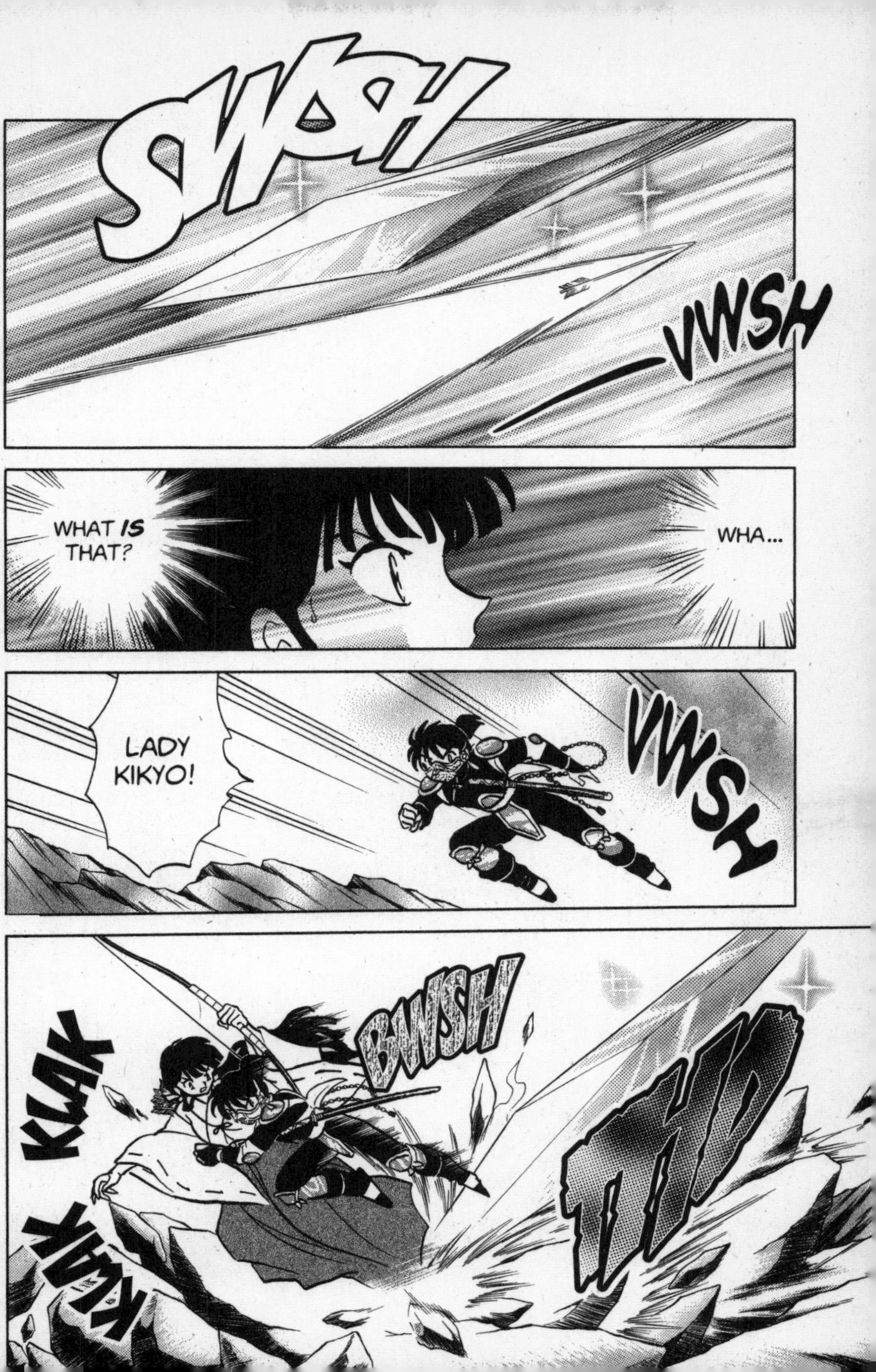
SWOSH
VWSH
WHA...
WHAT *IS* THAT?
VWSH
LADY KIKYO!
BWSH
KLAK
KLAK

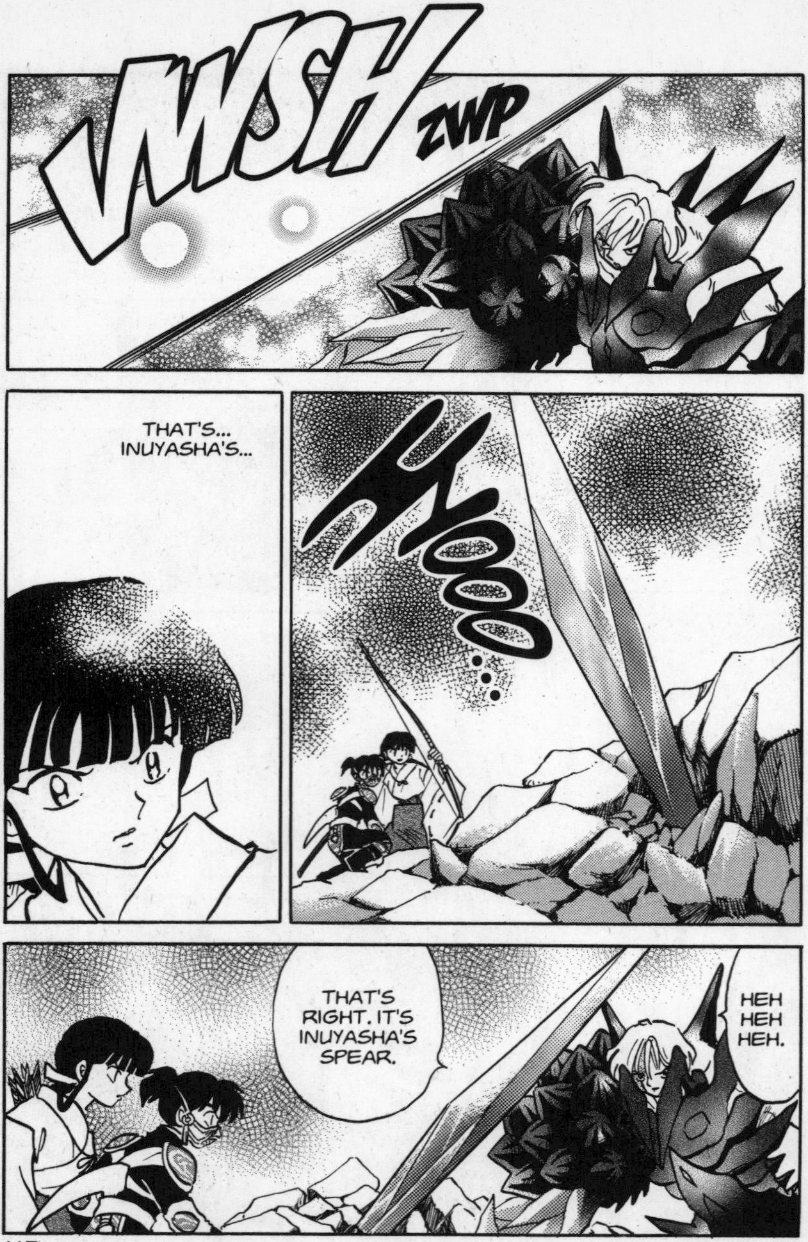
VWSH
ZWP
HYOOO...
THAT'S... INUYASHA'S...
HEH HEH HEH.
THAT'S RIGHT. IT'S INUYASHA'S SPEAR.

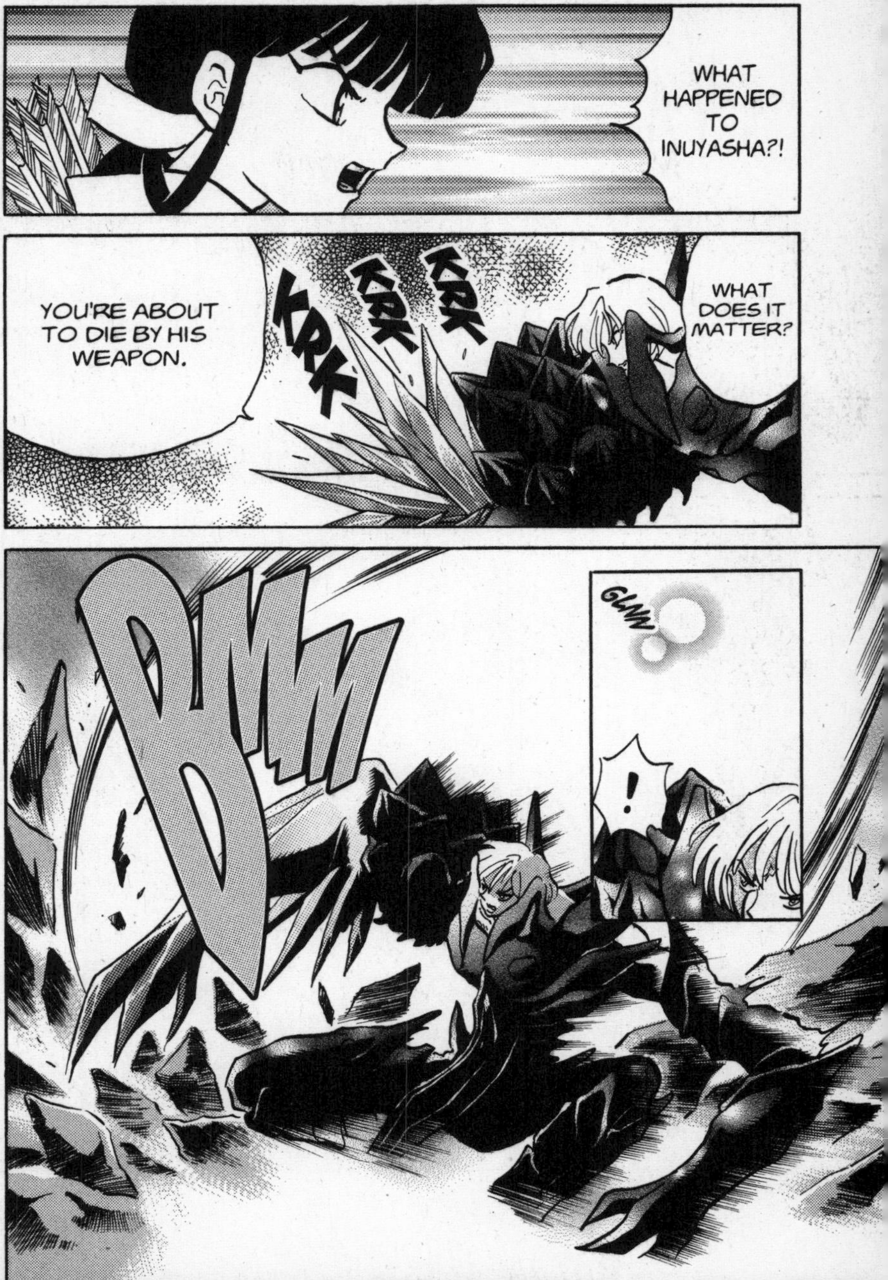
WHAT HAPPENED TO INUYASHA?!
WHAT DOES IT MATTER?
KRK KRK KRK
YOU'RE ABOUT TO DIE BY HIS WEAPON.
GLNN
!
BMMM

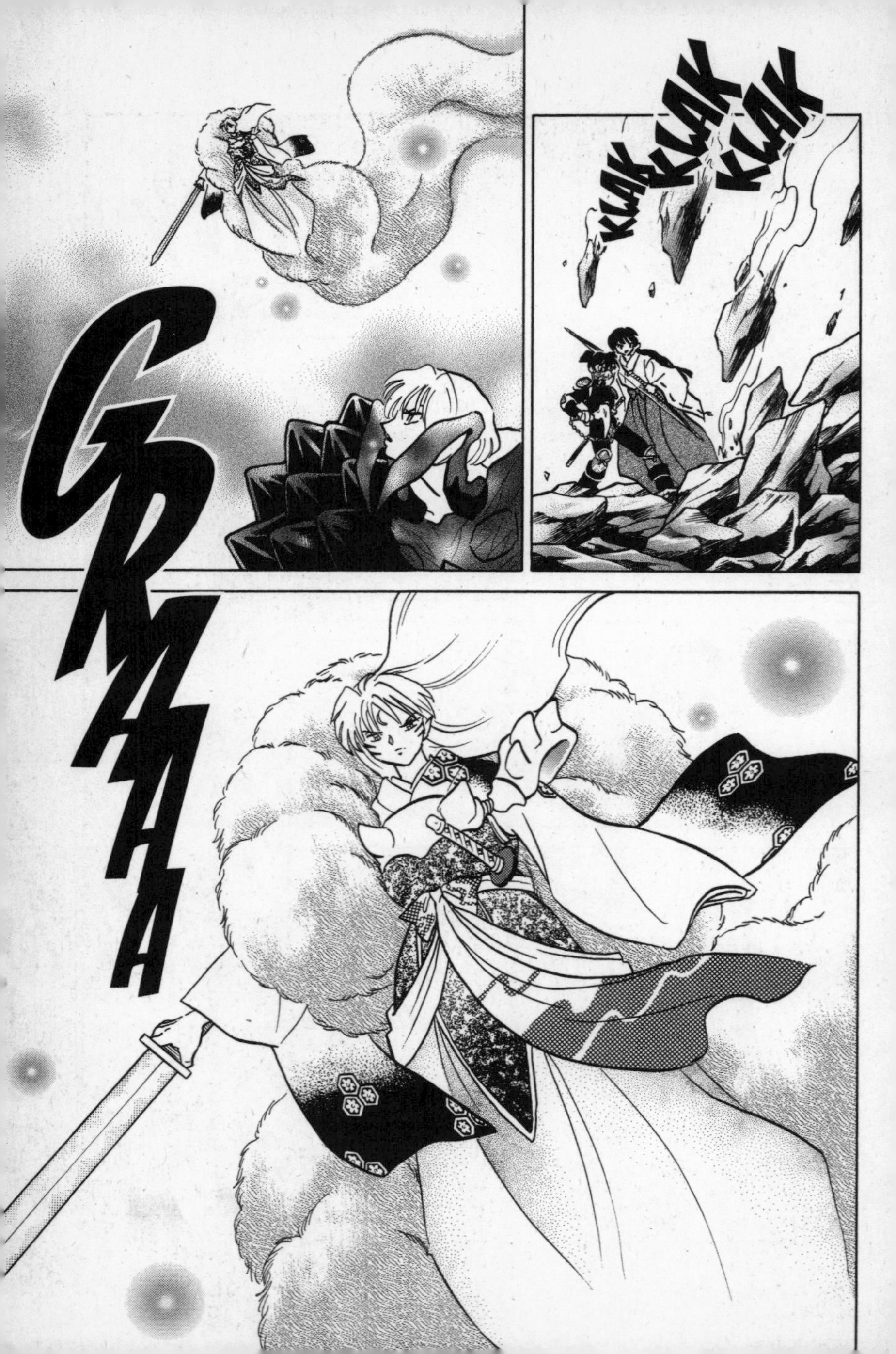
KLAK
KLAK
KLAK
GRMAAA

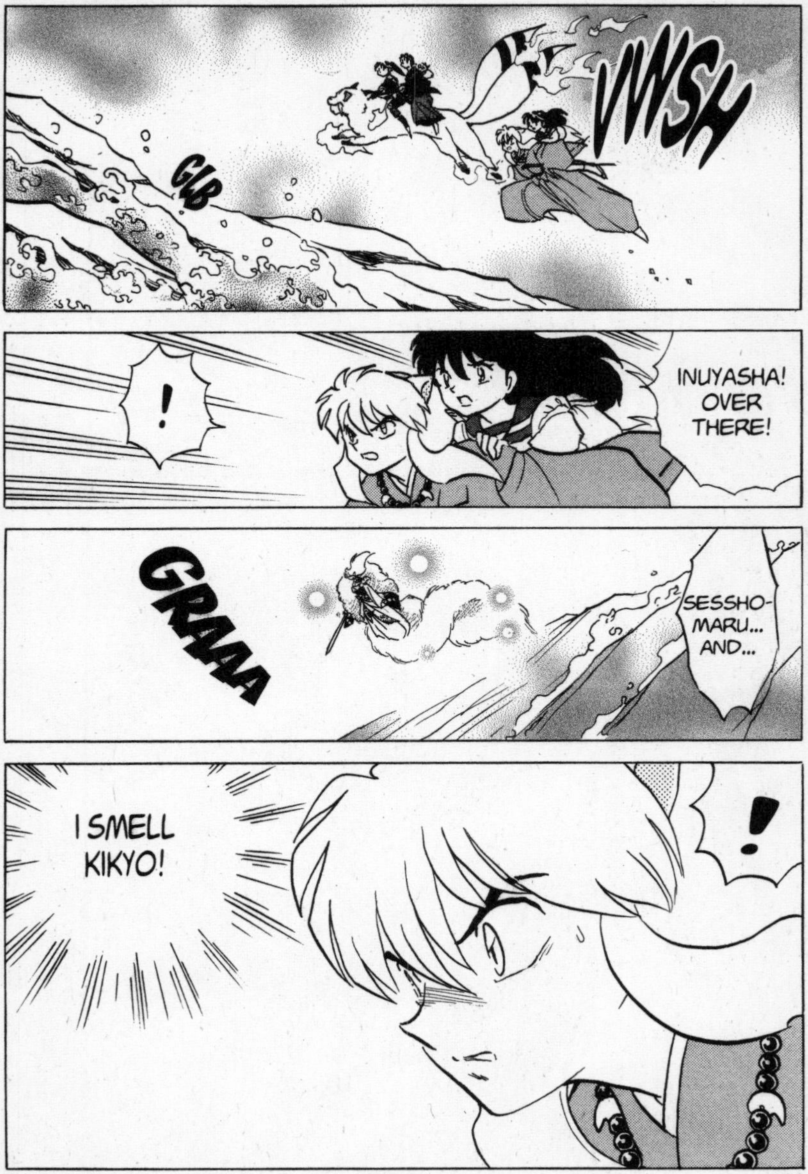
VWSH
GLB
!
INUYASHA! OVER THERE!
SESSHOMARU... AND...
GRAAA
!
I SMELL KIKYO!

SCROLL 7
RIVALRY

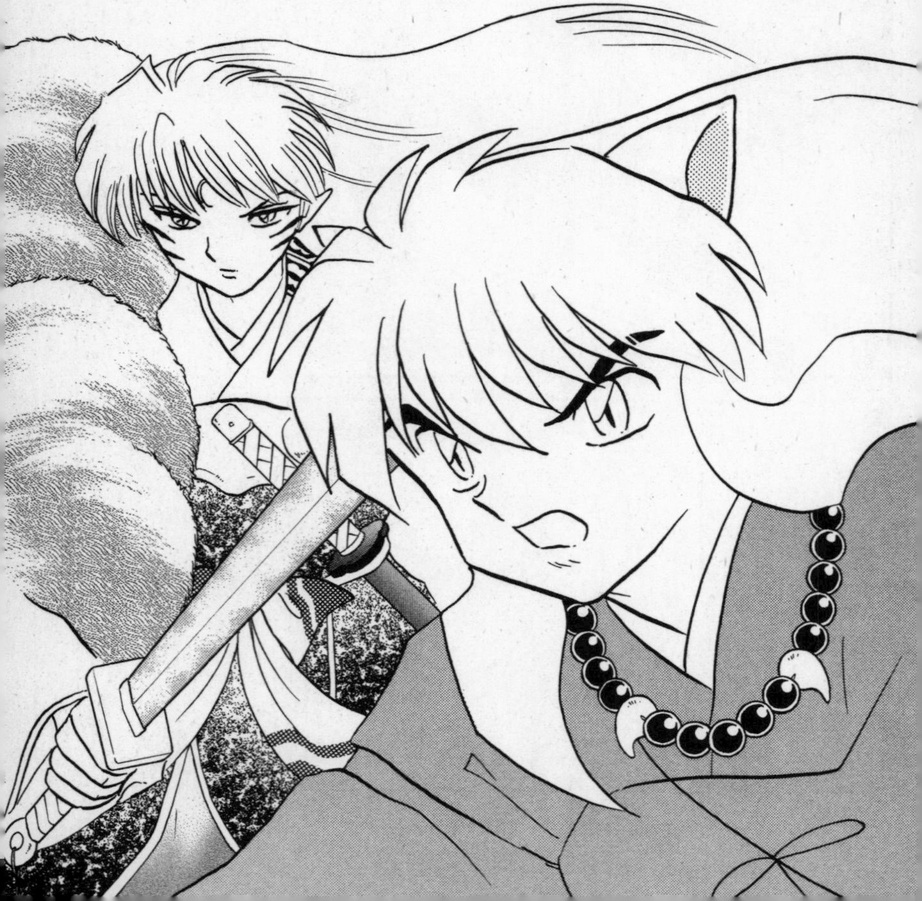

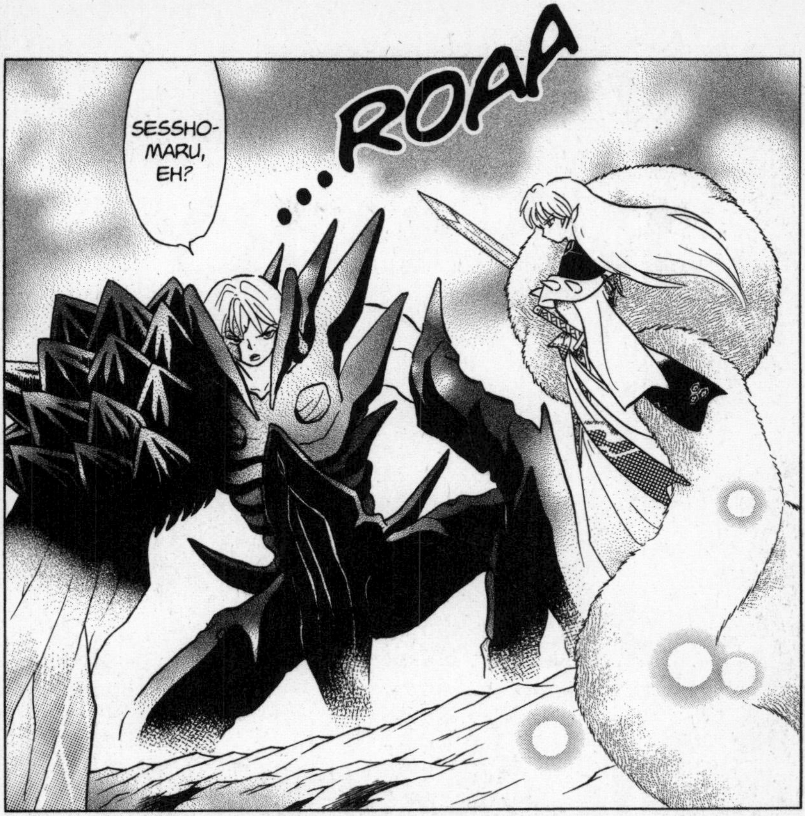
ROAA
...
SESSHO-MARU, EH?

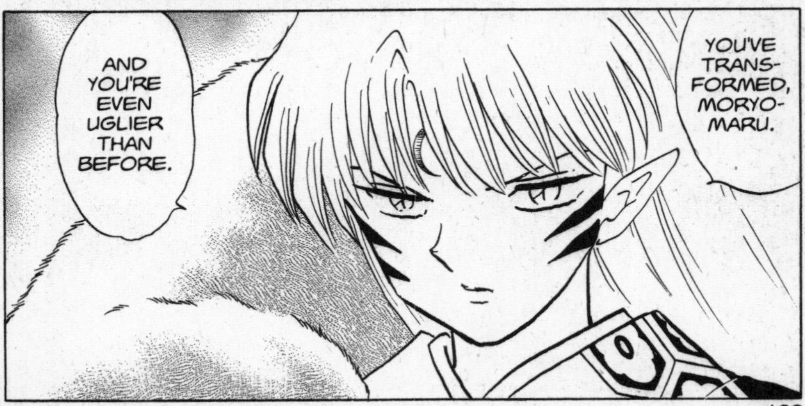
YOU'VE TRANS-FORMED, MORYO-MARU.
AND YOU'RE EVEN UGLIER THAN BEFORE.

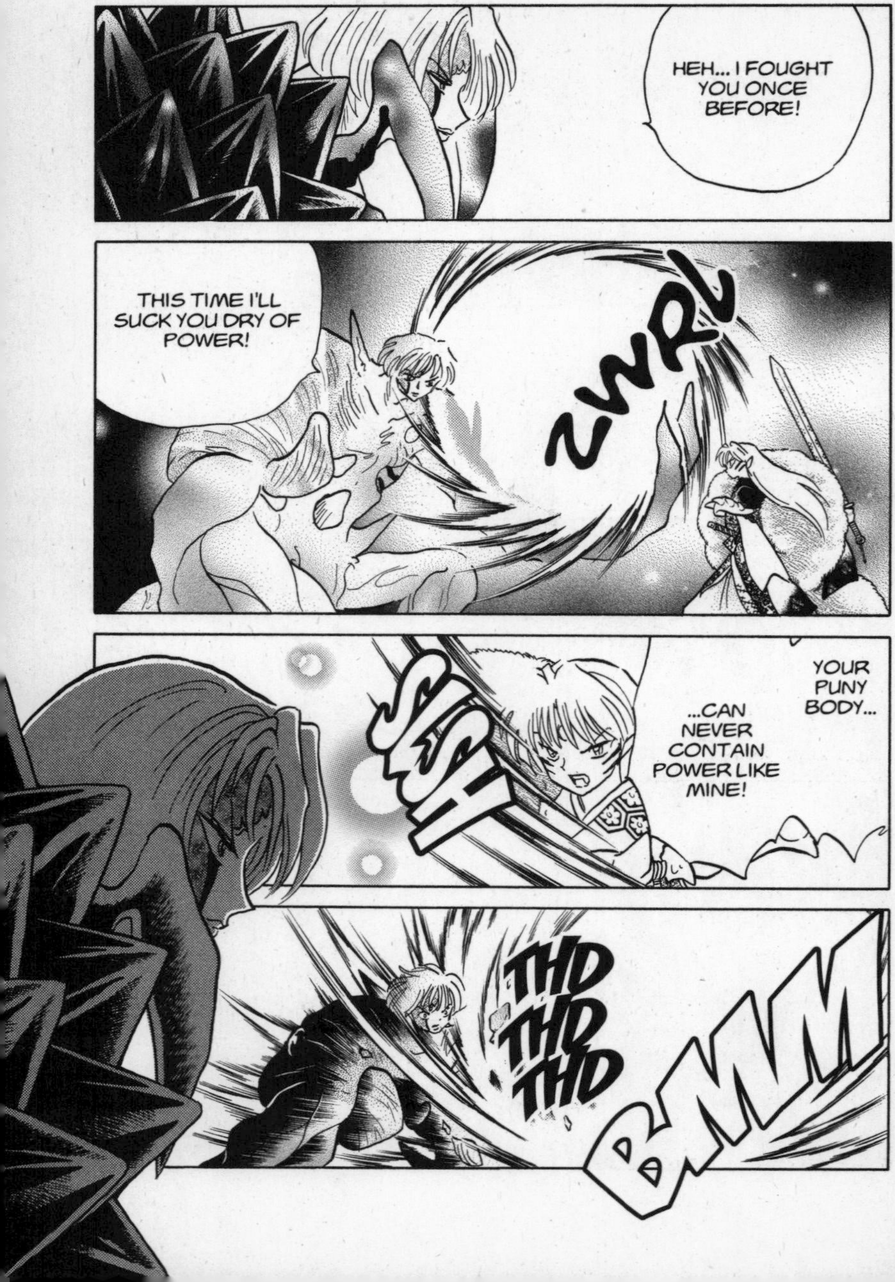
HEH... I FOUGHT YOU ONCE BEFORE!
THIS TIME I'LL SUCK YOU DRY OF POWER!
ZWRL
YOUR PUNY BODY...
...CAN NEVER CONTAIN POWER LIKE MINE!
SSH
BMMM
THD THD THD

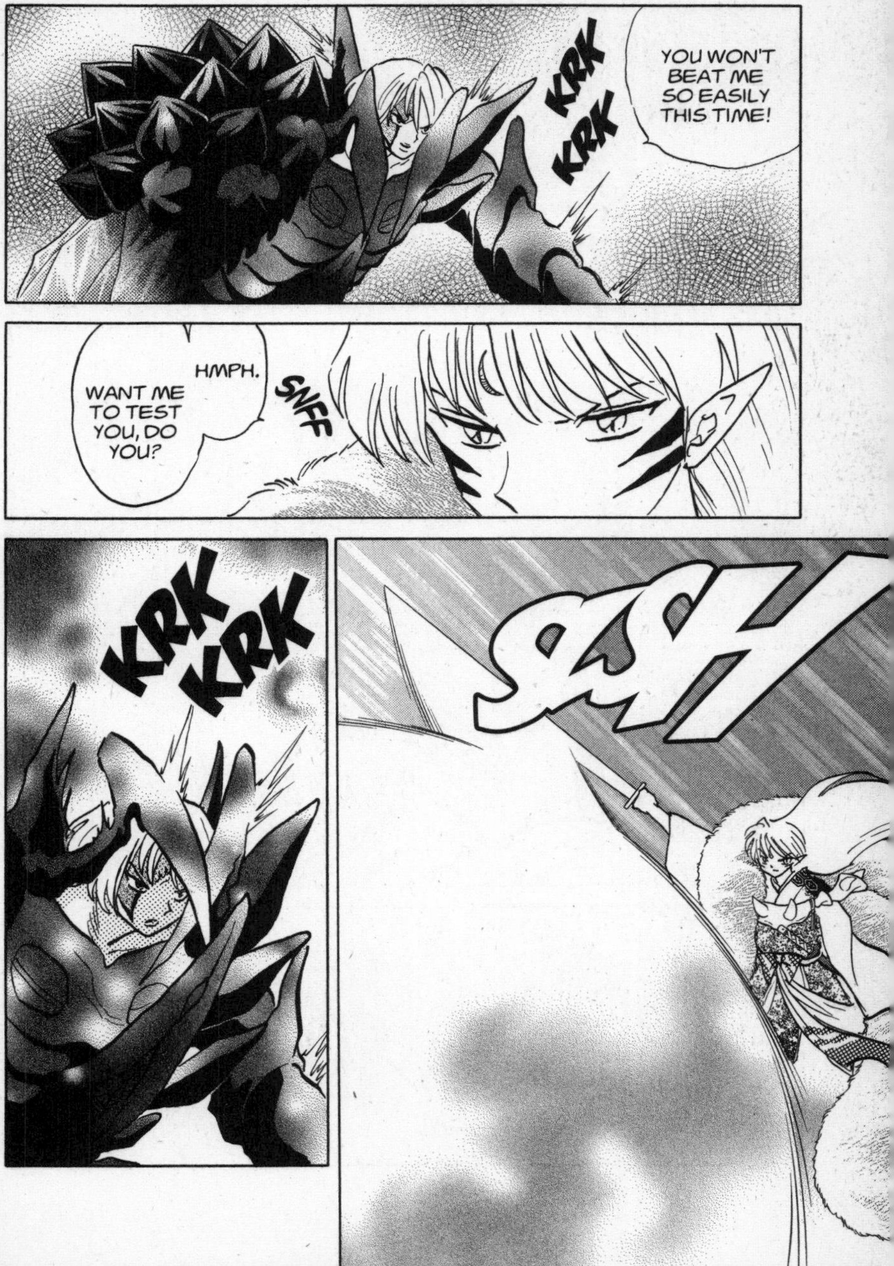
YOU WON'T BEAT ME SO EASILY THIS TIME!
KRK KRK
SNIFF
HMPH.
WANT ME TO TEST YOU, DO YOU?
SASH
KRK KRK

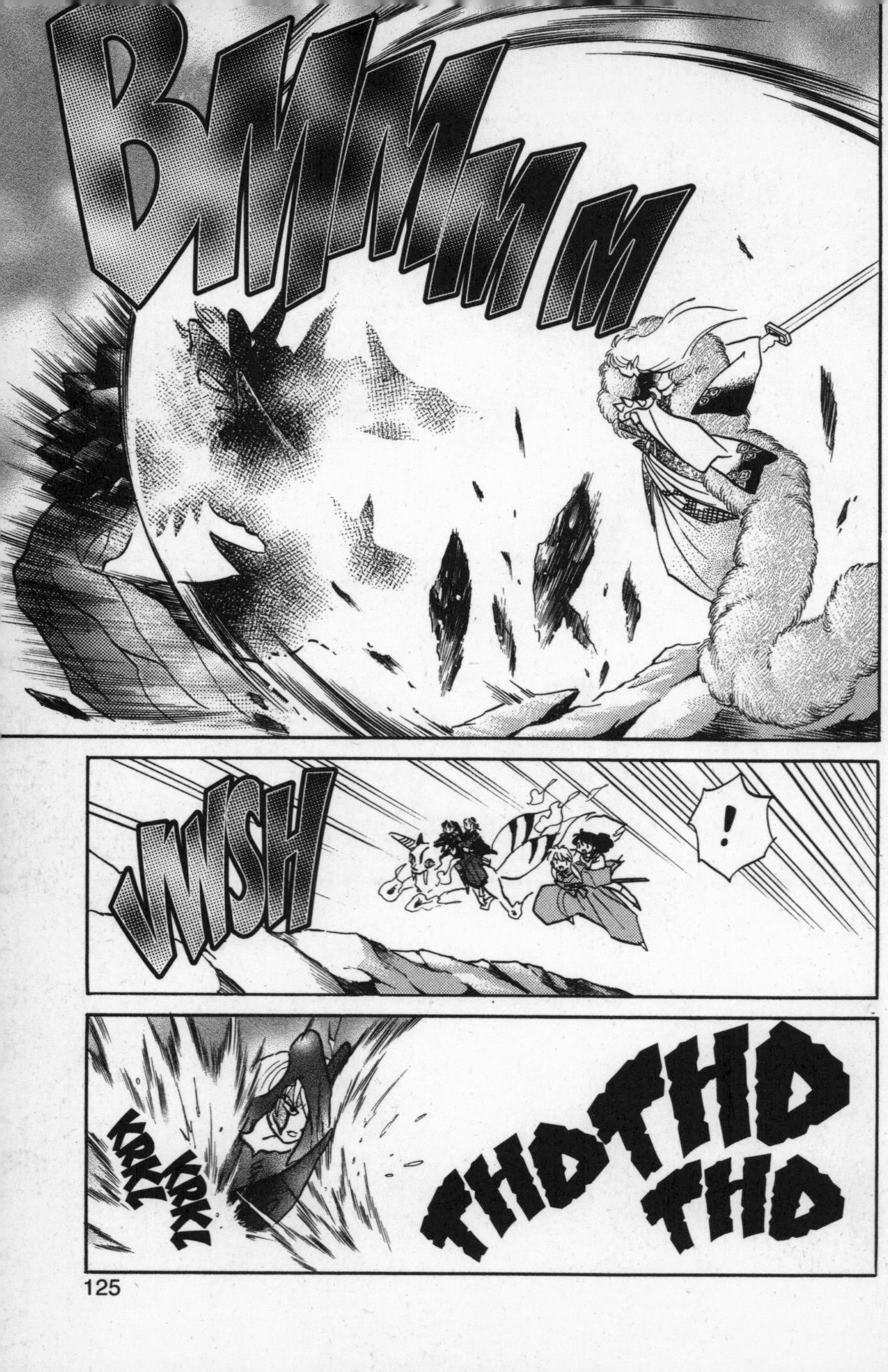
BMMMMMM
!
WSH
THDTHD
THD
KRKL KRKL

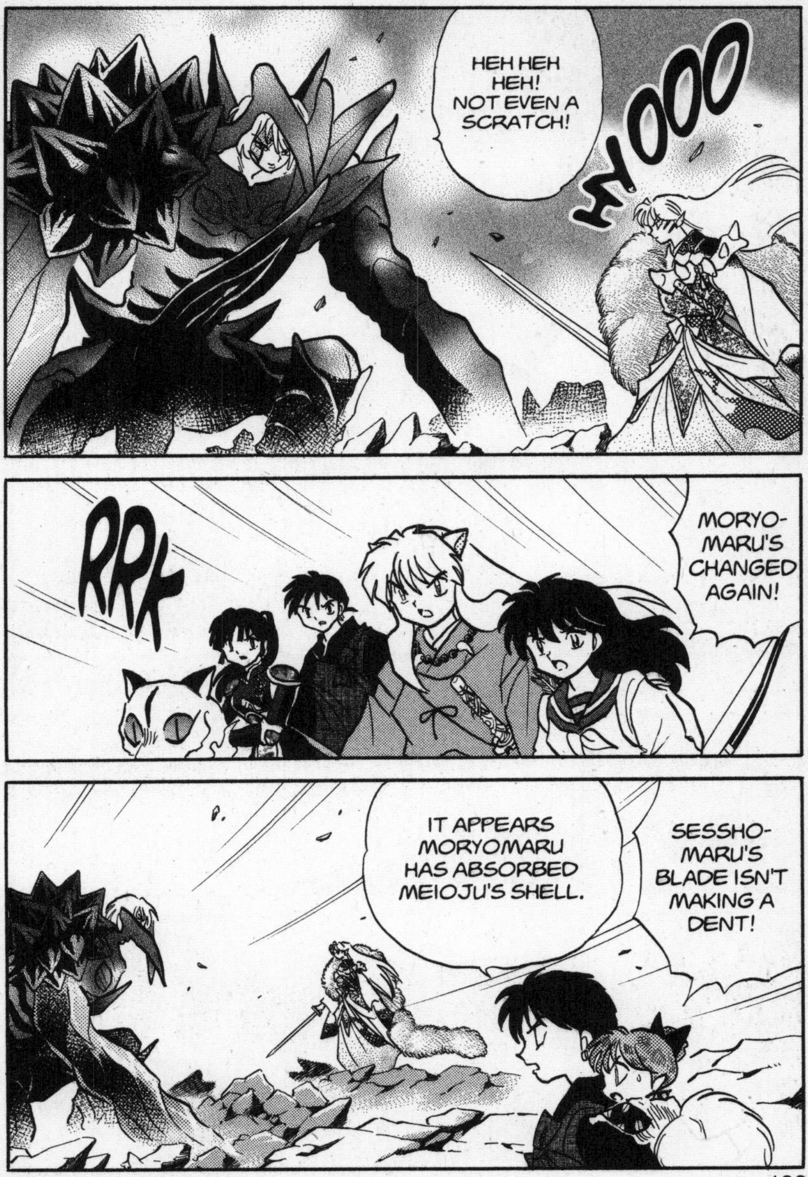
HYOOO
HEH HEH HEH! NOT EVEN A SCRATCH!
MORYO-MARU'S CHANGED AGAIN!
RRK
SESSHO-MARU'S BLADE ISN'T MAKING A DENT!
IT APPEARS MORYOMARU HAS ABSORBED MEIOJU'S SHELL.

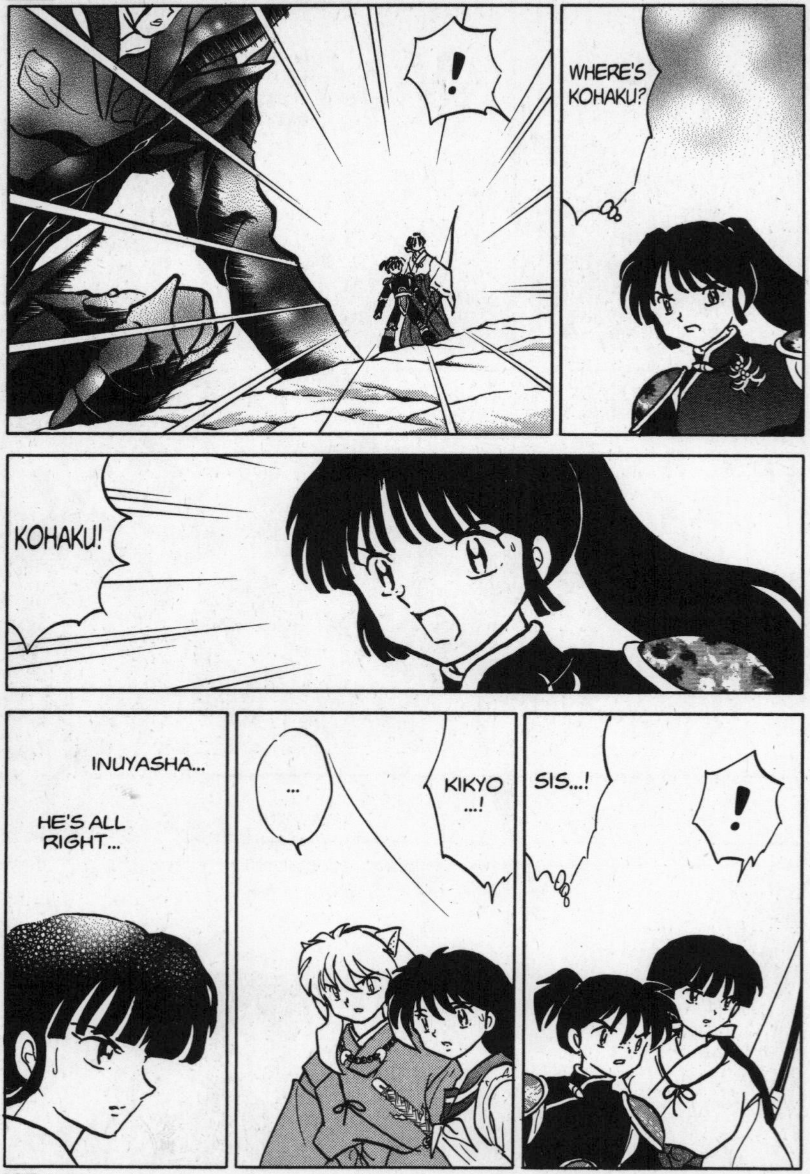
WHERE'S KOHAKU?
!
KOHAKU!
!
SIS...!
KIKYO ...!
...
INUYASHA...
HE'S ALL RIGHT...

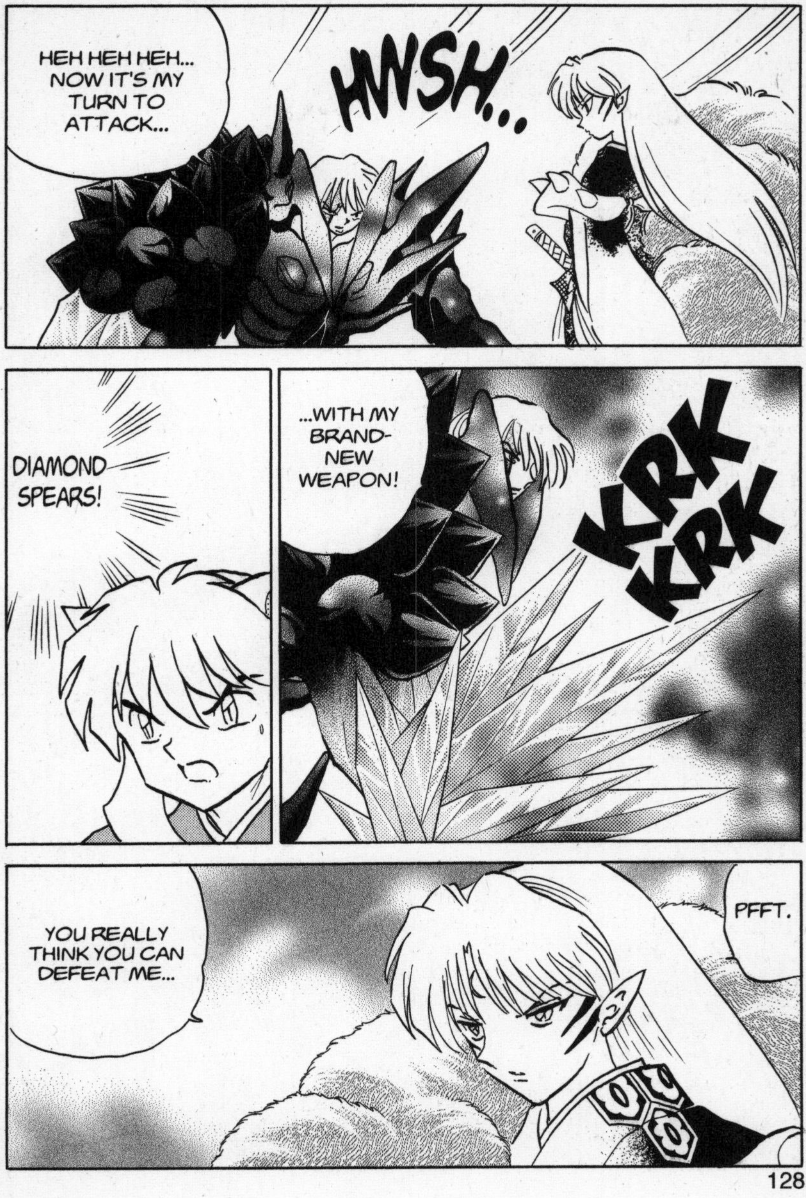
HWSH...
HEH HEH HEH... NOW IT'S MY TURN TO ATTACK...
...WITH MY BRAND-NEW WEAPON!
KRK KRK
DIAMOND SPEARS!
PFFT.
YOU REALLY THINK YOU CAN DEFEAT ME...

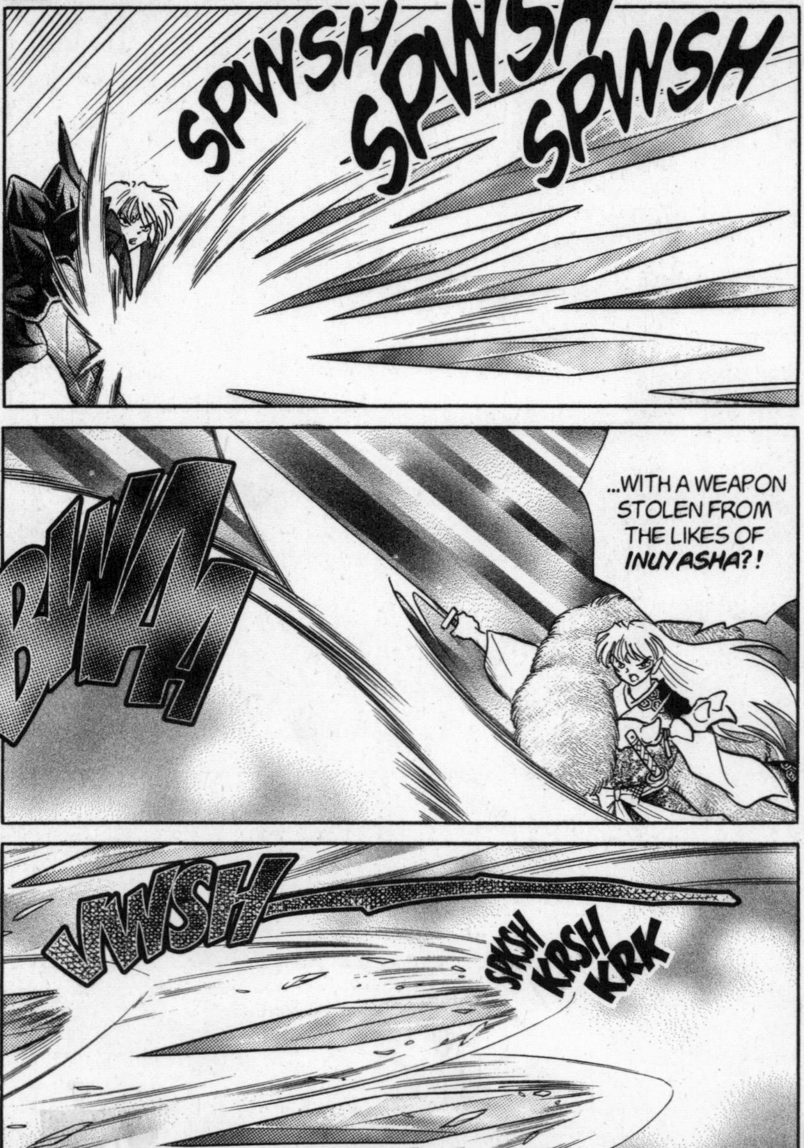
SPWSH SPWSH SPWSH
...WITH A WEAPON STOLEN FROM THE LIKES OF INUYASHA?!
BWAM
VWWSH
SPRSH KRSH KRK

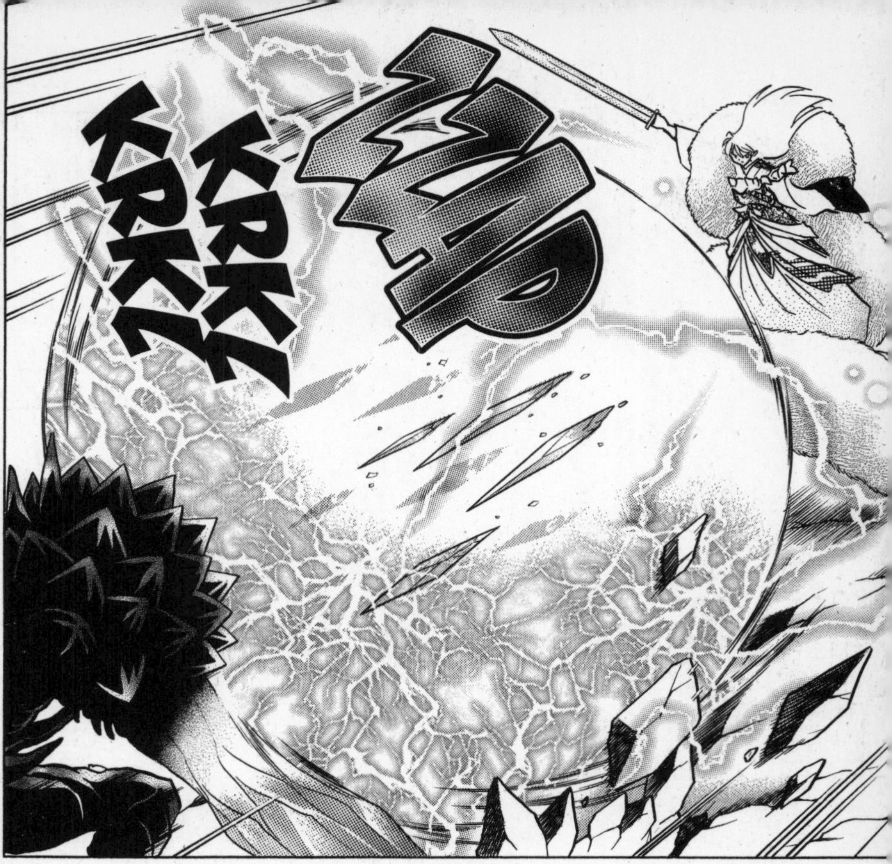

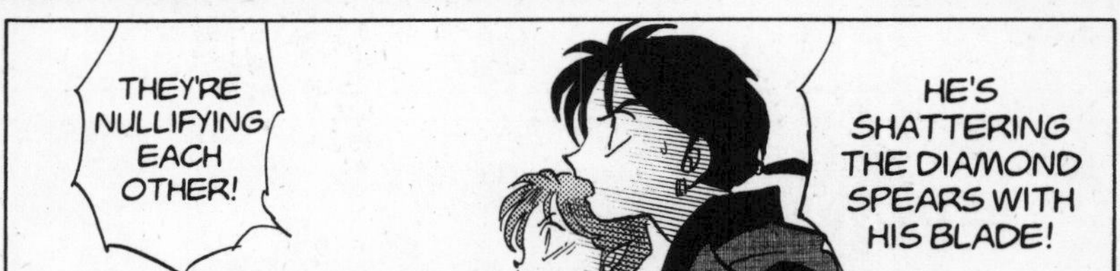
HE'S SHATTERING THE DIAMOND SPEARS WITH HIS BLADE!
THEY'RE NULLIFYING EACH OTHER!

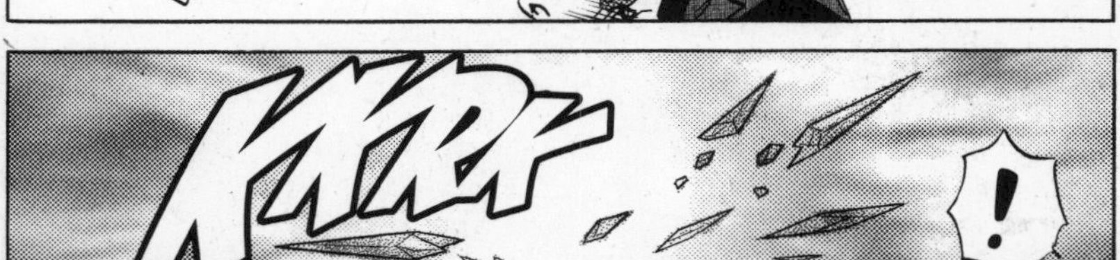
!

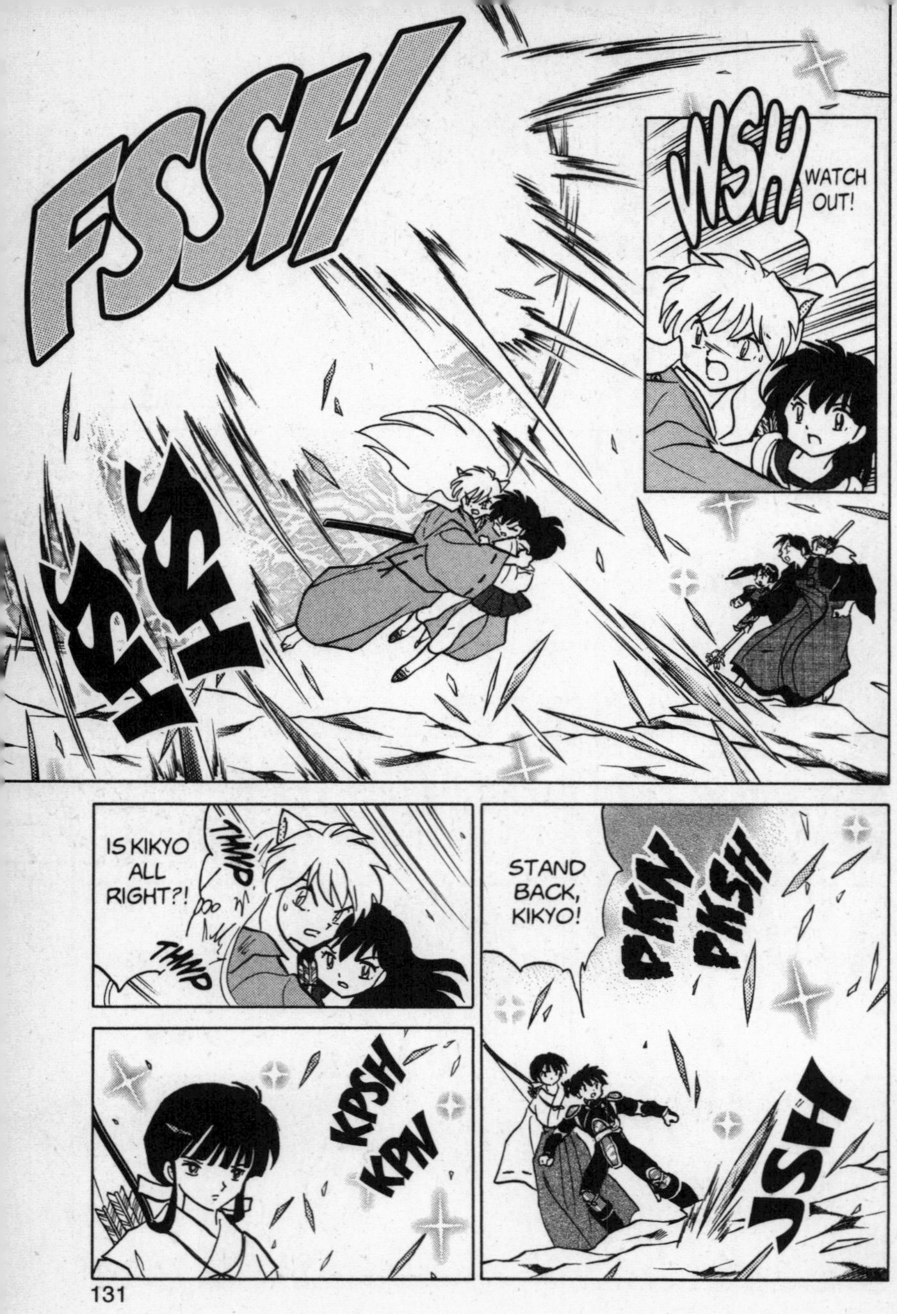

WSH
WATCH OUT!
FSSH
PKN
PKSH
STAND BACK, KIKYO!
IS KIKYO ALL RIGHT?!
THMP
THMP
JSH
KPSH
KPN

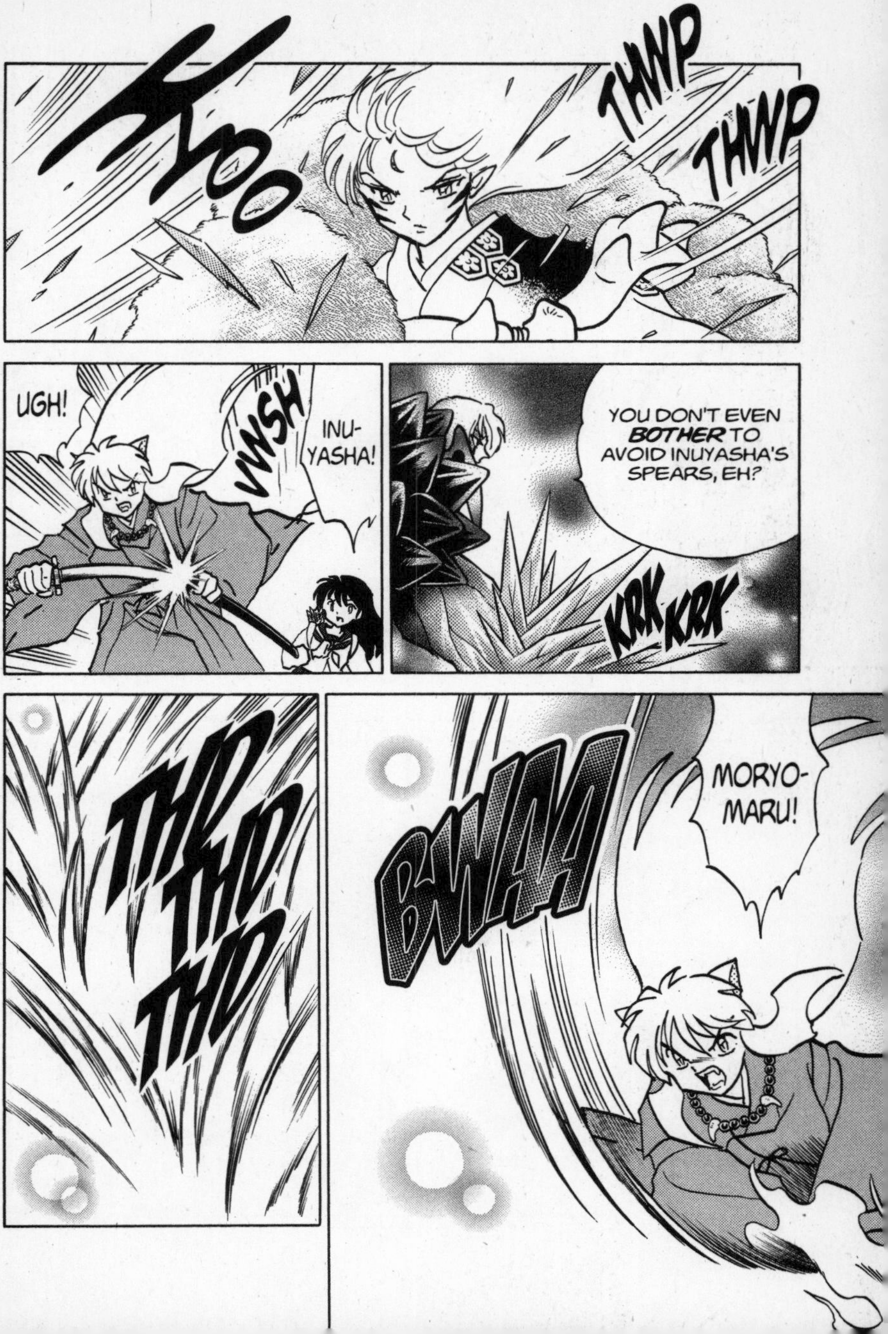
THWP
THWP
KYOO
YOU DON'T EVEN **BOTHER** TO AVOID INUYASHA'S SPEARS, EH?
KRK KRK
INU-YASHA!
VWSH
UGH!
MORYO-MARU!
BWAM
THD THD THD

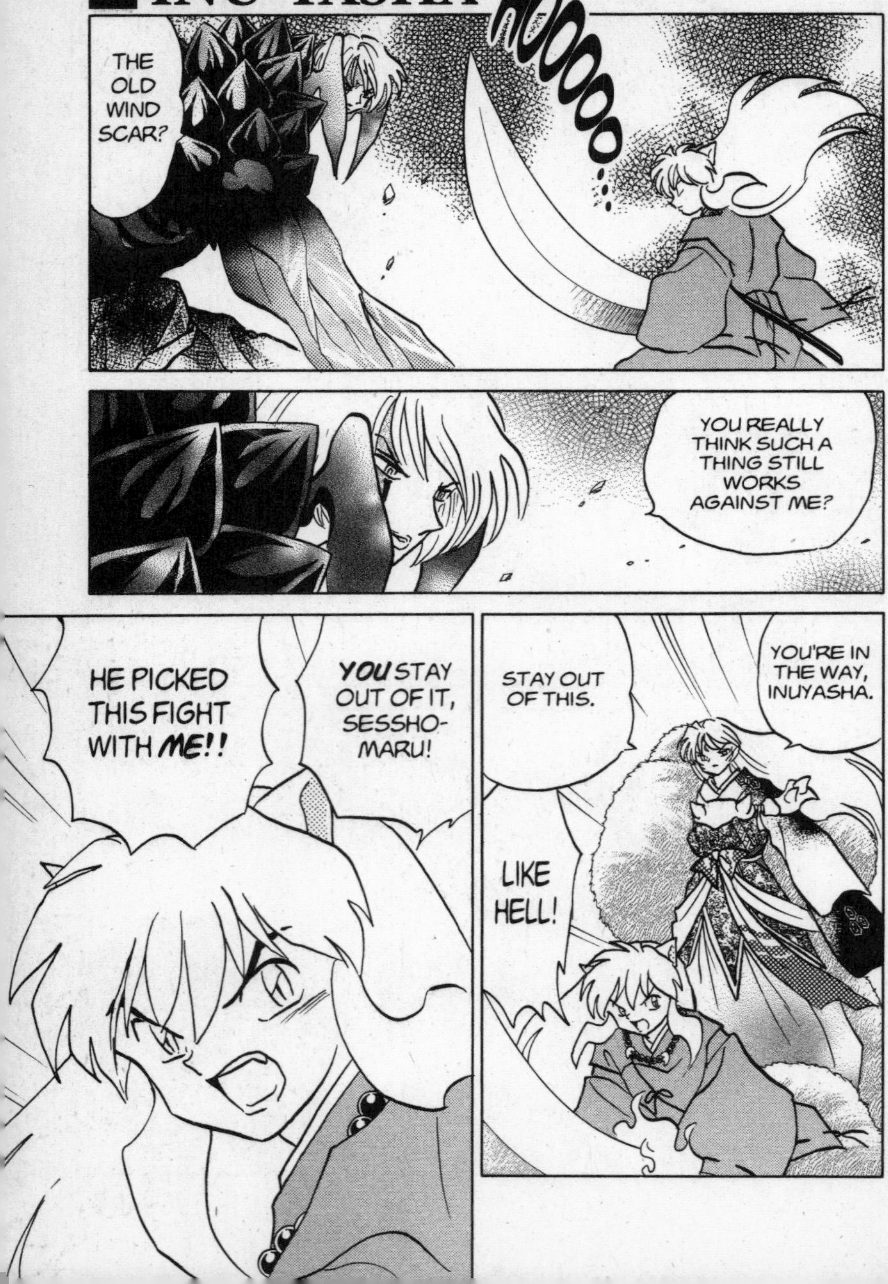
HOOOOO...
THE OLD WIND SCAR?
YOU REALLY THINK SUCH A THING STILL WORKS AGAINST ME?
YOU'RE IN THE WAY, INUYASHA.
STAY OUT OF THIS.
LIKE HELL!
YOU STAY OUT OF IT, SESSHO-MARU!
HE PICKED THIS FIGHT WITH ME!!

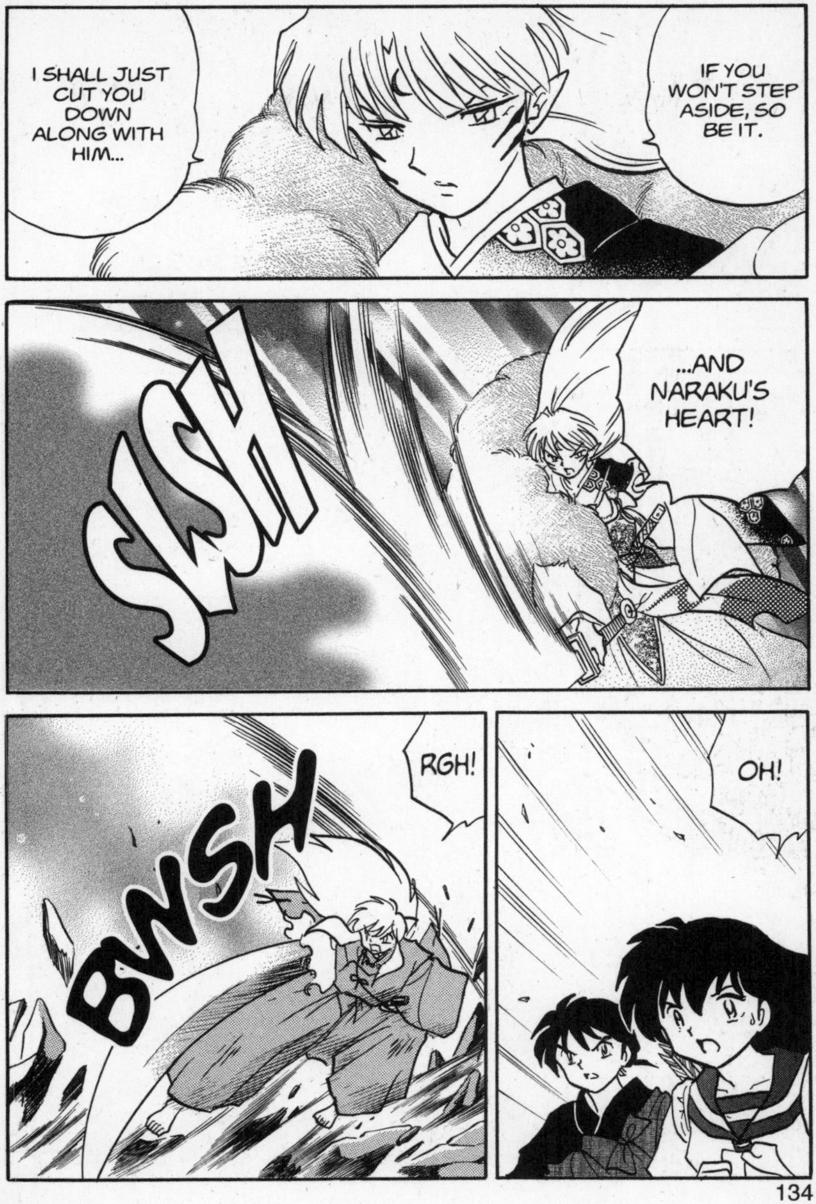
IF YOU WON'T STEP ASIDE, SO BE IT.
I SHALL JUST CUT YOU DOWN ALONG WITH HIM...
...AND NARAKU'S HEART!
SWSH
OH!
RGH!
BWSH

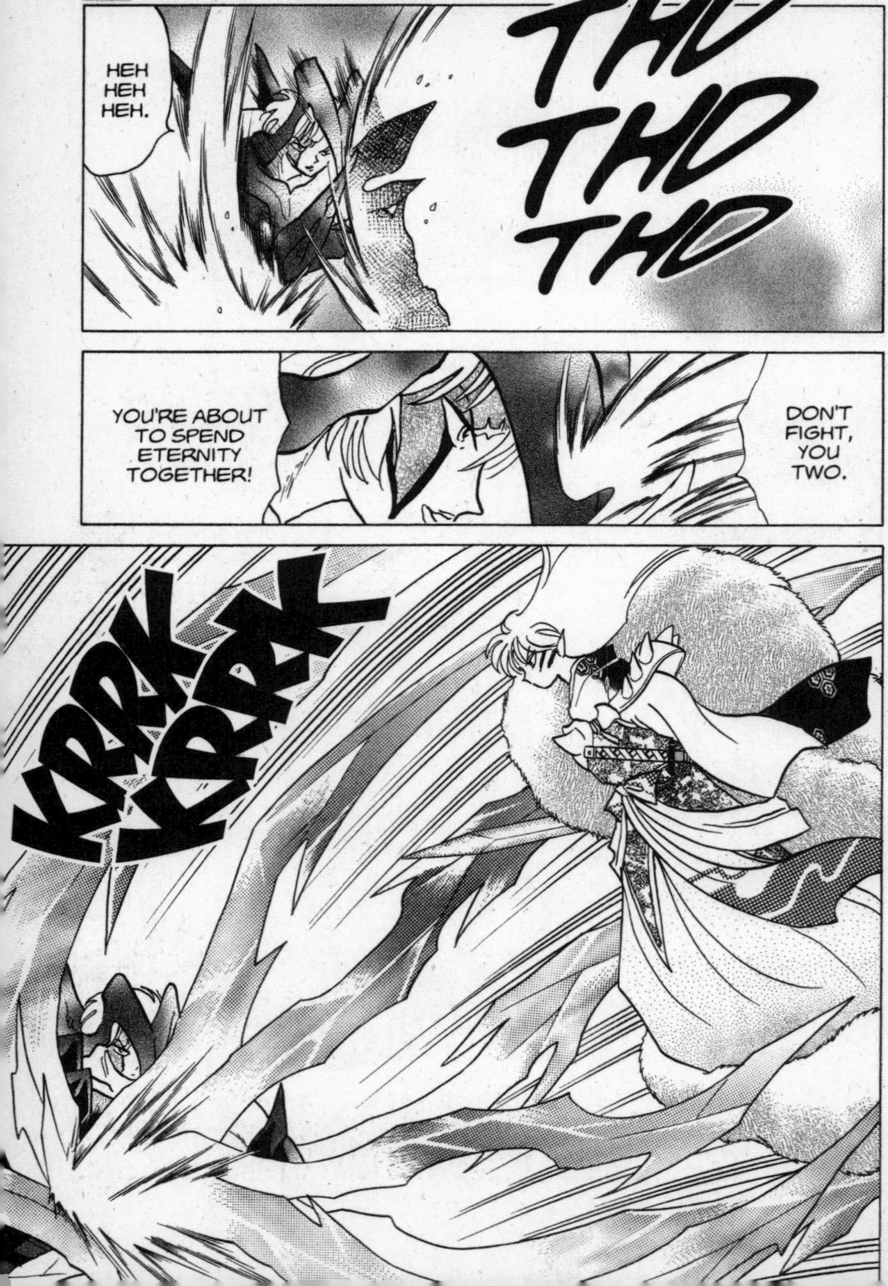
THD THD THD
HEH HEH HEH.
DON'T FIGHT, YOU TWO.
YOU'RE ABOUT TO SPEND ETERNITY TOGETHER!
KRRK KRRK

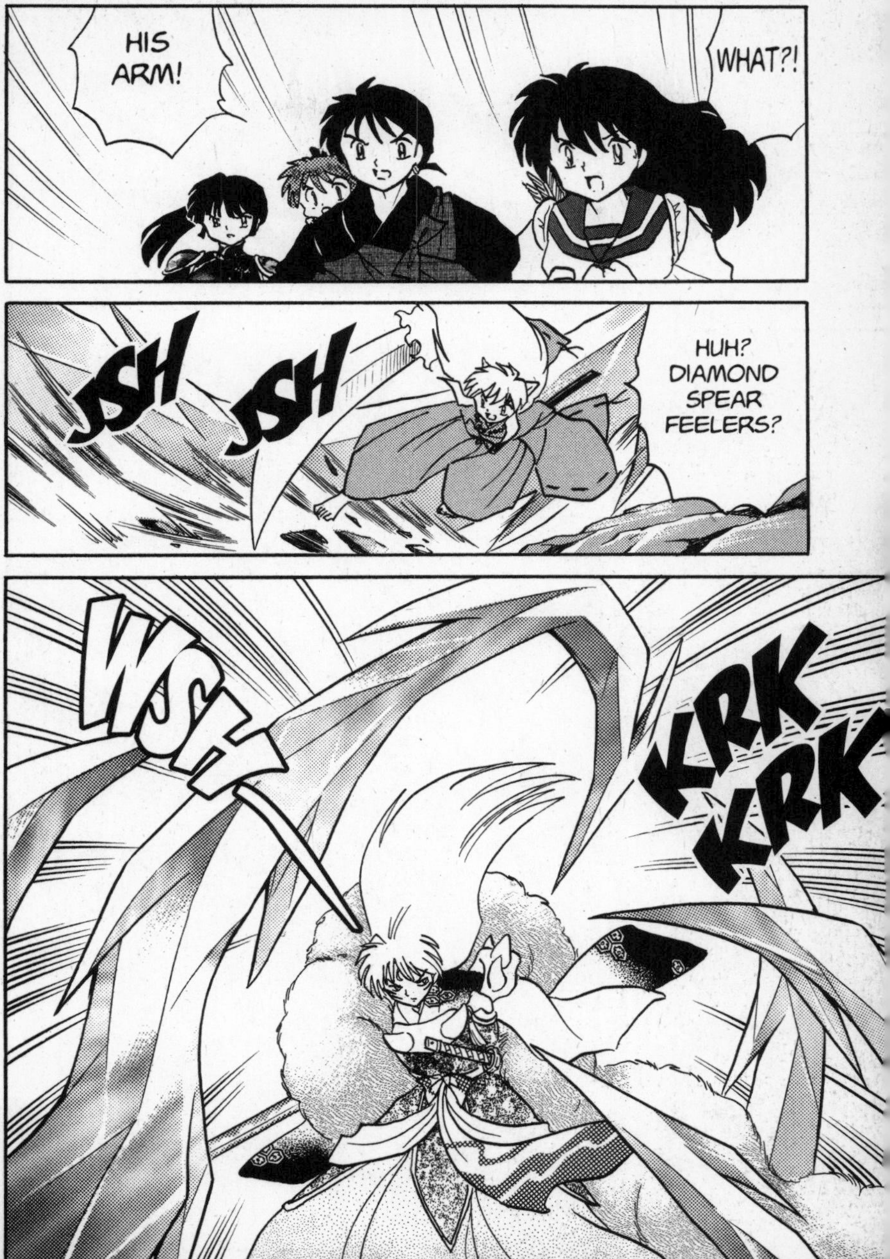
WHAT?!
HIS ARM!
HUH? DIAMOND SPEAR FEELERS?
JSH
JSH
KRK KRK
WSH

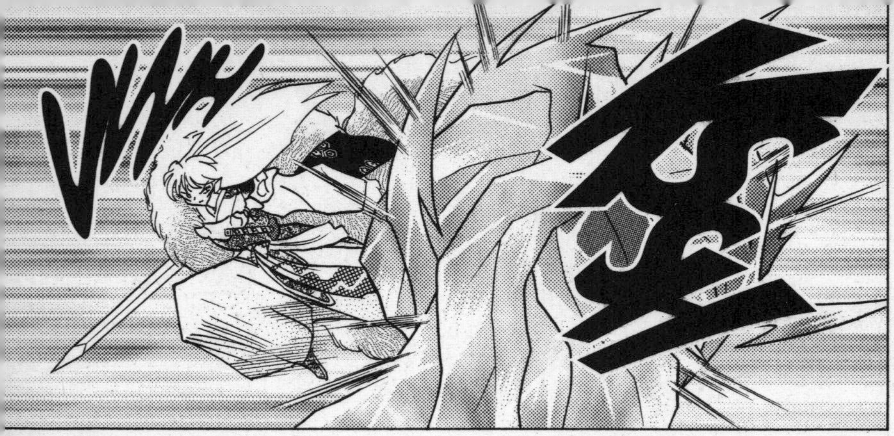

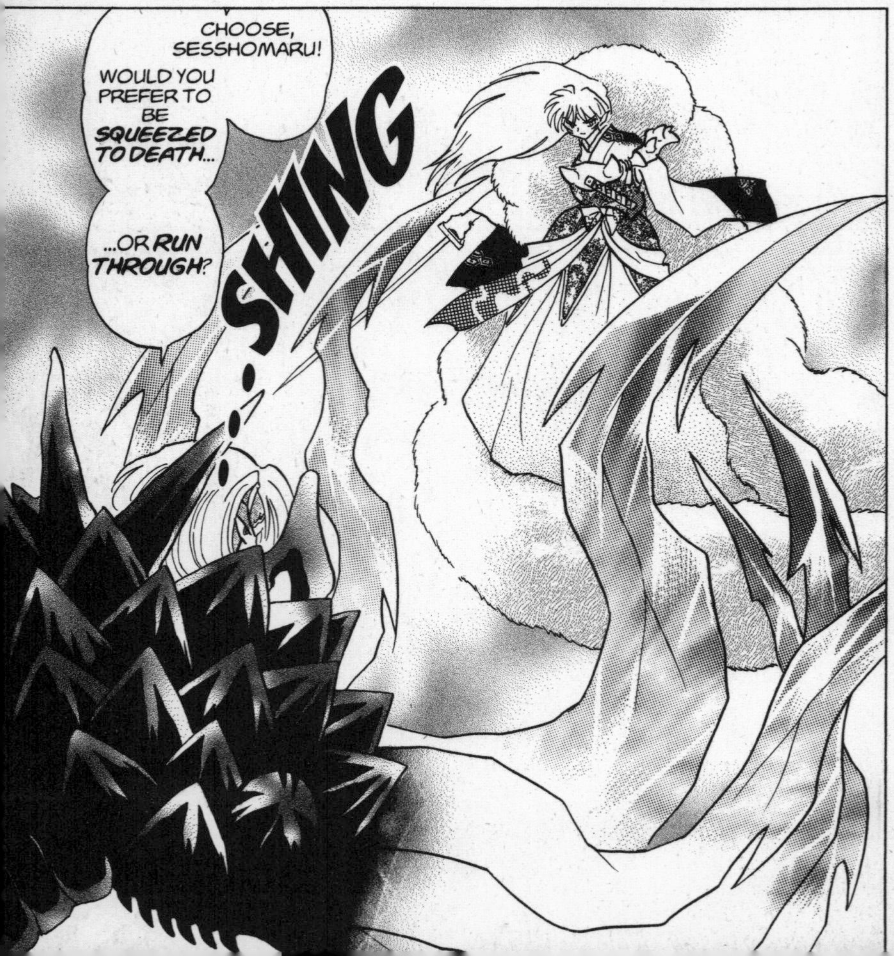
CHOOSE, SESSHOMARU!
WOULD YOU PREFER TO BE **SQUEEZED TO DEATH**...
...OR **RUN THROUGH**?
...SHING

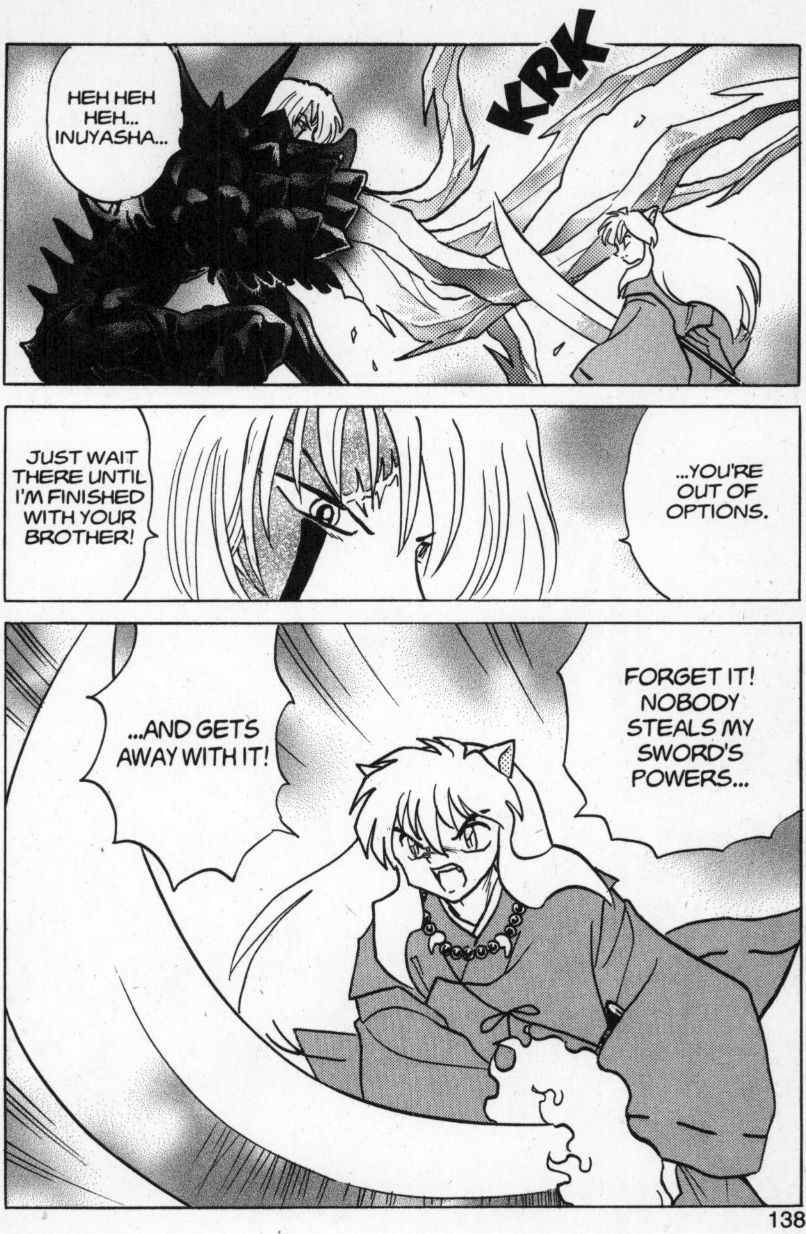
KRK
HEH HEH HEH... INUYASHA...
...YOU'RE OUT OF OPTIONS.
JUST WAIT THERE UNTIL I'M FINISHED WITH YOUR BROTHER!
FORGET IT! NOBODY STEALS MY SWORD'S POWERS...
...AND GETS AWAY WITH IT!

SCROLL 8
WRATH

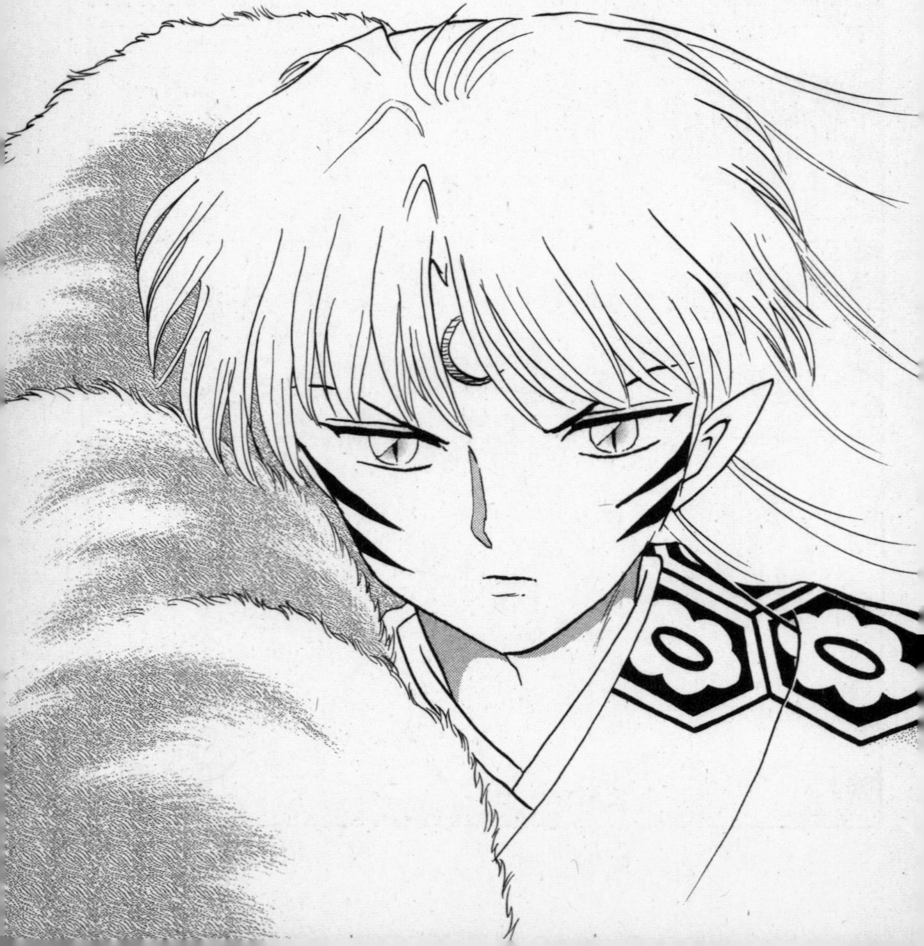

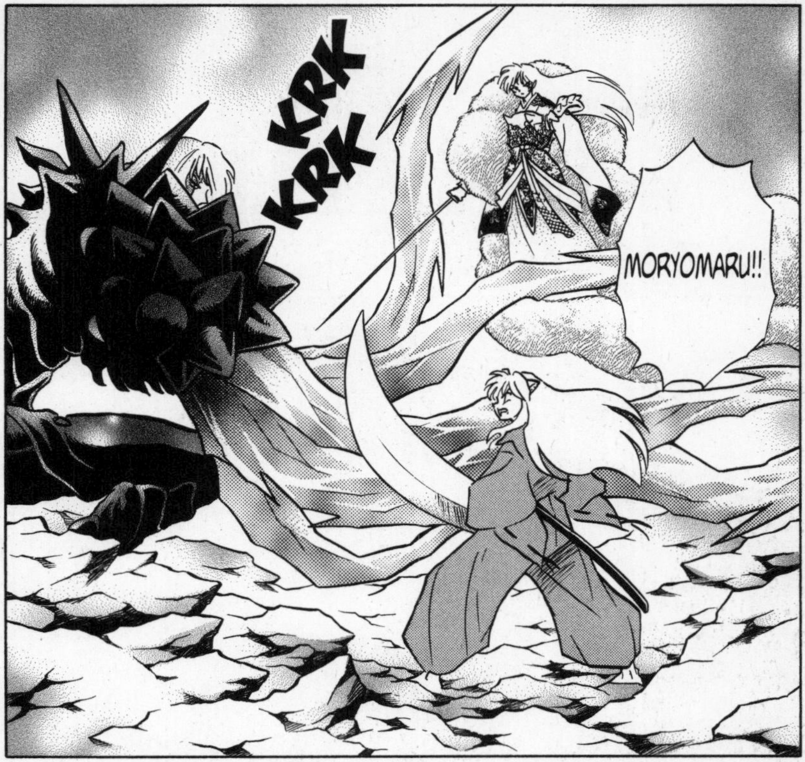
KRK KRK
MORYOMARU!!

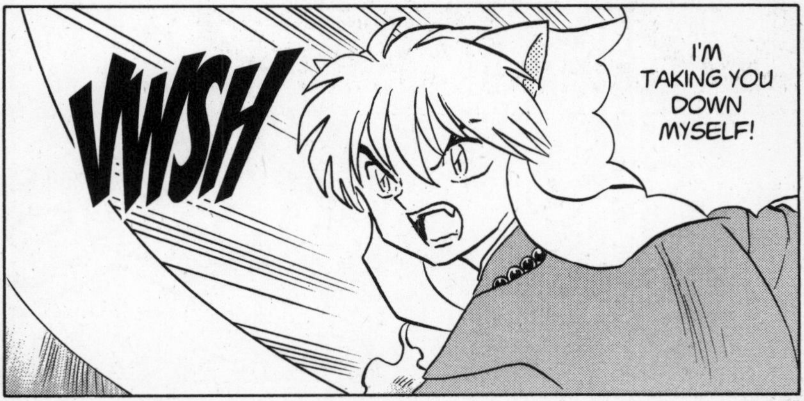
VWSH
I'M TAKING YOU DOWN MYSELF!

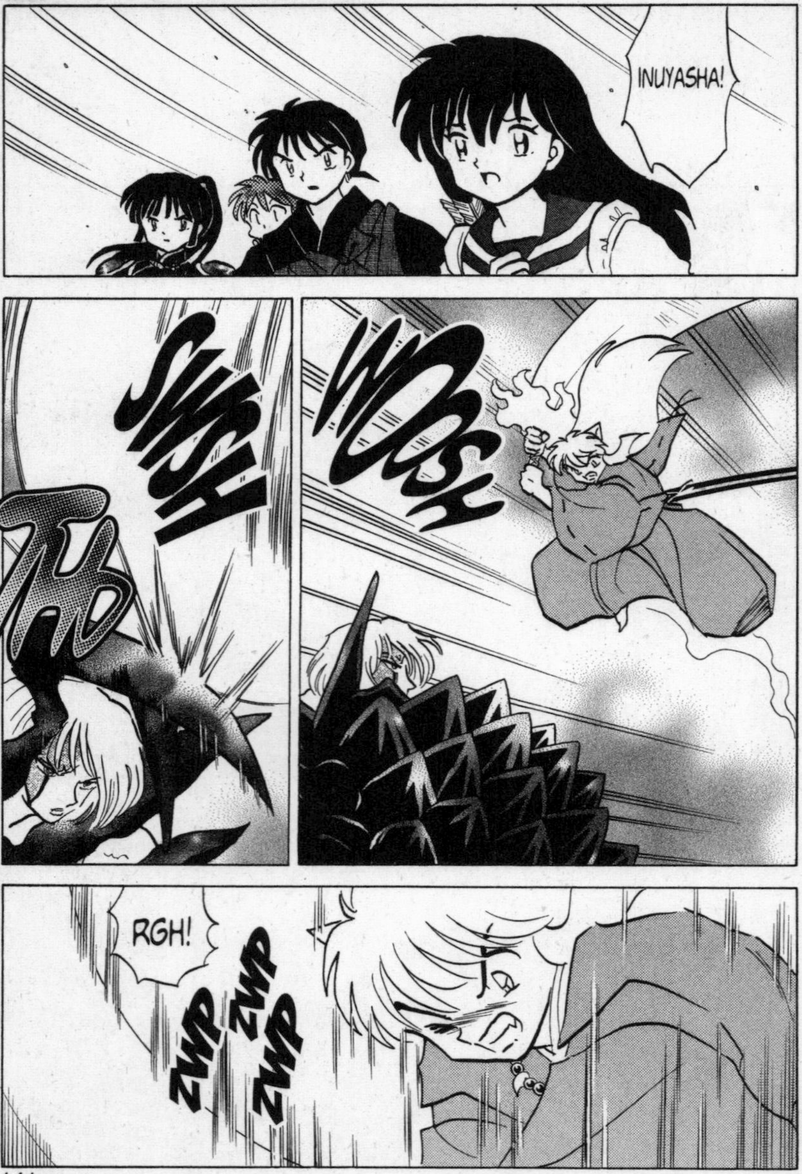
INUYASHA!
WOOSH
SWISH!
THD
RGH!
ZWP
ZWP
ZWP
ZWP

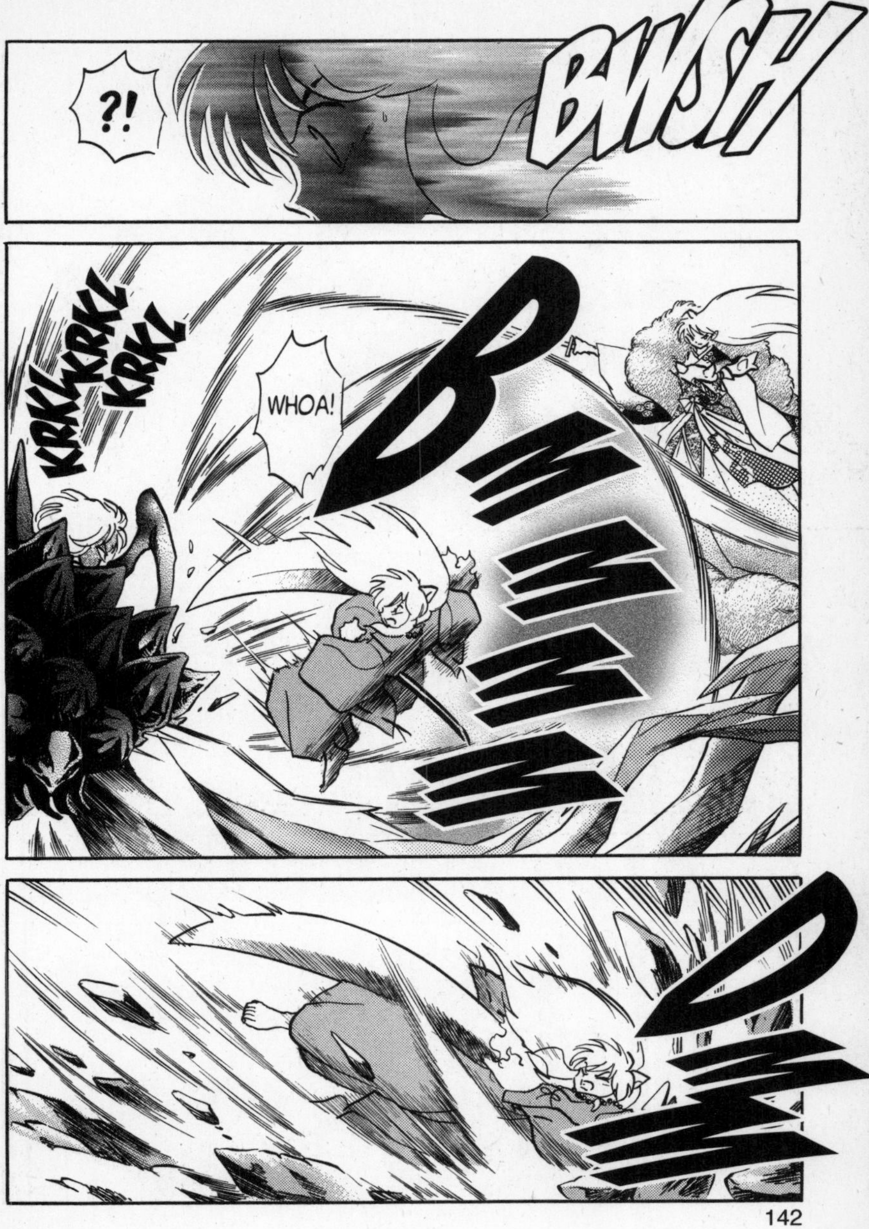
BWSH
?!
BMMMMM
WHOA!
KRKL KRKL KRKL
DMMM

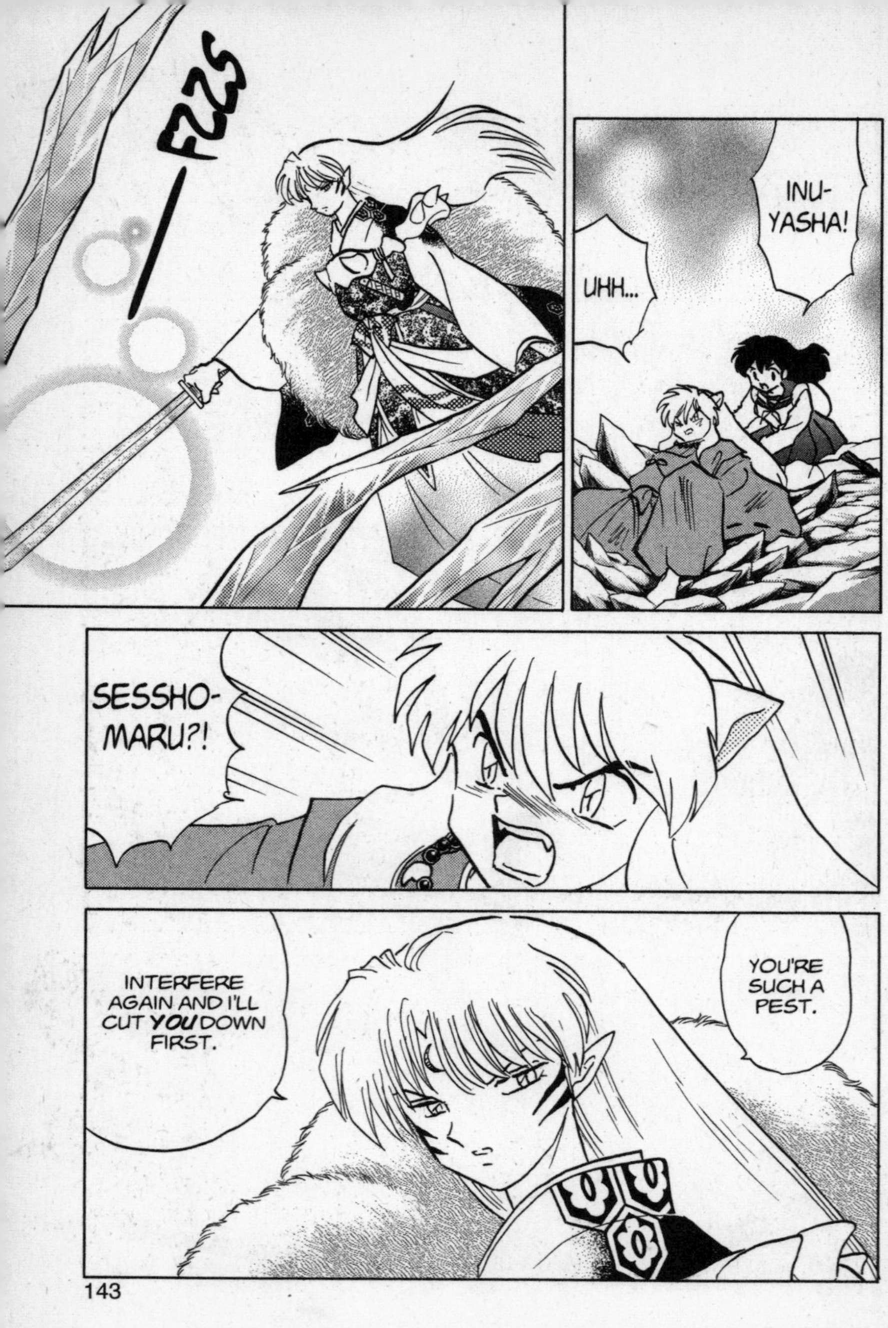
INU-YASHA!
UHH...
FZZS
SESSHO-MARU?!
YOU'RE SUCH A PEST.
INTERFERE AGAIN AND I'LL CUT **YOU** DOWN FIRST.

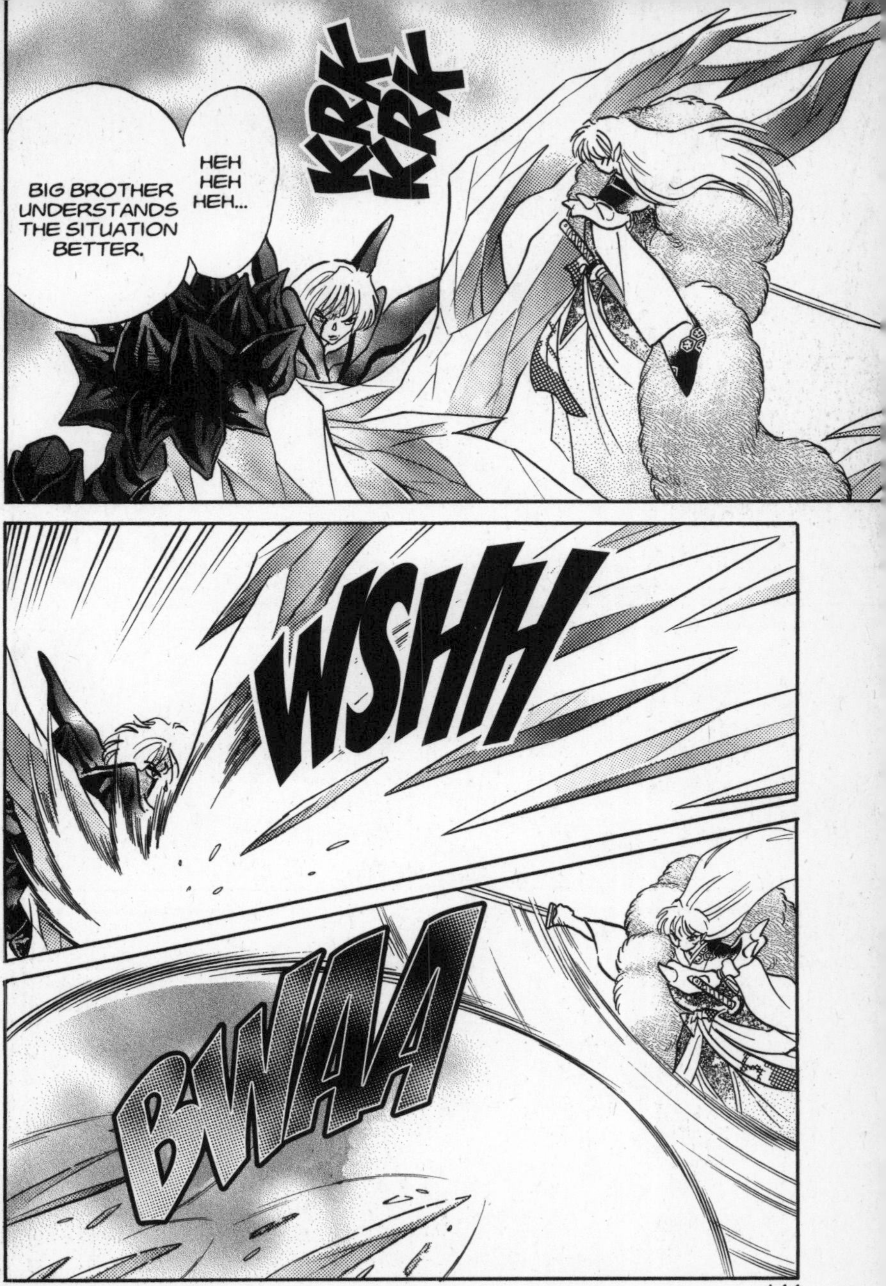
KRK KRK
HEH HEH HEH...
BIG BROTHER UNDERSTANDS THE SITUATION BETTER.
WSHH
BWAA

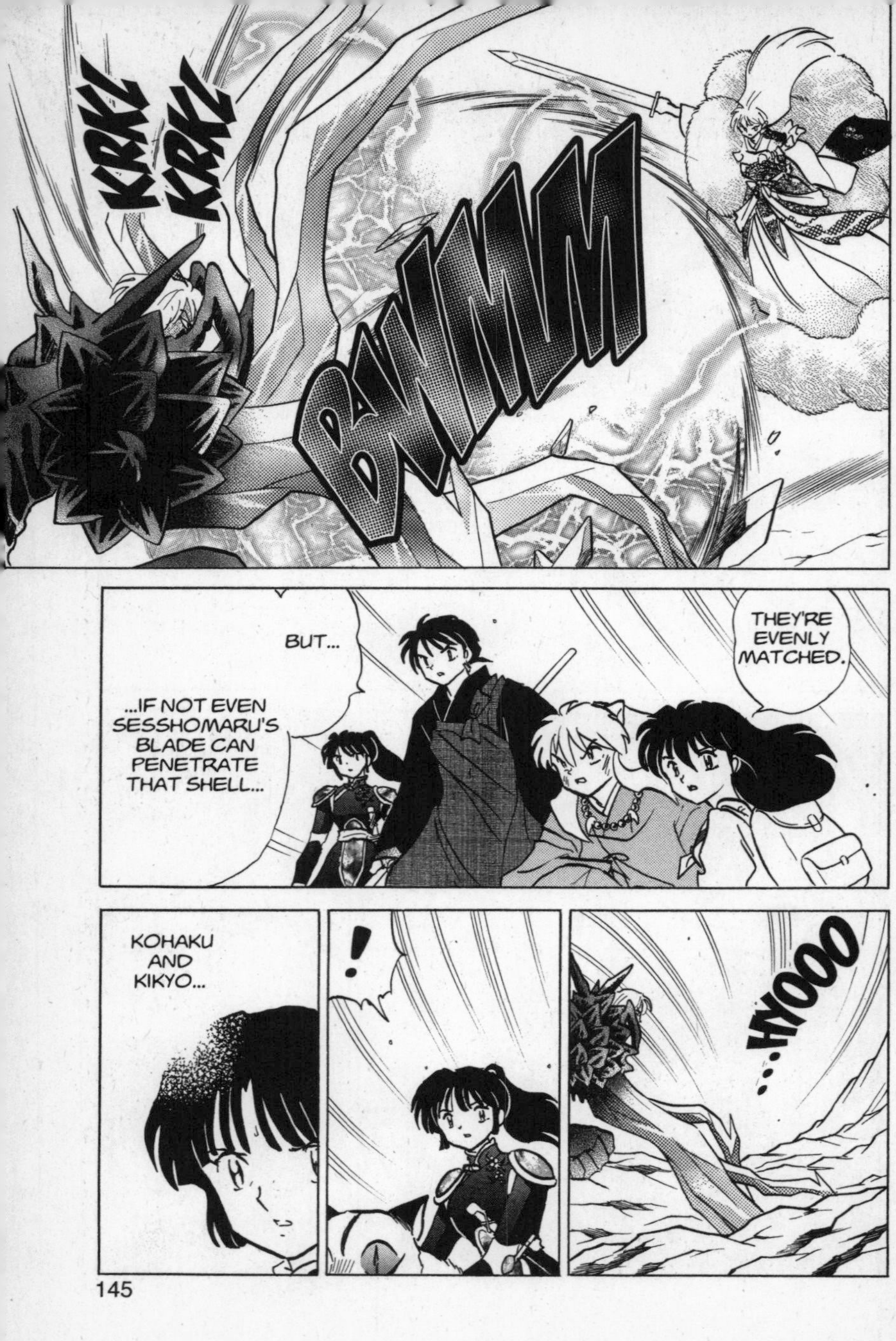
BWMMM
KRKL KRKL
THEY'RE EVENLY MATCHED.
BUT...
...IF NOT EVEN SESSHOMARU'S BLADE CAN PENETRATE THAT SHELL...
...HYOOO
!
KOHAKU AND KIKYO...

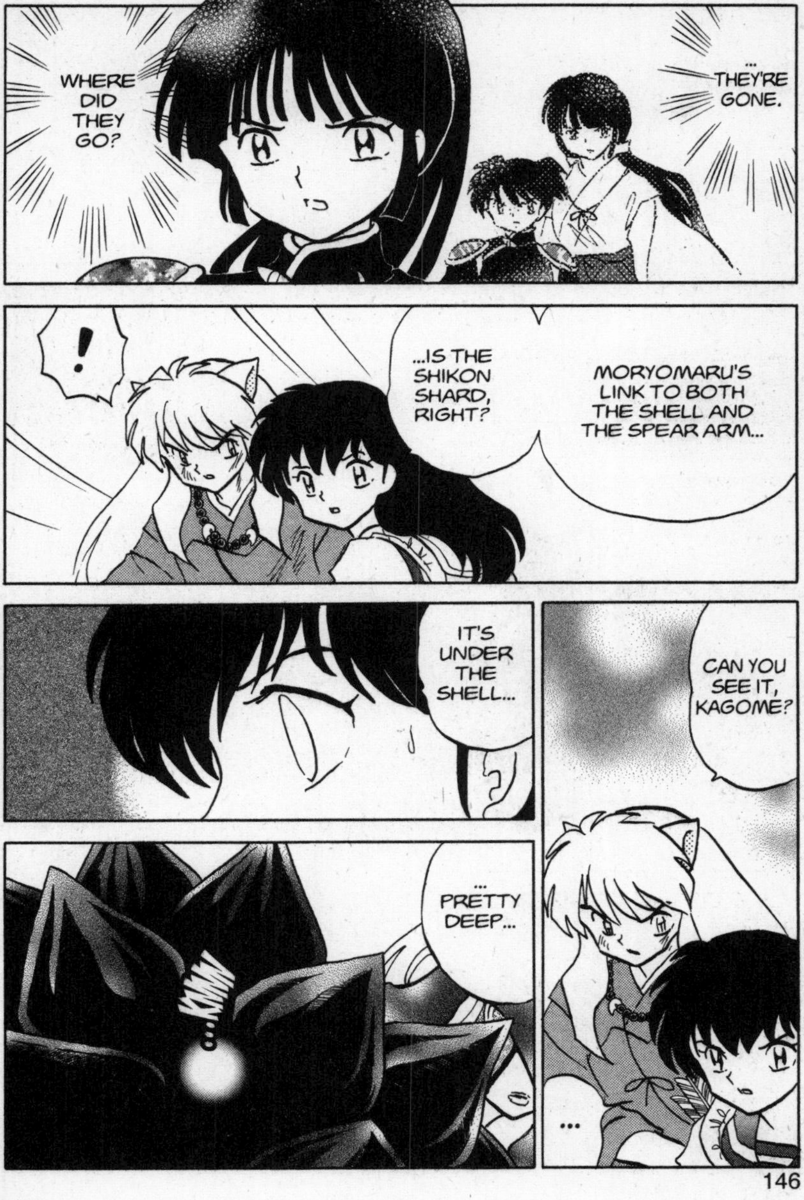
... THEY'RE GONE.
WHERE DID THEY GO?
MORYOMARU'S LINK TO BOTH THE SHELL AND THE SPEAR ARM...
...IS THE SHIKON SHARD, RIGHT?
!
CAN YOU SEE IT, KAGOME?
...
IT'S UNDER THE SHELL...
... PRETTY DEEP...

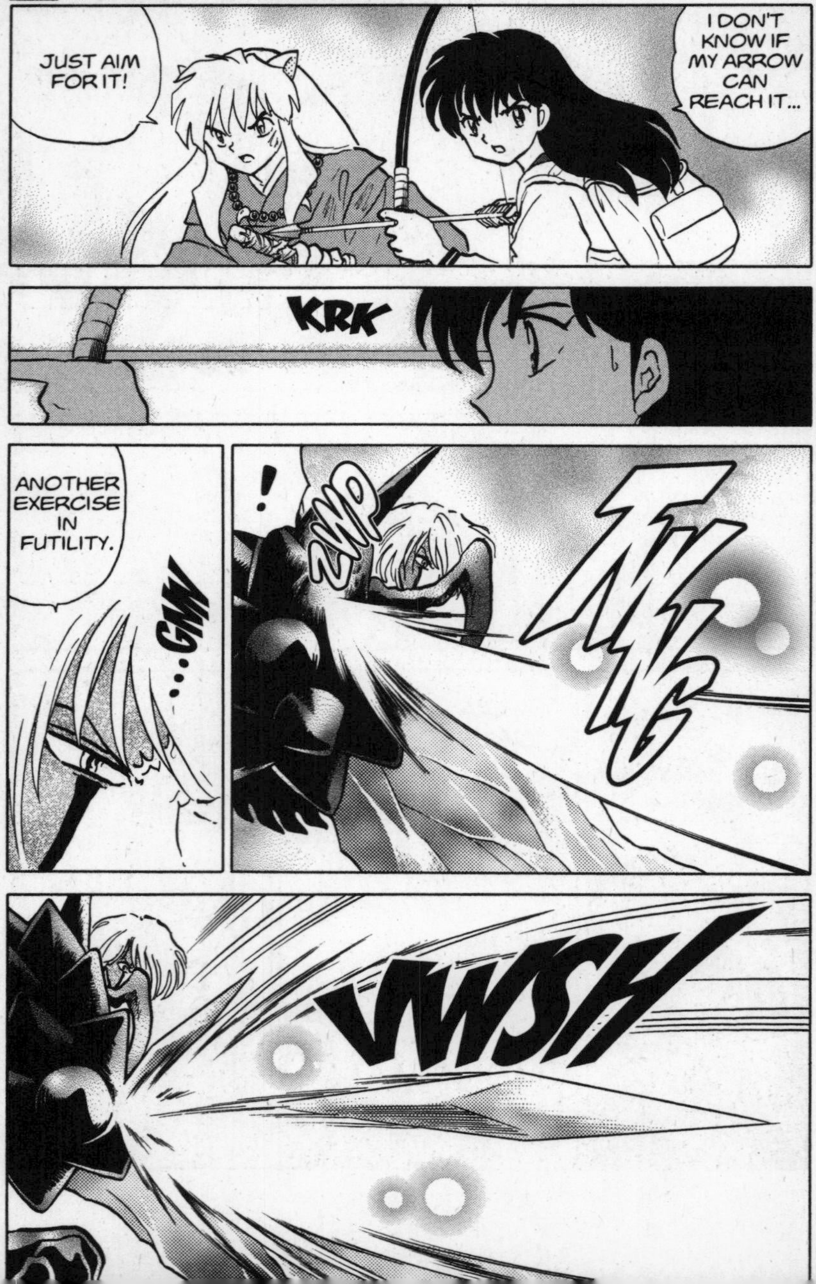
I DON'T KNOW IF MY ARROW CAN REACH IT...
JUST AIM FOR IT!
KRK
!
ZWP
TWNG
ANOTHER EXERCISE IN FUTILITY.
...GNN
VWSH

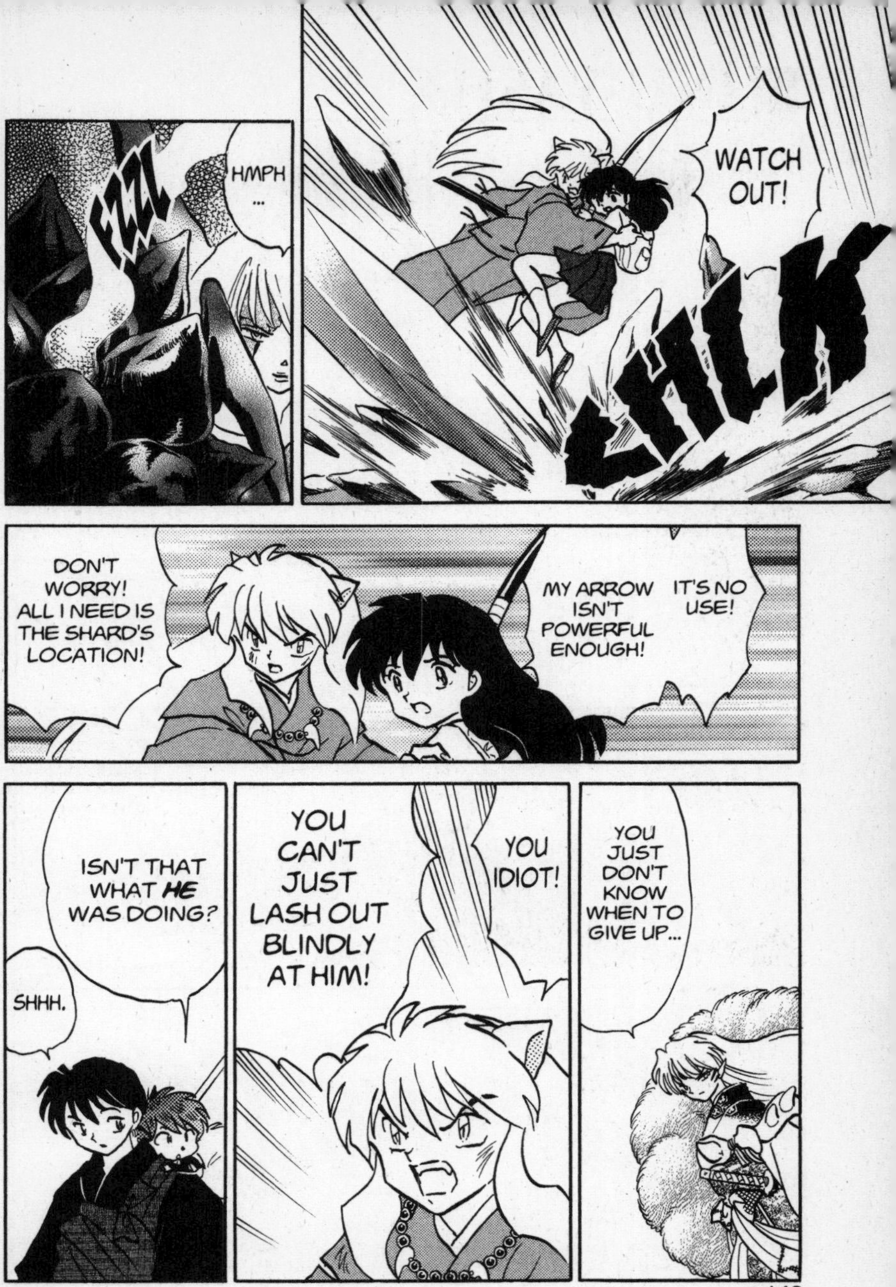
WATCH OUT!
CHLK
HMPH ...
FZZL
IT'S NO USE!
MY ARROW ISN'T POWERFUL ENOUGH!
DON'T WORRY! ALL I NEED IS THE SHARD'S LOCATION!
YOU JUST DON'T KNOW WHEN TO GIVE UP...
YOU IDIOT!
YOU CAN'T JUST LASH OUT BLINDLY AT HIM!
ISN'T THAT WHAT *HE* WAS DOING?
SHHH.

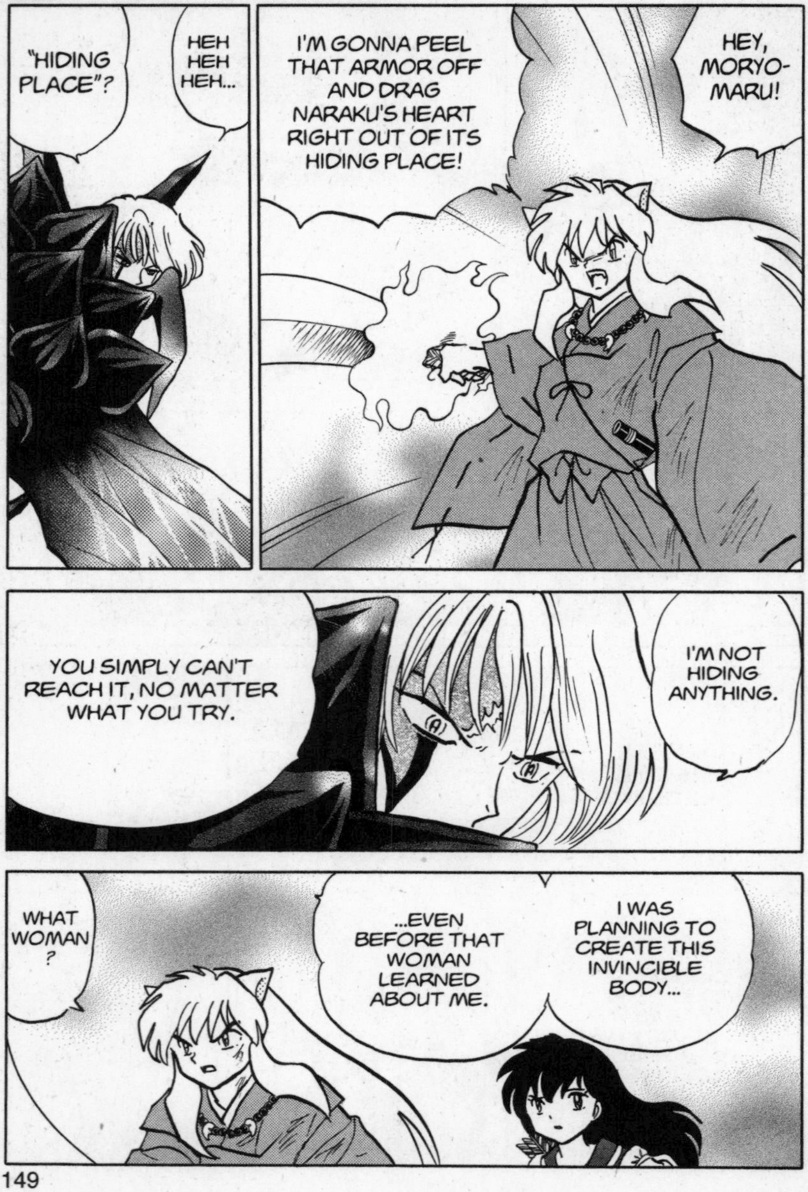
HEY, MORYO-MARU!
I'M GONNA PEEL THAT ARMOR OFF AND DRAG NARAKU'S HEART RIGHT OUT OF ITS HIDING PLACE!
HEH HEH HEH...
"HIDING PLACE"?
I'M NOT HIDING ANYTHING.
YOU SIMPLY CAN'T REACH IT, NO MATTER WHAT YOU TRY.
I WAS PLANNING TO CREATE THIS INVINCIBLE BODY...
...EVEN BEFORE THAT WOMAN LEARNED ABOUT ME.
WHAT WOMAN?

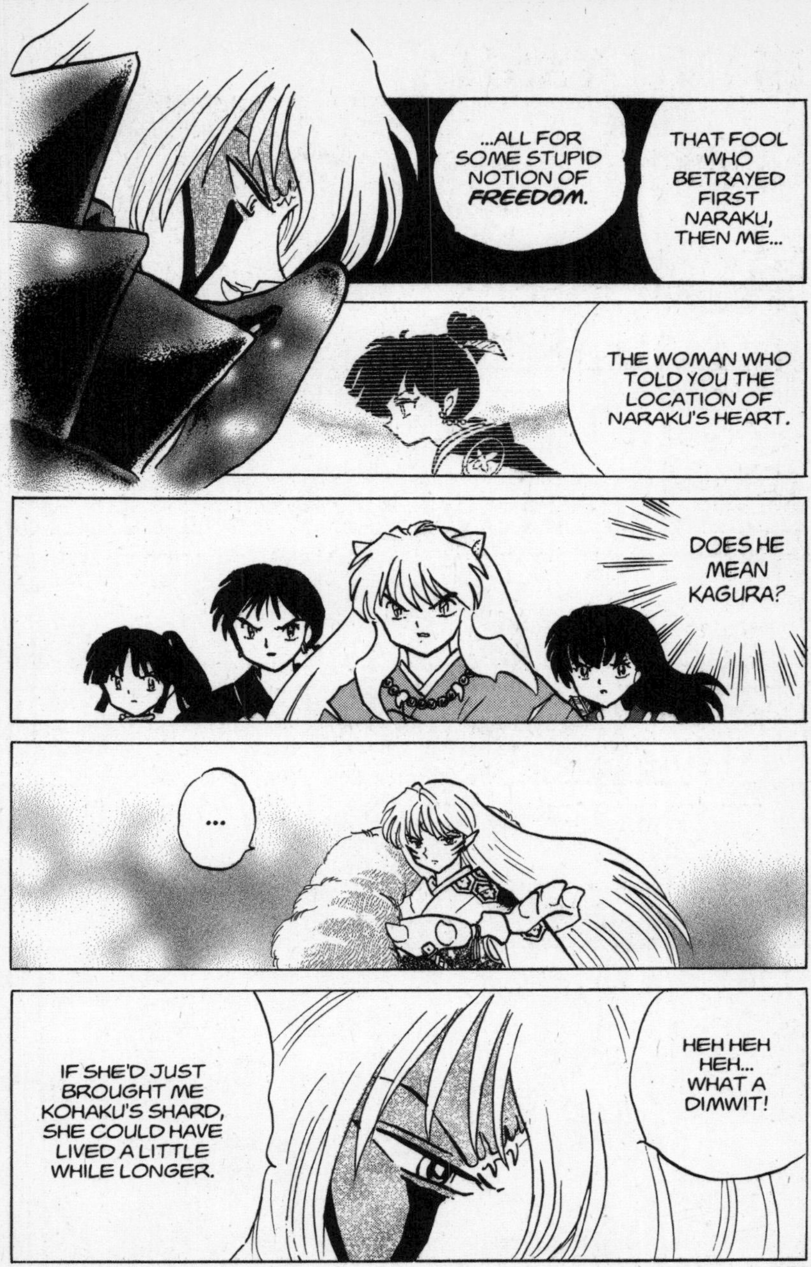
THAT FOOL WHO BETRAYED FIRST NARAKU, THEN ME...
...ALL FOR SOME STUPID NOTION OF *FREEDOM*.
THE WOMAN WHO TOLD YOU THE LOCATION OF NARAKU'S HEART.
DOES HE MEAN KAGURA?
...
HEH HEH HEH... WHAT A DIMWIT!
IF SHE'D JUST BROUGHT ME KOHAKU'S SHARD, SHE COULD HAVE LIVED A LITTLE WHILE LONGER.

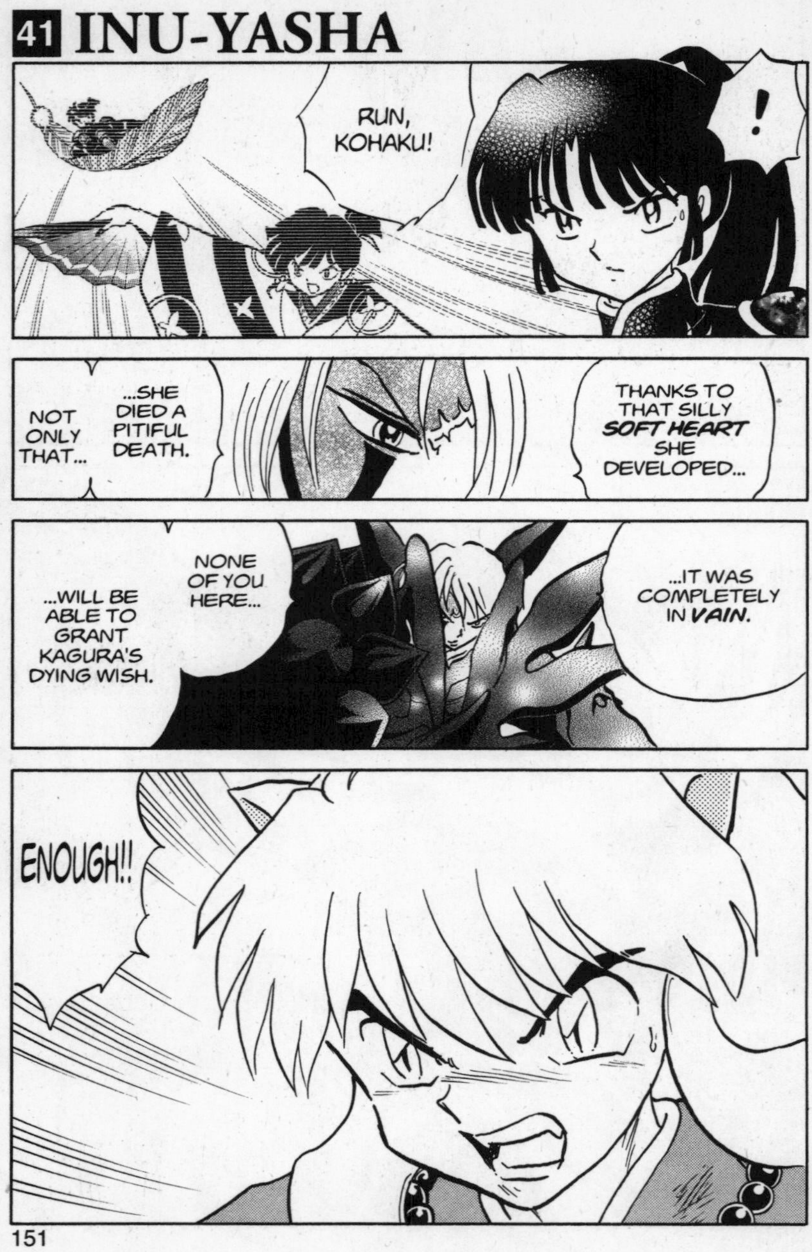
!
RUN, KOHAKU!
THANKS TO THAT SILLY SOFT HEART SHE DEVELOPED...
...SHE DIED A PITIFUL DEATH.
NOT ONLY THAT...
...IT WAS COMPLETELY IN VAIN.
NONE OF YOU HERE...
...WILL BE ABLE TO GRANT KAGURA'S DYING WISH.
ENOUGH!!

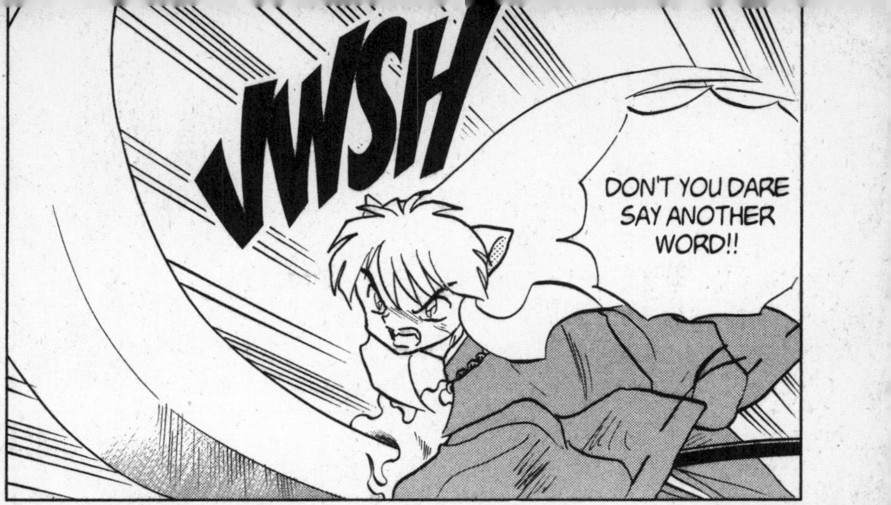
VWSH
DON'T YOU DARE SAY ANOTHER WORD!!

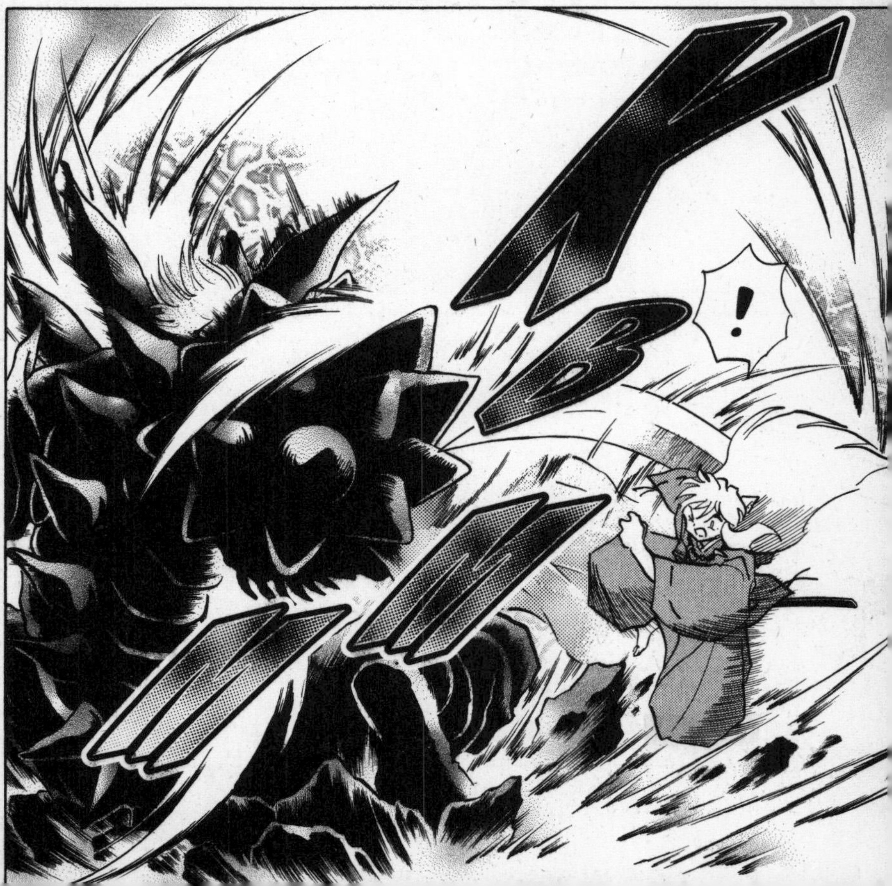
!

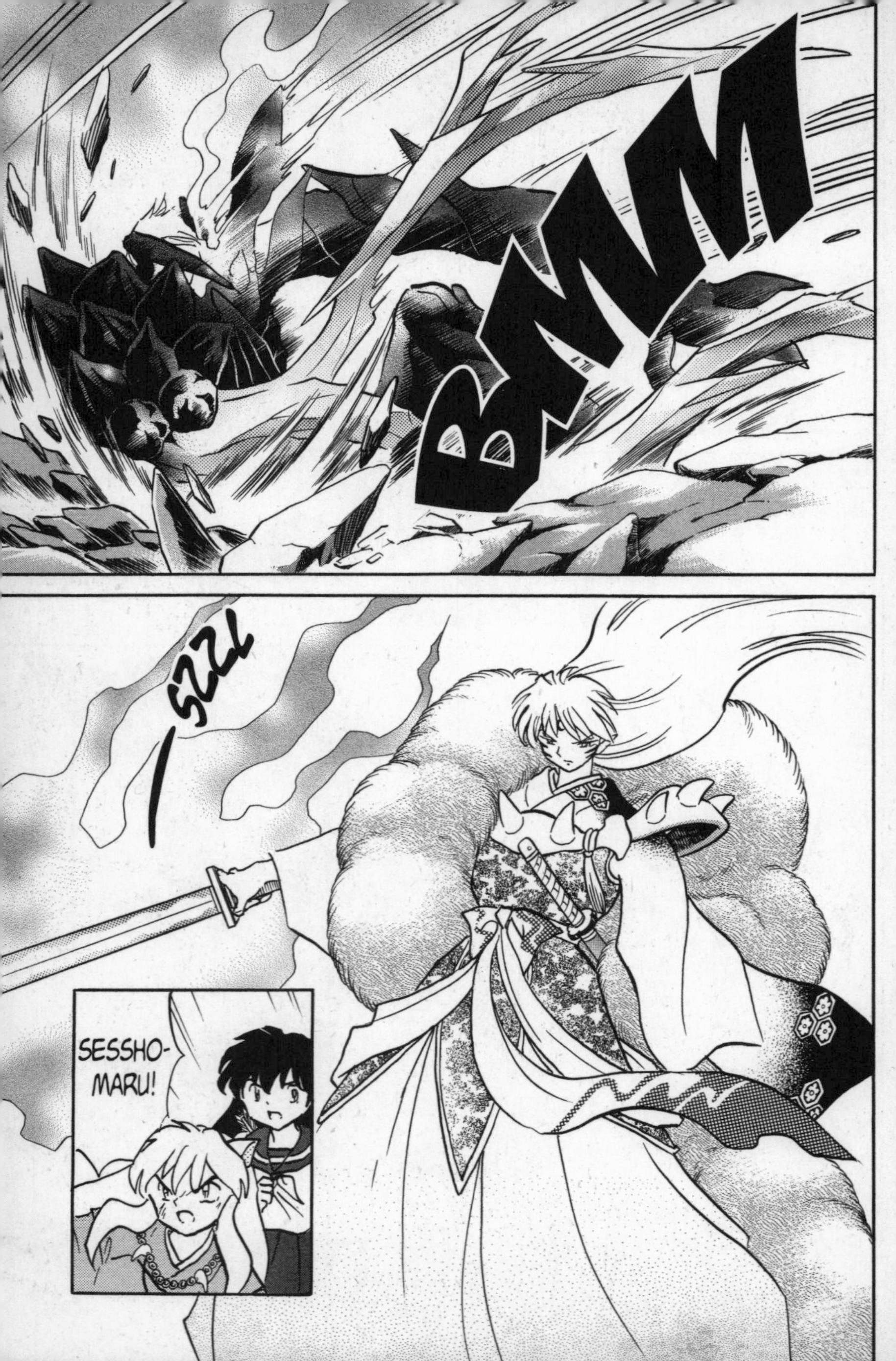
BAMM
-SZZZ
SESSHO-MARU!

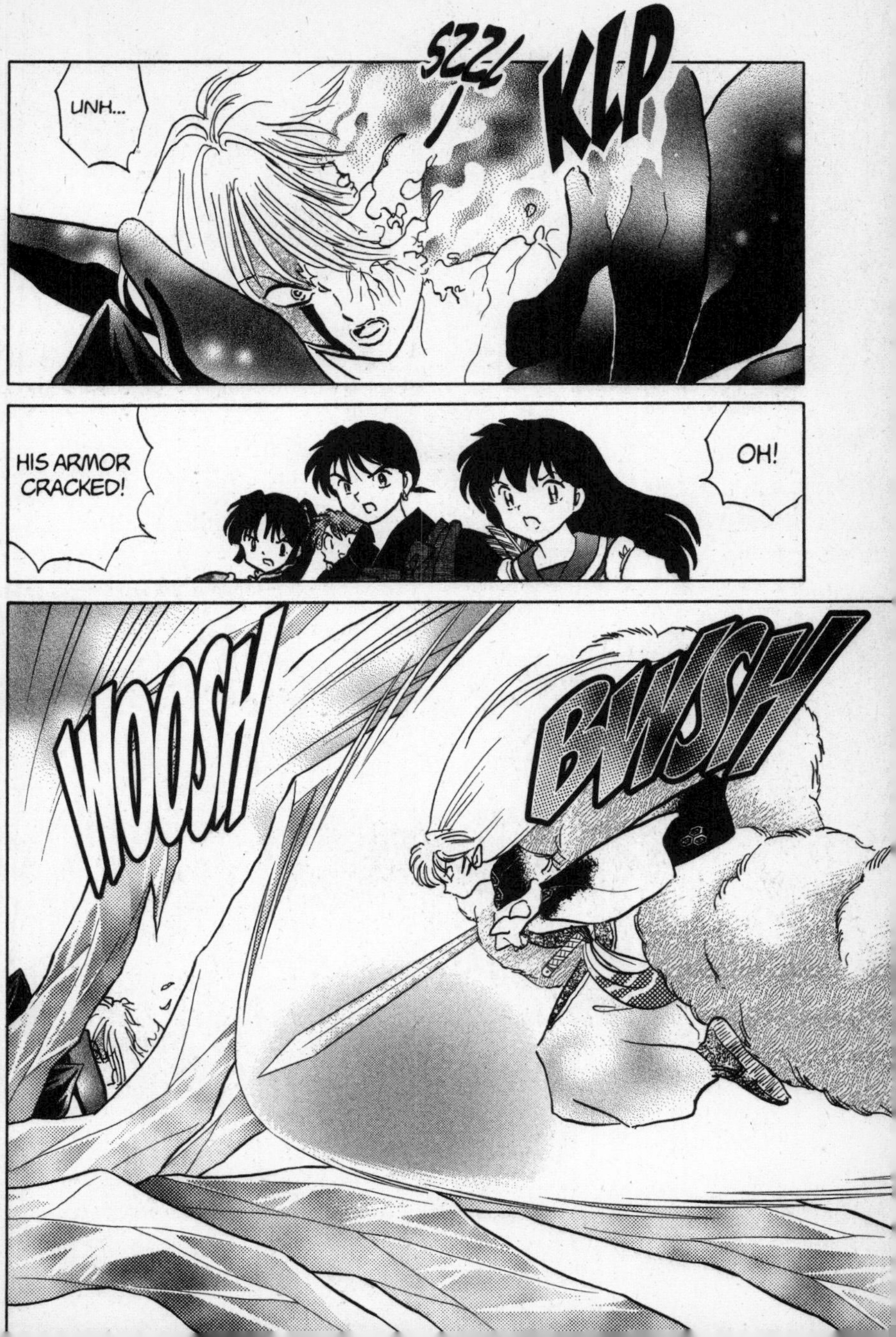
KLP
SZZZ
UNH...
OH!
HIS ARMOR CRACKED!
BWSH
WOOSH

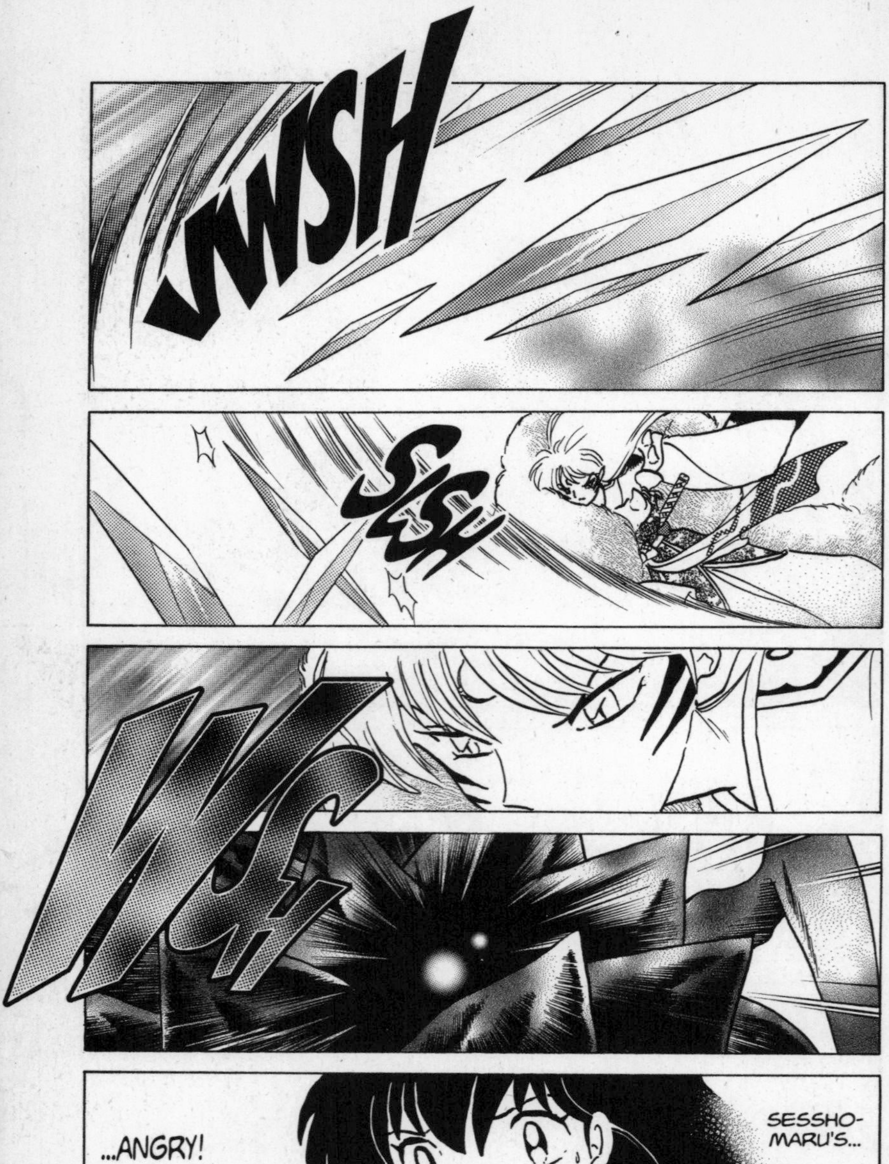
SESSHO-MARU'S...
...ANGRY!

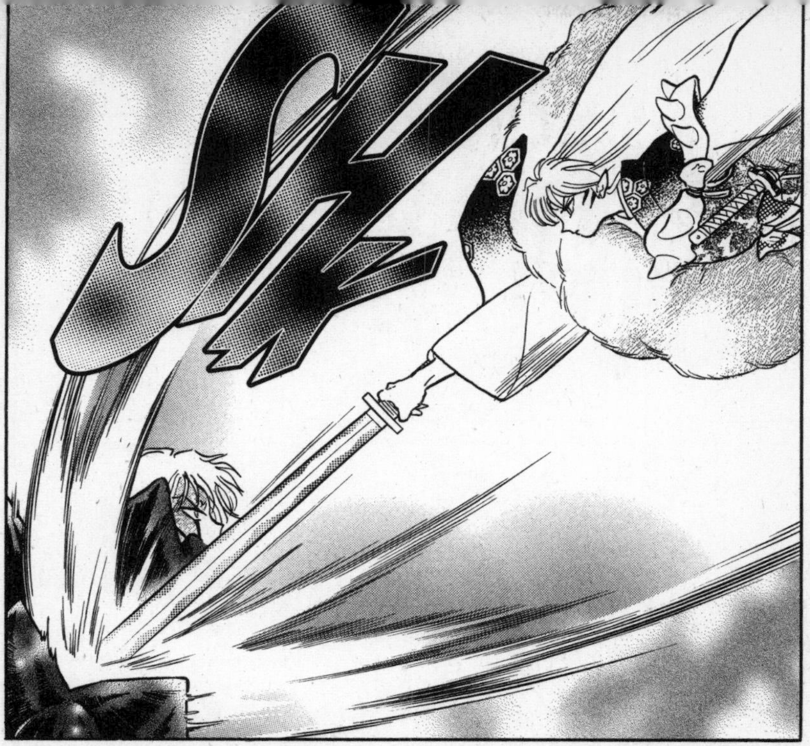

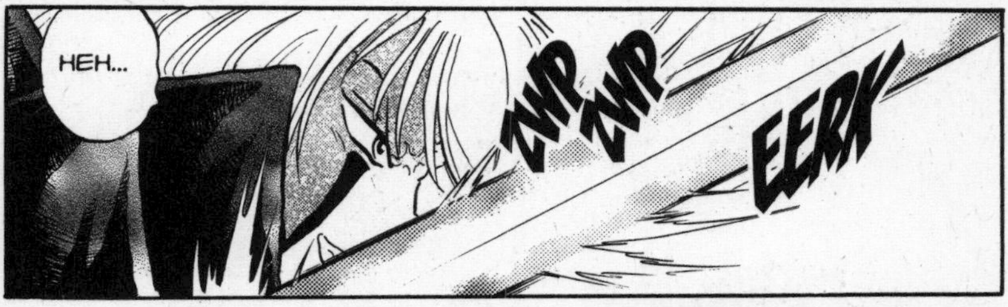
EERK
ZWP ZWP
HEH...

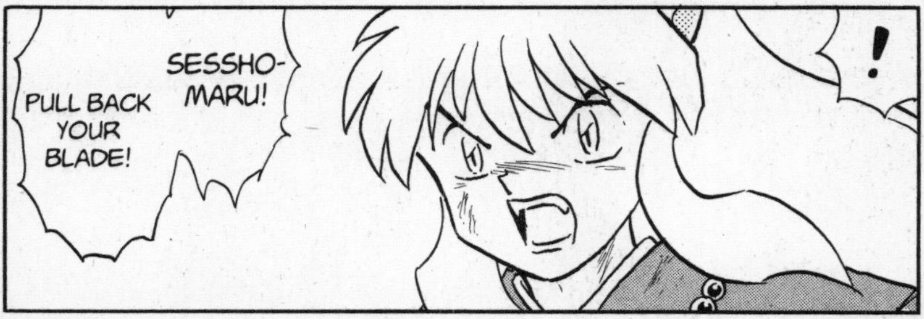
!
SESSHO-MARU!
PULL BACK YOUR BLADE!

SCROLL 9
SESSHOMARU'S PERIL

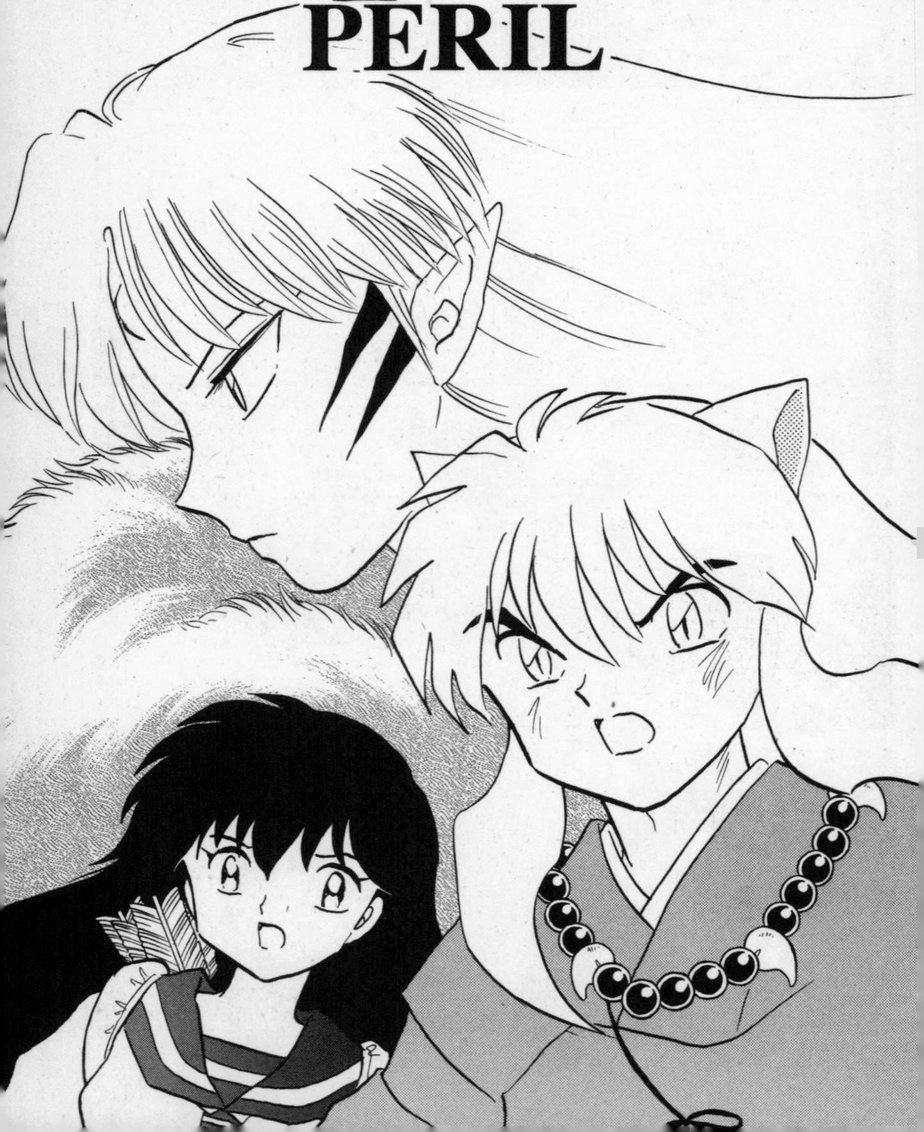

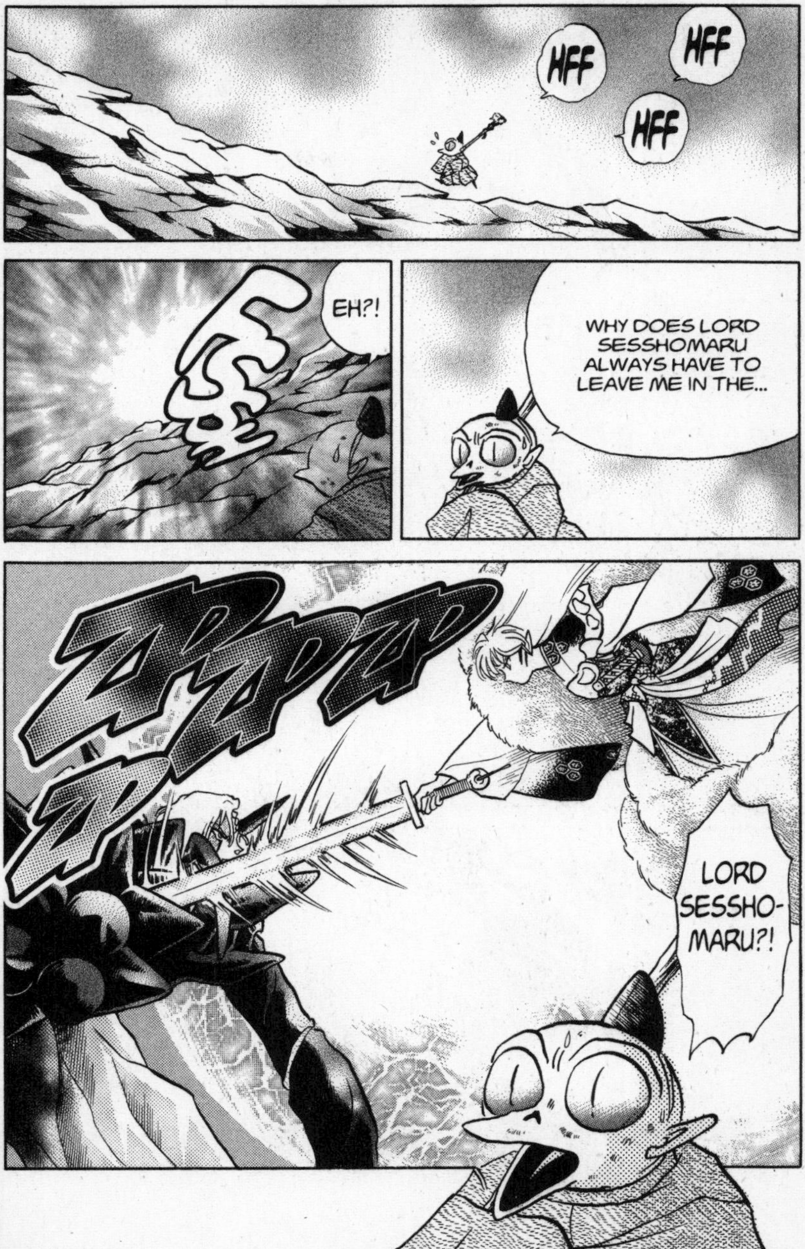
HFF
HFF
HFF
WHY DOES LORD SESSHOMARU ALWAYS HAVE TO LEAVE ME IN THE...
EH?!
ZAP ZAP ZAP
LORD SESSHO-MARU?!

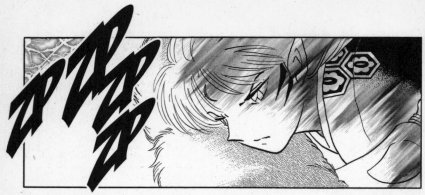

ZP ZP ZP ZP

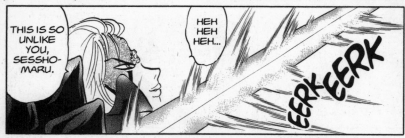

THIS IS SO UNLIKE YOU, SESSHO-MARU.

HEH HEH HEH...

EERK EERK

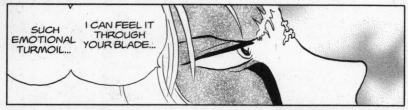

SUCH EMOTIONAL TURMOIL...

I CAN FEEL IT THROUGH YOUR BLADE...

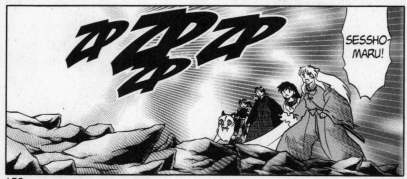

ZP ZP ZP ZP

SESSHO-MARU!

159

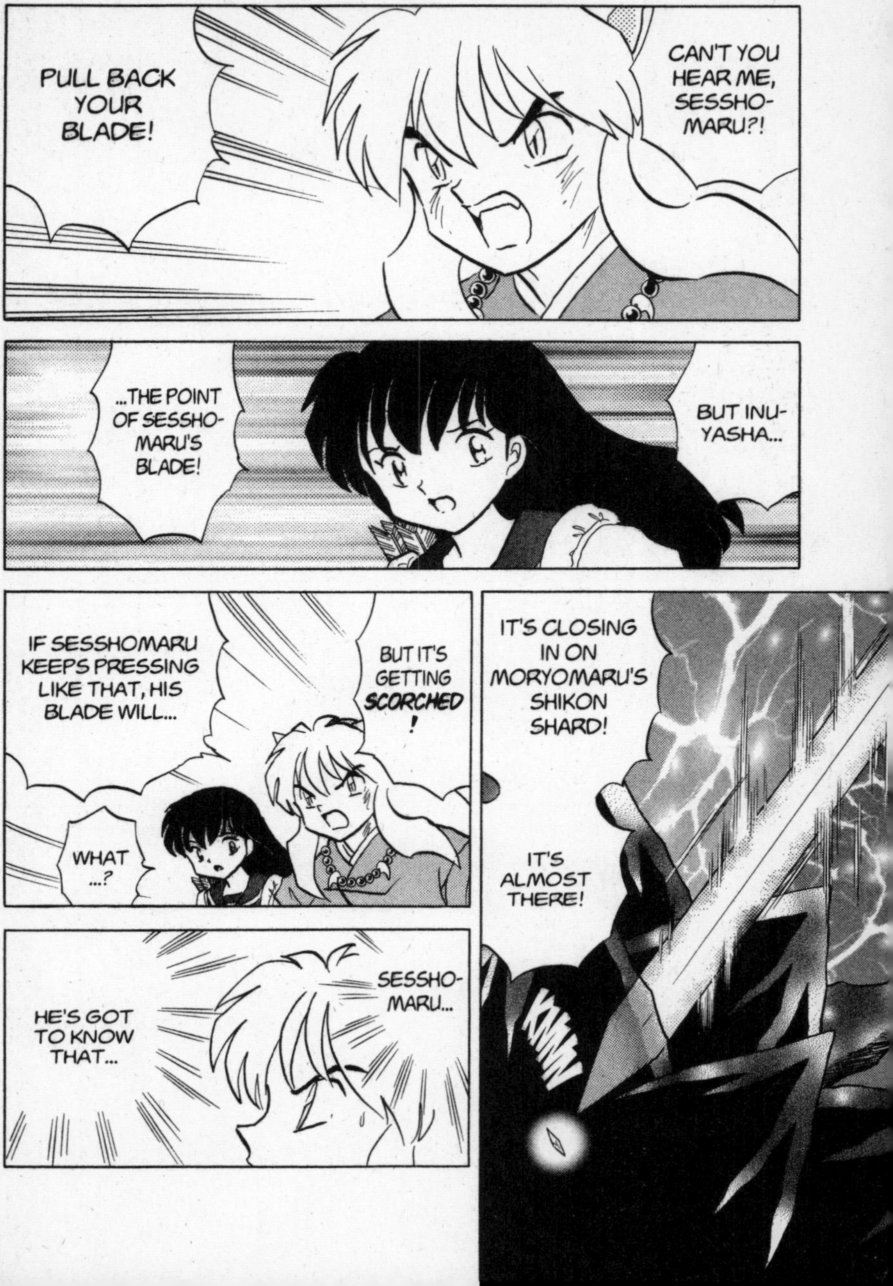
CAN'T YOU HEAR ME, SESSHO-MARU?!
PULL BACK YOUR BLADE!
BUT INU-YASHA...
...THE POINT OF SESSHO-MARU'S BLADE!
IT'S CLOSING IN ON MORYOMARU'S SHIKON SHARD!
IT'S ALMOST THERE!
KMM
BUT IT'S GETTING SCORCHED!
IF SESSHOMARU KEEPS PRESSING LIKE THAT, HIS BLADE WILL...
WHAT ...?
SESSHO-MARU...
HE'S GOT TO KNOW THAT...

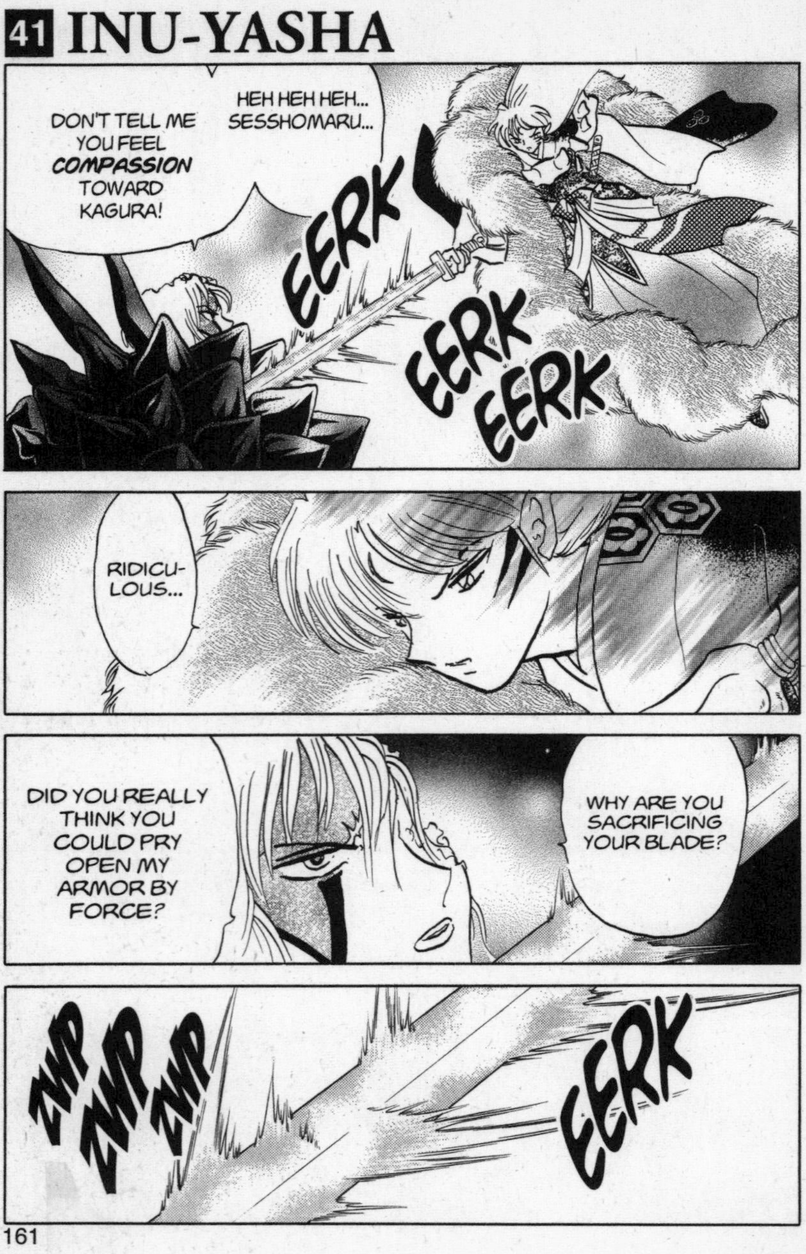
HEH HEH HEH... SESSHOMARU...
DON'T TELL ME YOU FEEL **COMPASSION** TOWARD KAGURA!
EERK
EERK
EERK
RIDICULOUS...
WHY ARE YOU SACRIFICING YOUR BLADE?
DID YOU REALLY THINK YOU COULD PRY OPEN MY ARMOR BY FORCE?
EERK
ZWP
ZWP
ZWP

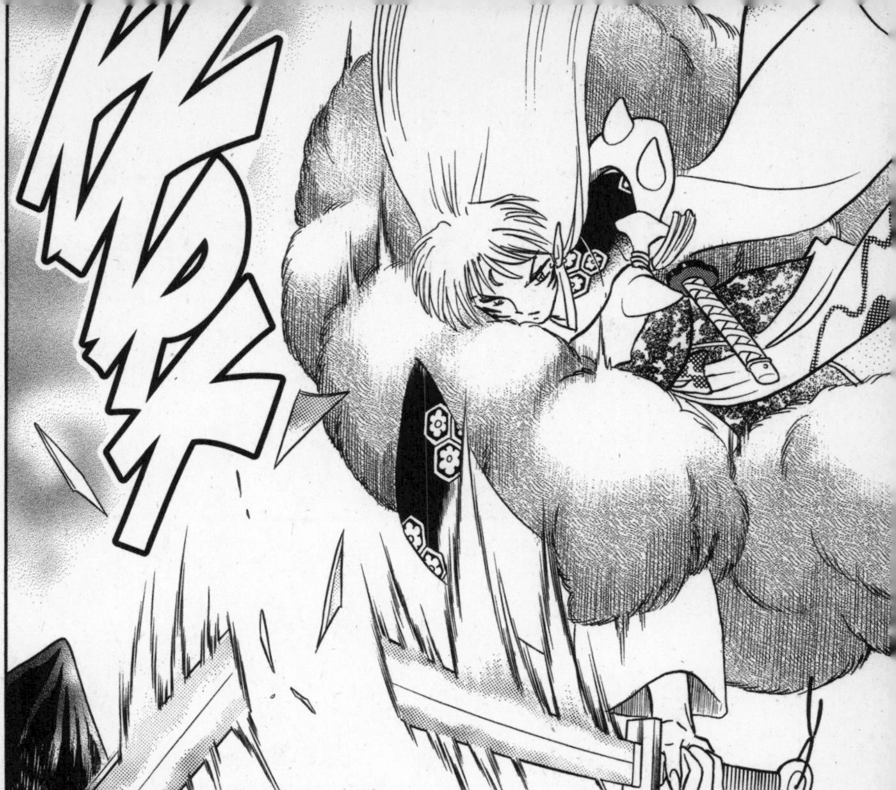

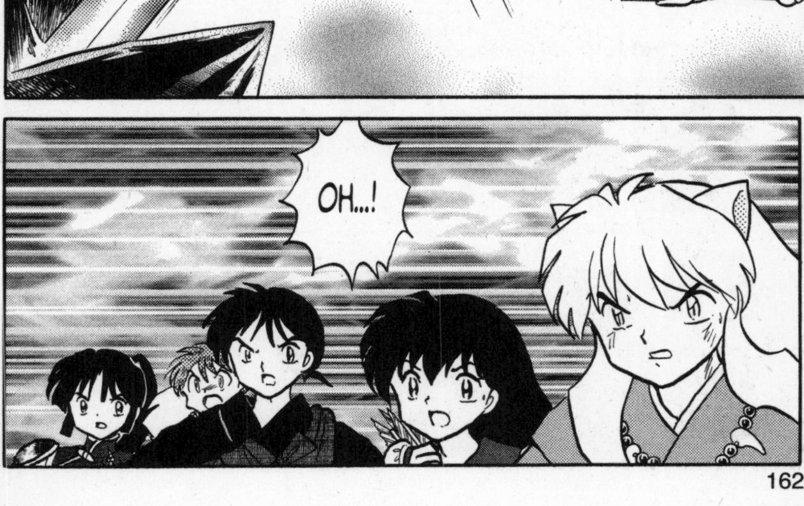
OH...!

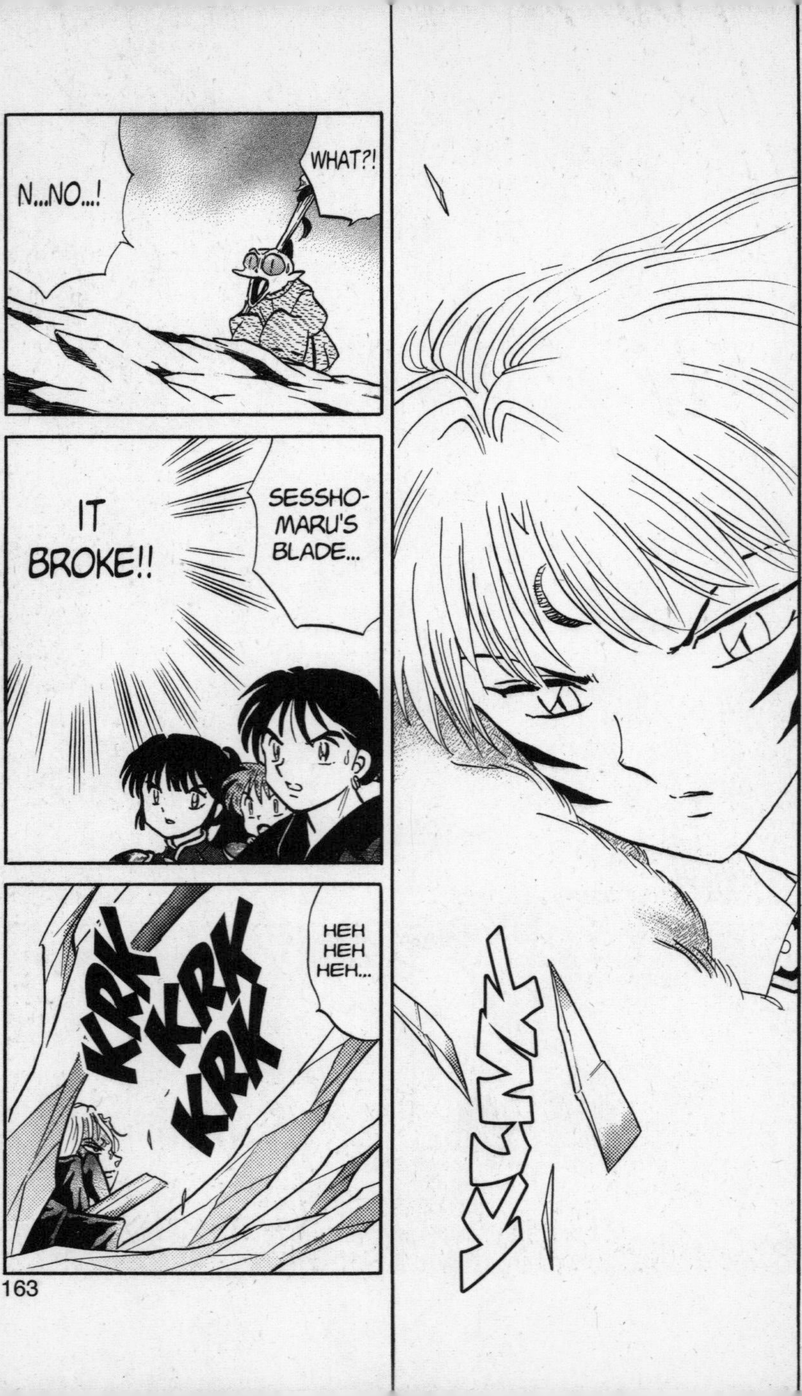
KLINK
WHAT?!
N...NO...!
SESSHO-MARU'S BLADE...
IT BROKE!!
HEH HEH HEH...
KRK KRK KRK

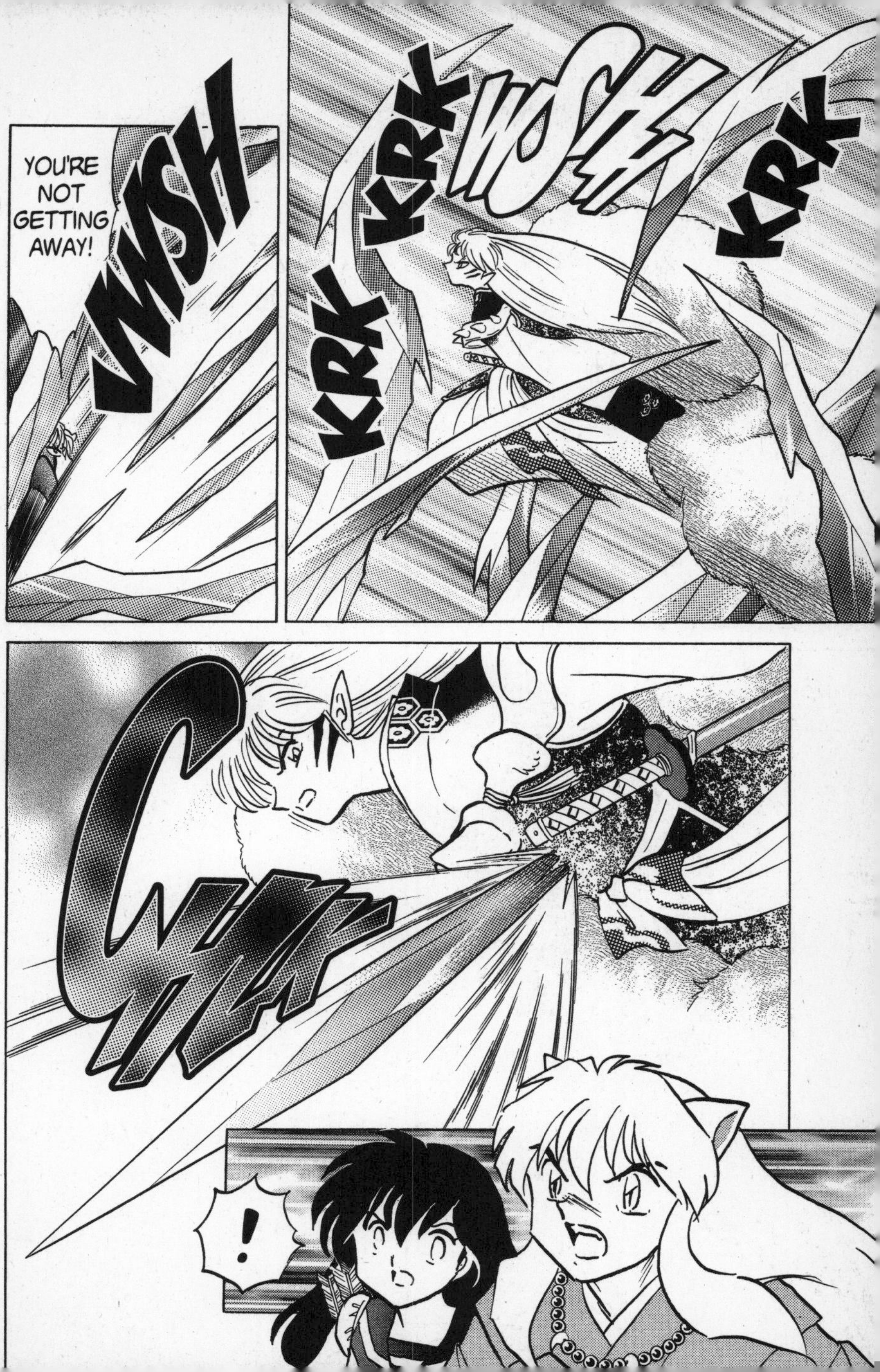
KRK
WOSH
KRK
KRK
VWSH
YOU'RE NOT GETTING AWAY!
GSHK
!

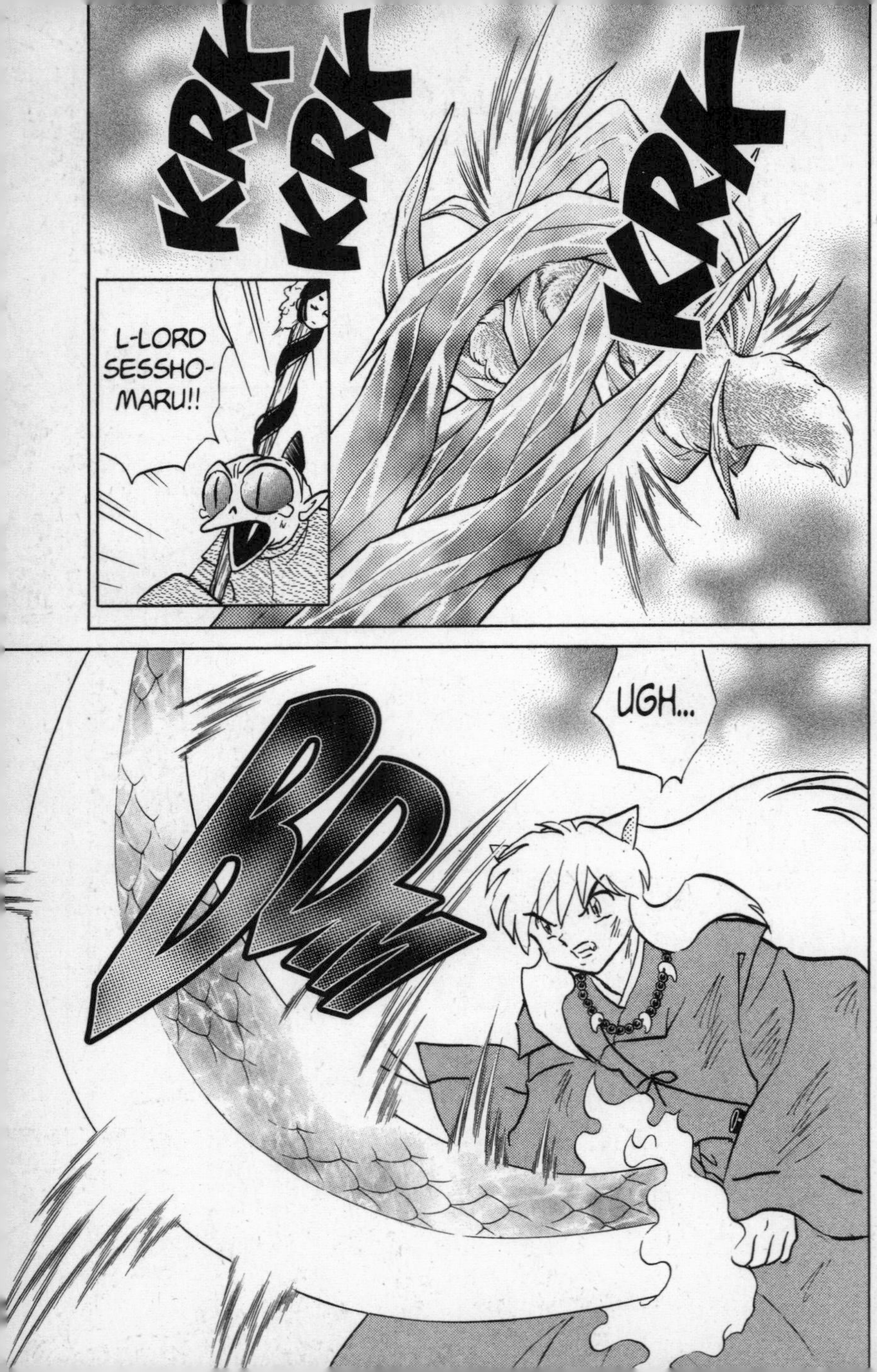
KRK KRK KRK
L-LORD SESSHO-MARU!!
UGH...
BRRM

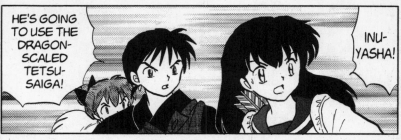

INU-YASHA!
HE'S GOING TO USE THE DRAGON-SCALED TETSU-SAIGA!
YOU CAN'T USE IT YET, INUYASHA!
YOU'LL BE HIT WITH AN ENERGY BACKLASH! YOU'LL GET HURT!
FEH!
NOW'S AS GOOD A TIME AS ANY!
VWSH
ANYWAY...
...IF SESSHOMARU GETS KILLED BY *MY* DIAMOND SPEARS...
...EERK
...IT'LL LEAVE A BAD TASTE IN MY MOUTH FOREVER!

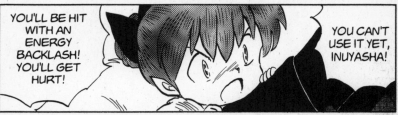

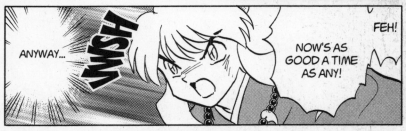

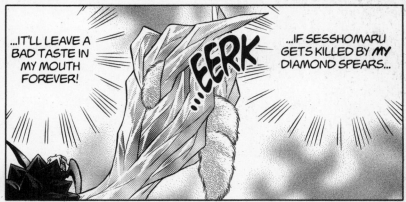

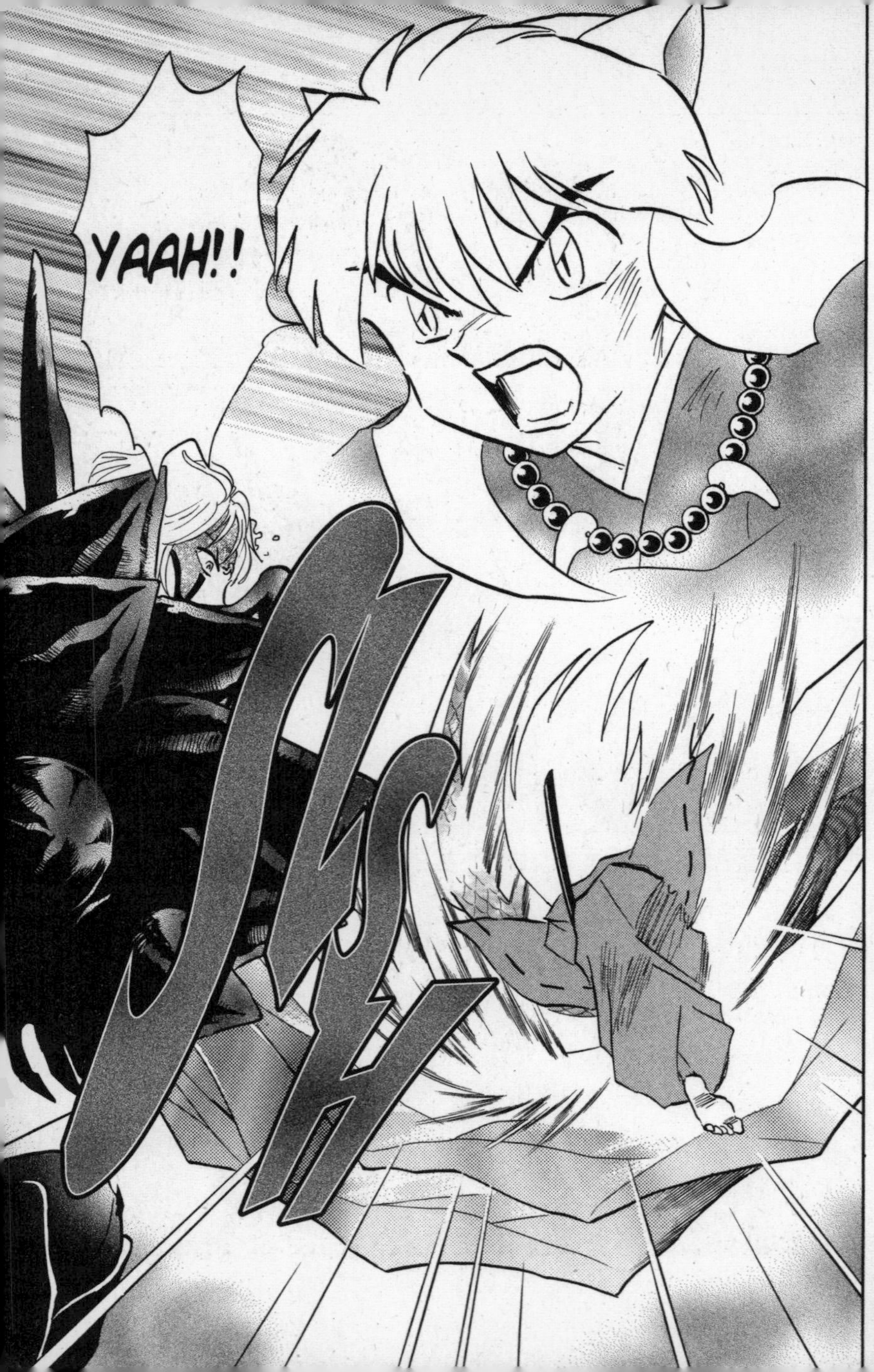
YAAH!!
SLASH

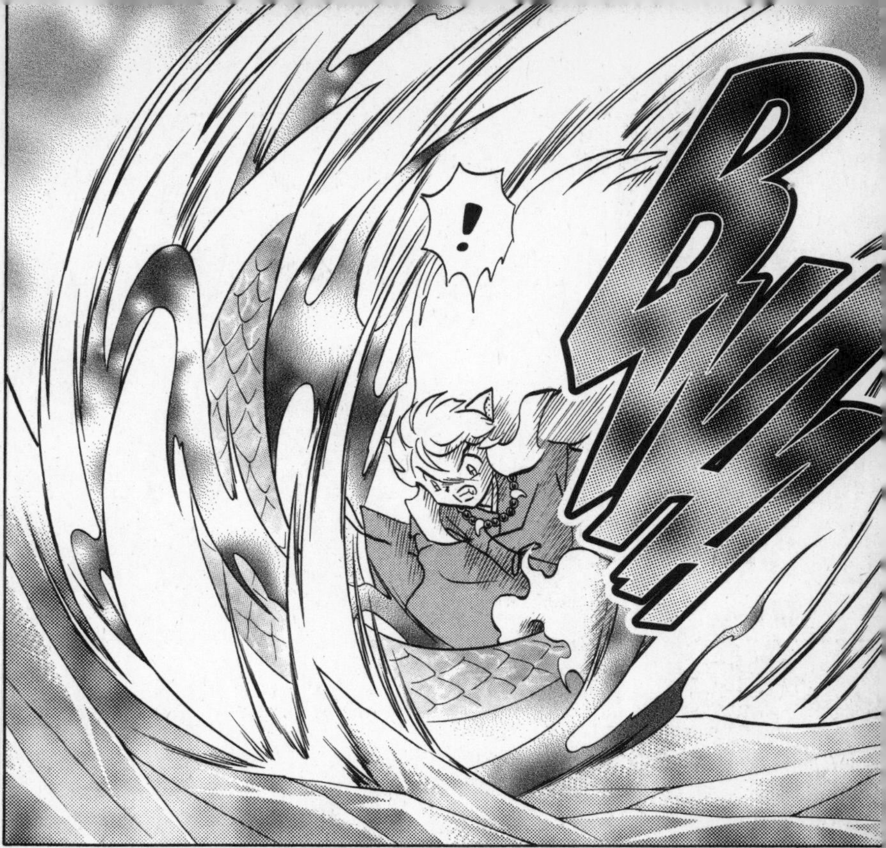
!
BA
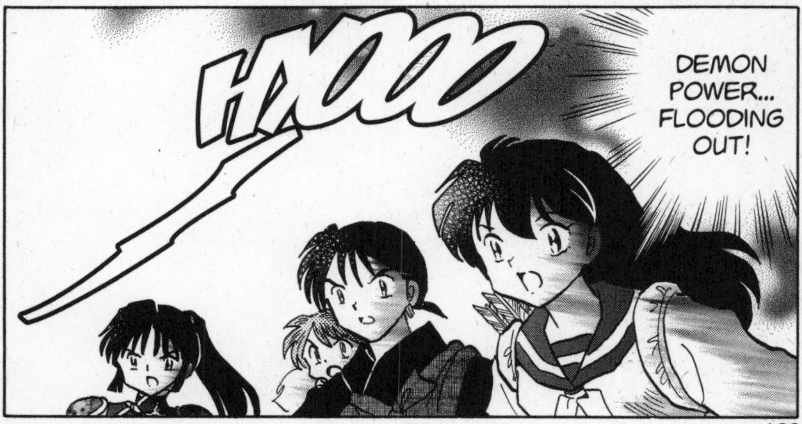
HOOO
DEMON POWER... FLOODING OUT!

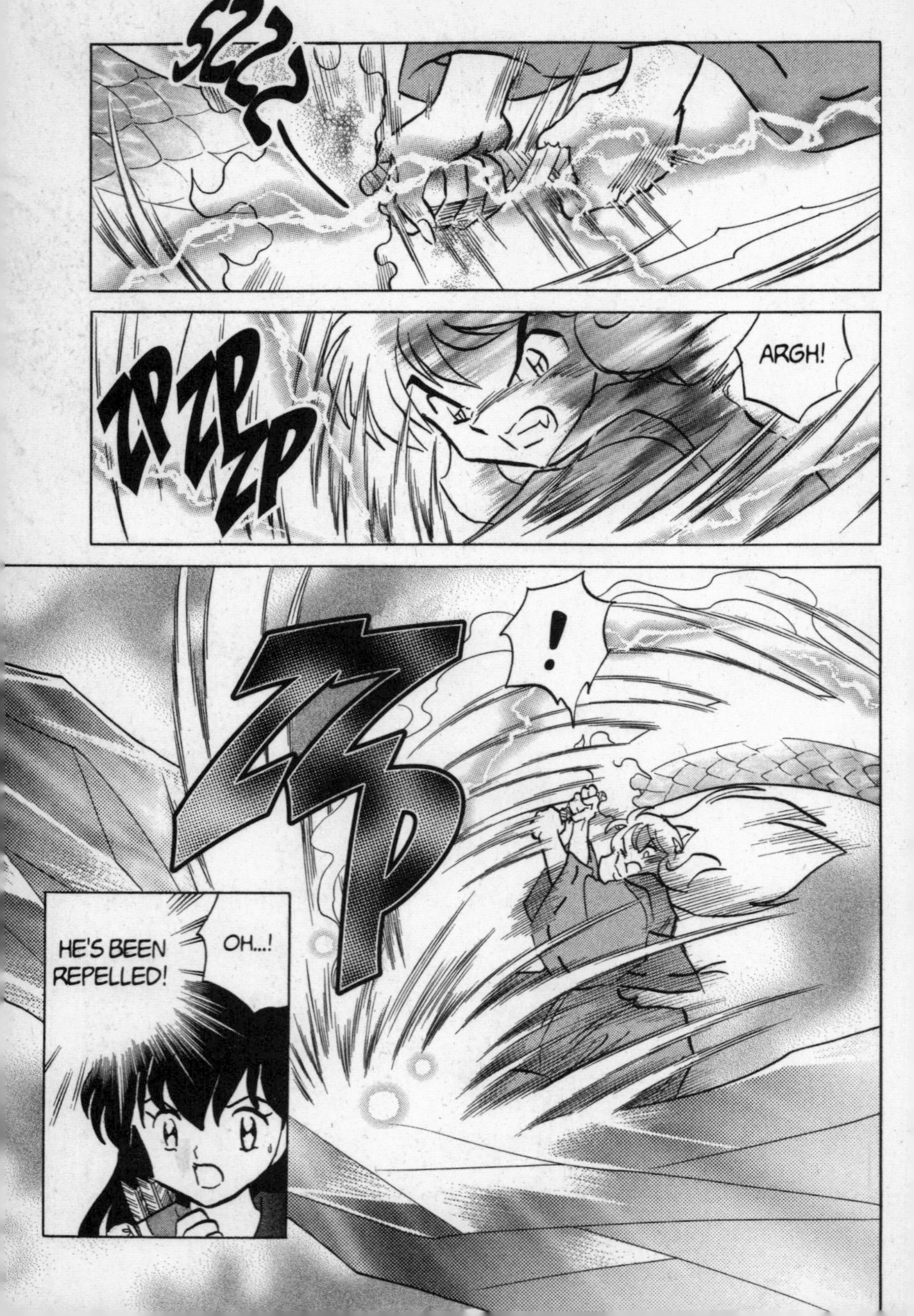
SZZZ
ARGH!
ZP ZP ZP
!
ZZP
OH...!
HE'S BEEN REPELLED!

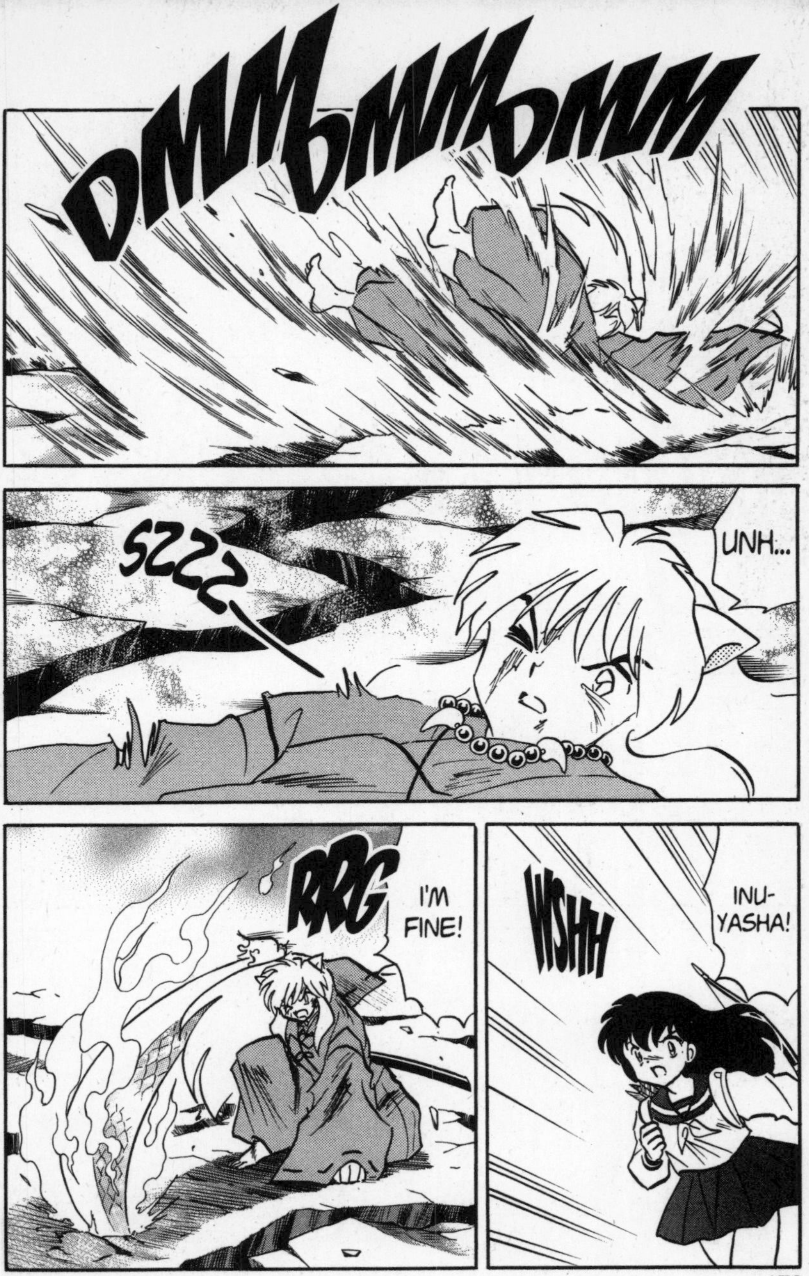
DMMDMMDMM
UNH...
SZZZ
INU-
YASHA!
WSHH
I'M
FINE!
RRG

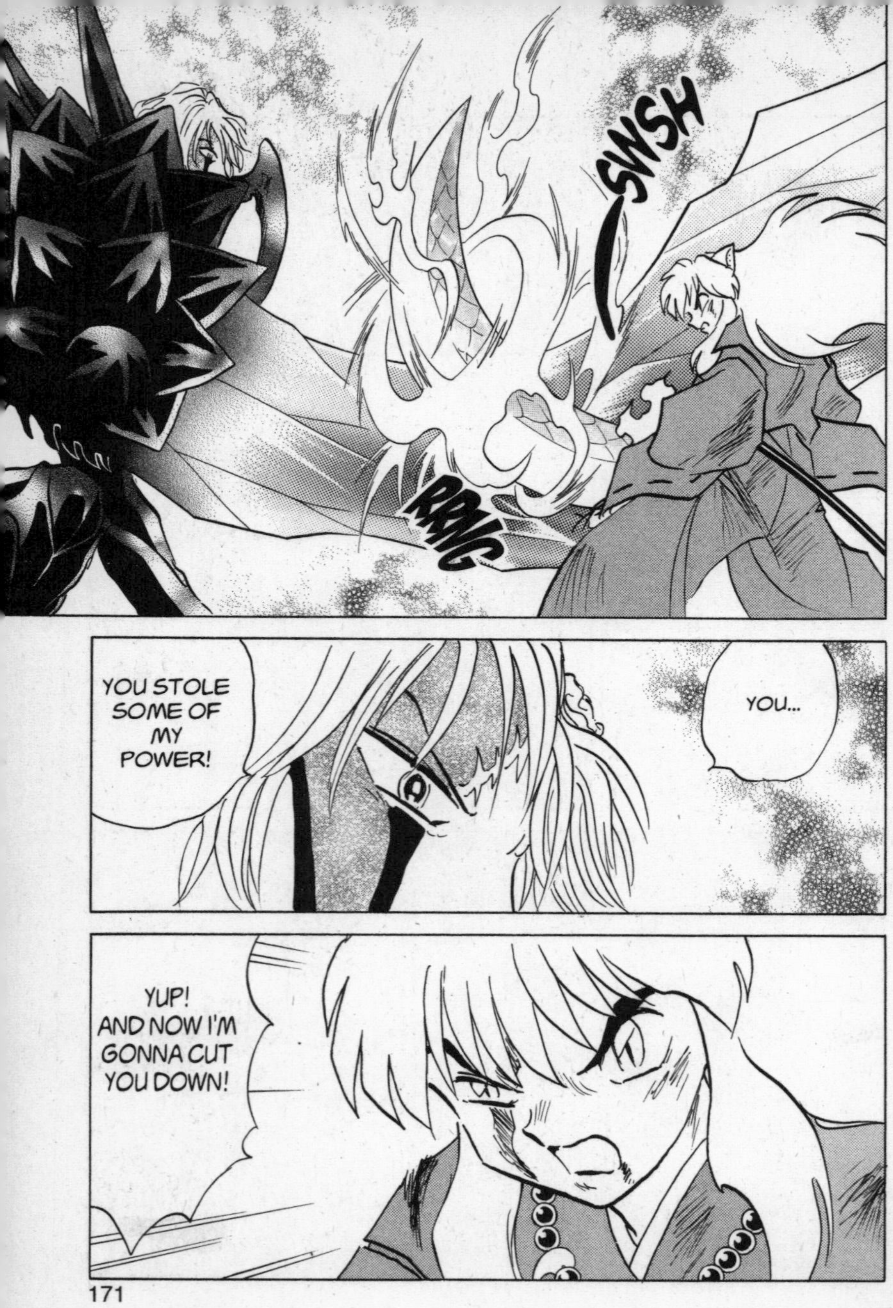
SWSH
RRING
YOU...
YOU STOLE SOME OF MY POWER!
YUP! AND NOW I'M GONNA CUT YOU DOWN!

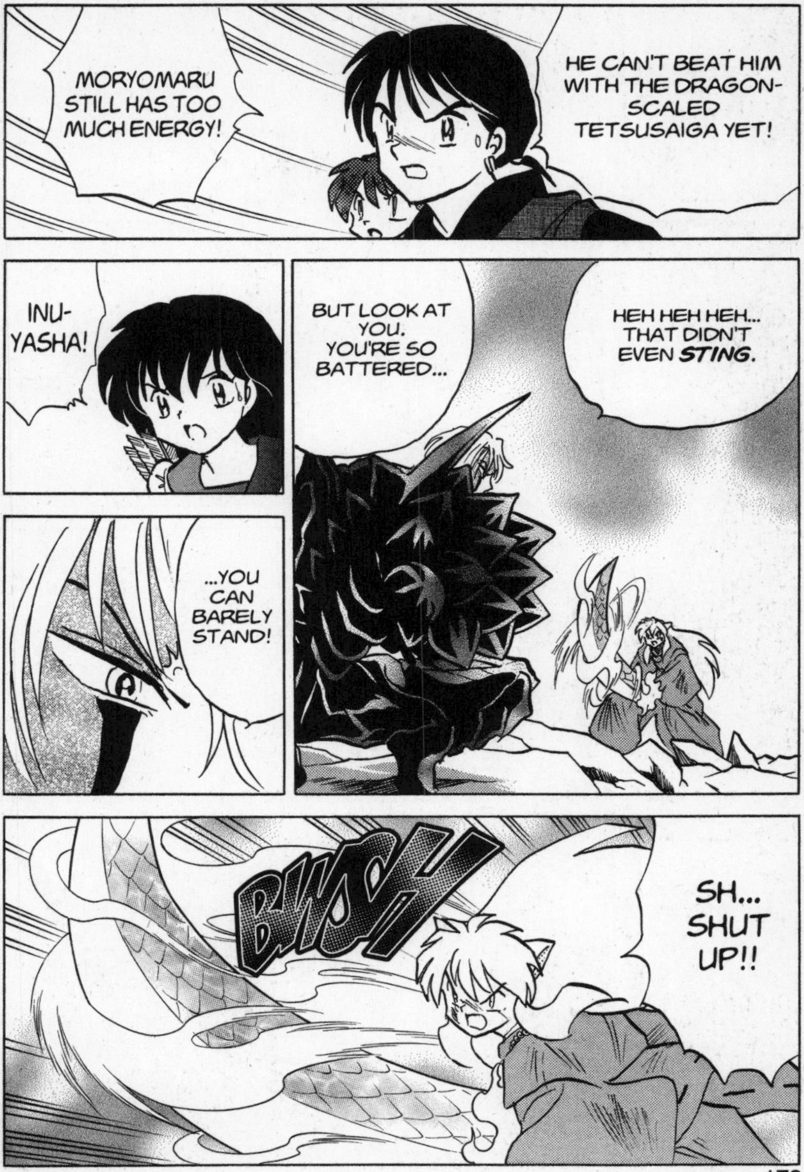
HE CAN'T BEAT HIM WITH THE DRAGON-SCALED TETSUSAIGA YET!
MORYOMARU STILL HAS TOO MUCH ENERGY!
HEH HEH HEH... THAT DIDN'T EVEN **STING**.
BUT LOOK AT YOU. YOU'RE SO BATTERED...
INU-YASHA!
...YOU CAN BARELY STAND!
SH... SHUT UP!!
BWOSH

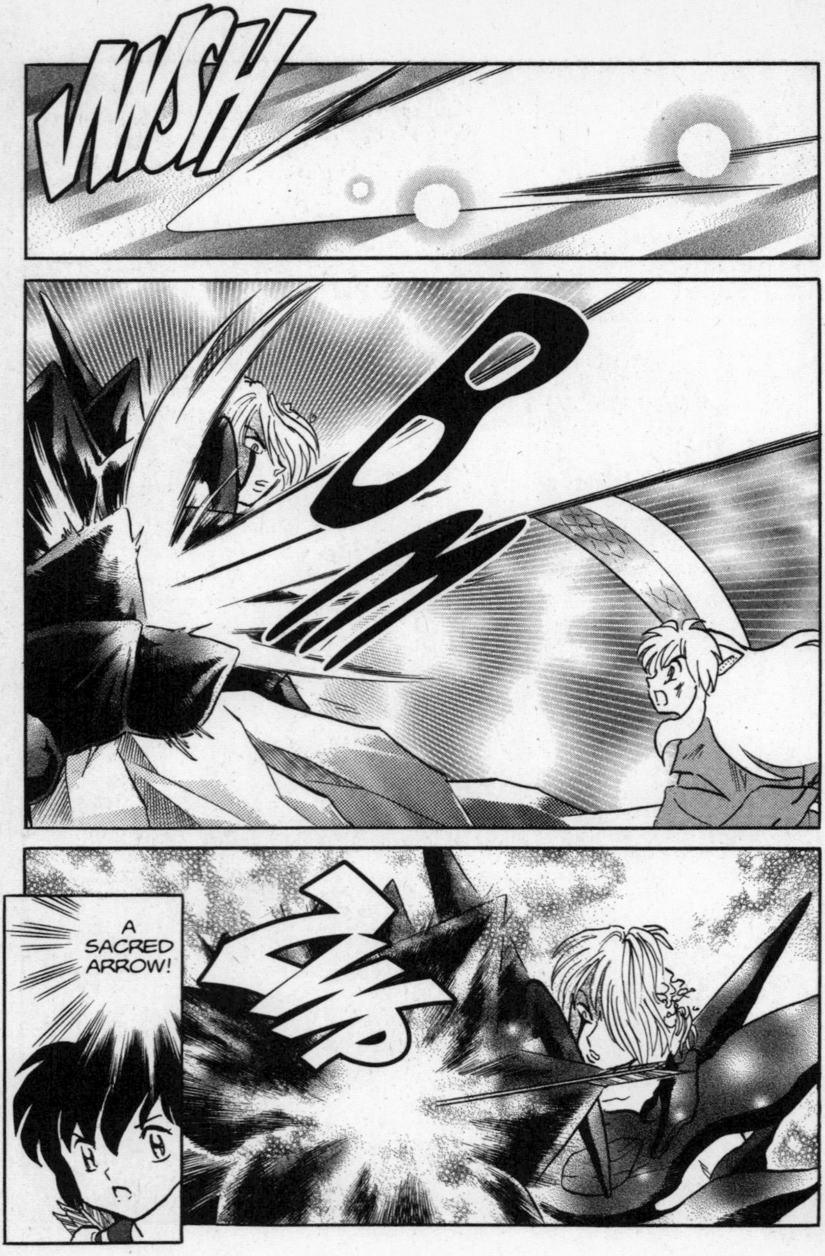
VWSH
BOM
ZWIP
A SACRED ARROW!

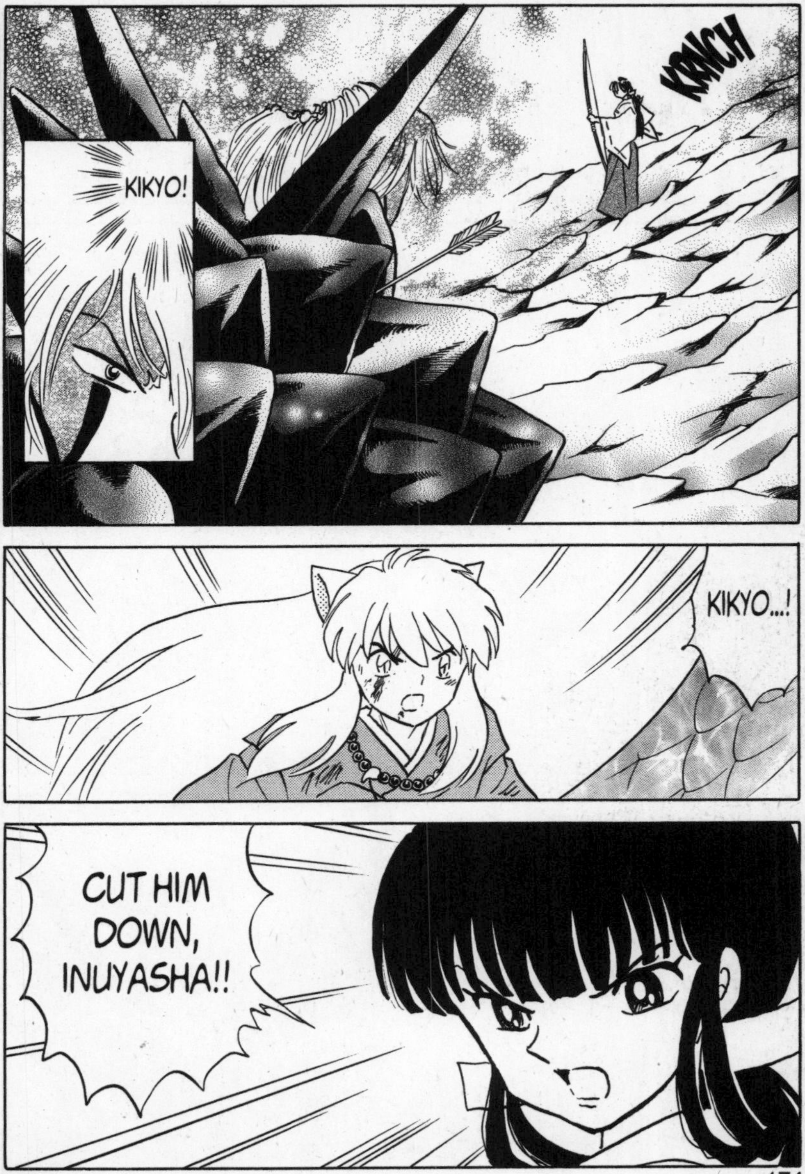
KRNCH
KIKYO!
KIKYO...!
CUT HIM DOWN, INUYASHA!!

SCROLL 10

FLIGHT

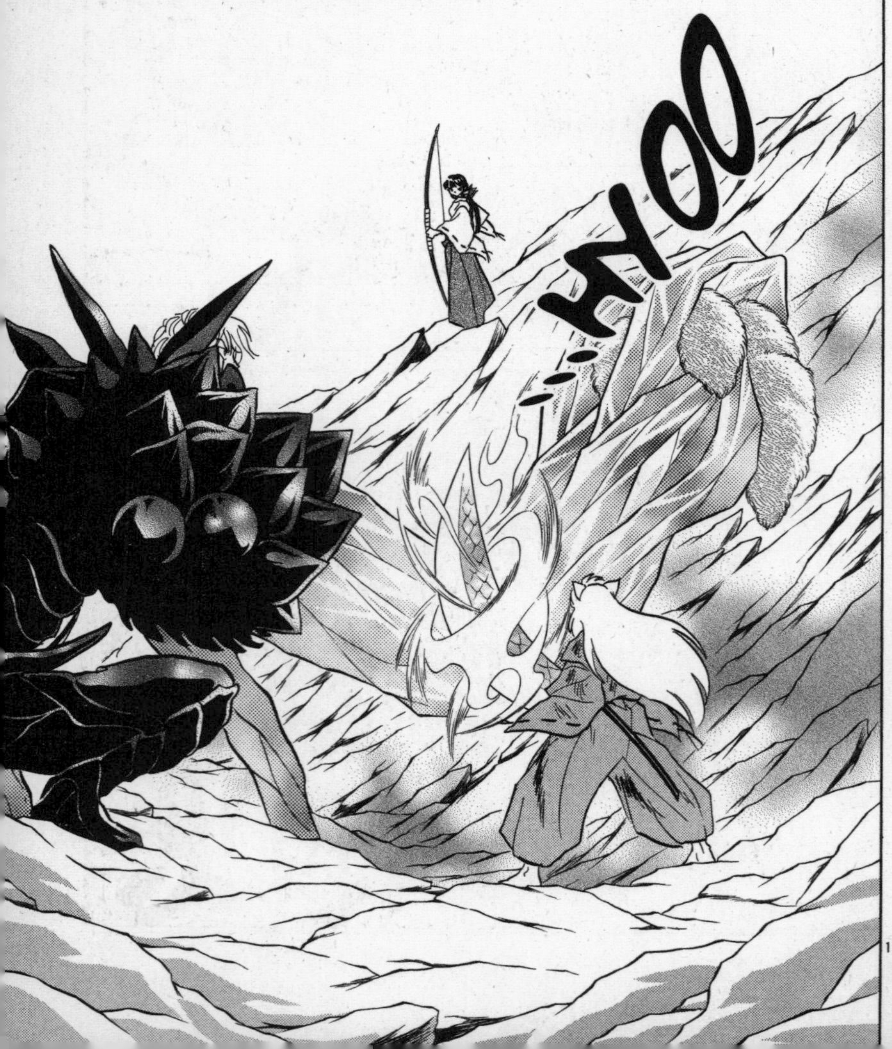
...HYOO

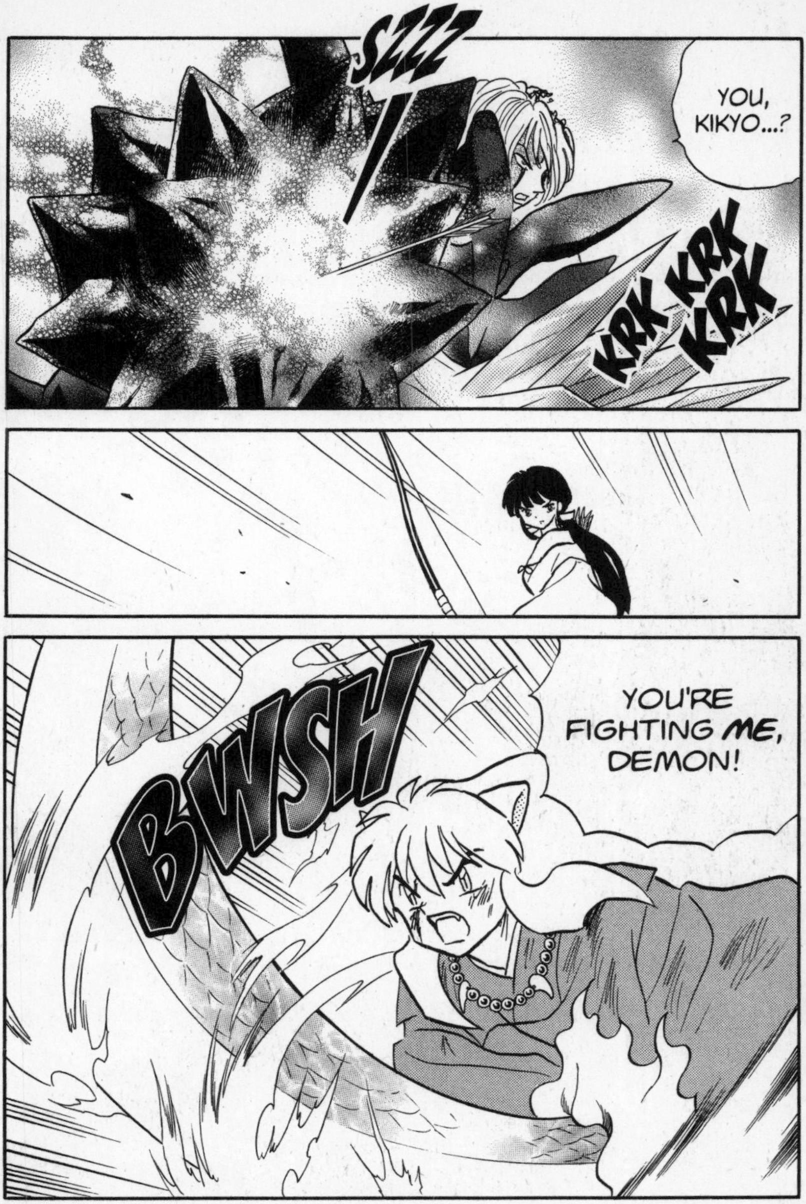
SZZZ
YOU, KIKYO...?
KRK KRK KRK
BWSH
YOU'RE FIGHTING *ME*, DEMON!

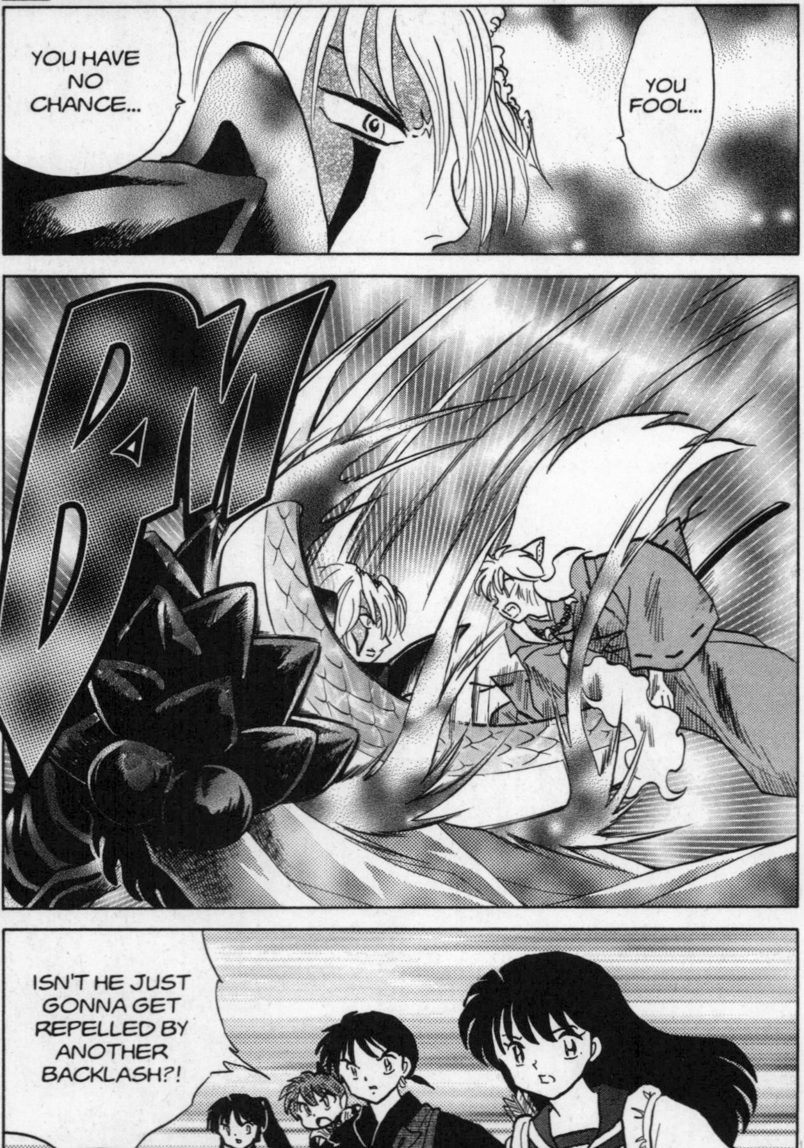
YOU FOOL...
YOU HAVE NO CHANCE...
BAM
ISN'T HE JUST GONNA GET REPELLED BY ANOTHER BACKLASH?!

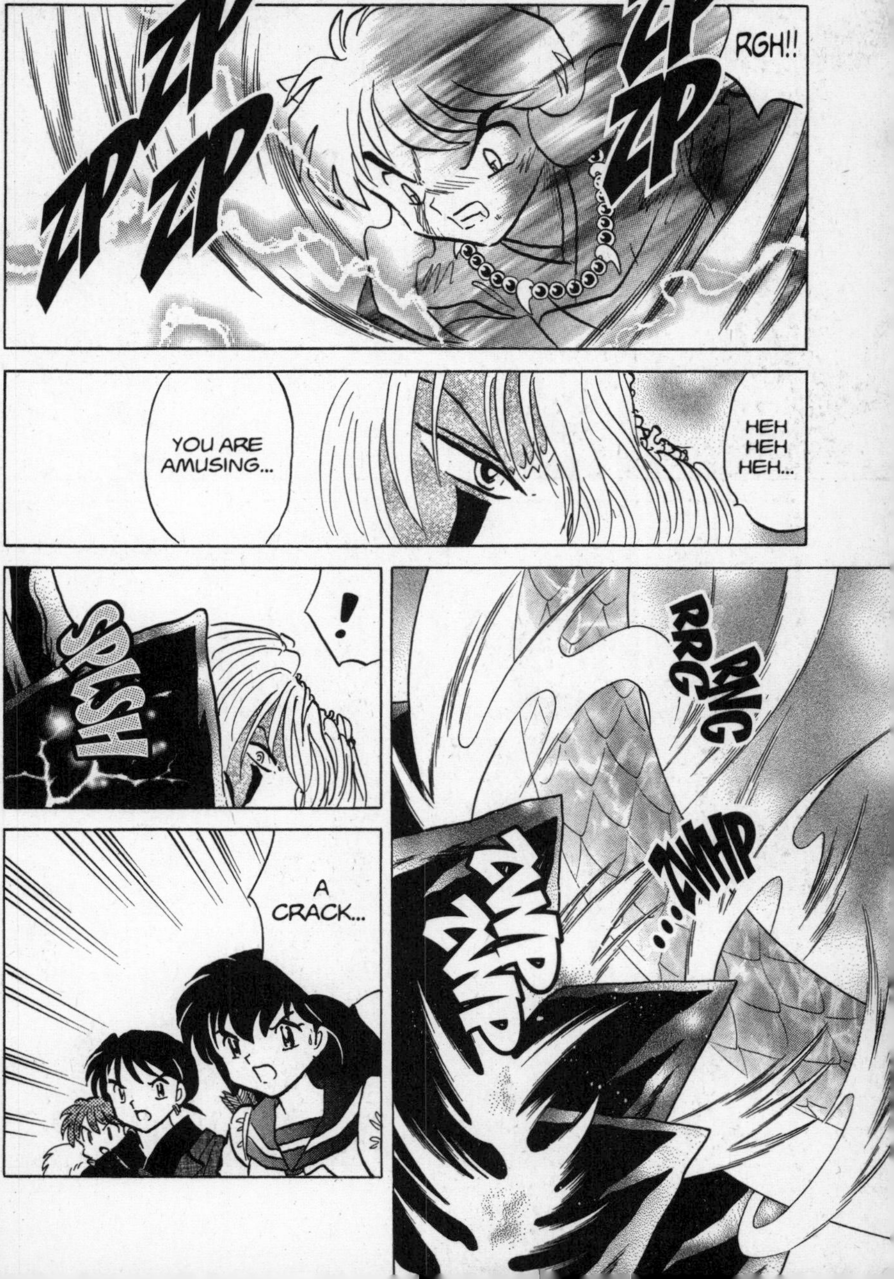
RGH!!
ZP ZP
ZP ZP ZP ZP
HEH HEH HEH...
YOU ARE AMUSING...
RRG RNG
...ZWHP
ZWP ZWP
!
SPLSH
A CRACK...

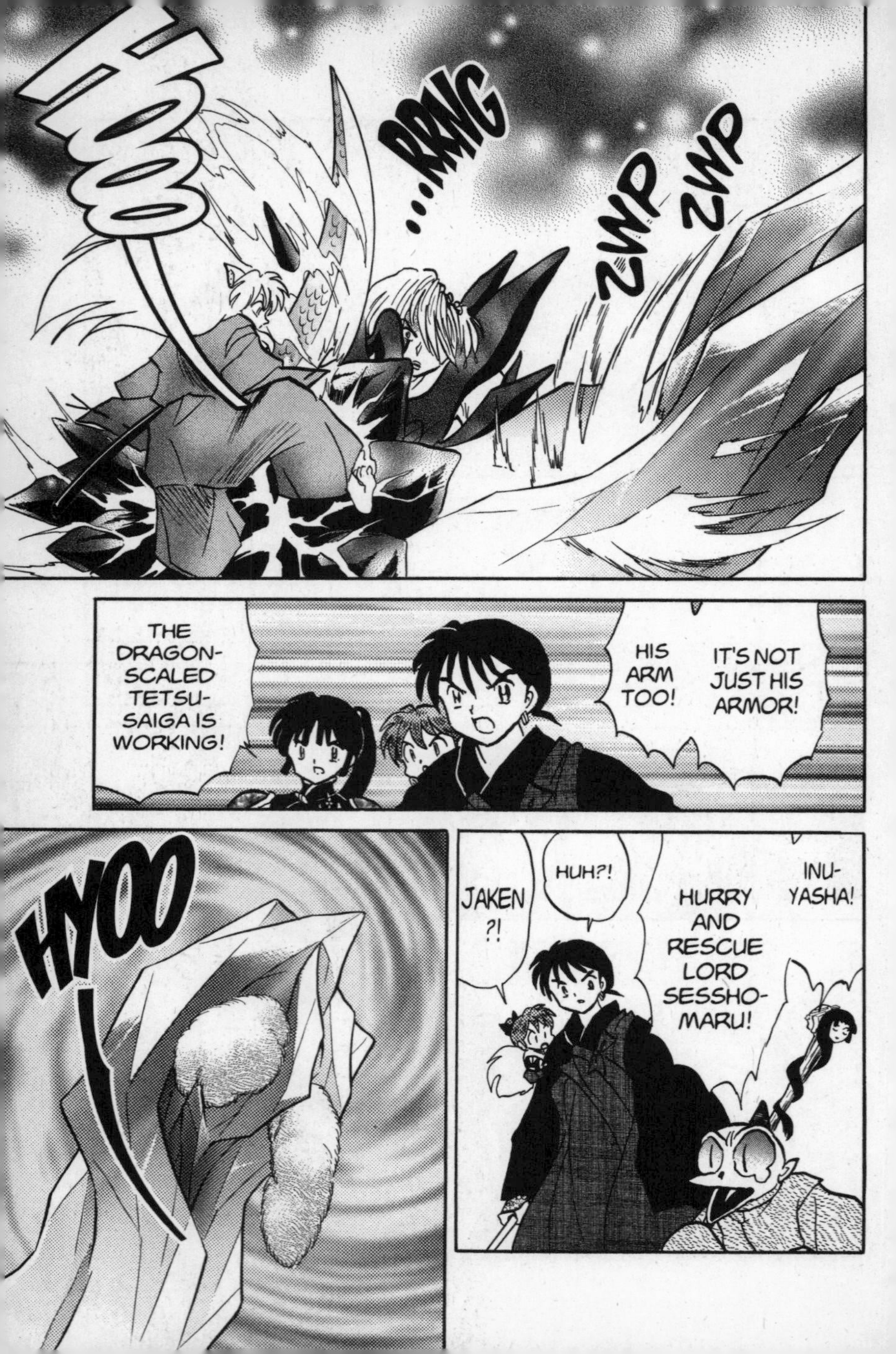
ZWP
ZWP
...RRNG
HOOO
IT'S NOT JUST HIS ARMOR!
HIS ARM TOO!
THE DRAGON-SCALED TETSU-SAIGA IS WORKING!
INU-YASHA!
HURRY AND RESCUE LORD SESSHO-MARU!
HUH?!
JAKEN ?!
HYOO

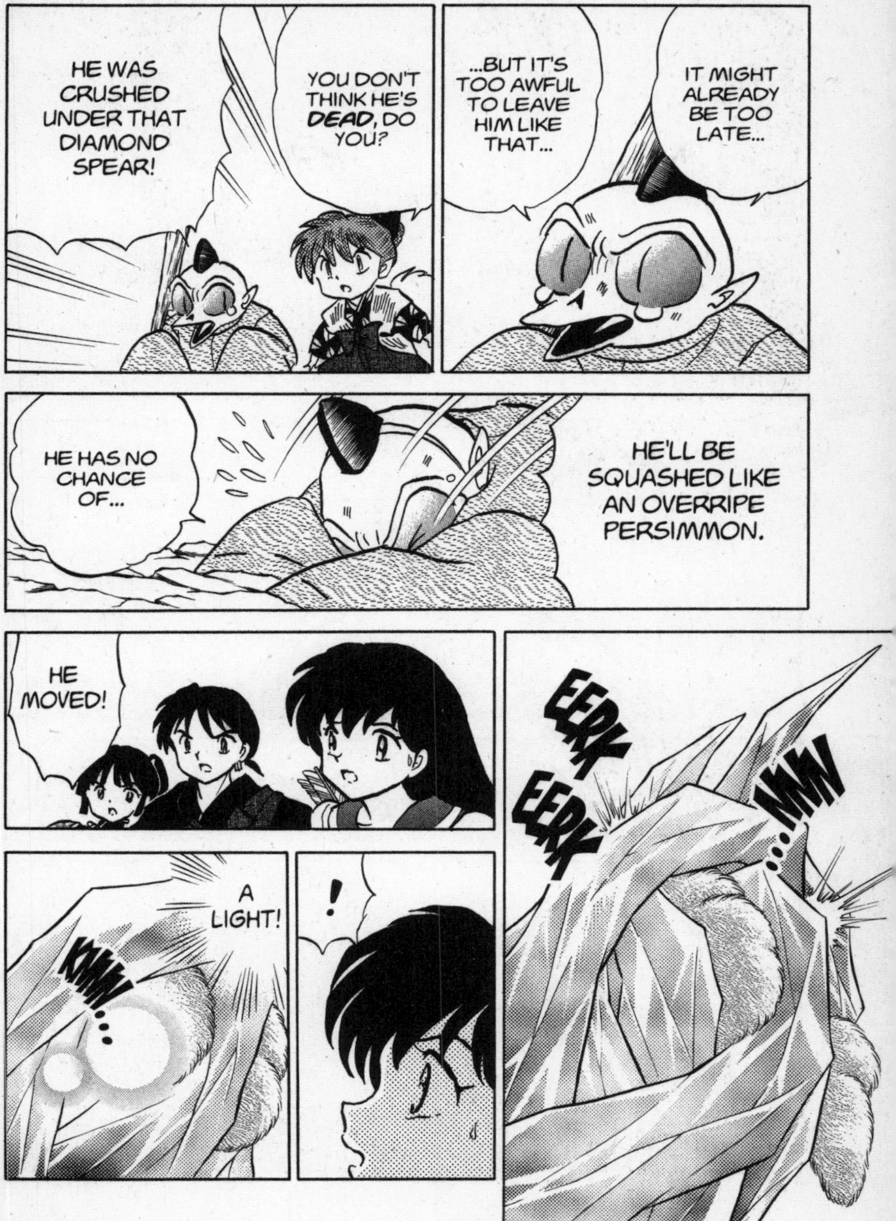
HE WAS CRUSHED UNDER THAT DIAMOND SPEAR!
YOU DON'T THINK HE'S *DEAD*, DO YOU?
IT MIGHT ALREADY BE TOO LATE...
...BUT IT'S TOO AWFUL TO LEAVE HIM LIKE THAT...
HE HAS NO CHANCE OF...
HE'LL BE SQUASHED LIKE AN OVERRIPE PERSIMMON.
HE MOVED!
A LIGHT!
KMM...
!
EERK EERK
...MMM

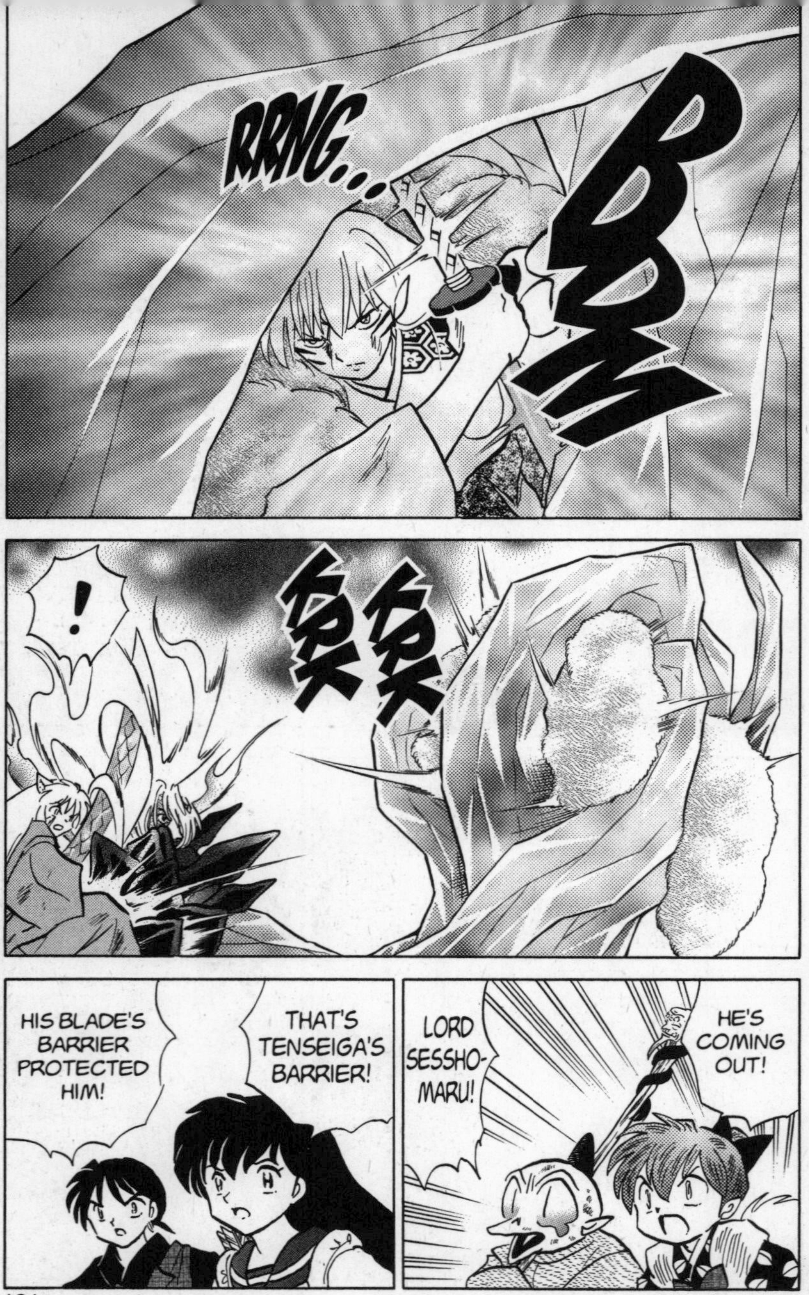
BDM
RRNG...
KRK KRK
!
HE'S COMING OUT!
LORD SESSHO-MARU!
THAT'S TENSEIGA'S BARRIER!
HIS BLADE'S BARRIER PROTECTED HIM!

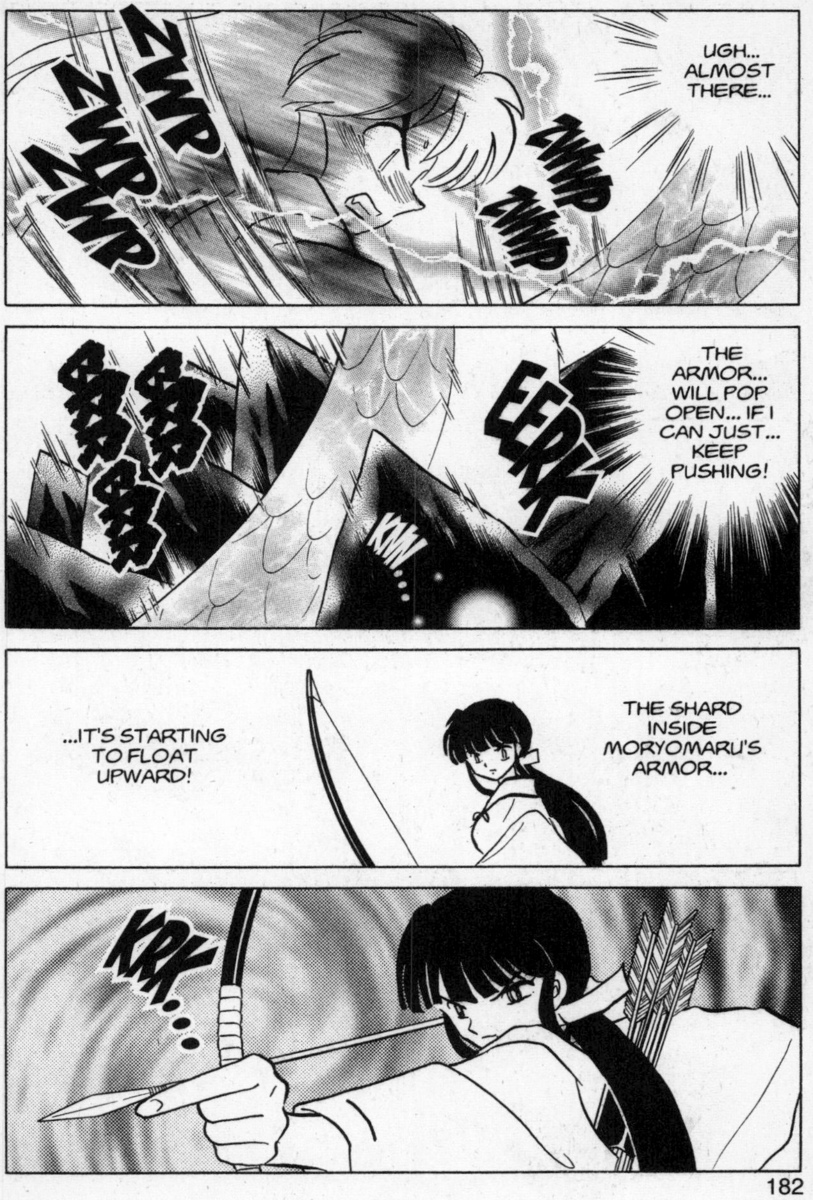
UGH... ALMOST THERE...
ZWMP ZWMP
ZWP ZWP ZWP
THE ARMOR... WILL POP OPEN... IF I CAN JUST... KEEP PUSHING!
EERK
KNN...
THE SHARD INSIDE MORYOMARU'S ARMOR...
...IT'S STARTING TO FLOAT UPWARD!
KRK...

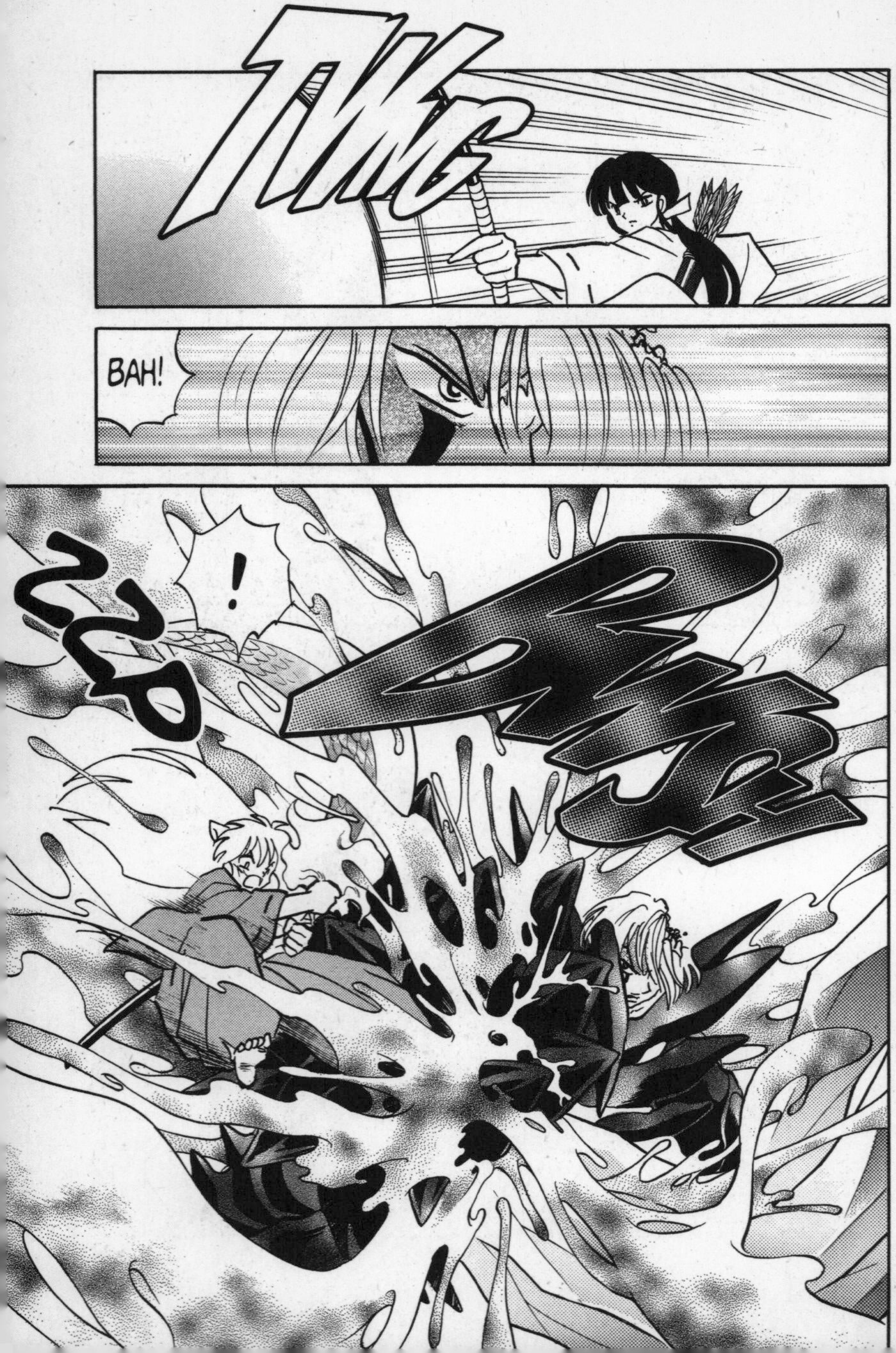
TWNG
BAH!
!
ZZZAP
SHHHK

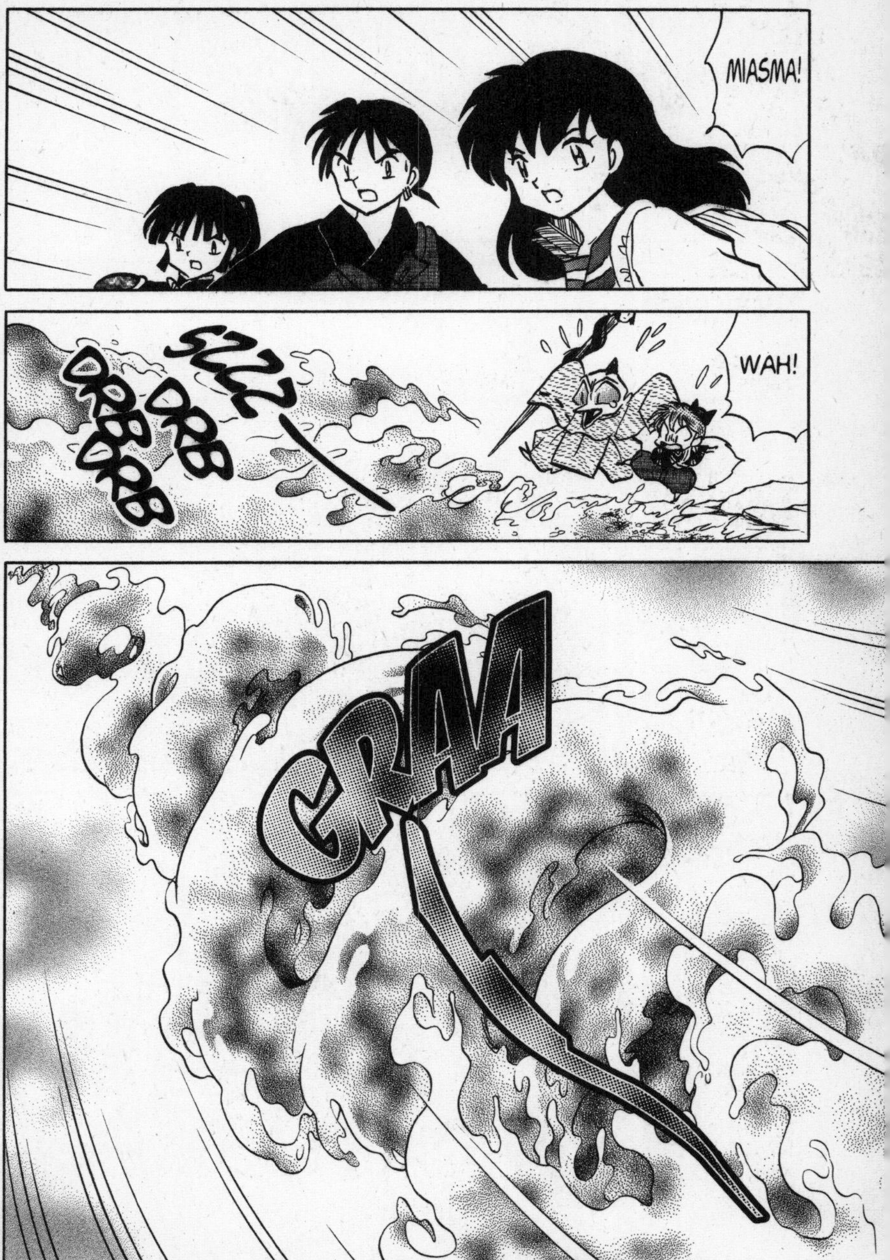
MIASMA!
WAH!
SZZZ
DRB
DRBDRB
CRAA

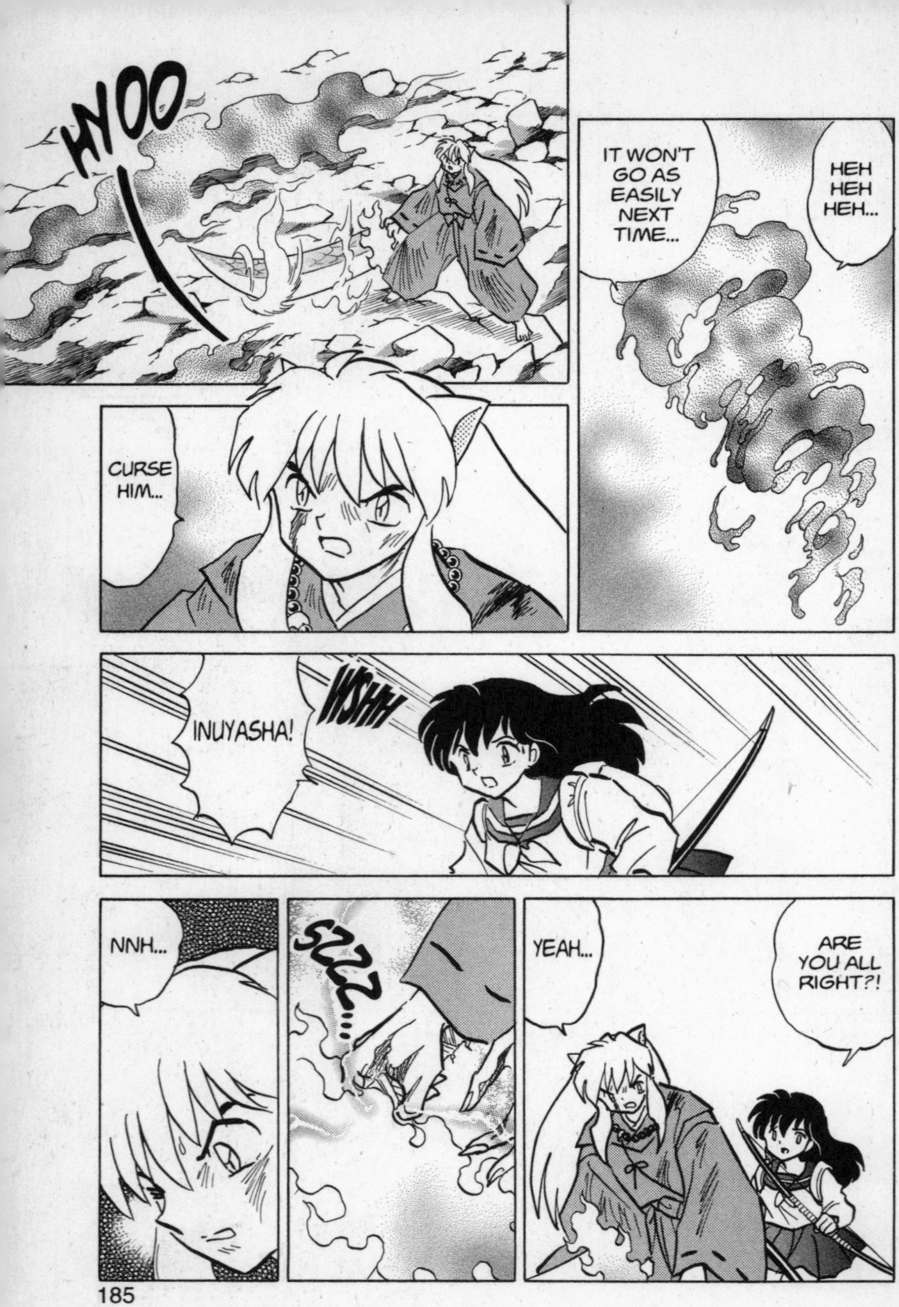
HEH HEH HEH...
IT WON'T GO AS EASILY NEXT TIME...
HYOO
CURSE HIM...
WHSHH
INUYASHA!
ARE YOU ALL RIGHT?!
YEAH...
SZZZ...
NNH...

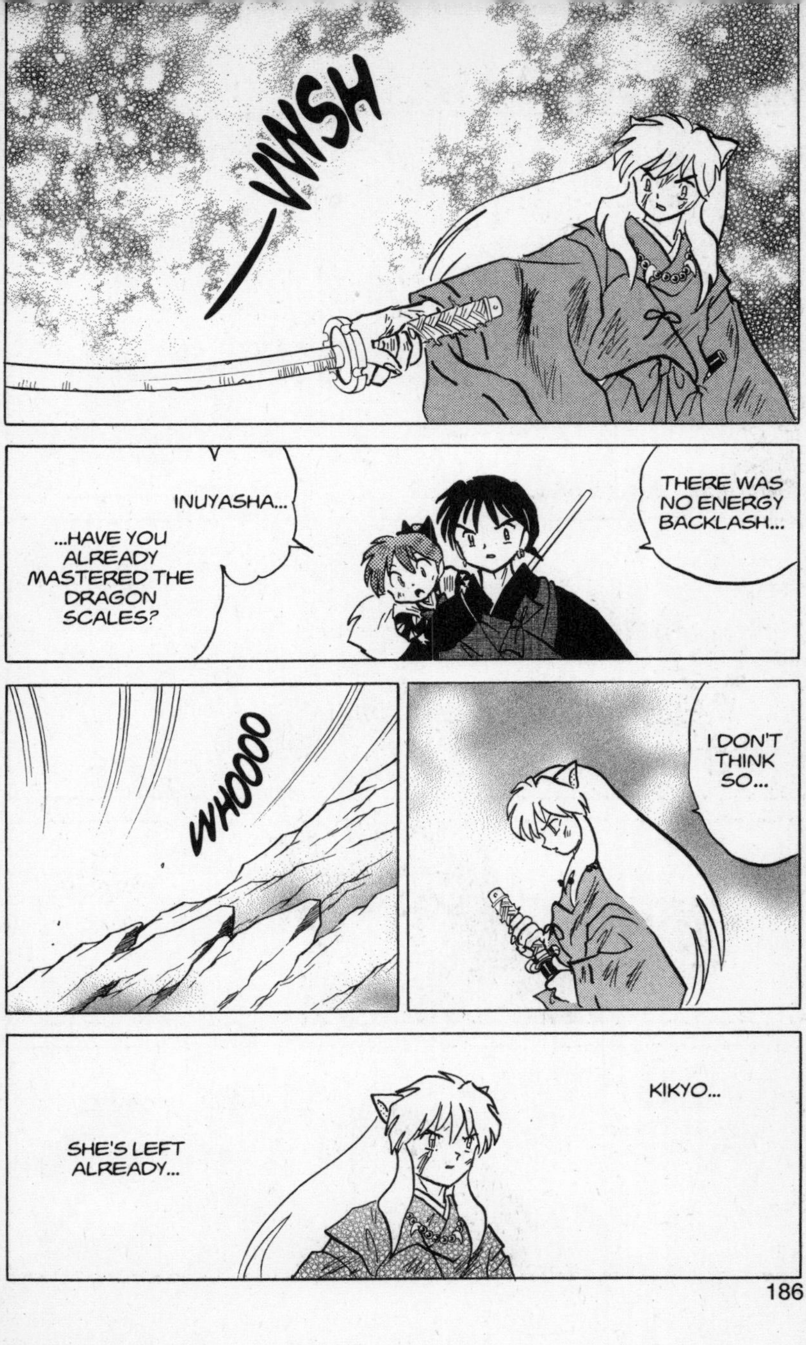
VWSH
THERE WAS NO ENERGY BACKLASH...
INUYASHA...
...HAVE YOU ALREADY MASTERED THE DRAGON SCALES?
I DON'T THINK SO...
WHOOOO
KIKYO...
SHE'S LEFT ALREADY...

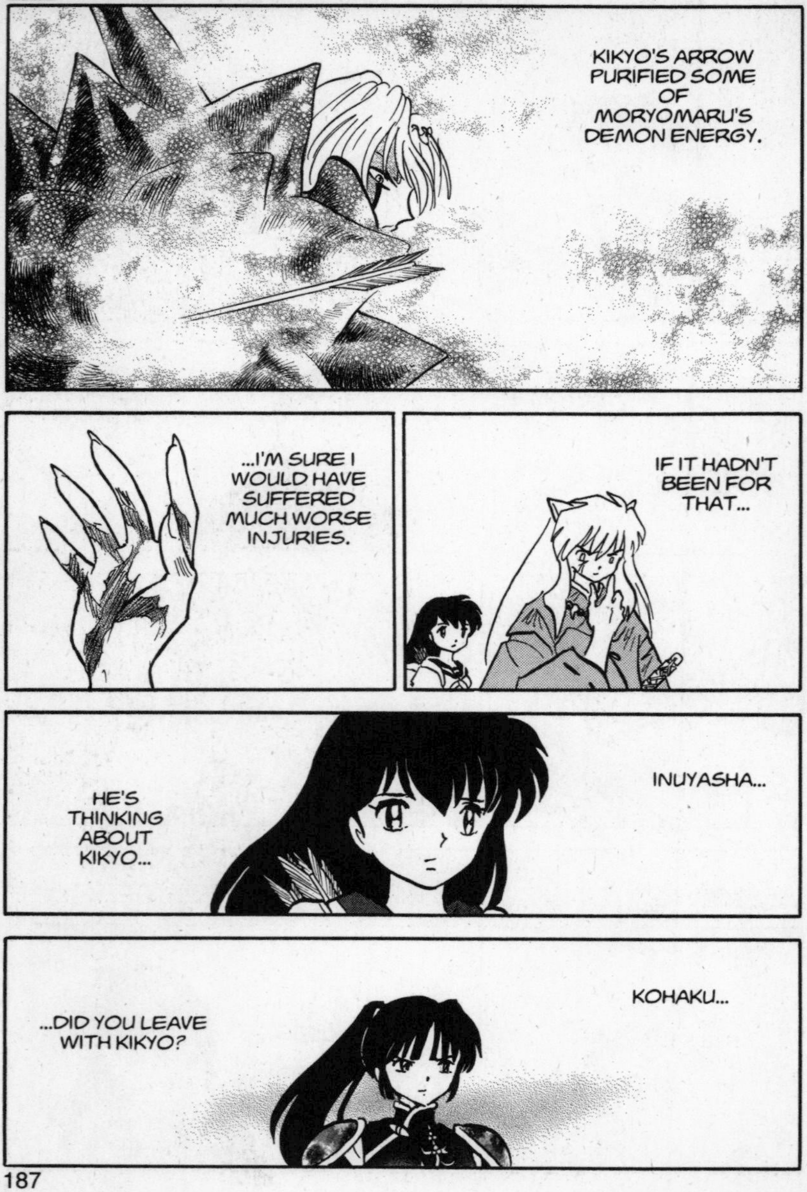
KIKYO'S ARROW PURIFIED SOME OF MORYOMARU'S DEMON ENERGY.
IF IT HADN'T BEEN FOR THAT...
...I'M SURE I WOULD HAVE SUFFERED MUCH WORSE INJURIES.
INUYASHA...
HE'S THINKING ABOUT KIKYO...
KOHAKU...
...DID YOU LEAVE WITH KIKYO?

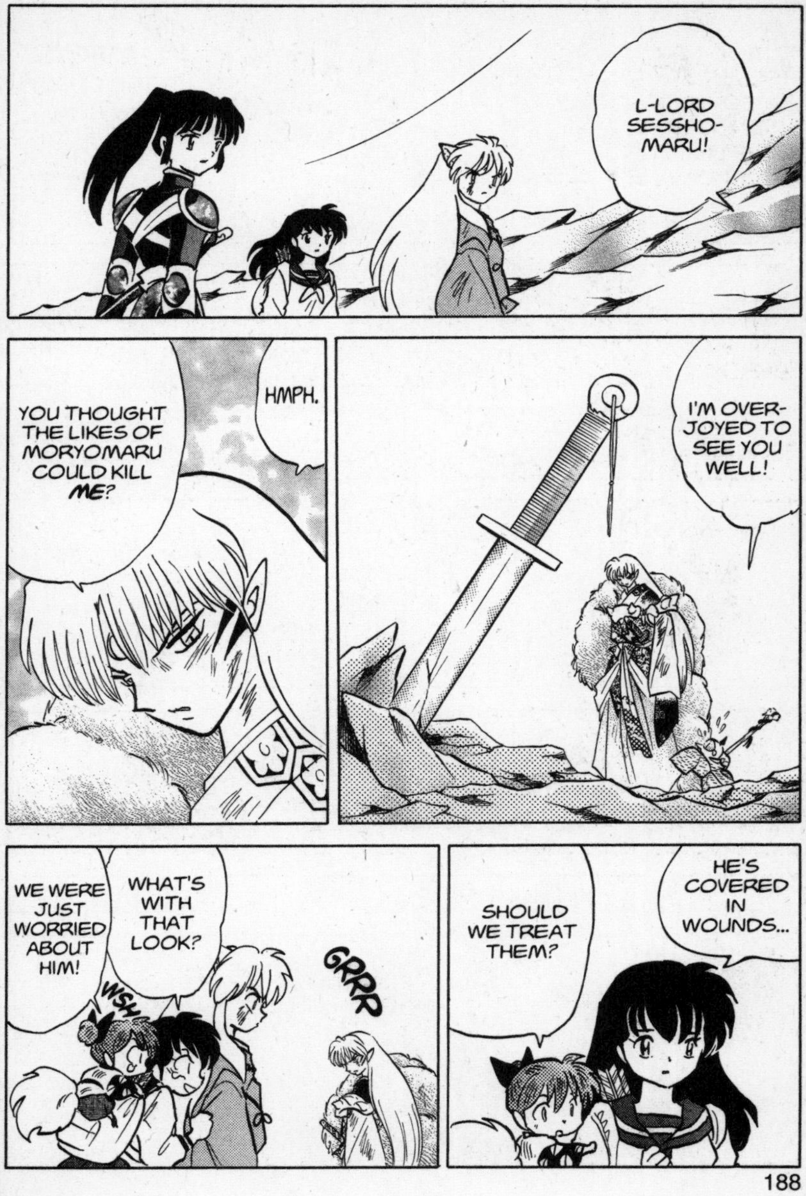
L-LORD SESSHO-MARU!
I'M OVER-JOYED TO SEE YOU WELL!
HMPH.
YOU THOUGHT THE LIKES OF MORYOMARU COULD KILL *ME*?
HE'S COVERED IN WOUNDS...
SHOULD WE TREAT THEM?
GRRR
WHAT'S WITH THAT LOOK?
WE WERE JUST WORRIED ABOUT HIM!
WSH

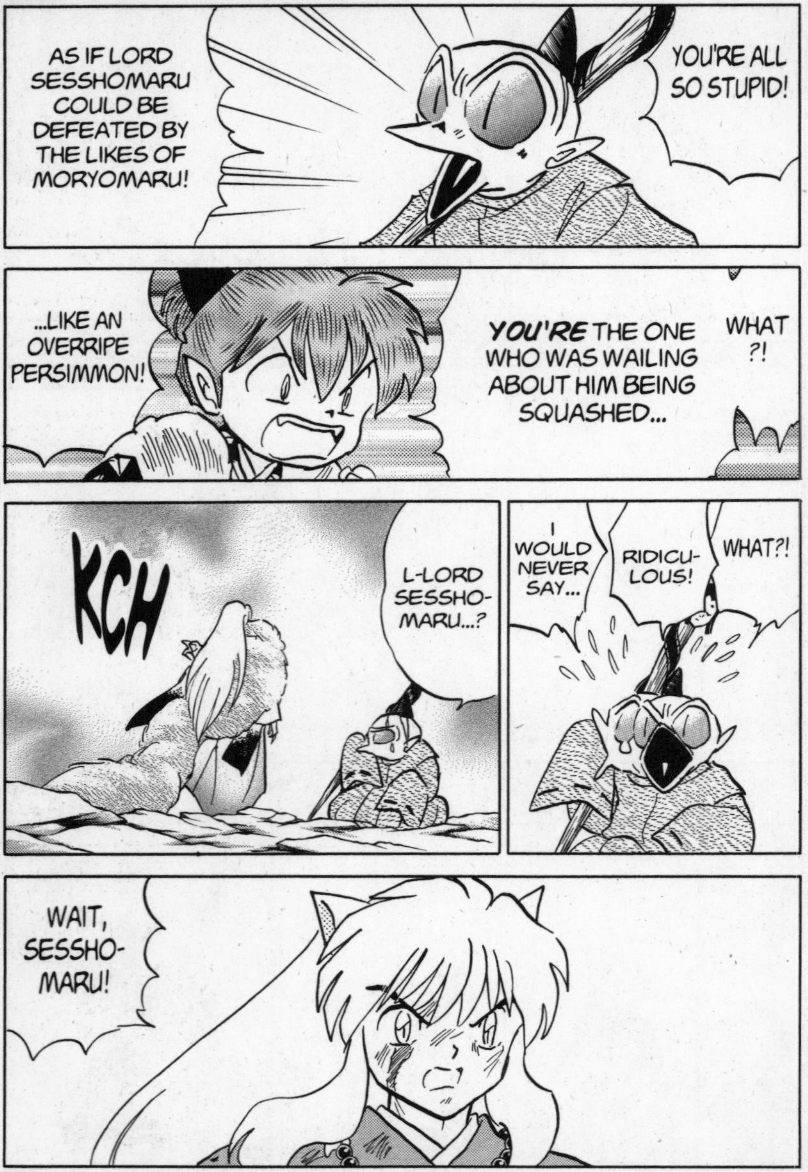
YOU'RE ALL SO STUPID!
AS IF LORD SESSHOMARU COULD BE DEFEATED BY THE LIKES OF MORYOMARU!
WHAT ?!
YOU'RE THE ONE WHO WAS WAILING ABOUT HIM BEING SQUASHED...
...LIKE AN OVERRIPE PERSIMMON!
WHAT?!
RIDICU-LOUS!
I WOULD NEVER SAY...
L-LORD SESSHO-MARU...?
KCH
WAIT, SESSHO-MARU!

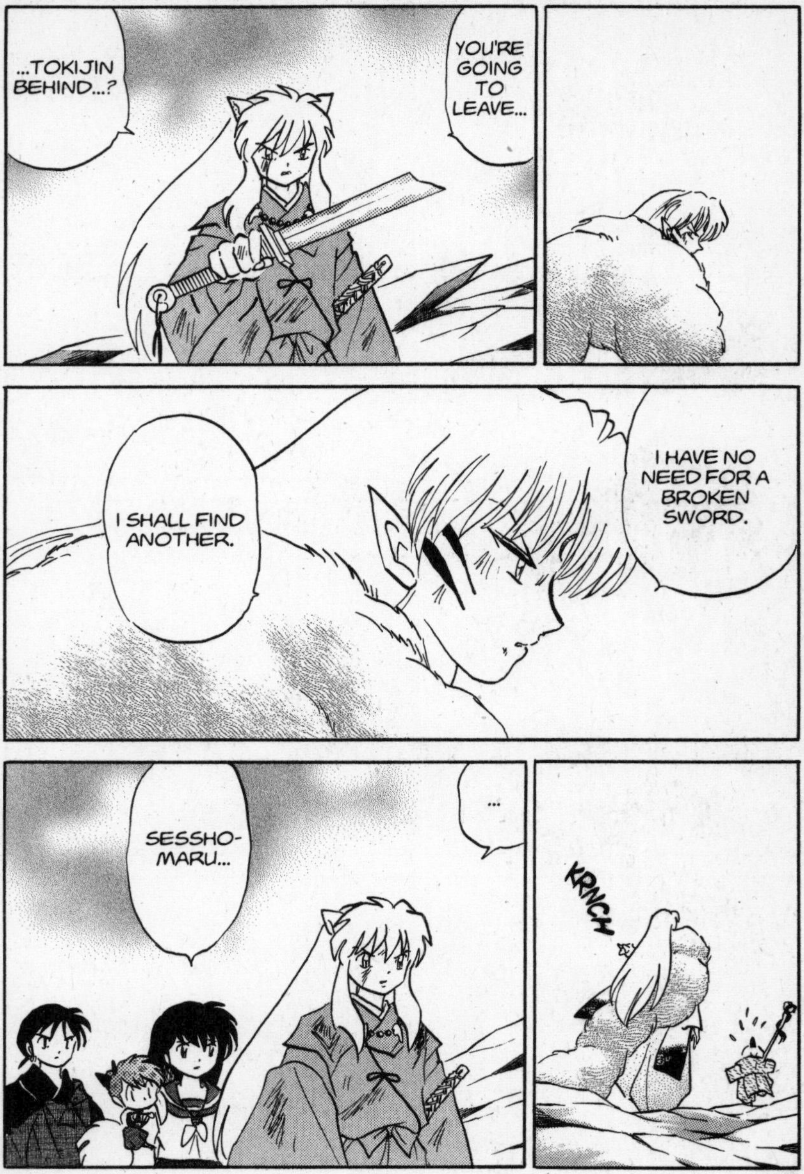
YOU'RE GOING TO LEAVE...
...TOKIJIN BEHIND...?
I HAVE NO NEED FOR A BROKEN SWORD.
I SHALL FIND ANOTHER.
KRNCH
...
SESSHO-MARU...

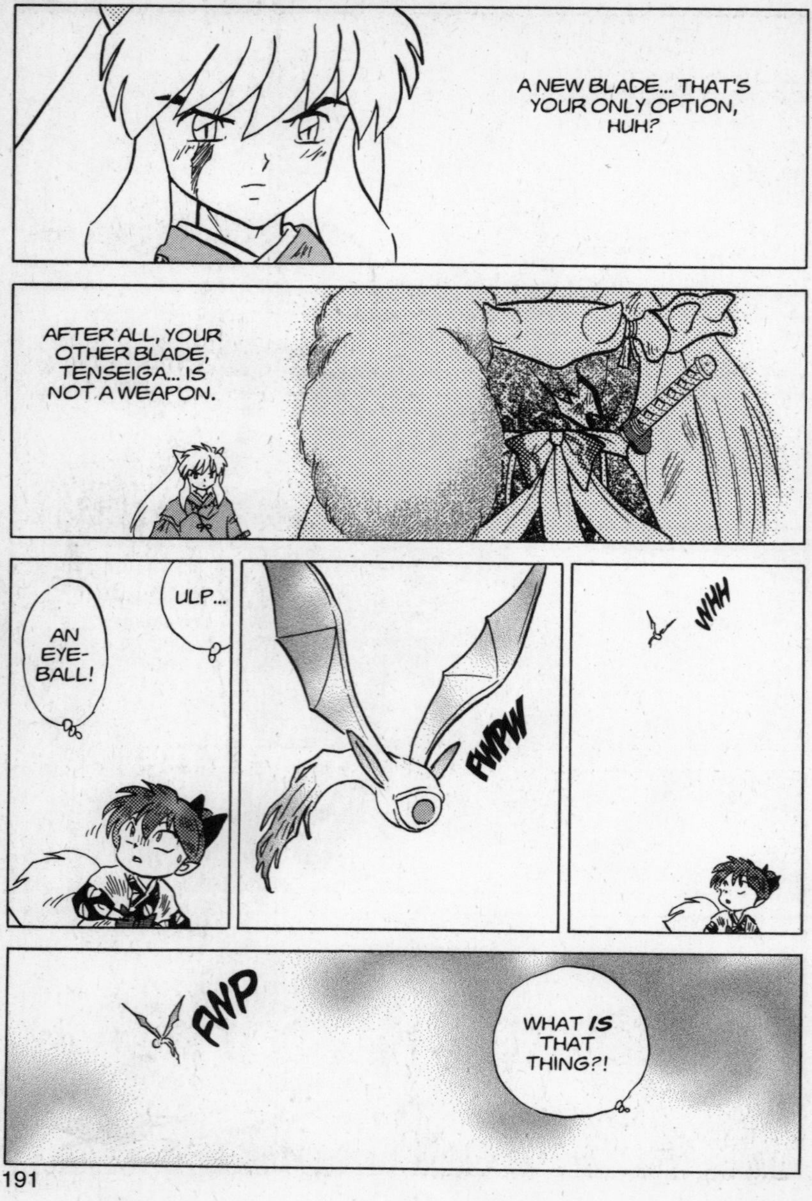
A NEW BLADE... THAT'S YOUR ONLY OPTION, HUH?
AFTER ALL, YOUR OTHER BLADE, TENSEIGA... IS NOT A WEAPON.
WHH
FWPW
ULP...
AN EYE-BALL!
WHAT IS THAT THING?!
FWP

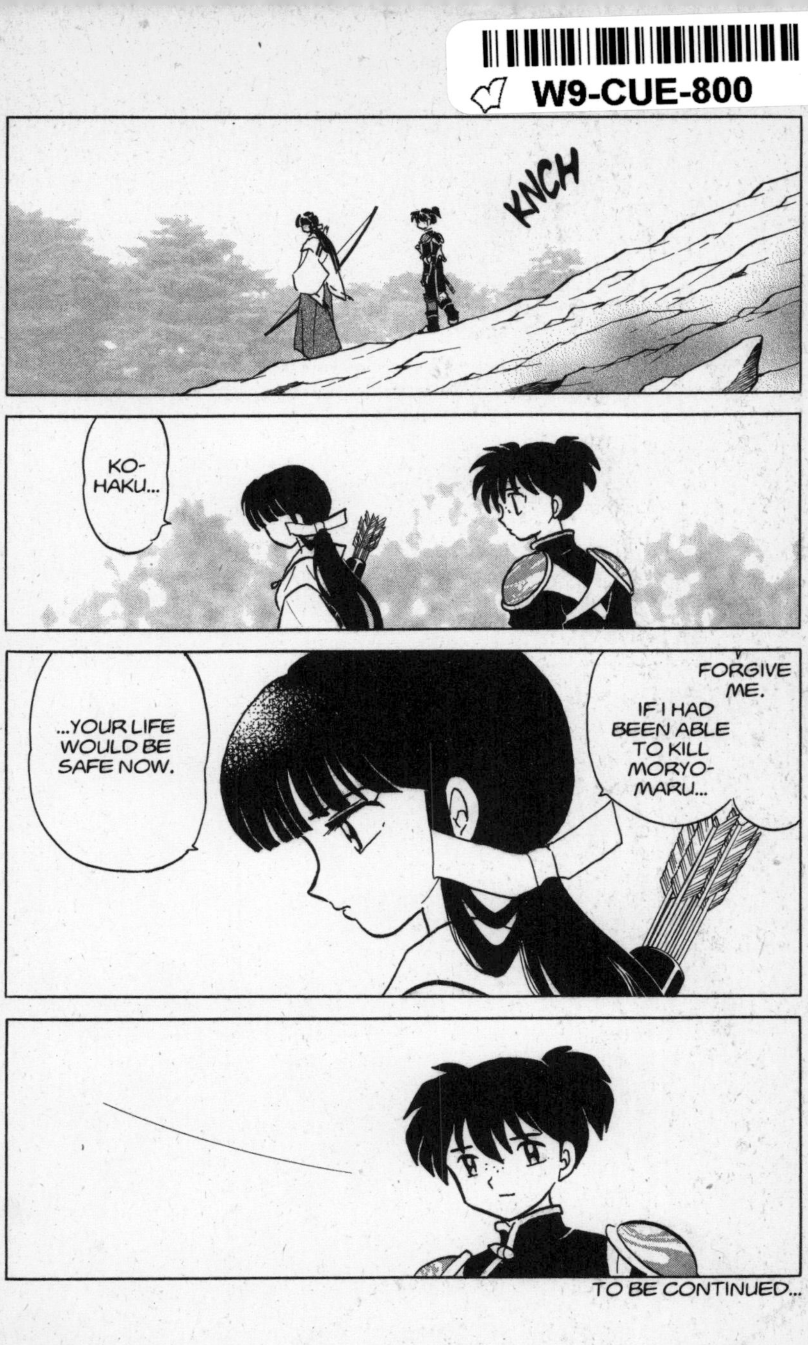
KNCH
KO-HAKU...
FORGIVE ME.
IF I HAD BEEN ABLE TO KILL MORYO-MARU...
...YOUR LIFE WOULD BE SAFE NOW.

TO BE CONTINUED...